CORK

The Beauty of the Rebel County

Michael Prior

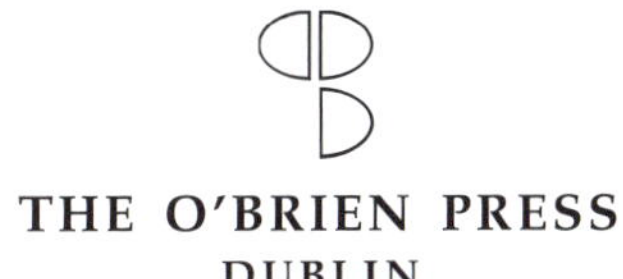

THE O'BRIEN PRESS
DUBLIN

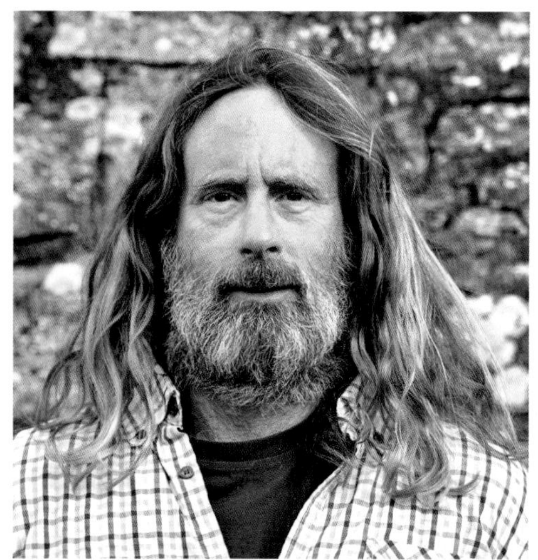

MICHAEL PRIOR has been a photographer for over twenty-five years. He has travelled extensively in South Africa, Asia and India, but Cork – his native home – is his favourite place.

A former sailing, windsurfing and canoeing instructor, he surfs a couple of times a week, when time allows. He lives between Kinsale and Clonakilty with his wife and two children.

michaelpriorphotography.net

To my wonderful mother, Olive: thank you for all your help

First published 2025 by The O'Brien Press Ltd,
12 Terenure Road East, Rathgar, Dublin 6, D06 HD27, Ireland.
Tel: +353 1 4923333; e-mail: books@obrien.ie; website: obrien.ie
The O'Brien Press is a member of Publishing Ireland.

ISBN: 978-1-78849-557-8

8 7 6 5 4 3 2 1
29 28 27 26 25

Printed and bound by L&C Printing Group, Poland.
The paper in this book is produced using pulp from managed forests.

To the best of our knowledge, this book complies in full with the requirements of the General Product Safety Regulation (GPSR). For further information and help with any safety queries, please contact us at productsafety@obrien.ie

Published in

DUBLIN UNESCO
City of Literature

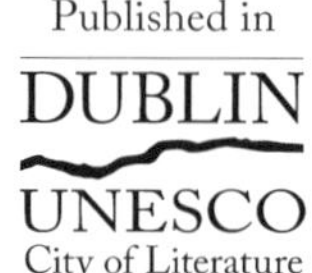

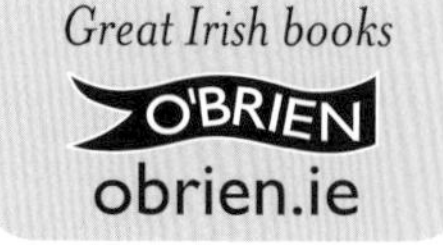

CONTENTS

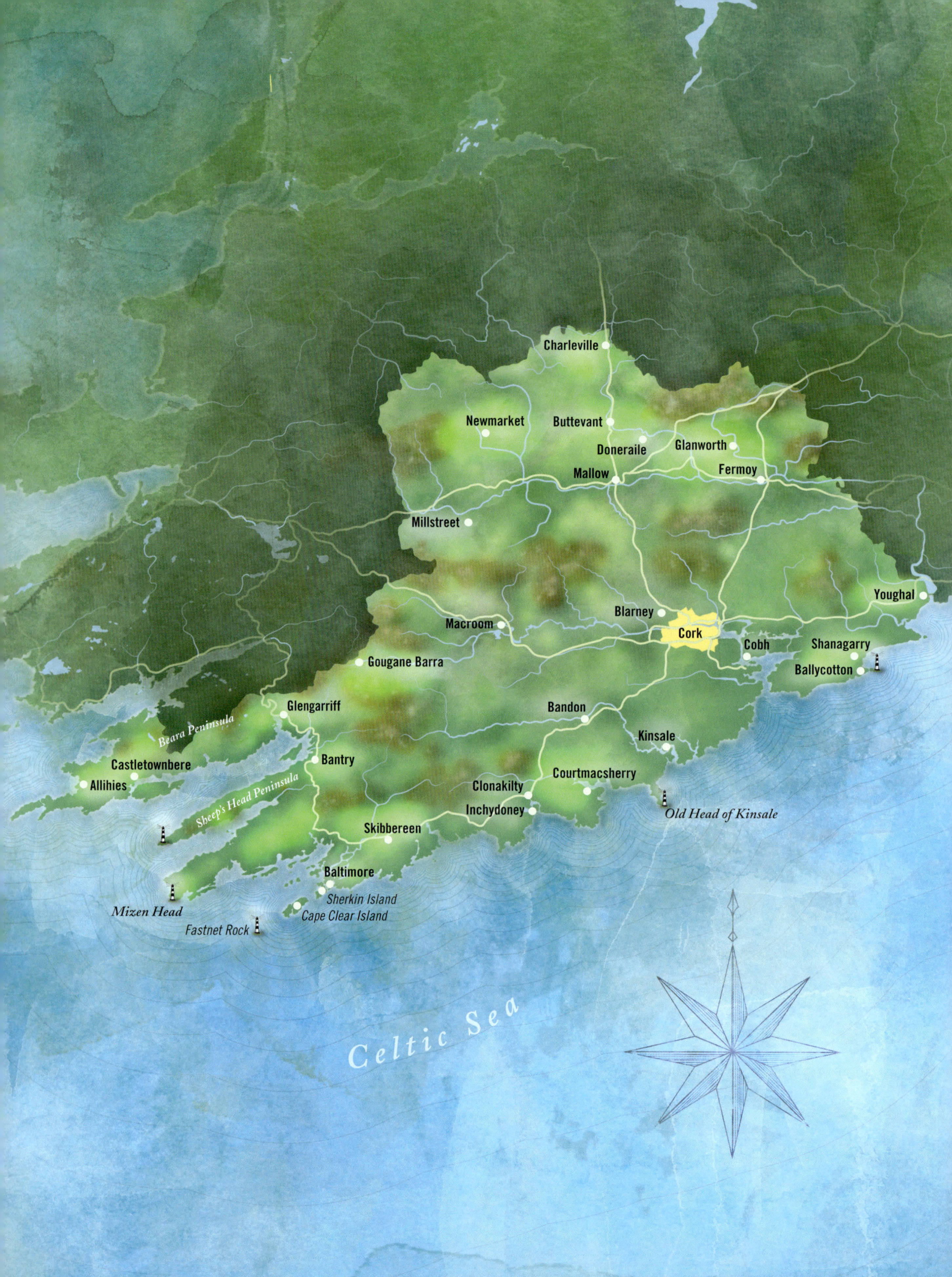

Charleville
Newmarket
Buttevant
Doneraile
Glanworth
Mallow
Fermoy
Millstreet
Youghal
Macroom
Blarney
Cork
Cobh
Shanagarry
Gougane Barra
Ballycotton
Glengarriff
Bandon
Beara Peninsula
Kinsale
Castletownbere
Bantry
Allihies
Courtmacsherry
Sheep's Head Peninsula
Clonakilty
Inchydoney
Skibbereen
Old Head of Kinsale
Baltimore
Mizen Head
Sherkin Island
Cape Clear Island
Fastnet Rock
Celtic Sea

INTRODUCTION

County Cork, situated in the south of the country is, at nearly three thousand square miles, the largest county in Ireland, and, with a population of six hundred thousand, the country's second most populated county after Dublin. The county's landscape varies greatly: the southwest is known for its mountainous and rugged terrain and is one of Ireland's main tourist destinations, while the rest of the county is rich in pastureland.

Cork's coastline stretches for almost twelve hundred kilometres and is dotted with beautiful beaches, such as Garrylucas, Long Strand and Barleycove. Its many islands range from little gems such as Fastnet, with its iconic lighthouse, to larger, inhabited ones such Dursey, famed for having Ireland's only cable car which connects it to the mainland, and the Irish-speaking Cape Clear. The Wild Atlantic Way starts in the historic town of Kinsale from where it winds its way west along the coastline.

Cork is renowned for its festivals dedicated to music, arts and food, both in the city and throughout the towns and villages, especially during the summer months. To mention just a few, Doneraile hosts a world-famous horse fair, Bantry a mussel festival and the West Cork Music festival, which draws people from far and wide. The county's regattas include a vintage boat regatta in Baltimore.

As for me, I am a proud Corkman. I began my photography journey in a darkroom in the 1990s. I started off on 35mm film, developing and printing my photographs in my darkroom. In 1999, I travelled to South Africa with a backpack and fifty rolls of black-and-white film. It went well: I got some good wildlife and landscape shots while having a great adventure. The photographs were well received, and earned some awards. The following year I was off travelling again, this time spending three months in India and again with fifty rolls of black-and-white film, and I have been hooked ever since. For the next few years, I concentrated mainly on black-and-white, printing all my own photographs, as well as printing for other photographers. It was only when I changed to digital that I started working mostly in colour. Over the years, I have returned to Africa and Asia on many occasions and have been lucky enough to watch the sun rise over Mount Everest.

While I have seen many beautiful countries, for me Ireland is the prettiest, and from a more than slightly biased point of view, I believe Cork is the prettiest part of the country. I live between Kinsale and Clonakilty in west Cork with my beautiful wife and our two wonderful children. My gallery workshop is there and you are always welcome to visit.

Michael Prew

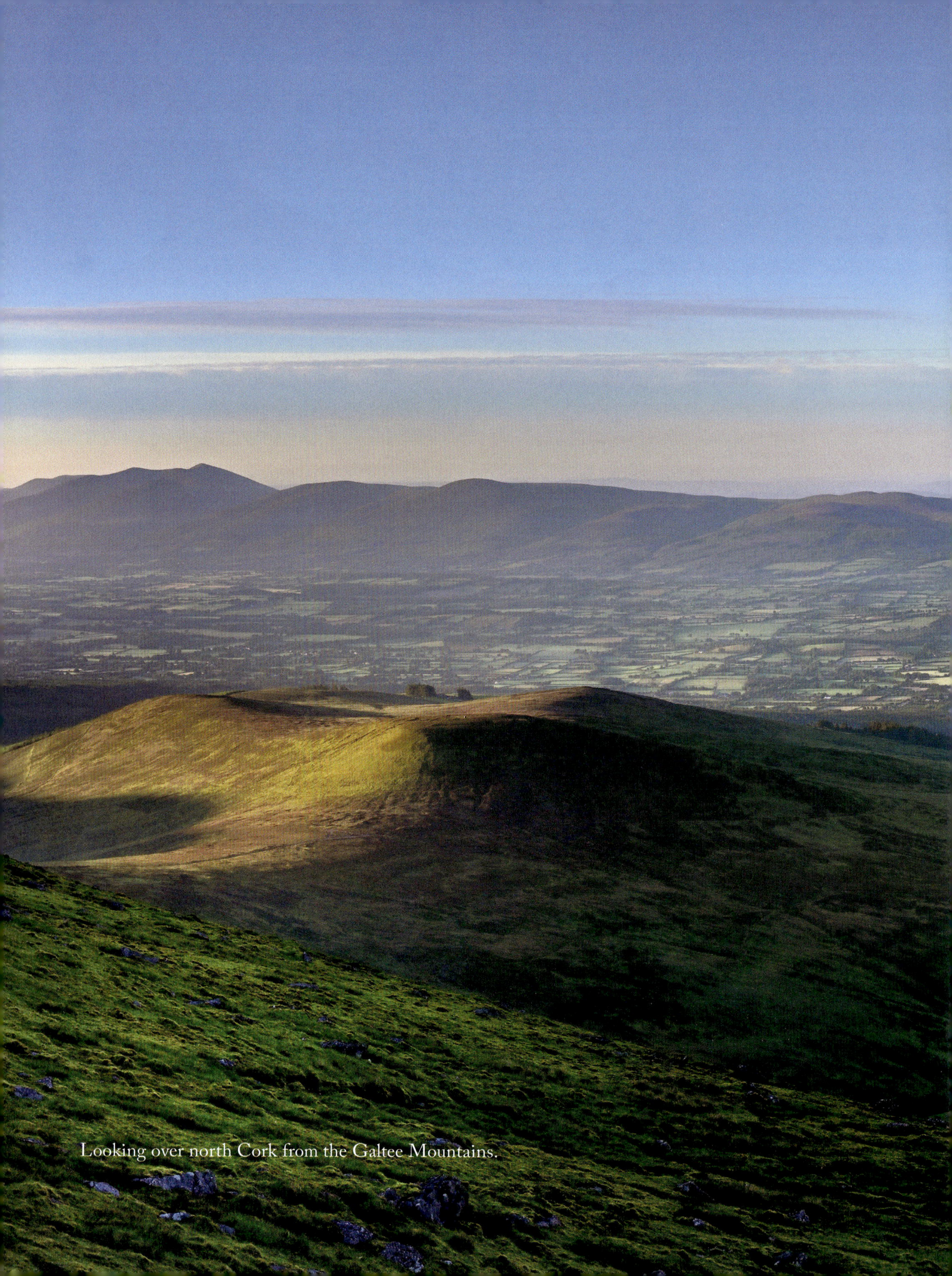

Looking over north Cork from the Galtee Mountains.

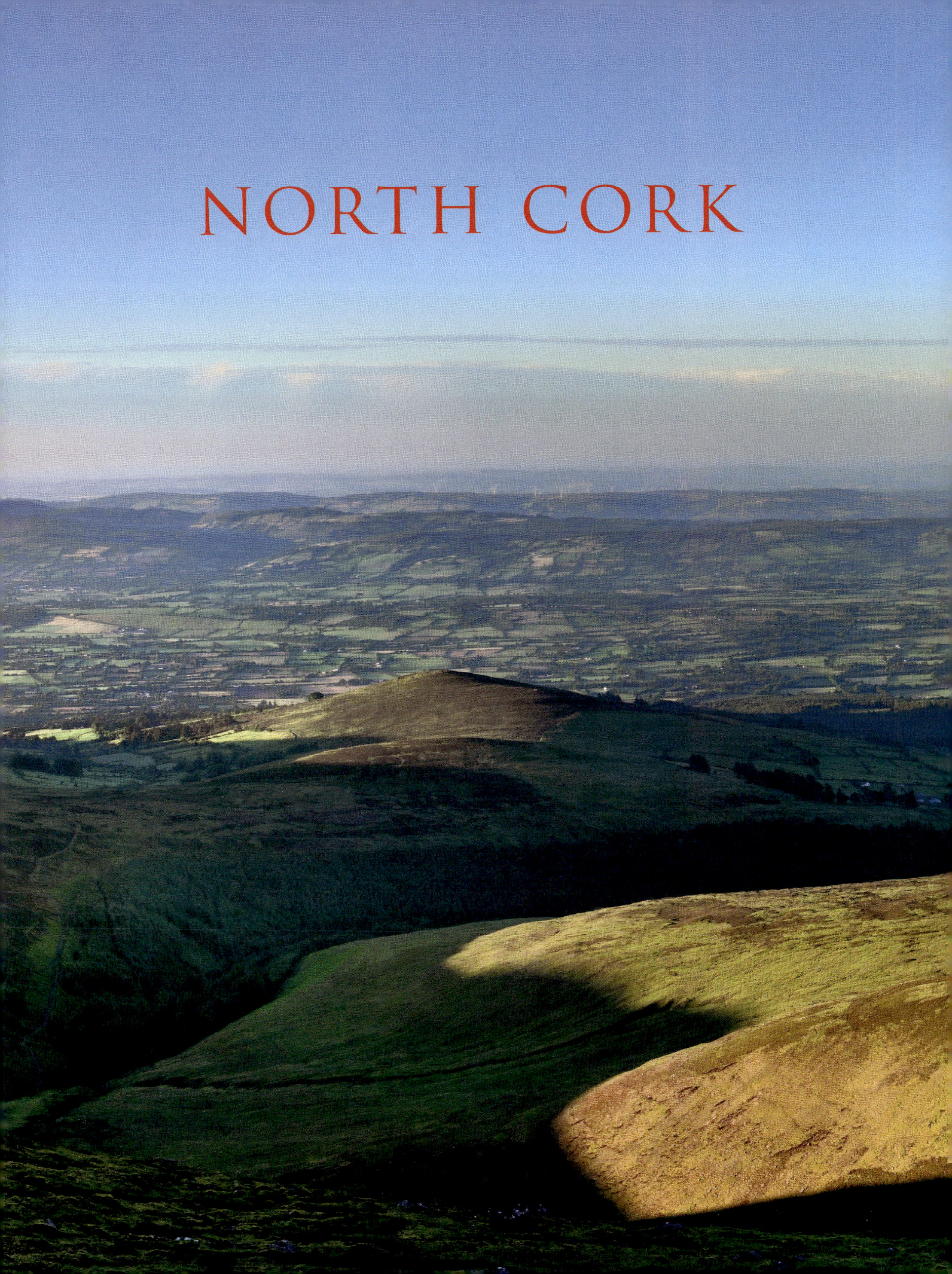

NORTH CORK

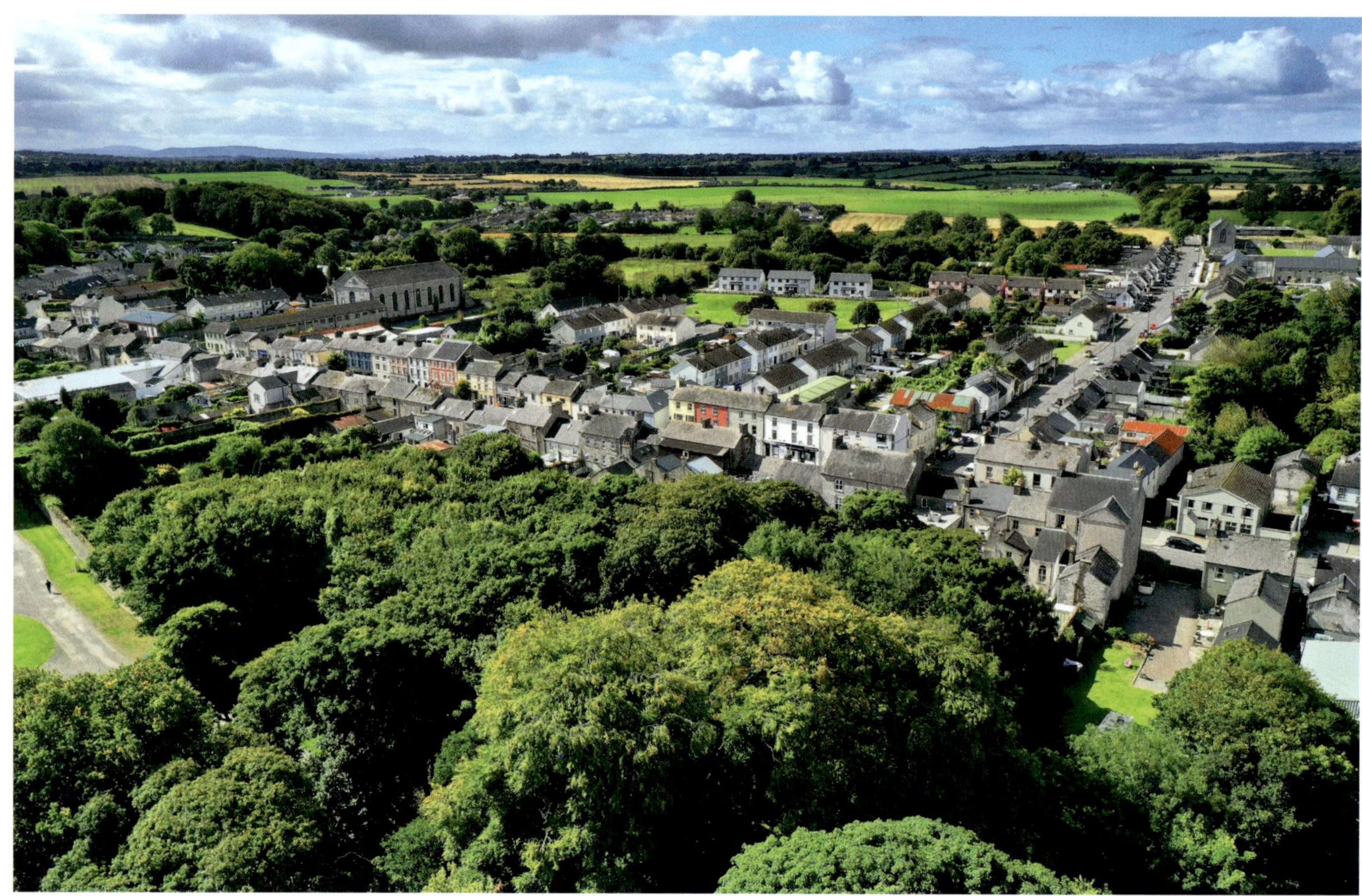

Above: The farming village of Doneraile is probably best known for its connection with horse racing: in 1752, a wager was placed by two gentlemen on a four-mile race between the steeples of St John's Church in Buttevant and St Mary's in Doneraile, and the steeplechase was born.

Opposite: Aerial view of Doneraile Court and its magnificent parklands. It was built in the seventeenth century by the St Leger family.

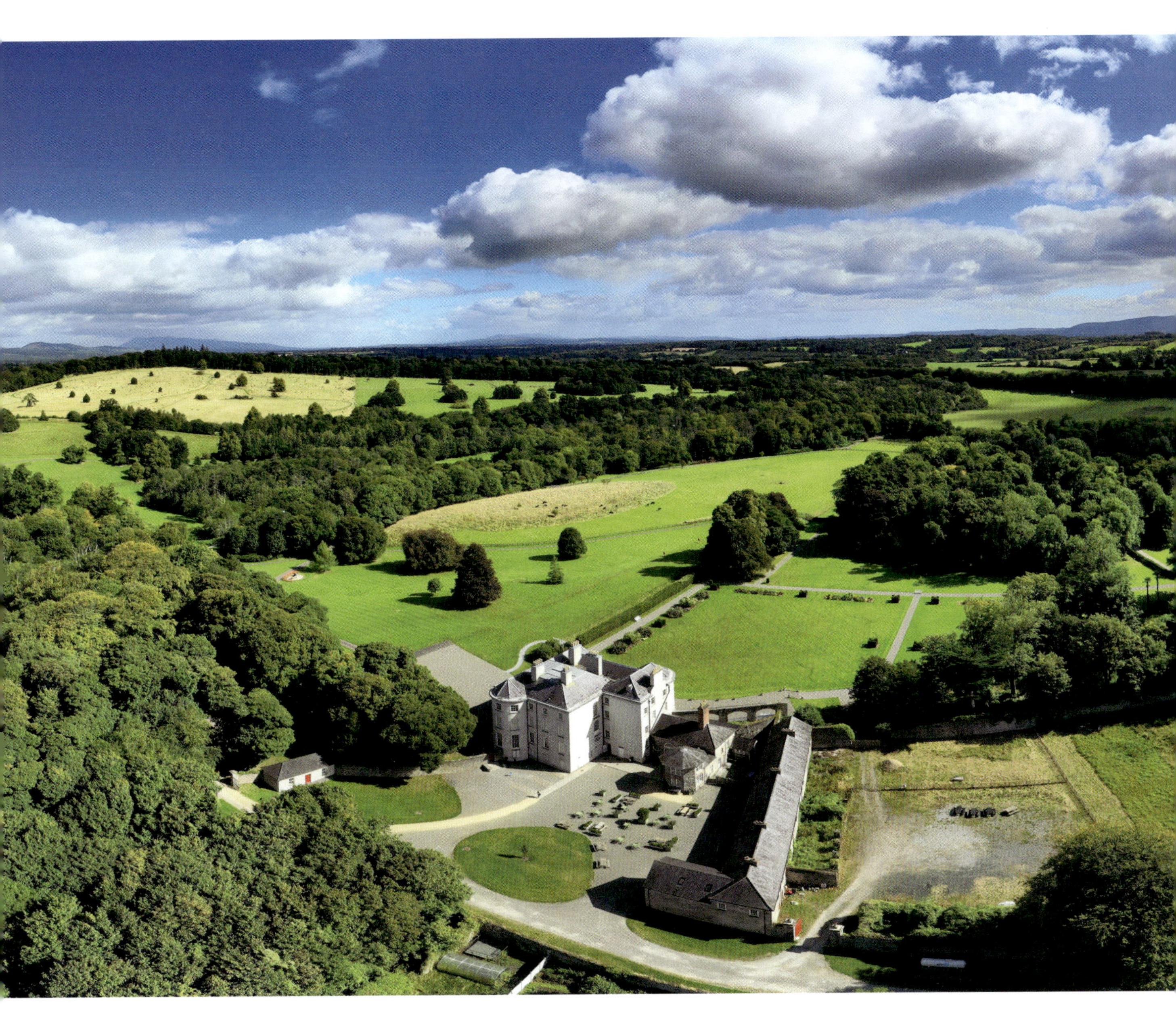

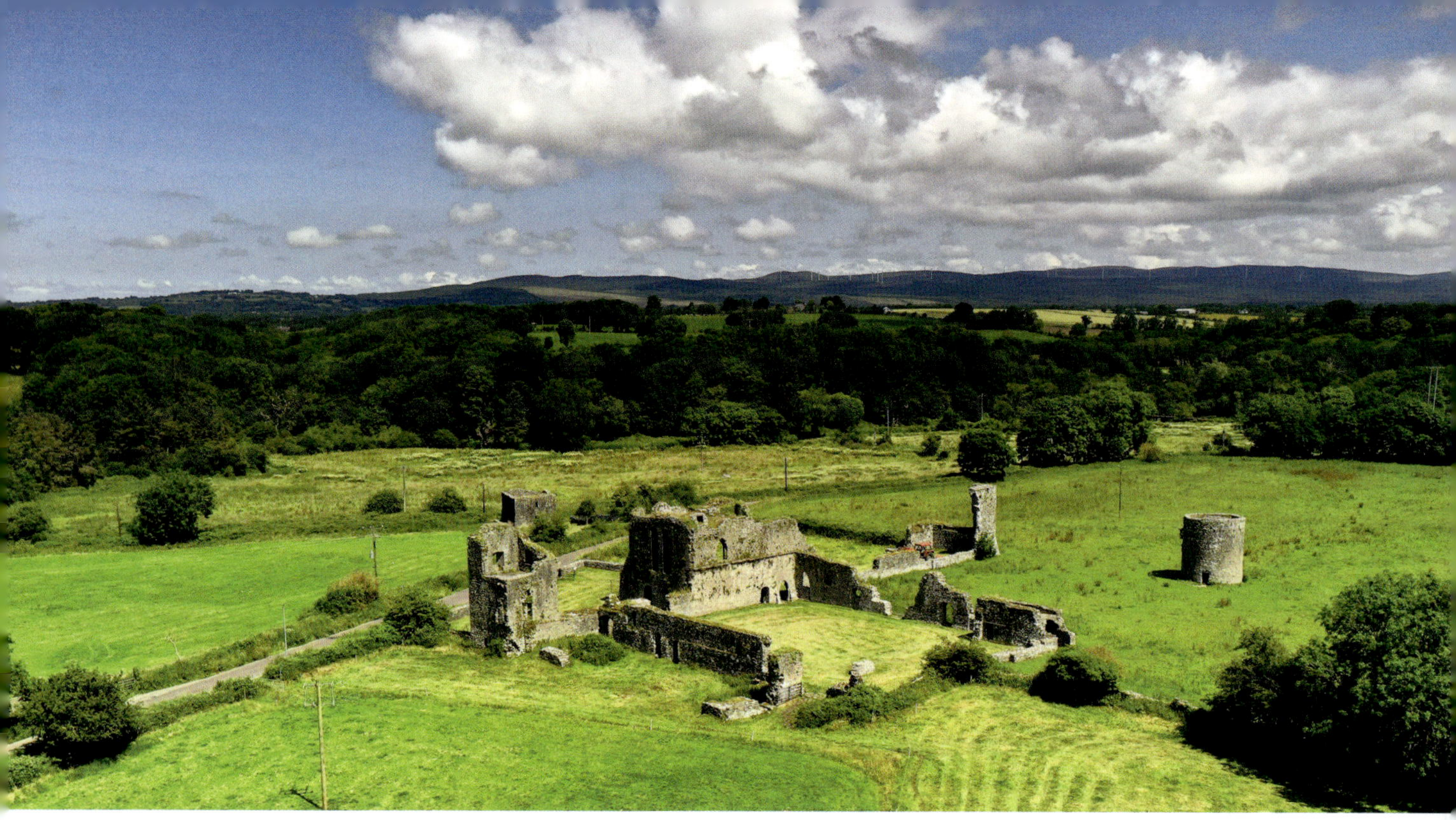

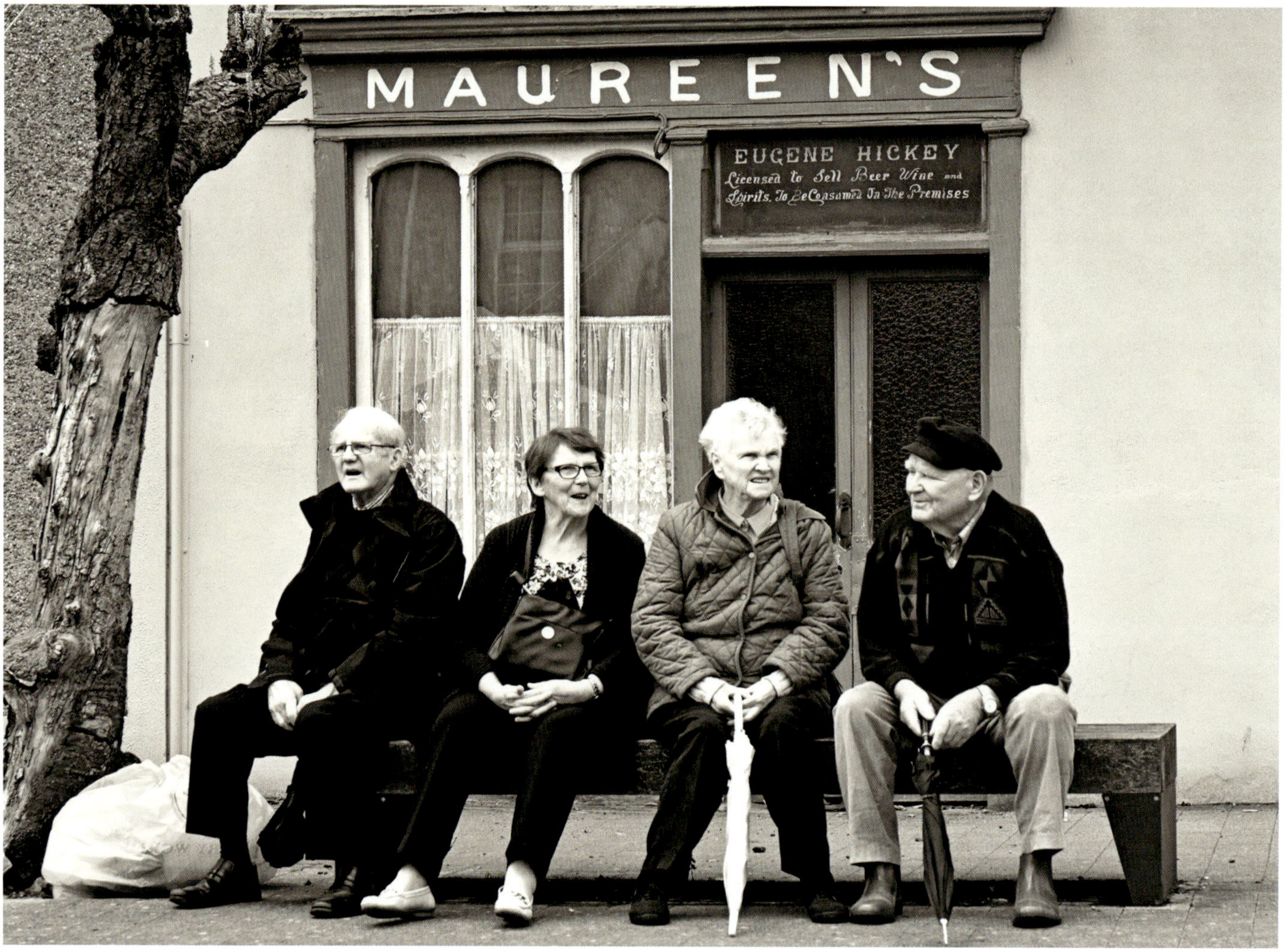
MAUREEN'S
EUGENE HICKEY
Licensed to Sell Beer Wine and
Spirits. To Be Consumed On The Premises

Opposite, top: Ballybeg Priory. This thirteenth-century priory is one of two Augustinian monasteries in Cork.

Opposite, bottom: Old friends catching up, outside Maureen's in Buttevant.

Below: Liscarroll Castle. Built in the thirteenth century, it was once was Ireland's third-largest castle.

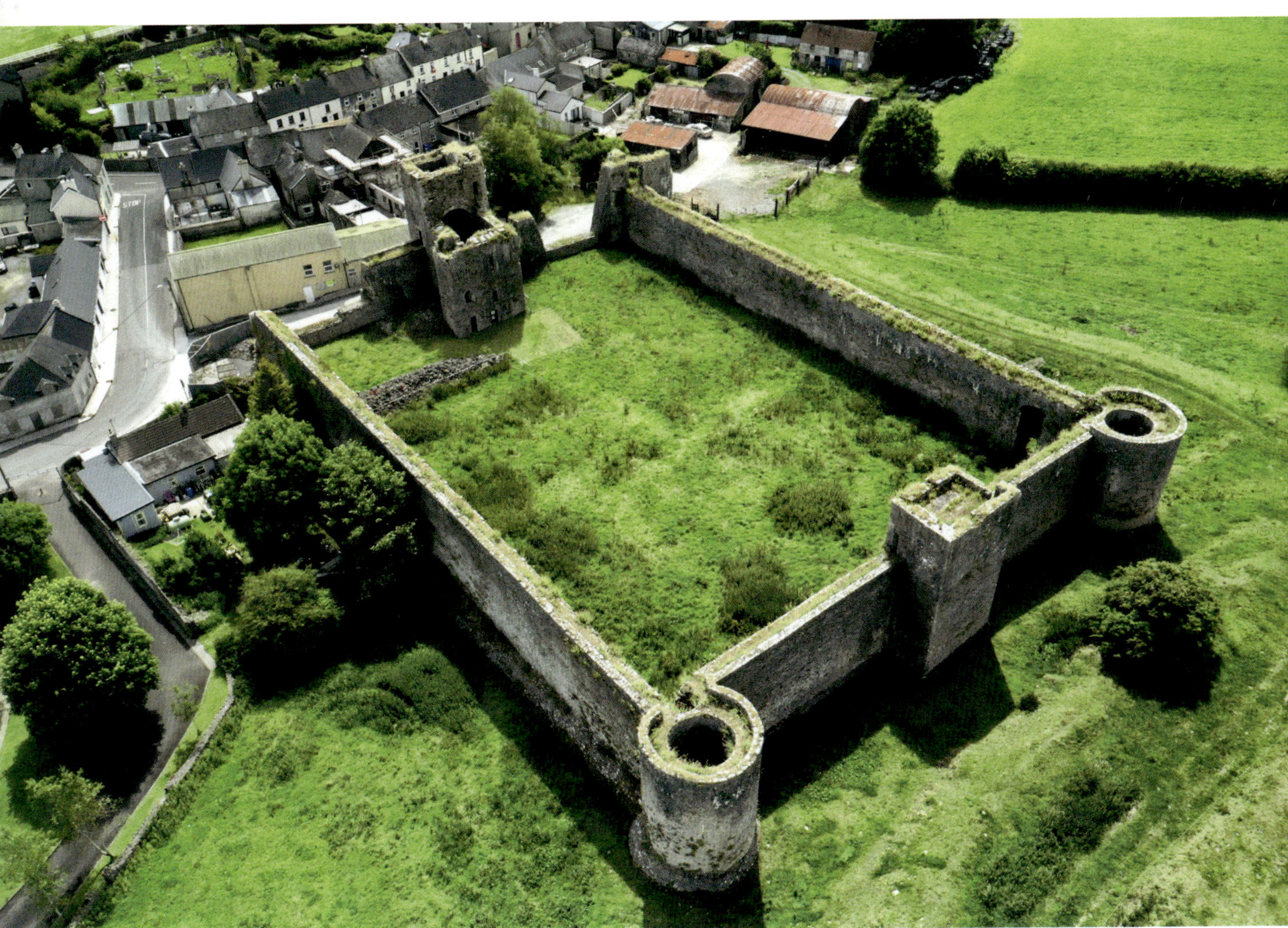

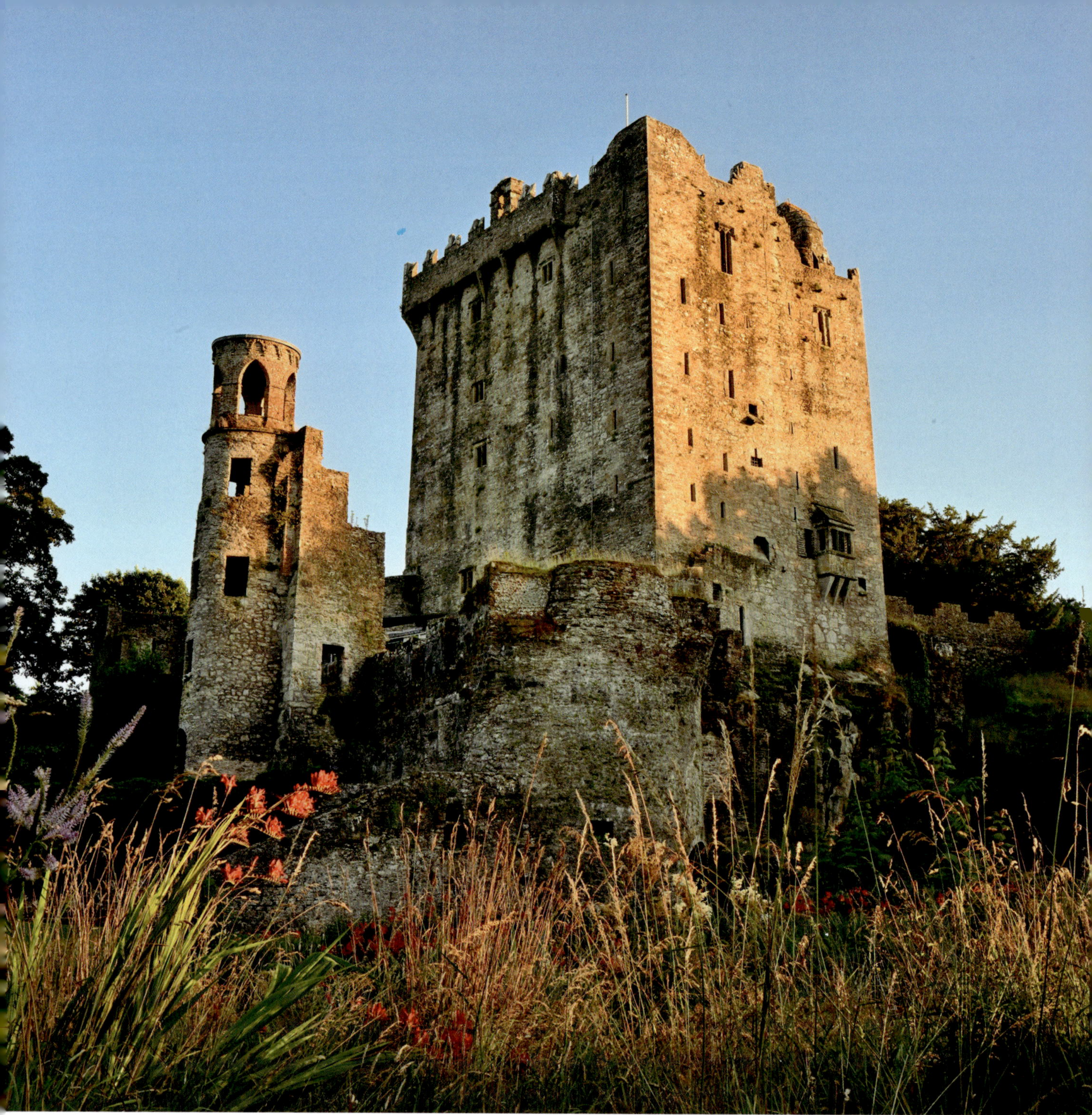

Blarney Castle is one of Ireland's top tourist attractions. At the top is the stone of eloquence, or Blarney Stone, which reputedly bestows the gift of the gab on those who kiss it.

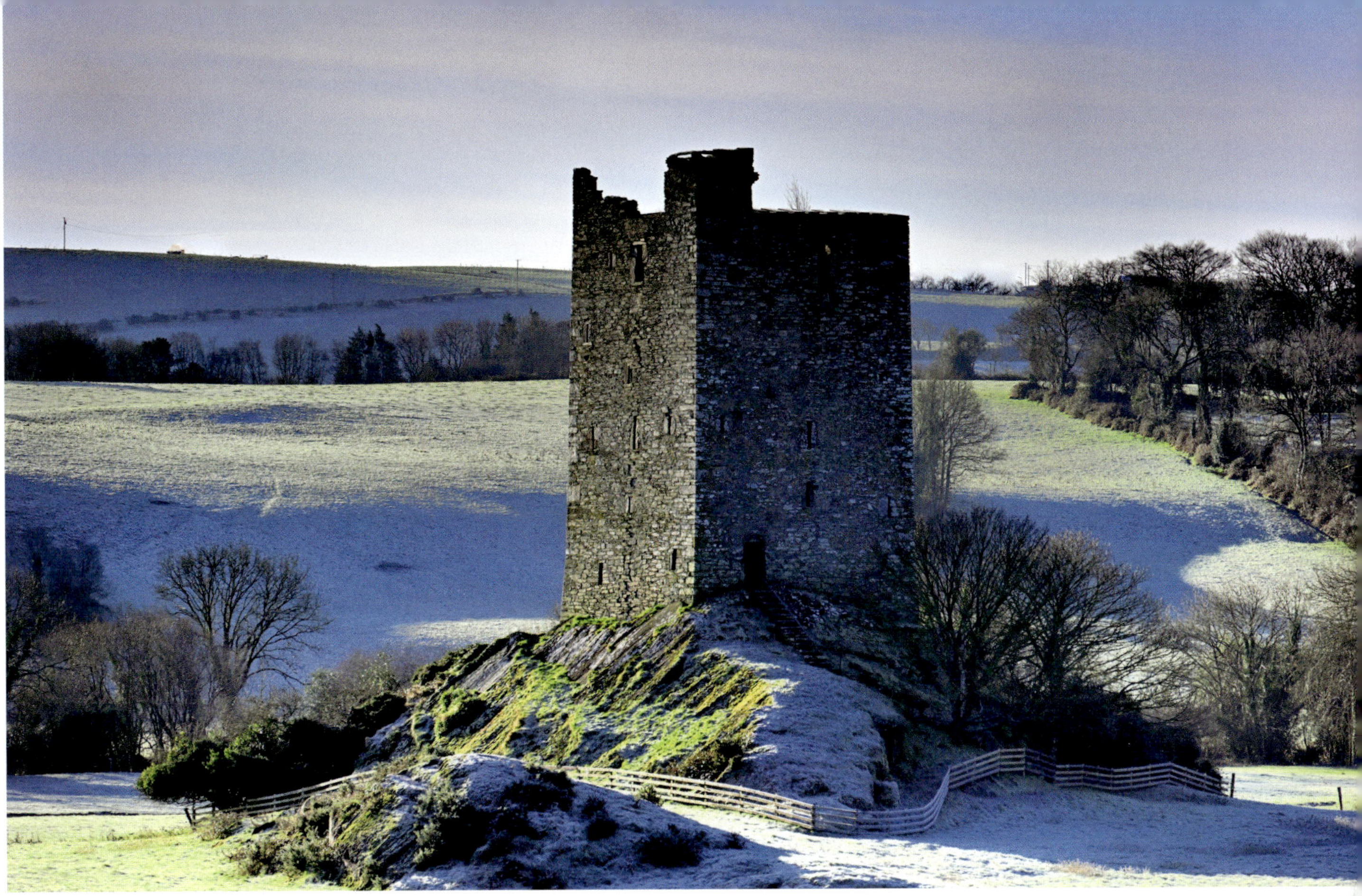

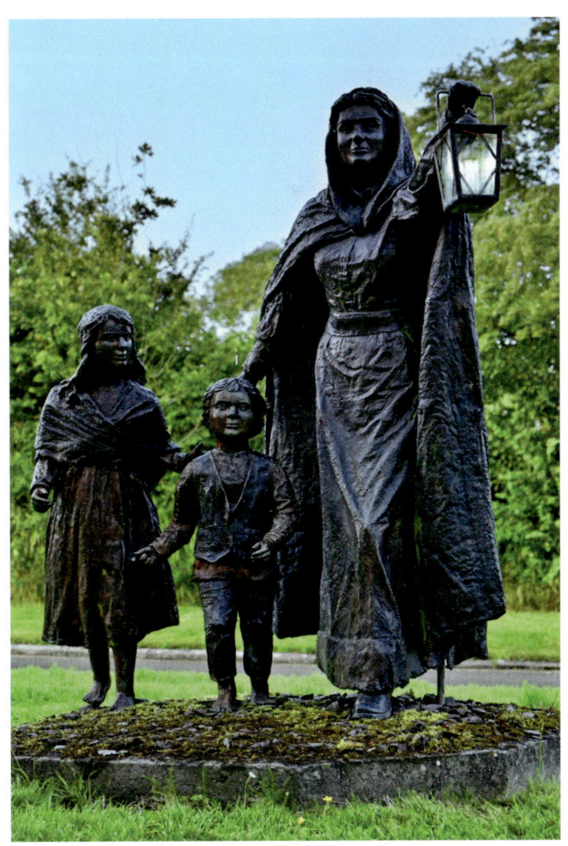

Top: Carrigaphooca Castle. This ruined five-storey tower house, situated on a steep-sided outcrop overlooking the River Sullane near Macroom, was built in the mid-fifteenth century. In English, its name means 'castle of the fairy'.

Right: The Nano Nagle statue marks the birthplace in Ballygriffin, Mallow, of the founder of the Presentation Sisters order. Nano Nagle (1718–84) championed Catholic education during the time of the Penal Laws.

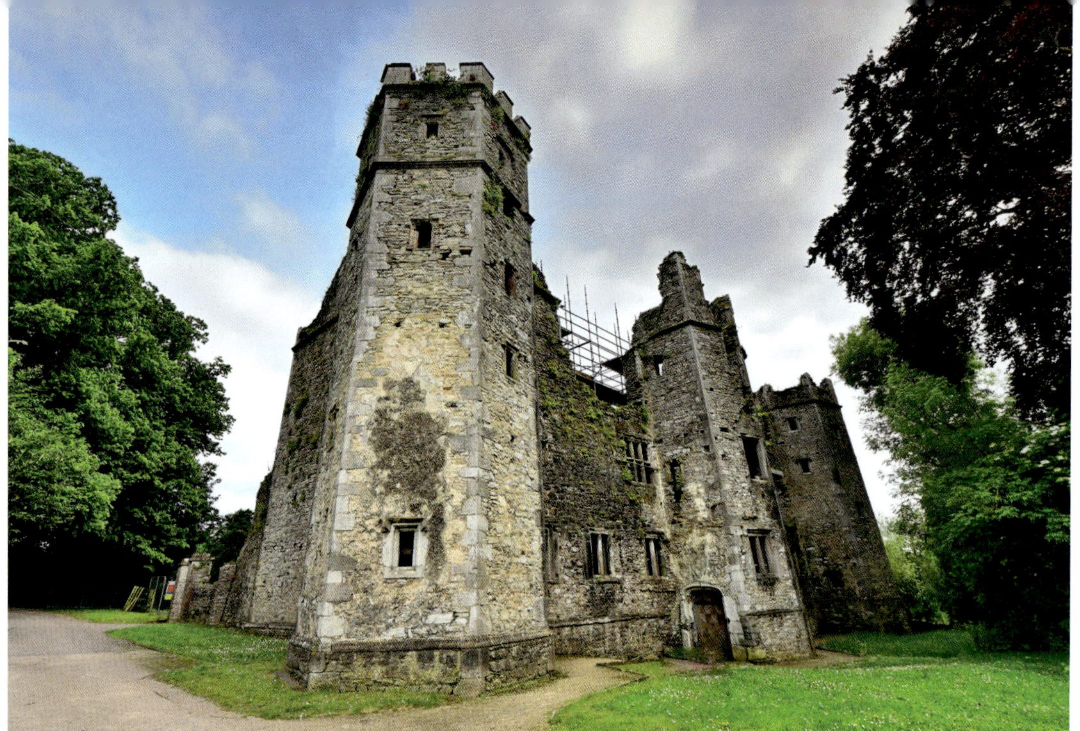

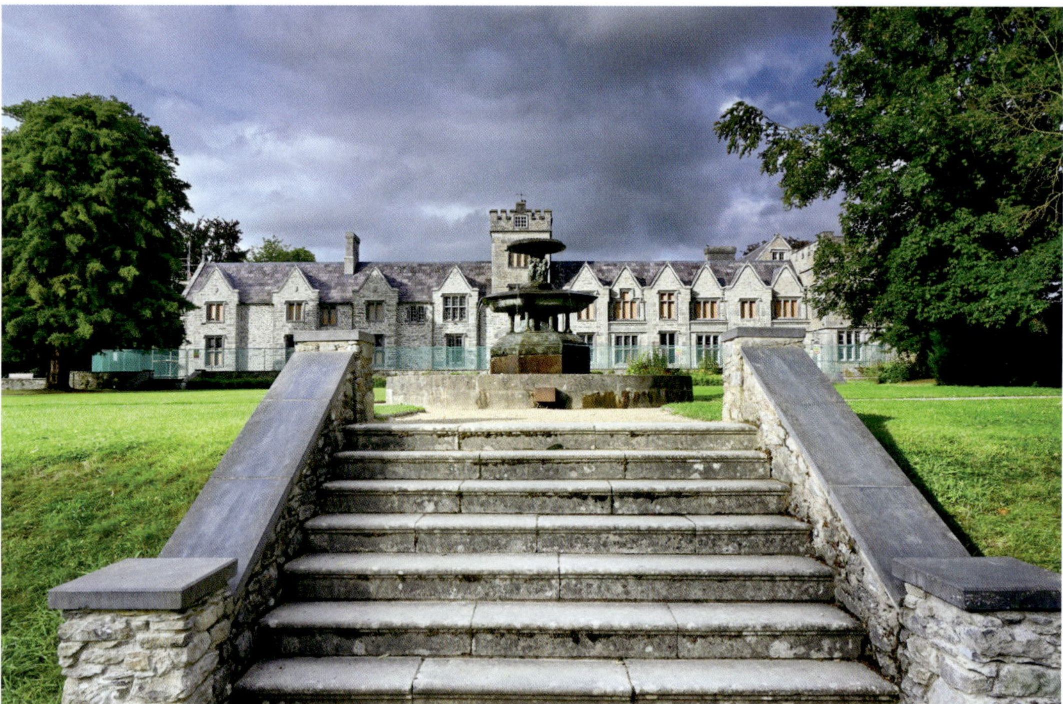

Top: Old Mallow Castle. Now a picturesque ruin, this castle was built in the sixteenth century.

Bottom: Nineteenth-century Mallow Castle is a fine baronial mansion.

Opposite: The Clock House in Mallow. This beautiful building in the heart of the town was constructed in 1855. The clock tower was restored in 1995.

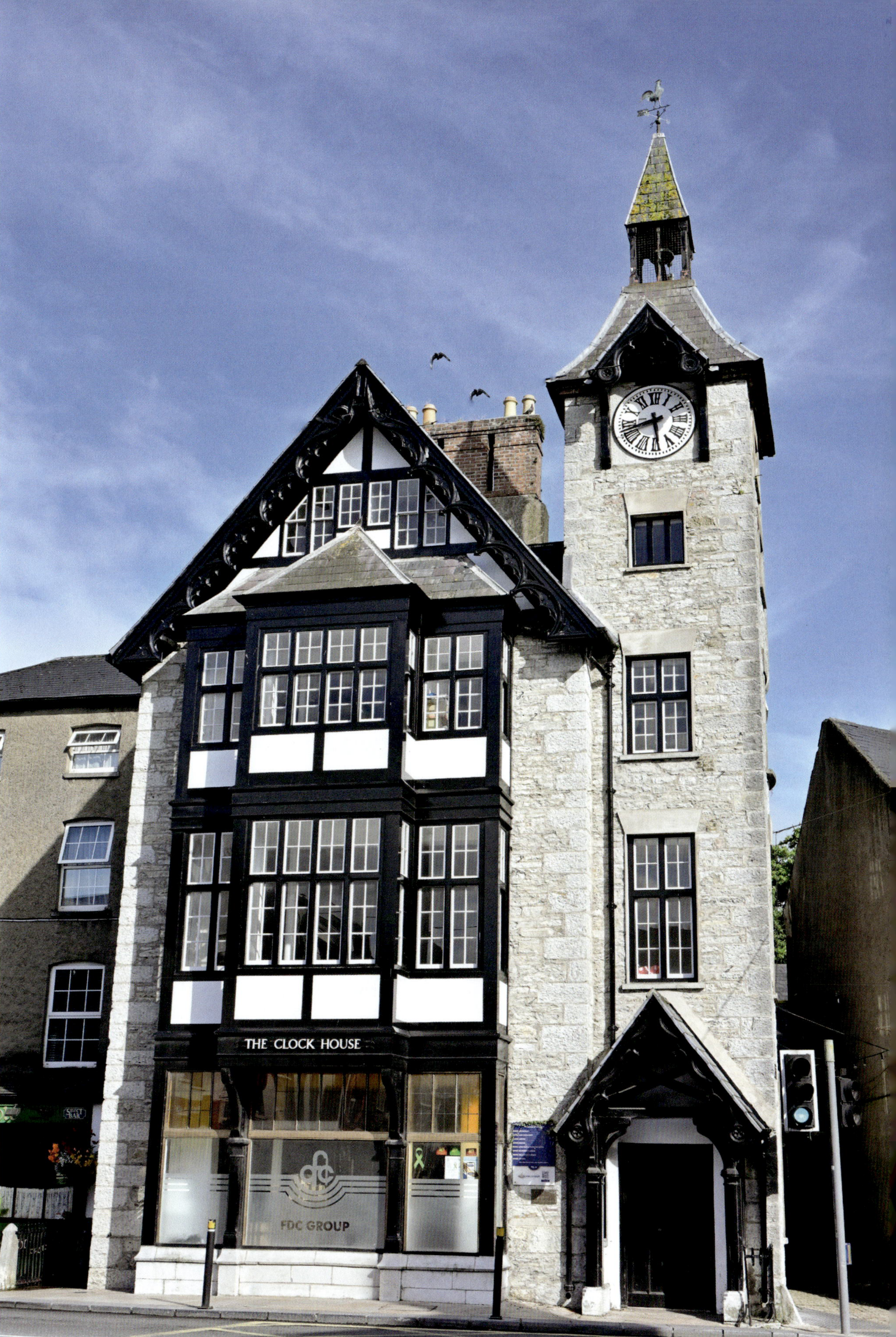

THE CLOCK HOUSE
FDC GROUP

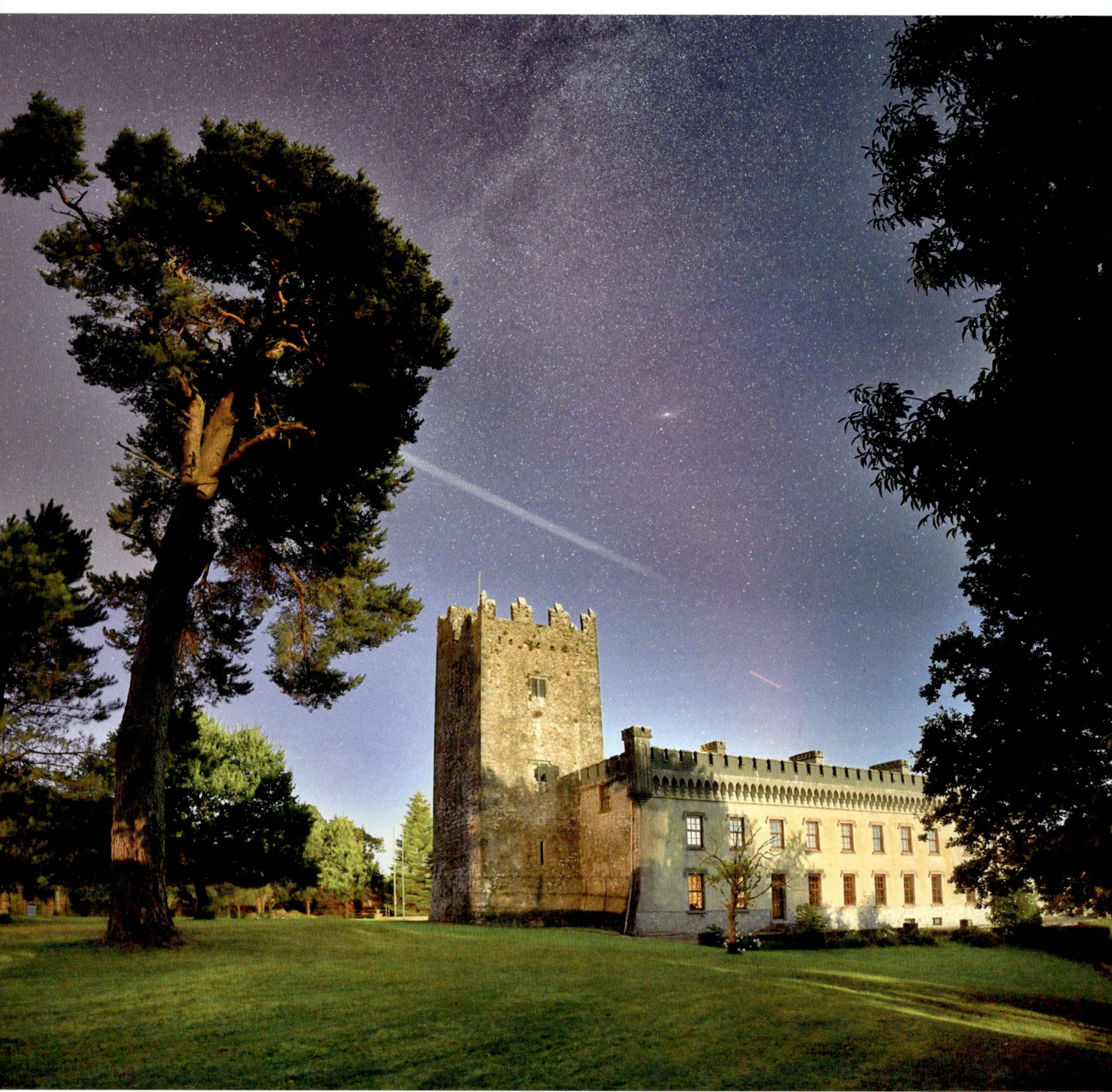

Top and opposite top: Two views of Blackwater Castle in Castletownroche. The main structure dates to the fifteenth century, while the tower was built in the twelfth century.

Opposite bottom: Castletownroche Mill. Constructed in 1828 on the site of an older mill, this building was renovated in the 1990s and is now a work hub for the local community.

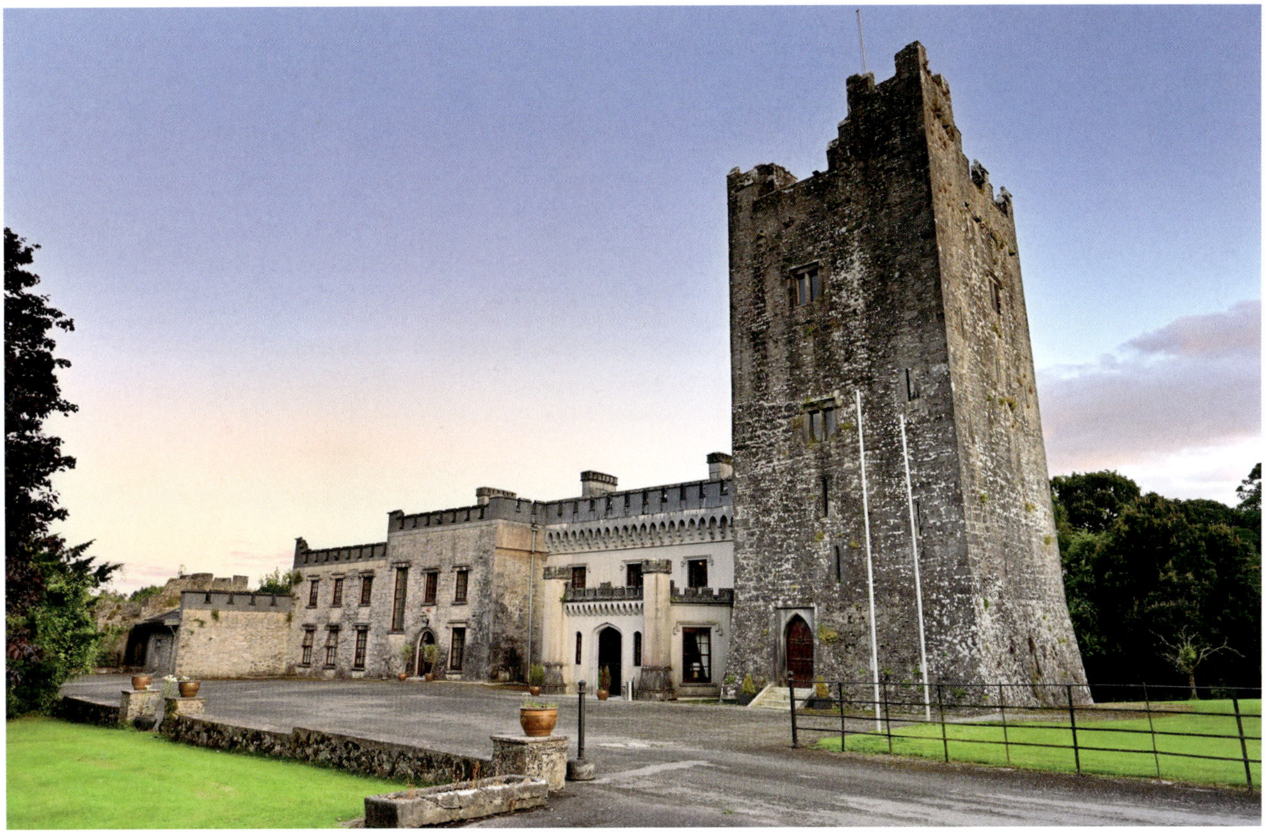

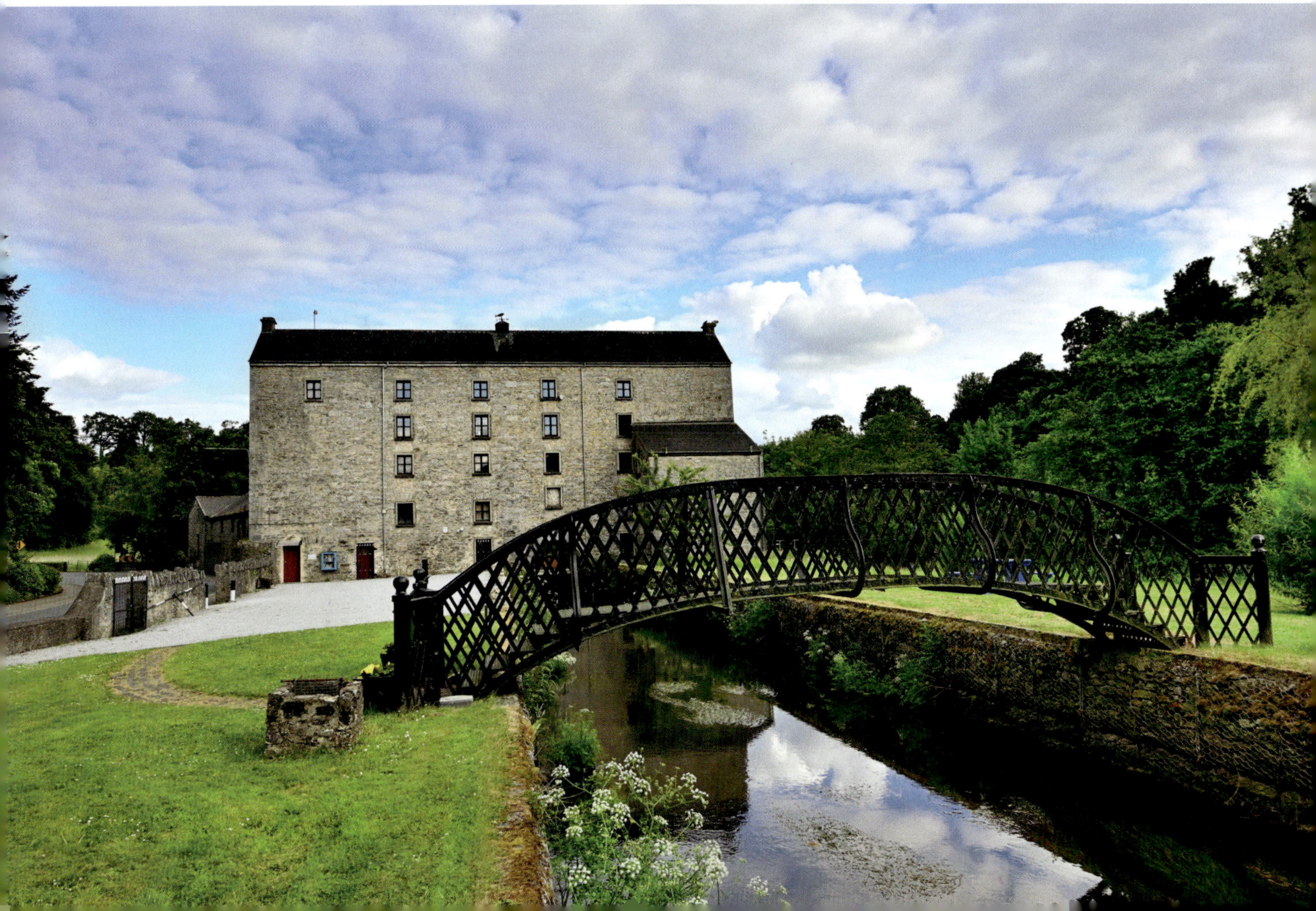

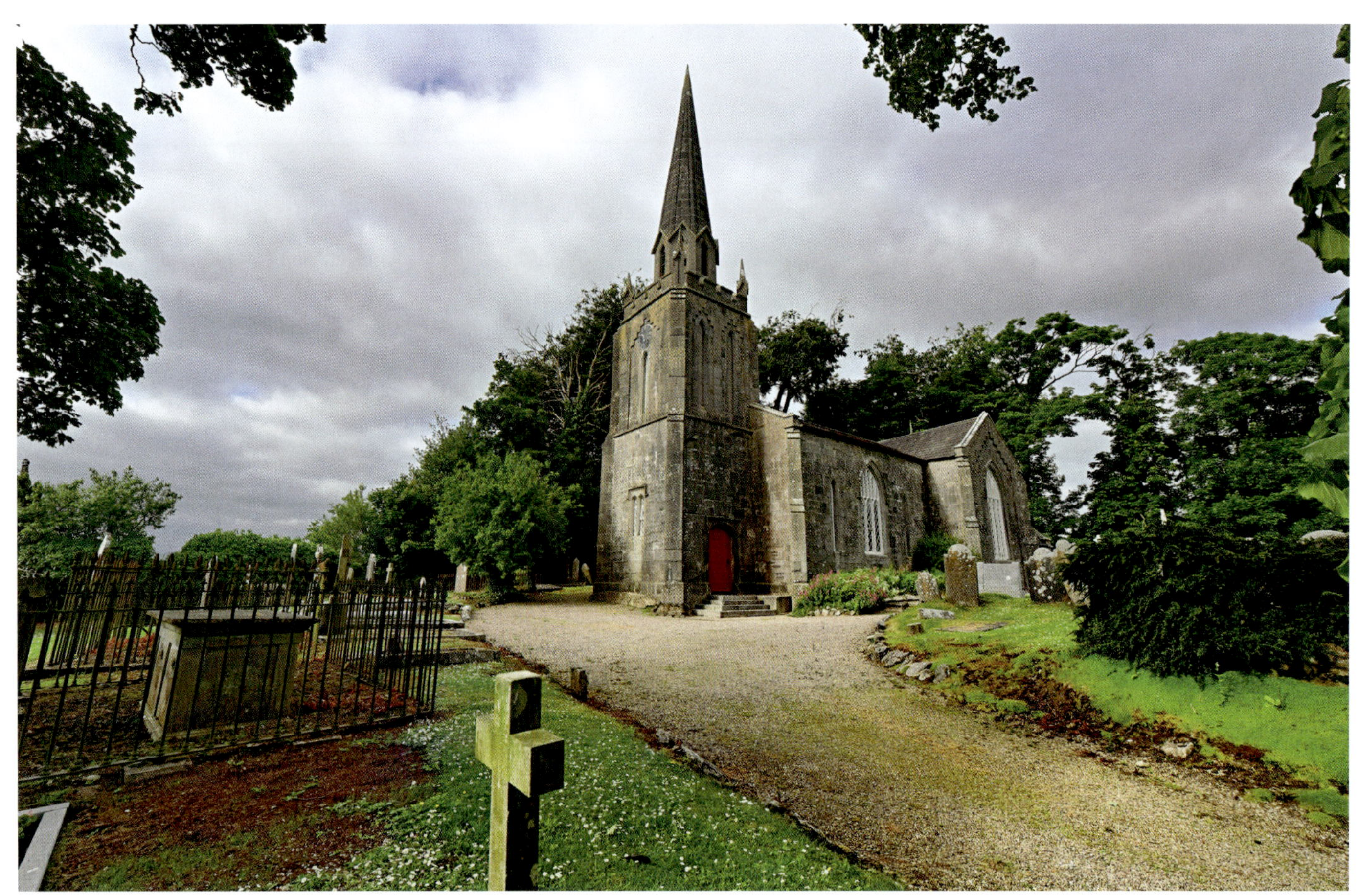

St Mary's Church of Ireland church in Castletownroche. It was built in 1825 in the Gothic Revival style on the site of a medieval church, on a hill overlooking the River Awbeg.

Bridgetown Abbey, near where the rivers Awbeg and Blackwater meet, is a fine example of a thirteenth-century Augustinian monastery.

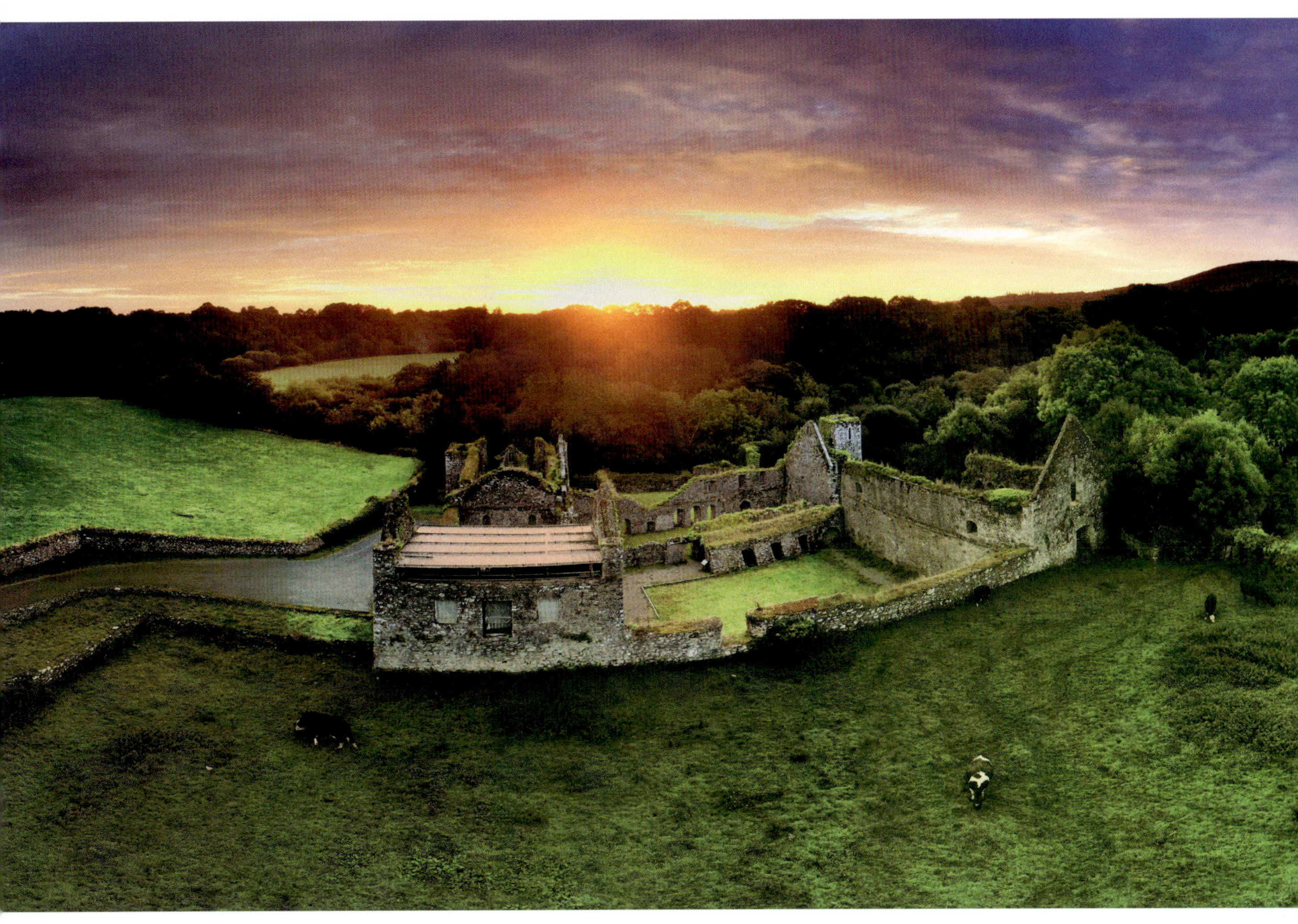

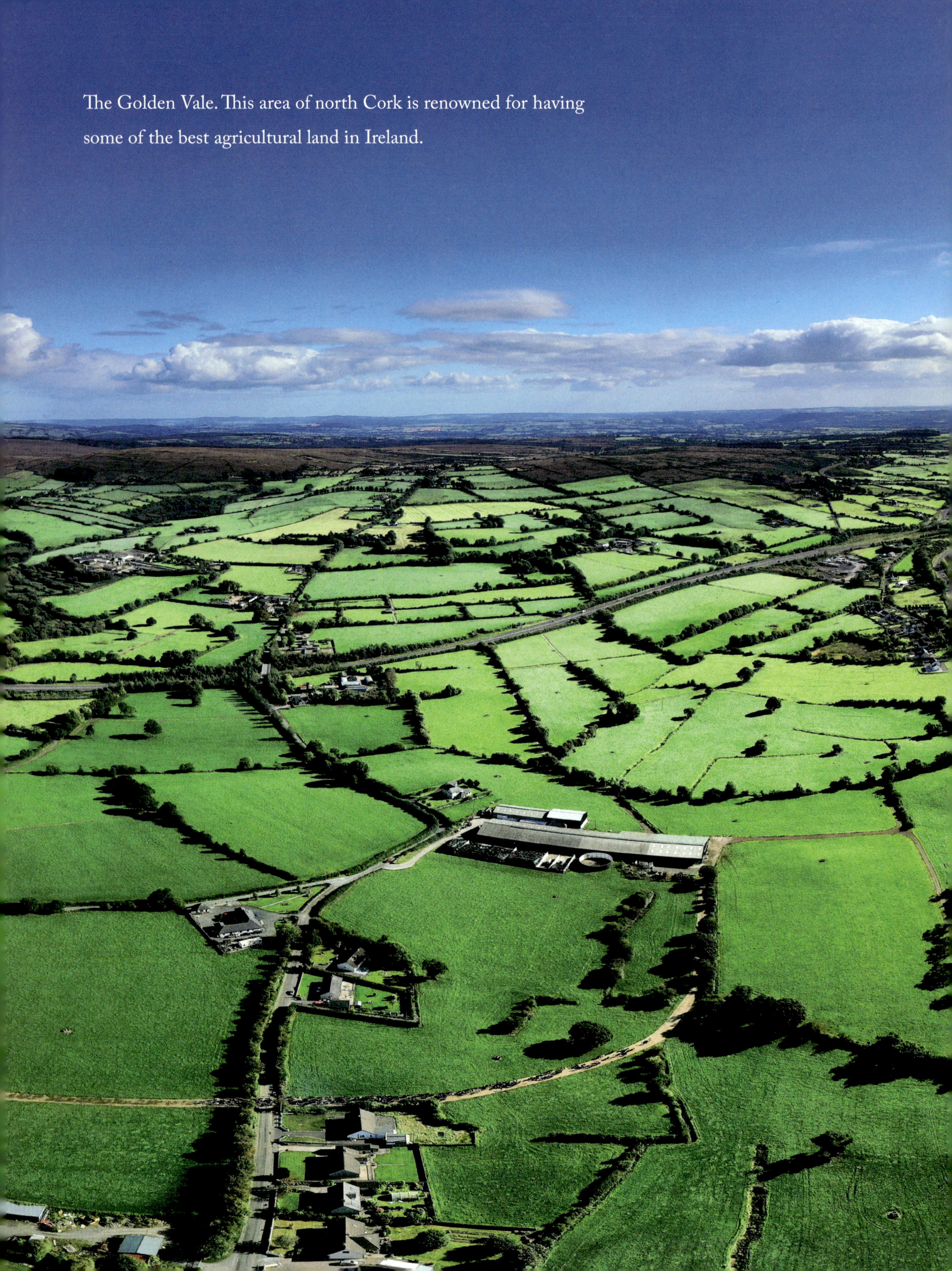

The Golden Vale. This area of north Cork is renowned for having some of the best agricultural land in Ireland.

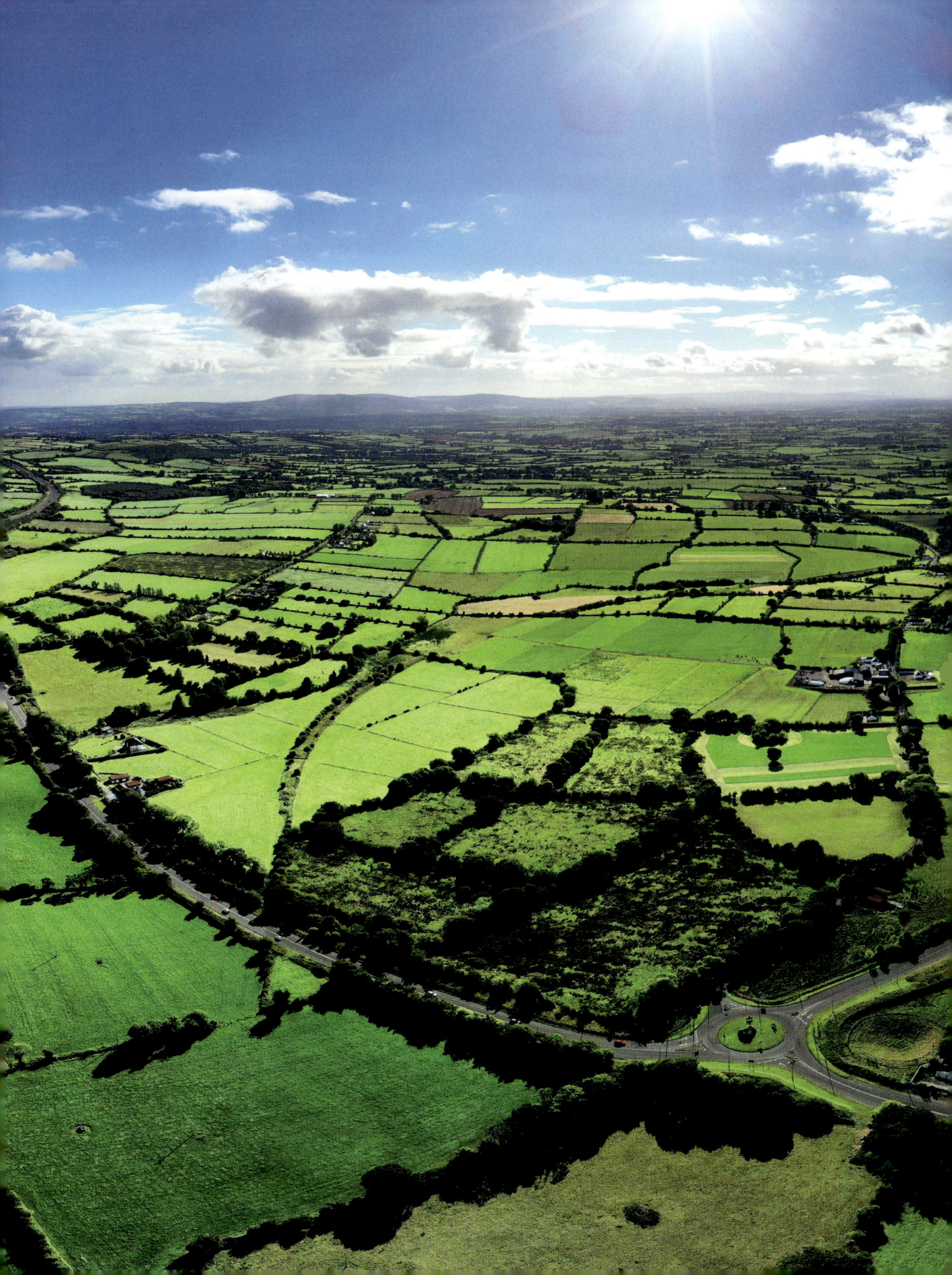

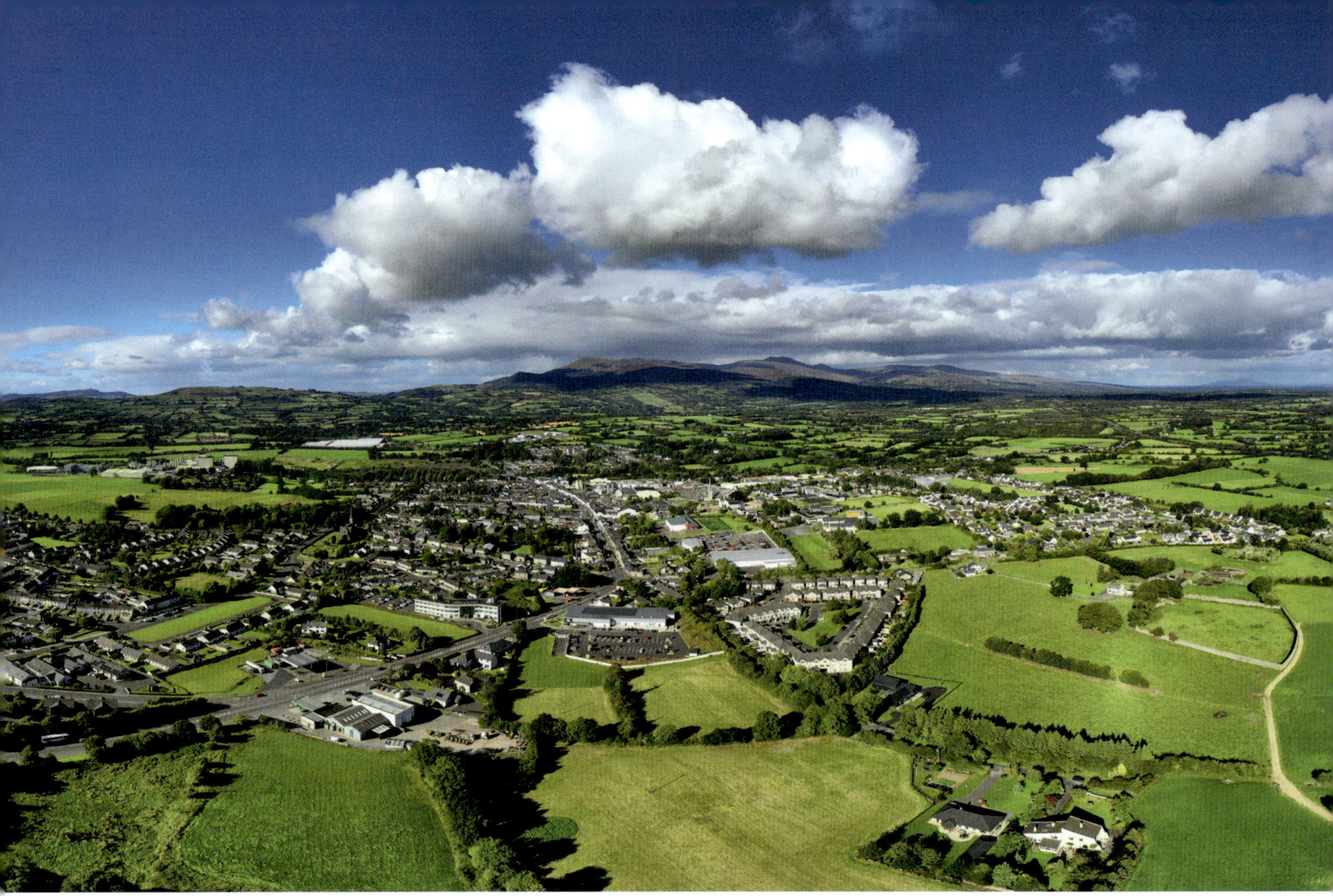

Above: Mitchelstown from the air. Sitting under the Galtee Mountains, this town is best known for its large limestone cave, twelve kilometres northeast of the town.

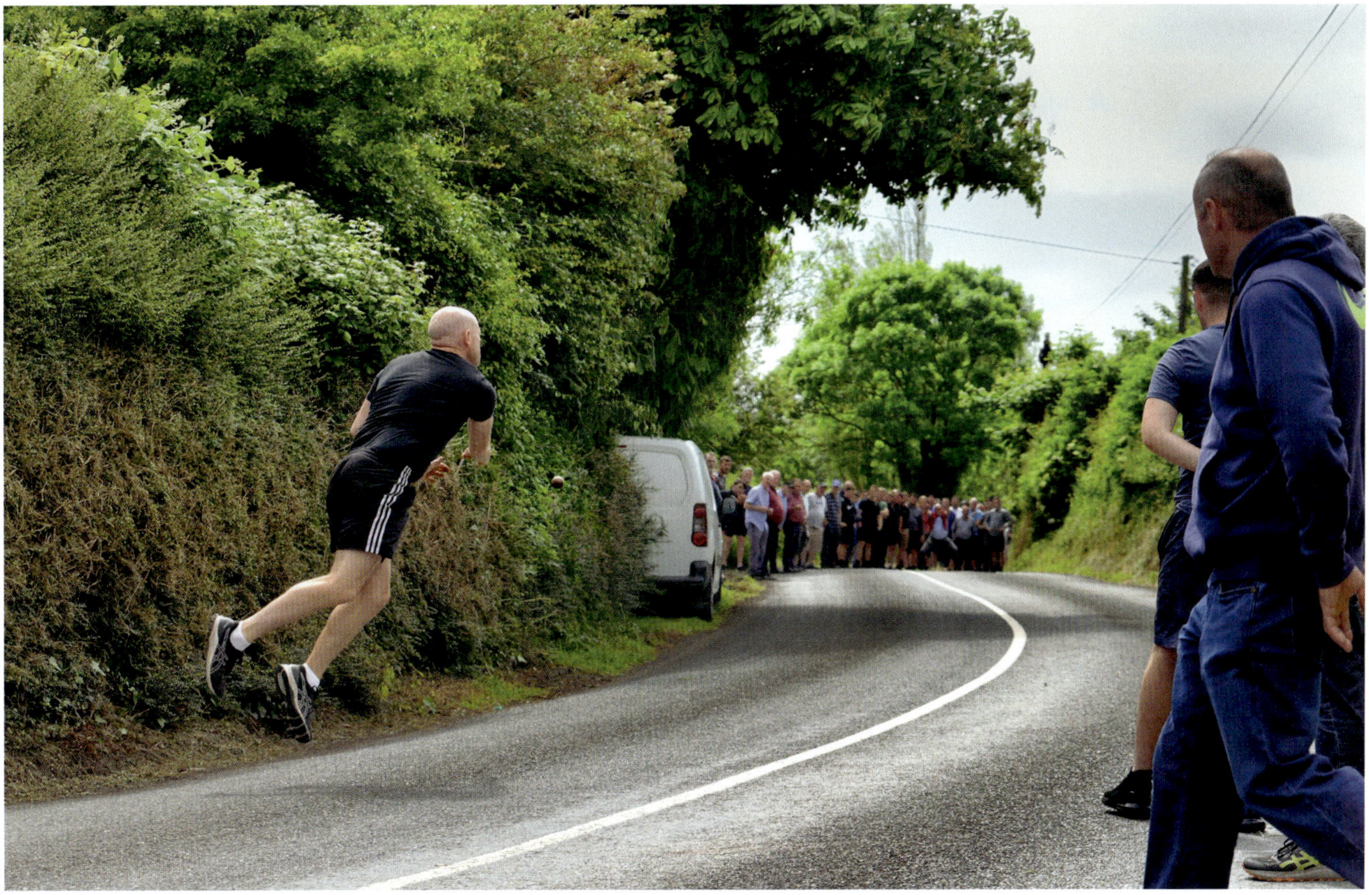

Above: Road bowling is a game for two people, who each throw an iron ball along a course on public back roads. Whoever completes the course in the fewest throws wins.

Right: Conna Castle. A tower house dating from the sixteenth century, it was used as a music venue in the 1980s and 1990s. It presently under restoration.

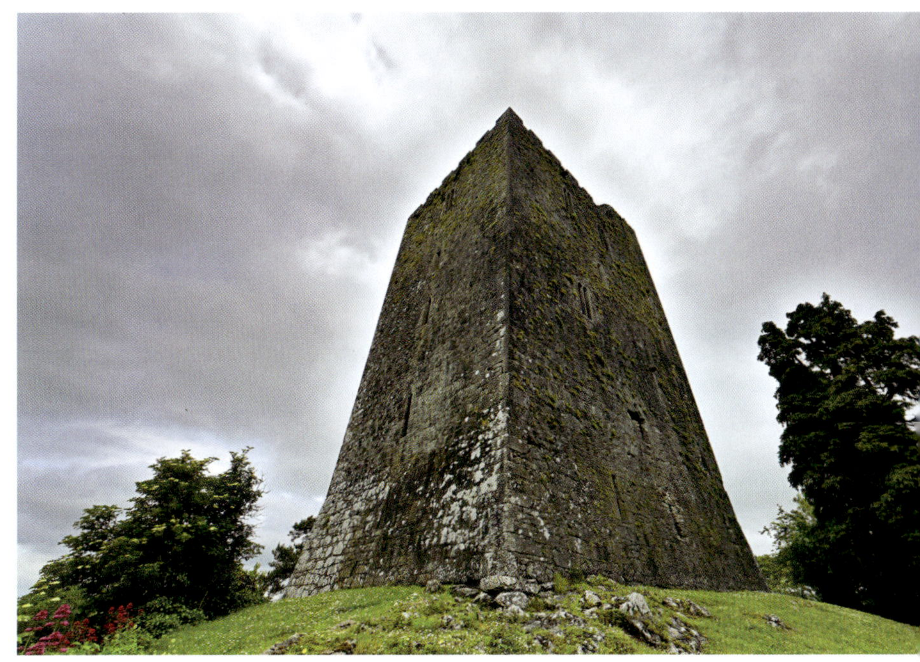

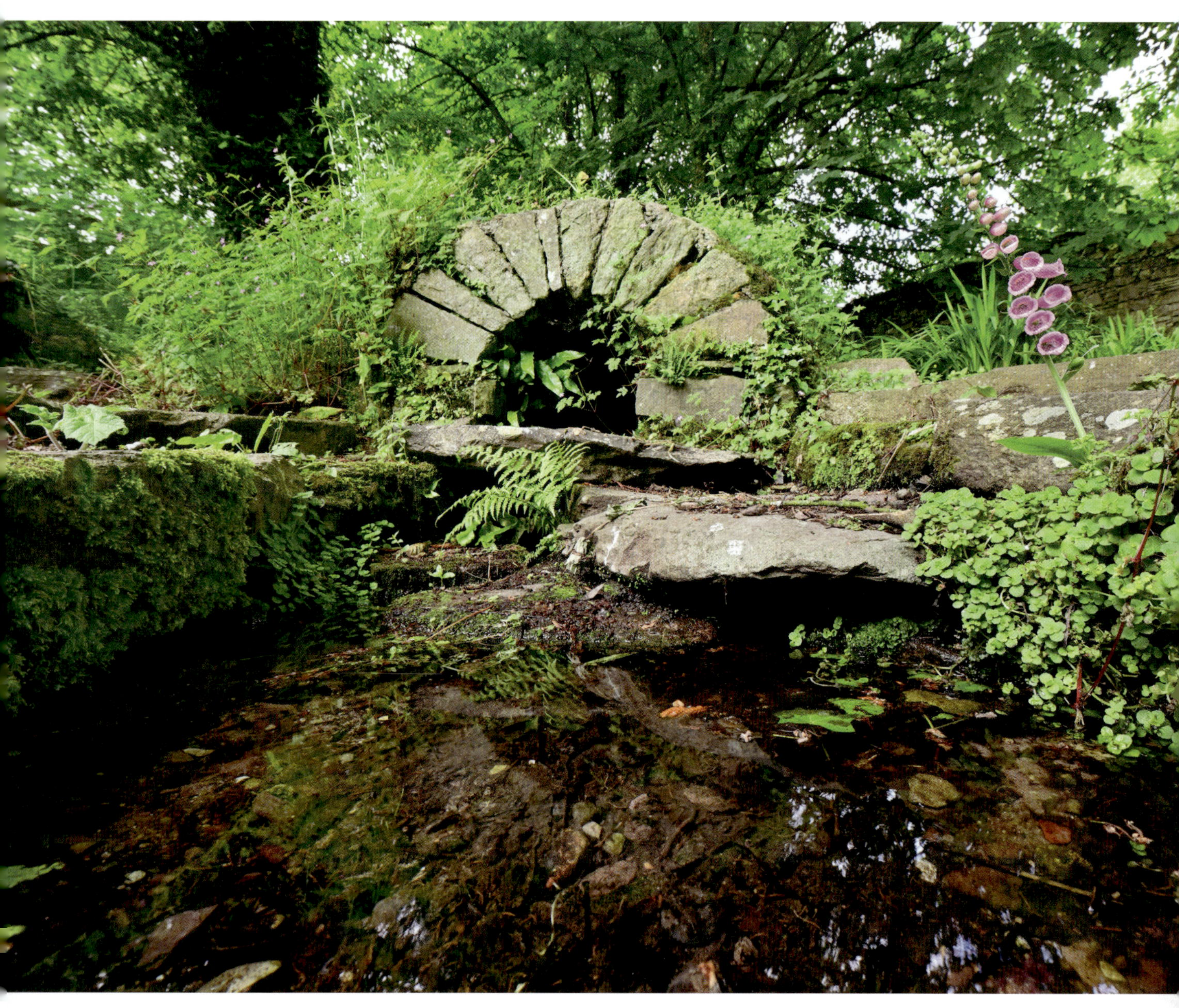

One of the many wishing wells in north Cork.

Kanturk Castle. This Irish chieftain's house dates from the 1580s and is located just outside the market town of Kanturk.

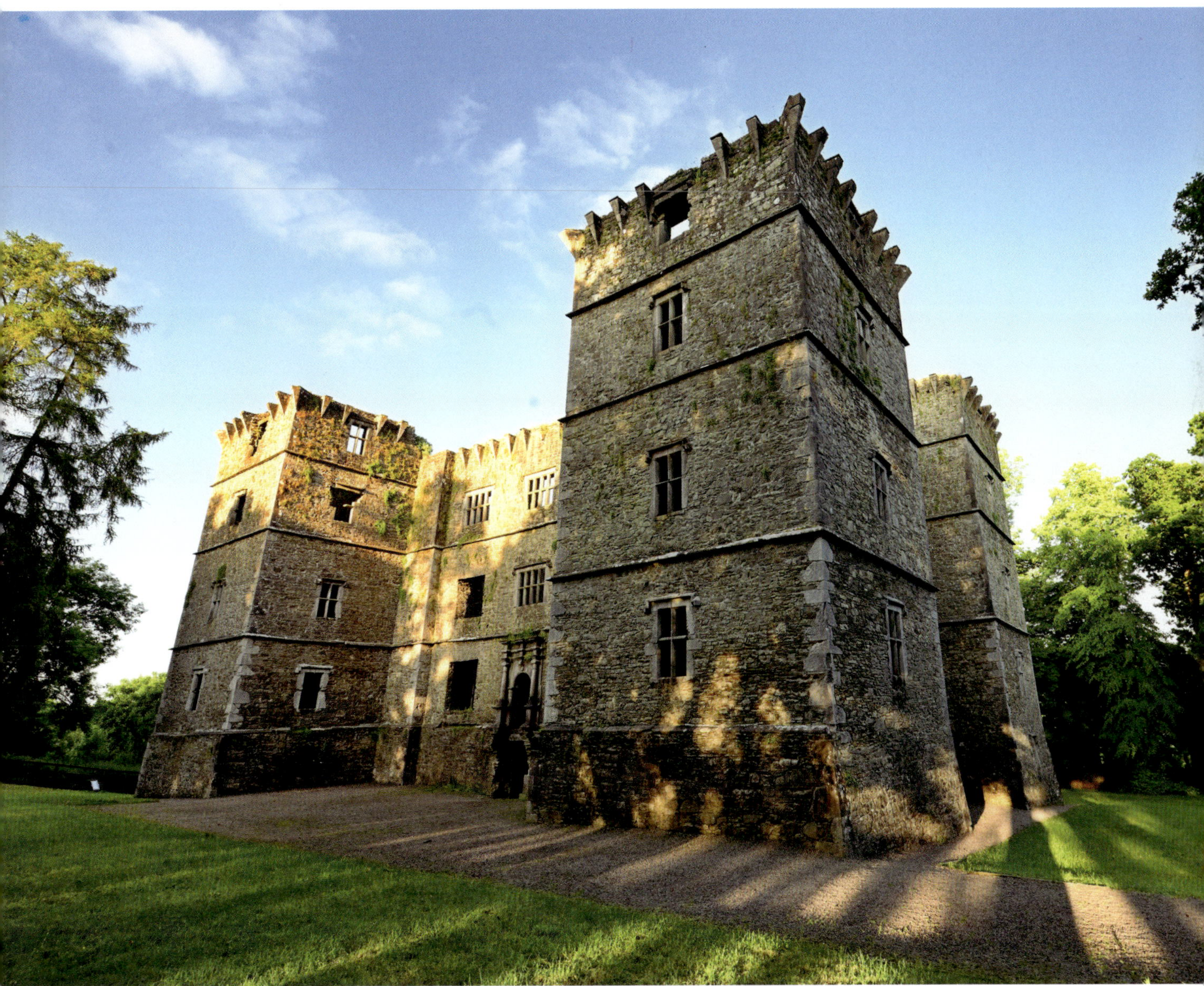

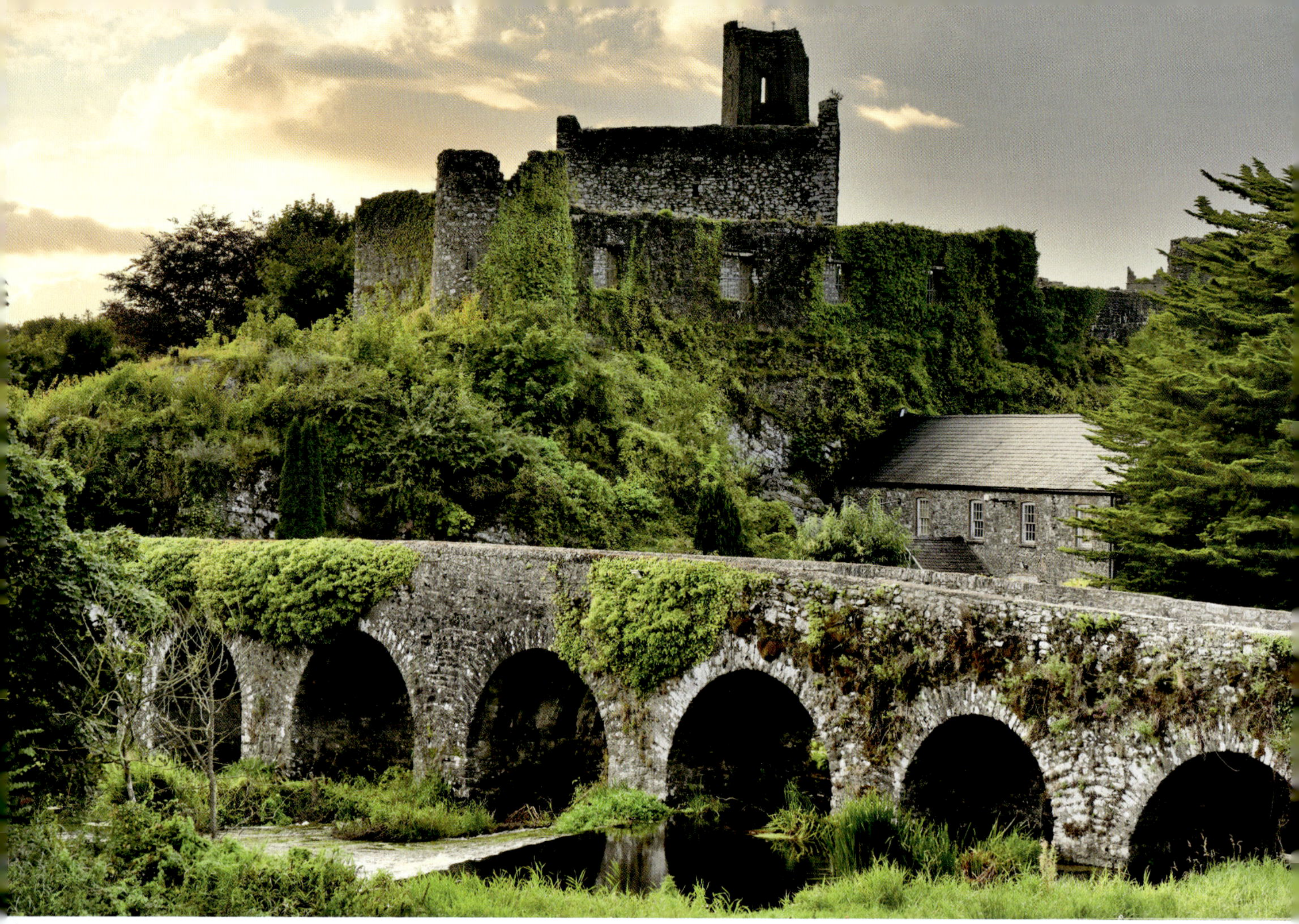

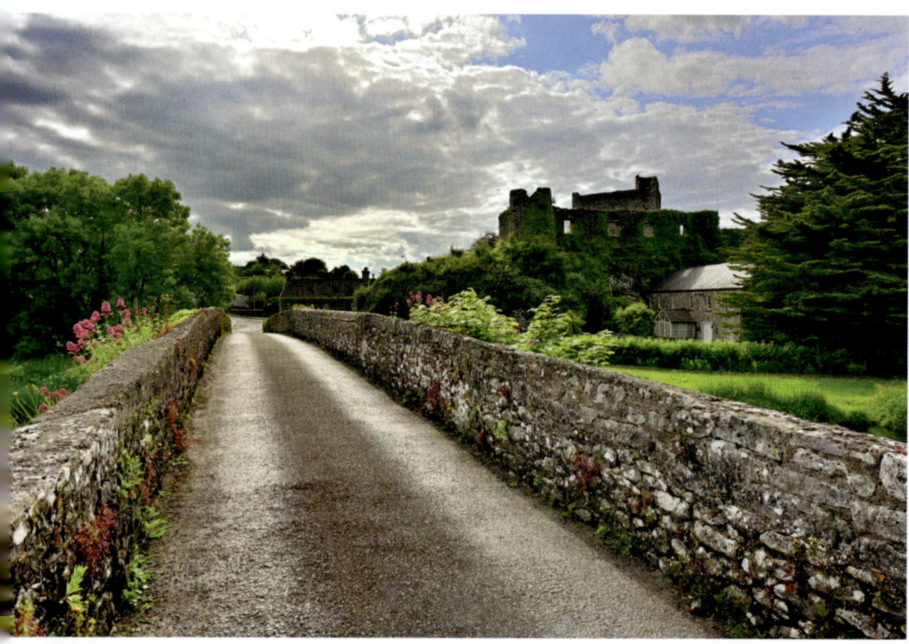

Above and left: Glanworth Castle and bridge. The thirteen-arch bridge is believed to be the oldest and narrowest working bridge in Europe.

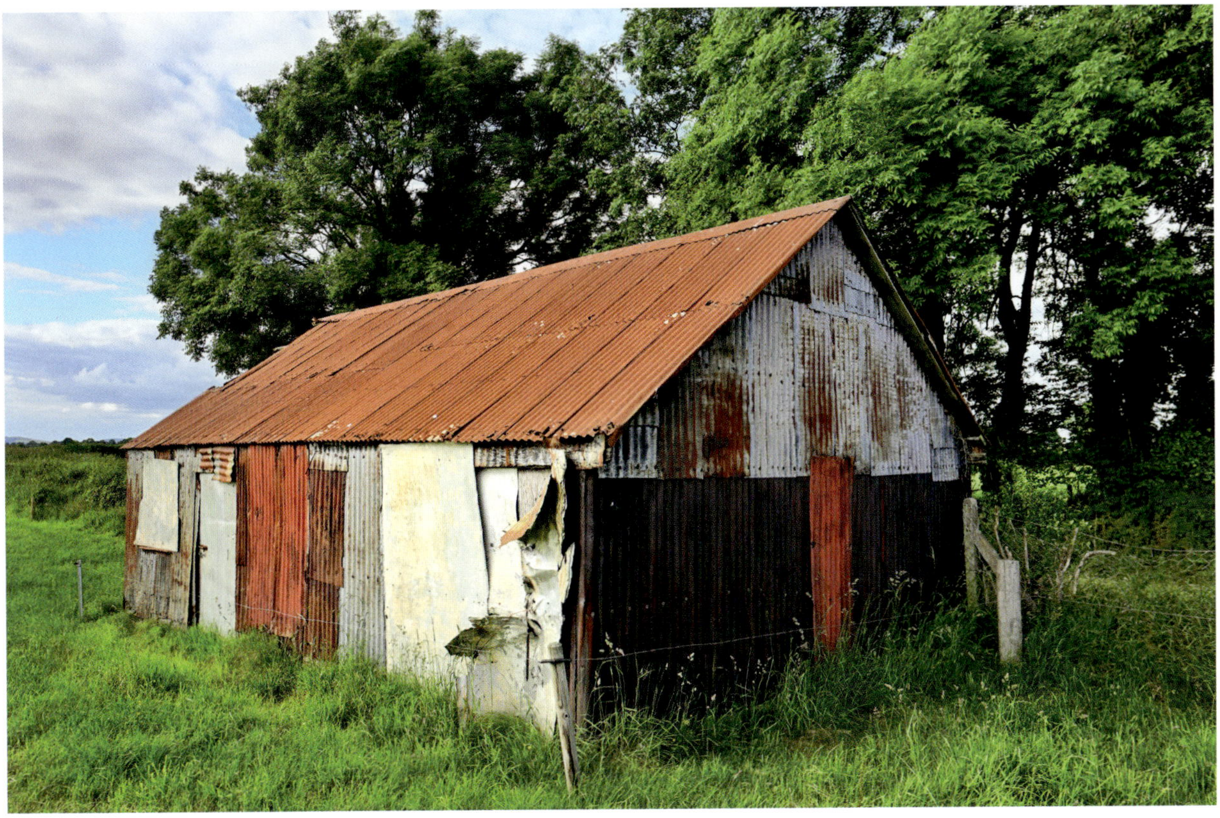

Above: A patchwork barn, near Kildorrery.

Below: Kilcummer Viaduct in evening sunshine.

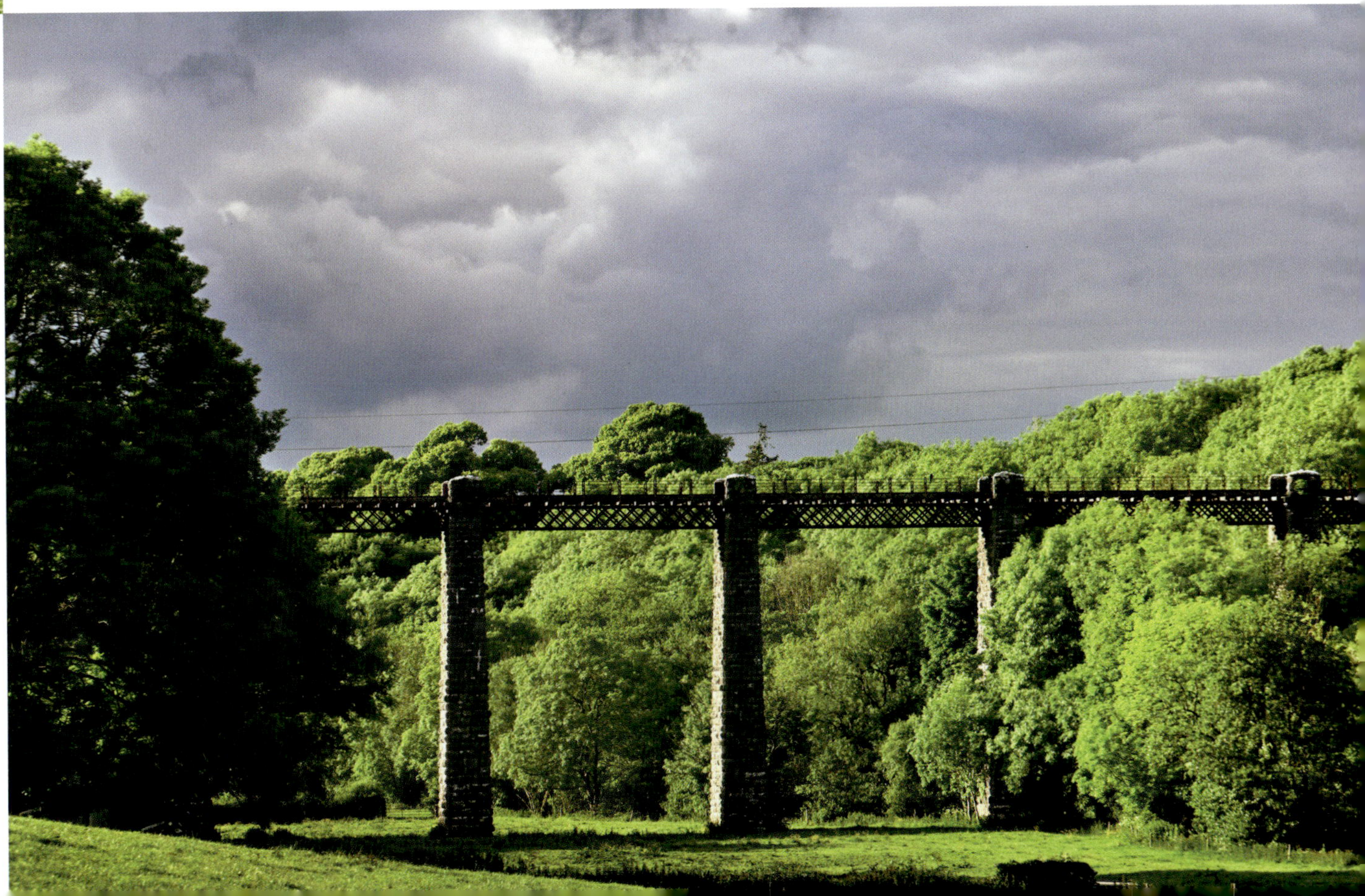

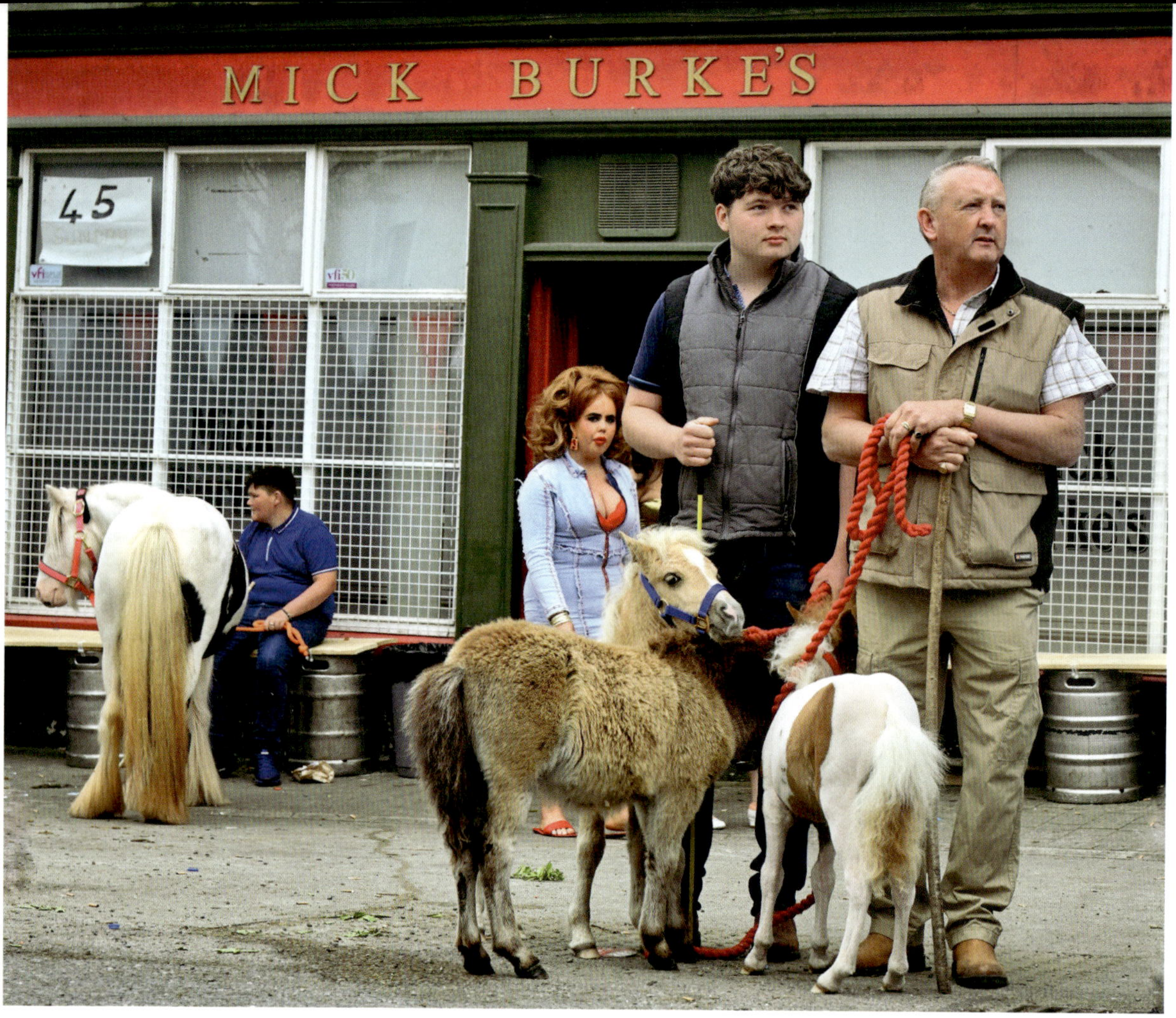

Above: Father and son at Cahirmee horse fair. **Below:** Lively ponies at Cahirmee horse fair.

Opposite: A harvest sunset.

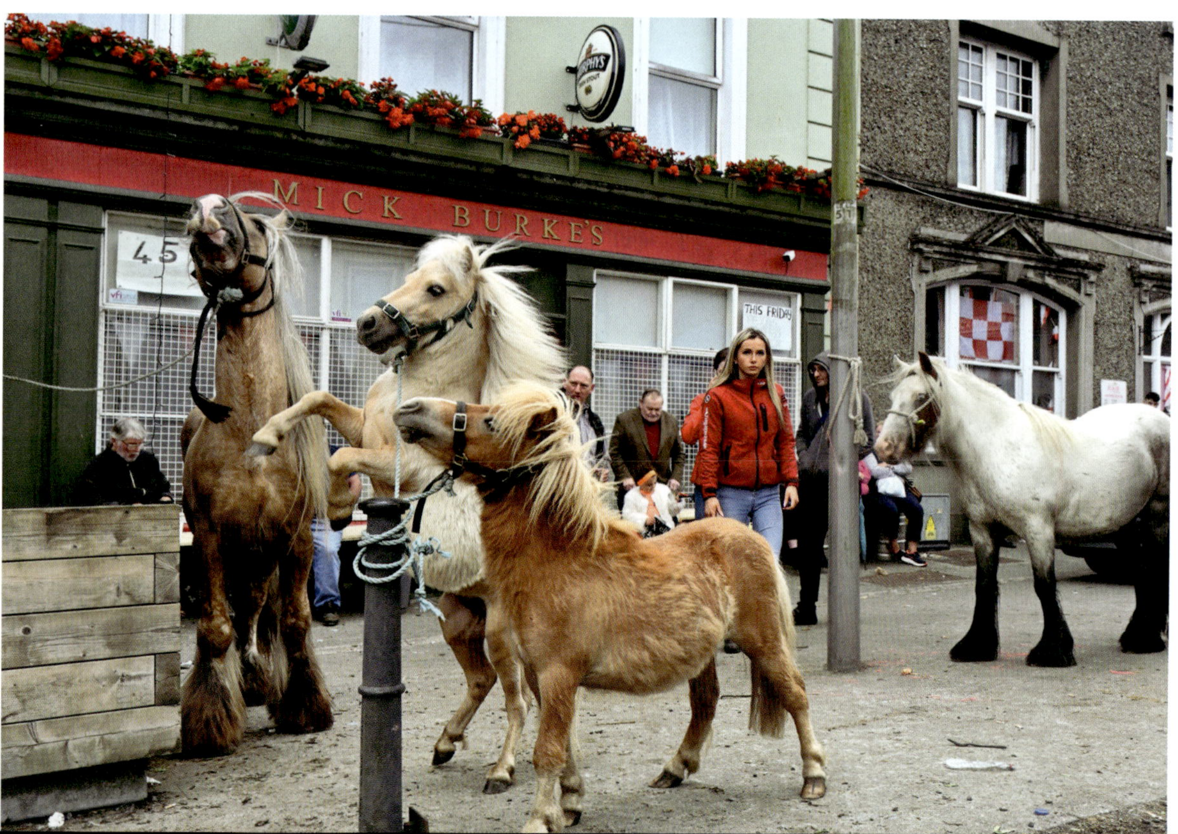

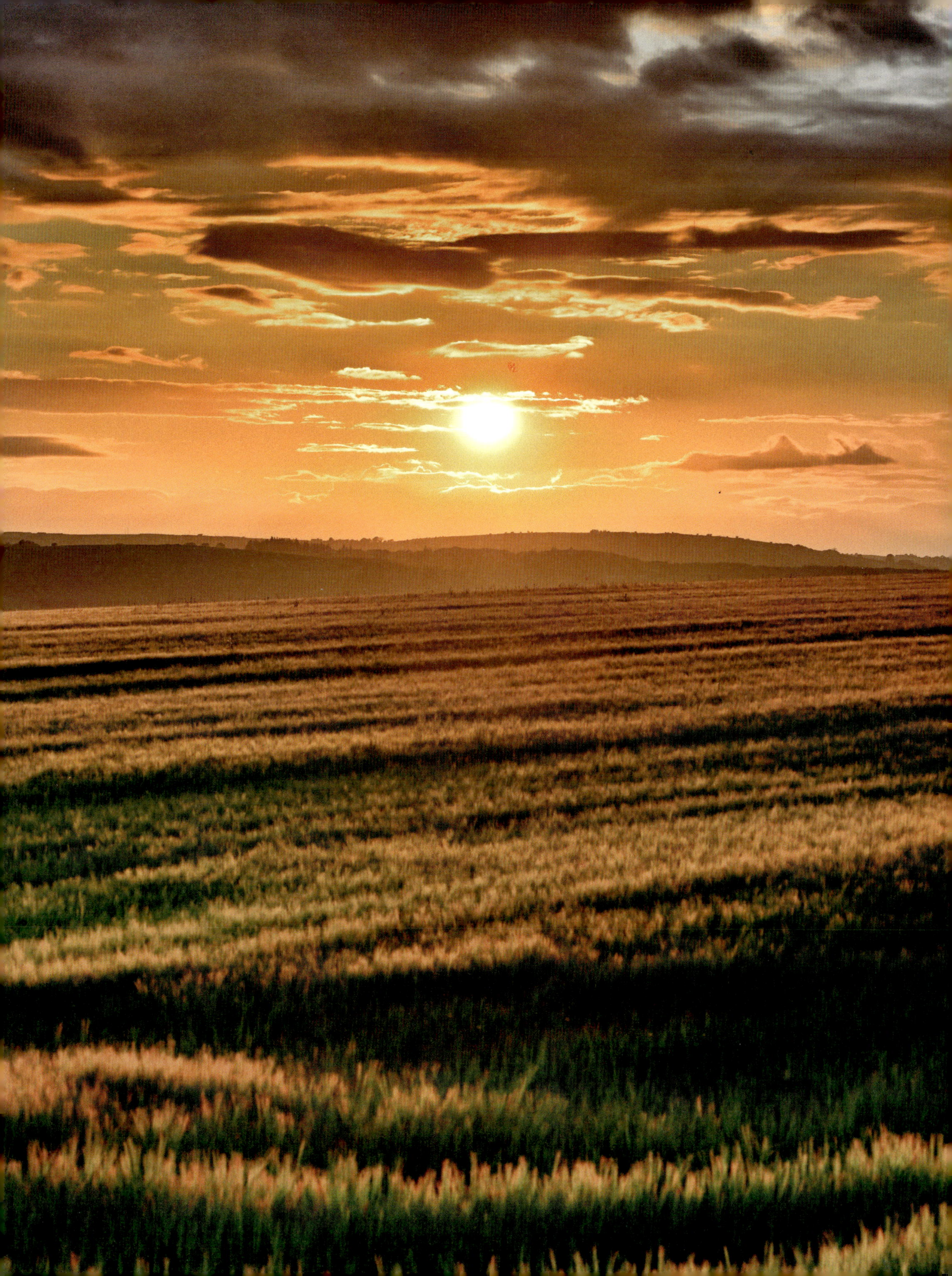

Aerial view of Gougane Barra, nestled in the Shehy Mountains, about 20 kilometres west of Macroom.

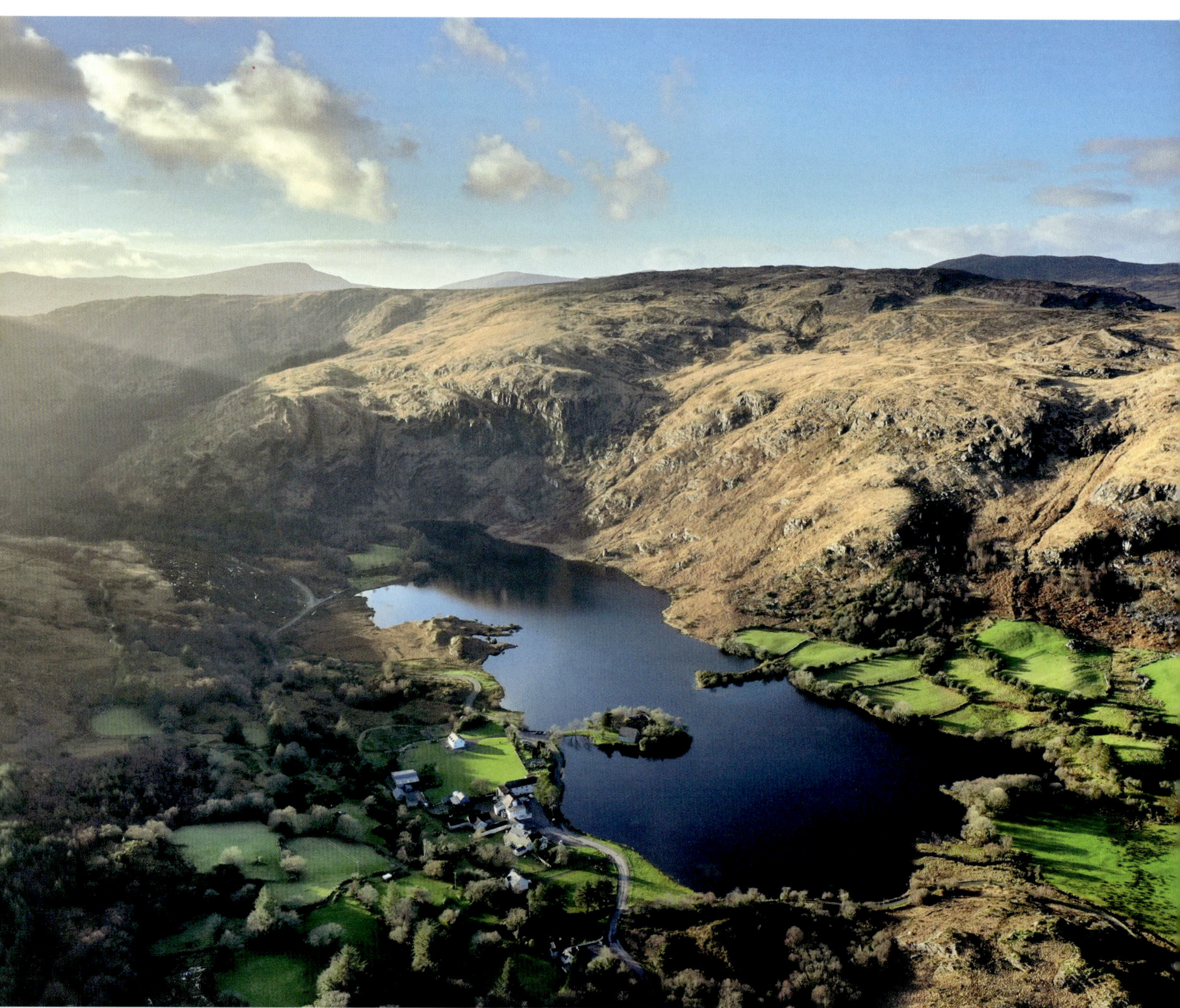

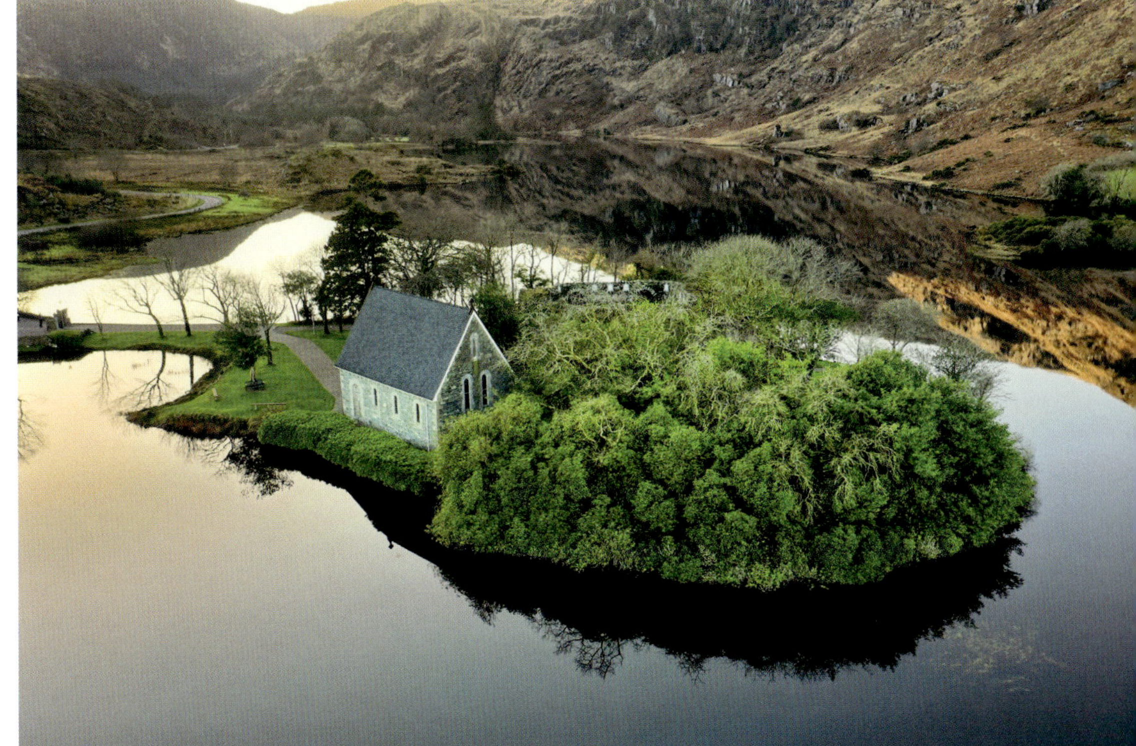

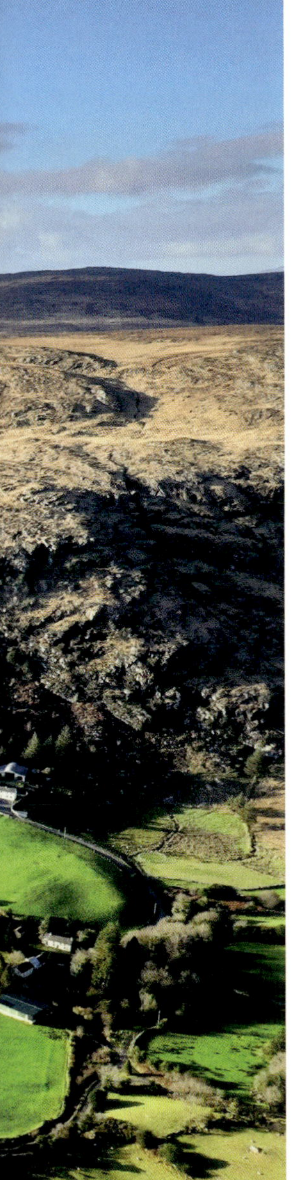

St Finbarr's Oratory in Gougane Barra. The tiny chapel, built in 1903, is reputedly on the site of a sixth-century monastic settlement.

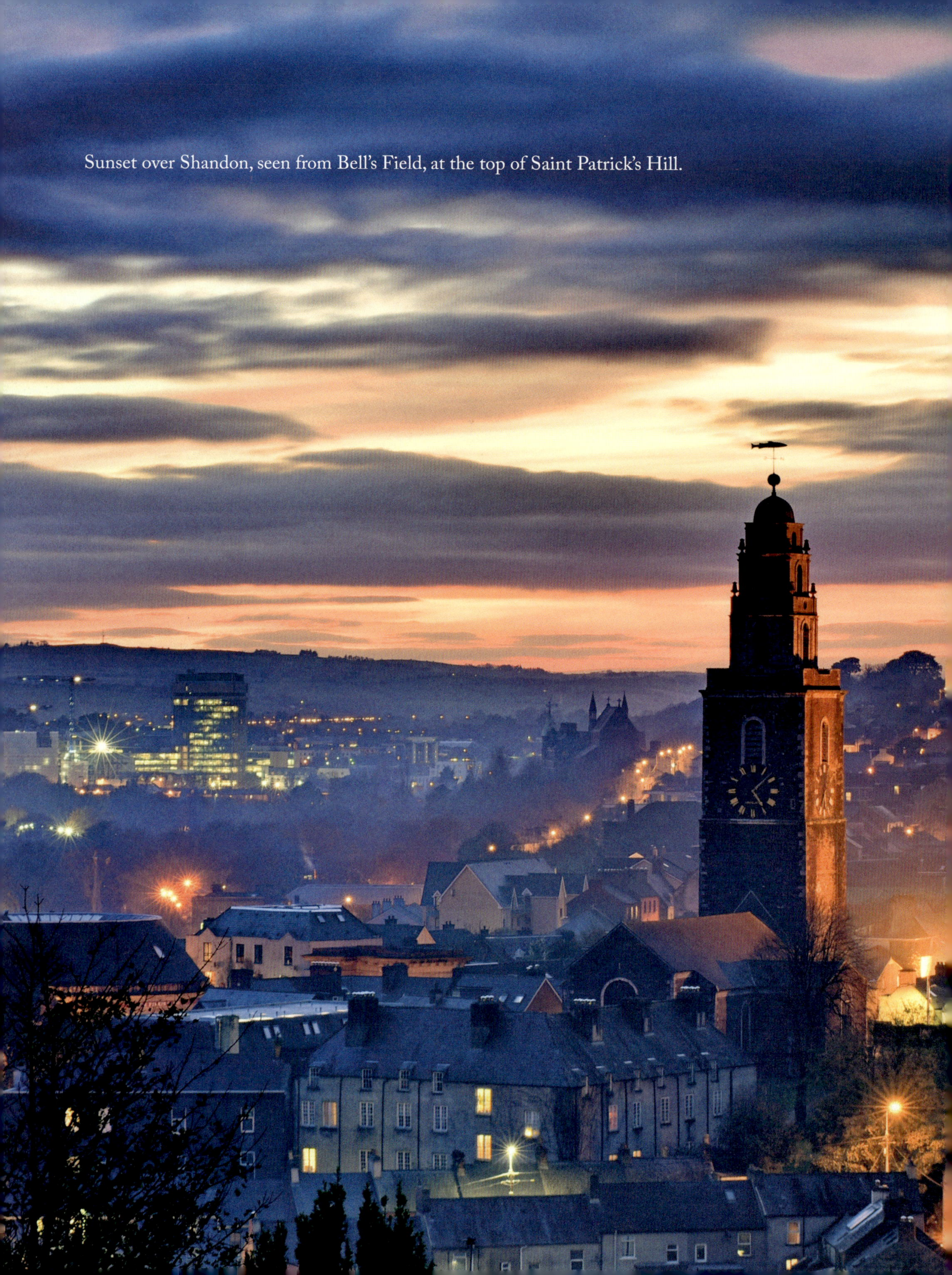

Sunset over Shandon, seen from Bell's Field, at the top of Saint Patrick's Hill.

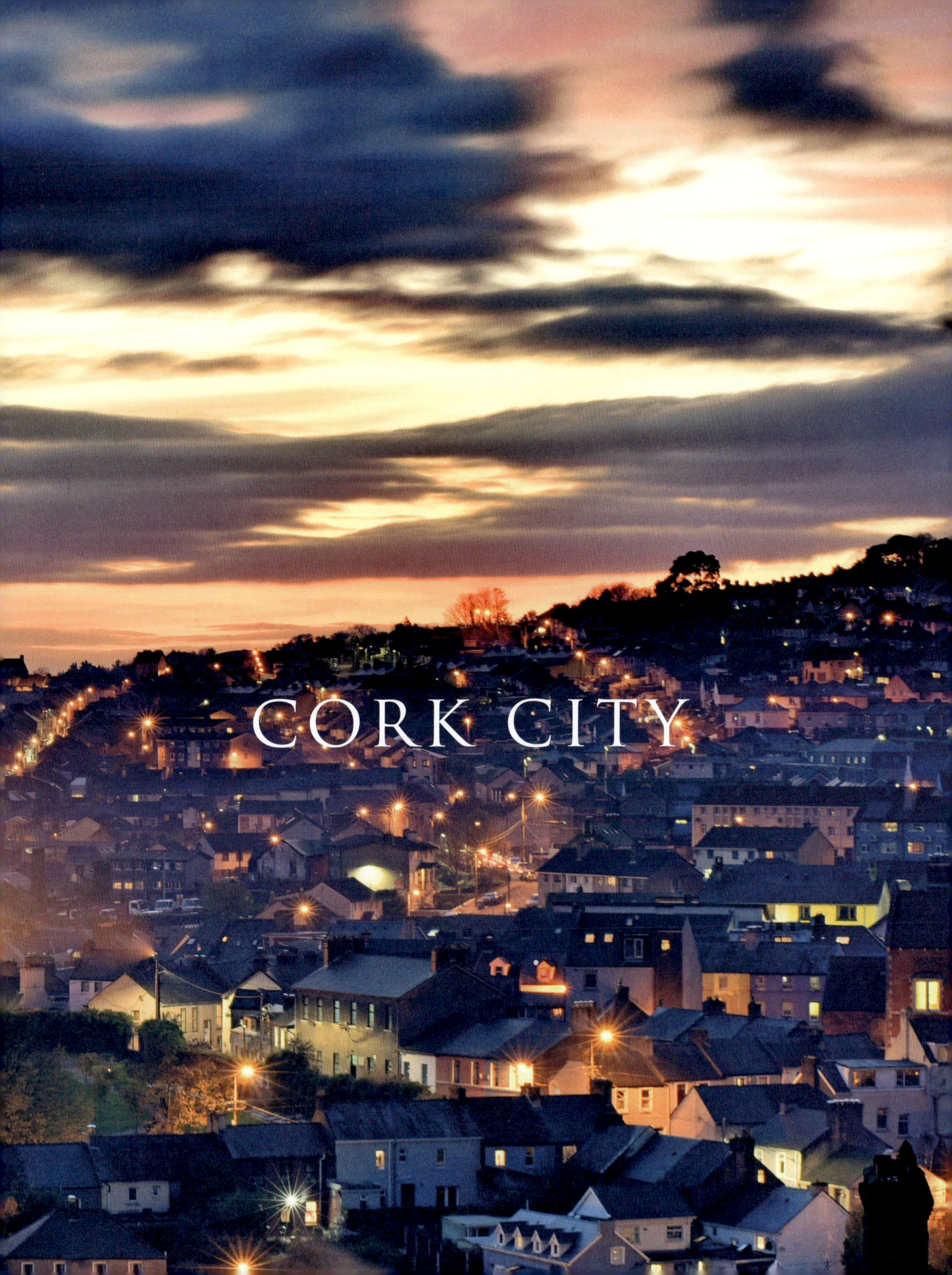

CORK CITY

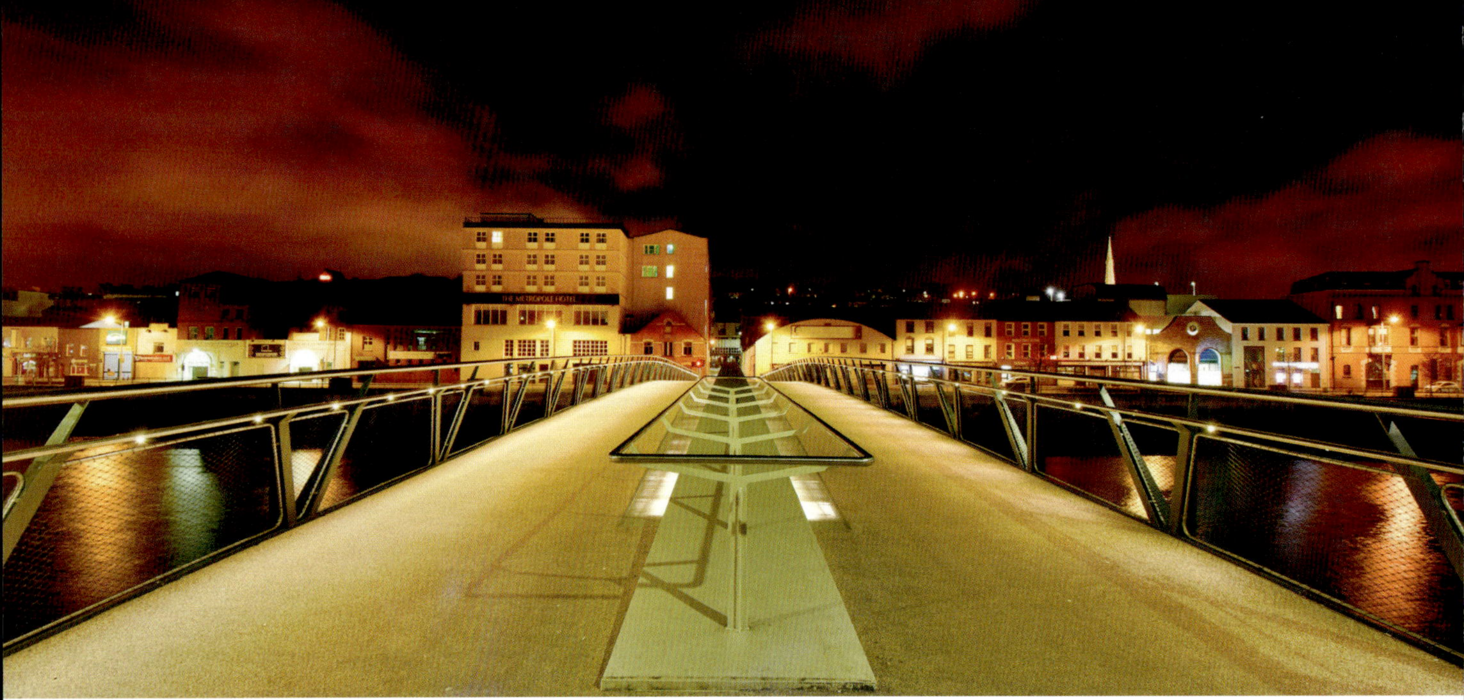

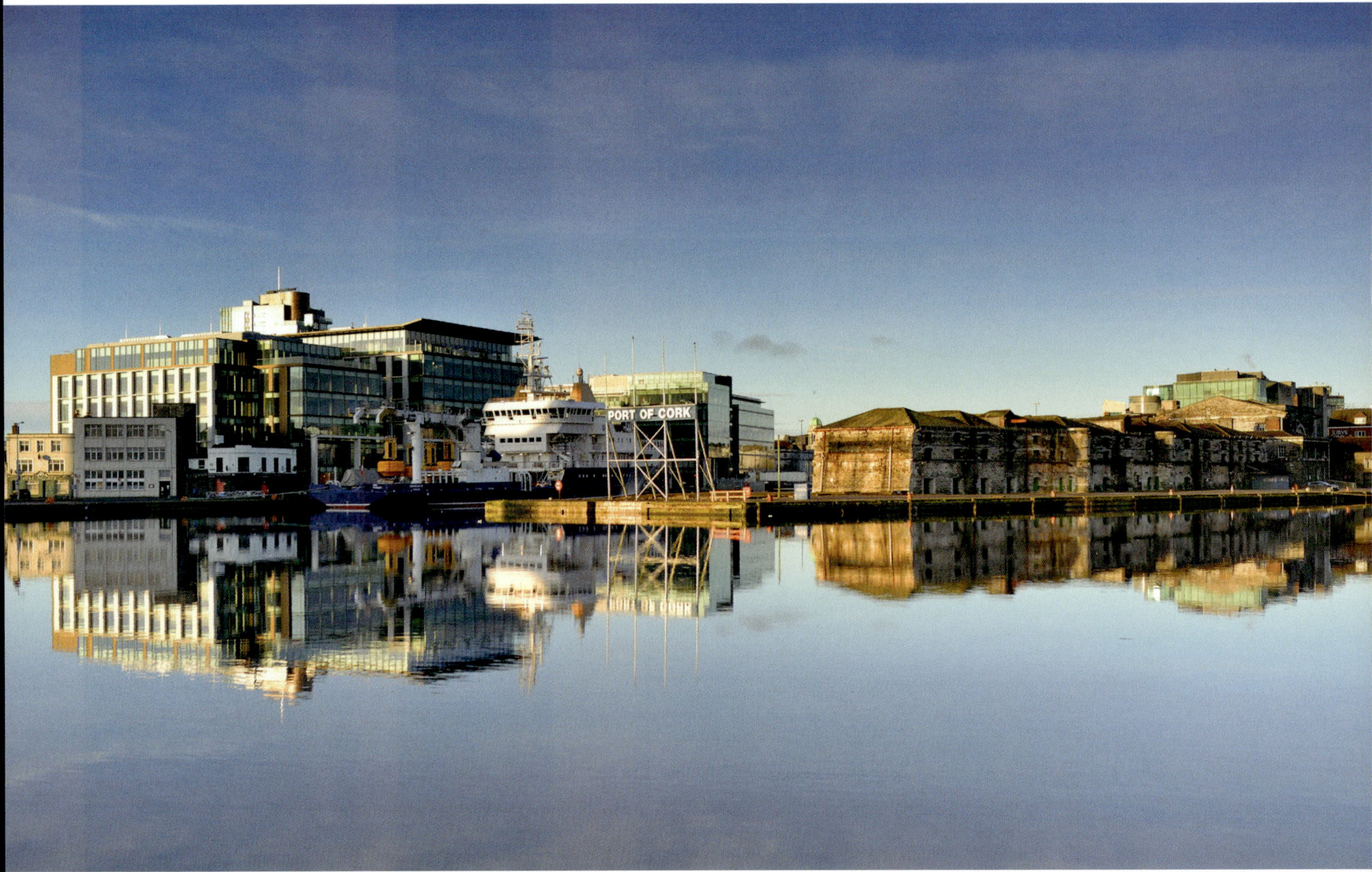

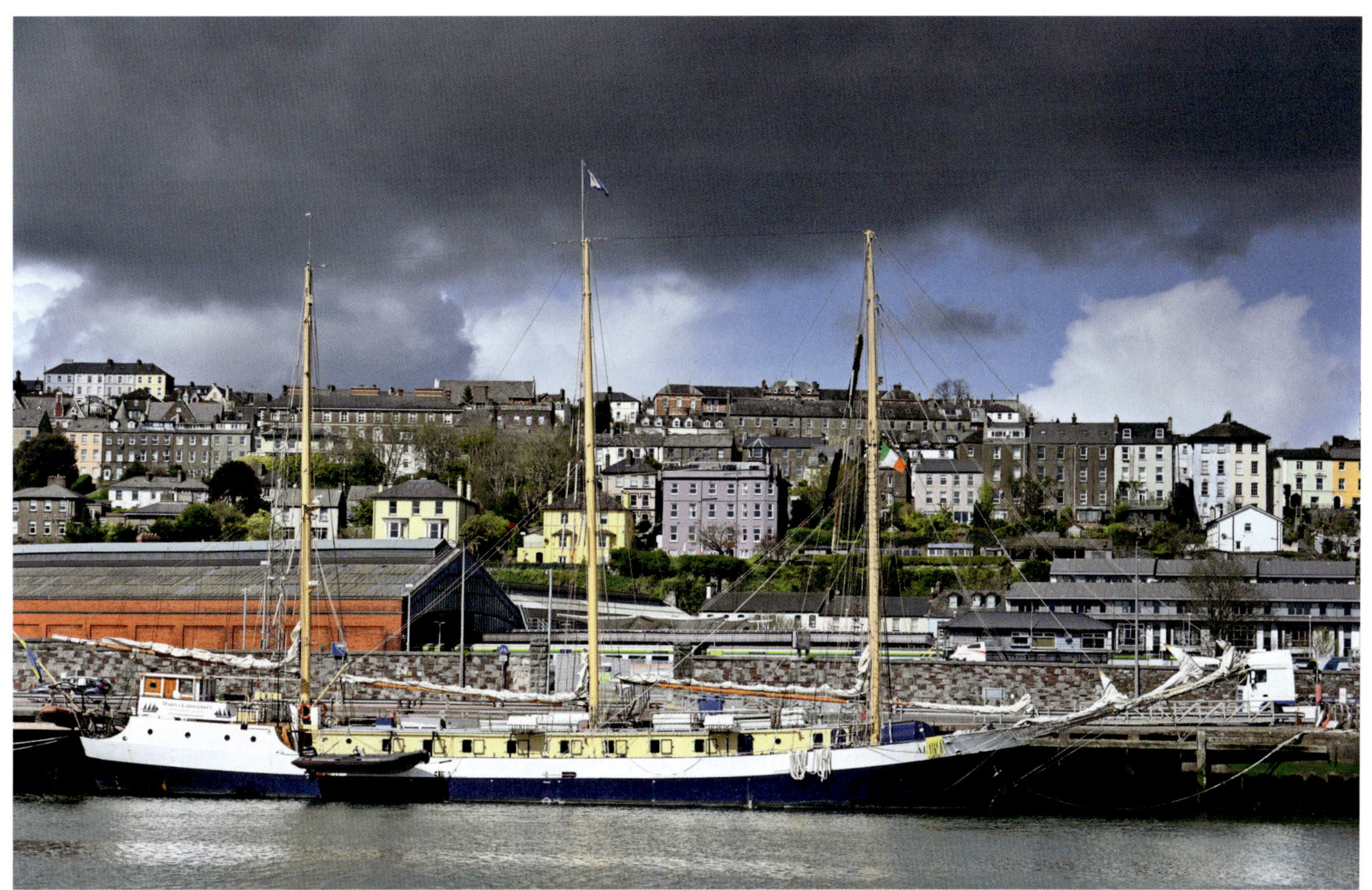

Above: The tall ship *Älva* moored outside Cork Kent Railway station. The Swedish sail-training vessel is a three-masted schooner, built in 1939.

Opposite top: Mary Elmes Bridge, built in 2019, is the newest bridge in the city and spans the River Lee between Merchant's Quay and Saint Patrick's Quay. Its name honours Cork woman Mary Elmes (1908–2002) who was a humanitarian aid worker in both the Spanish Civil War and Second World War.

Opposite bottom: A tranquil morning at the Port of Cork.

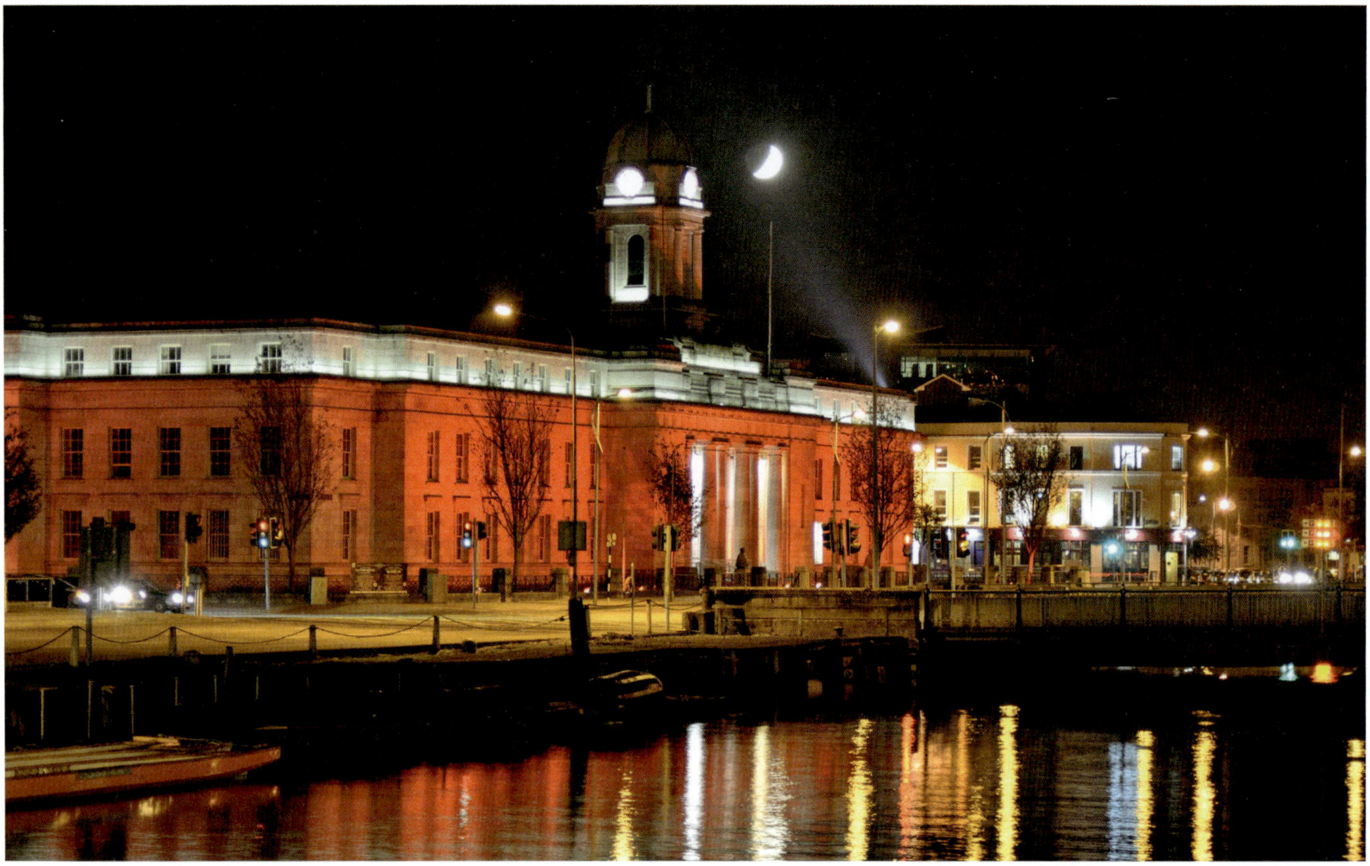

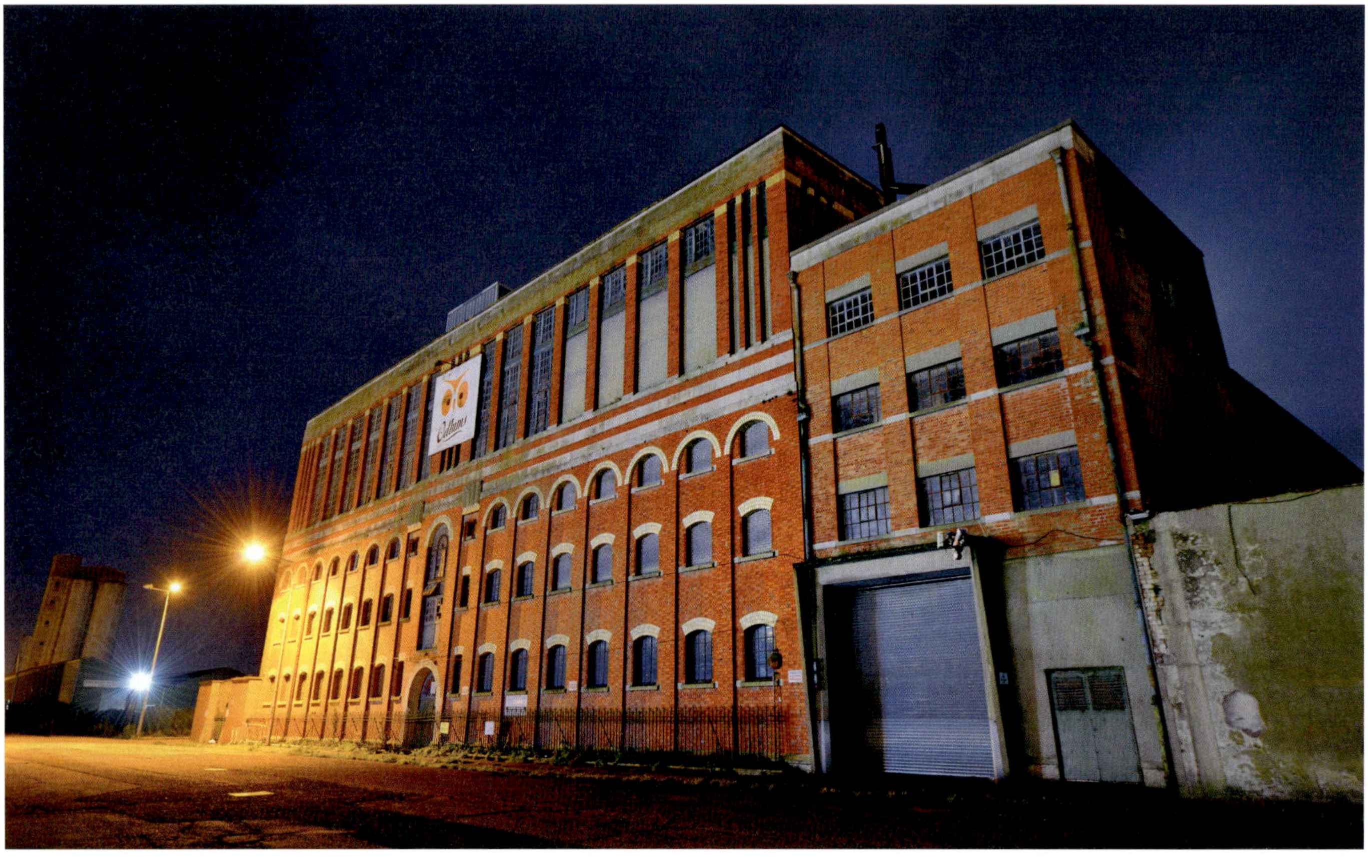

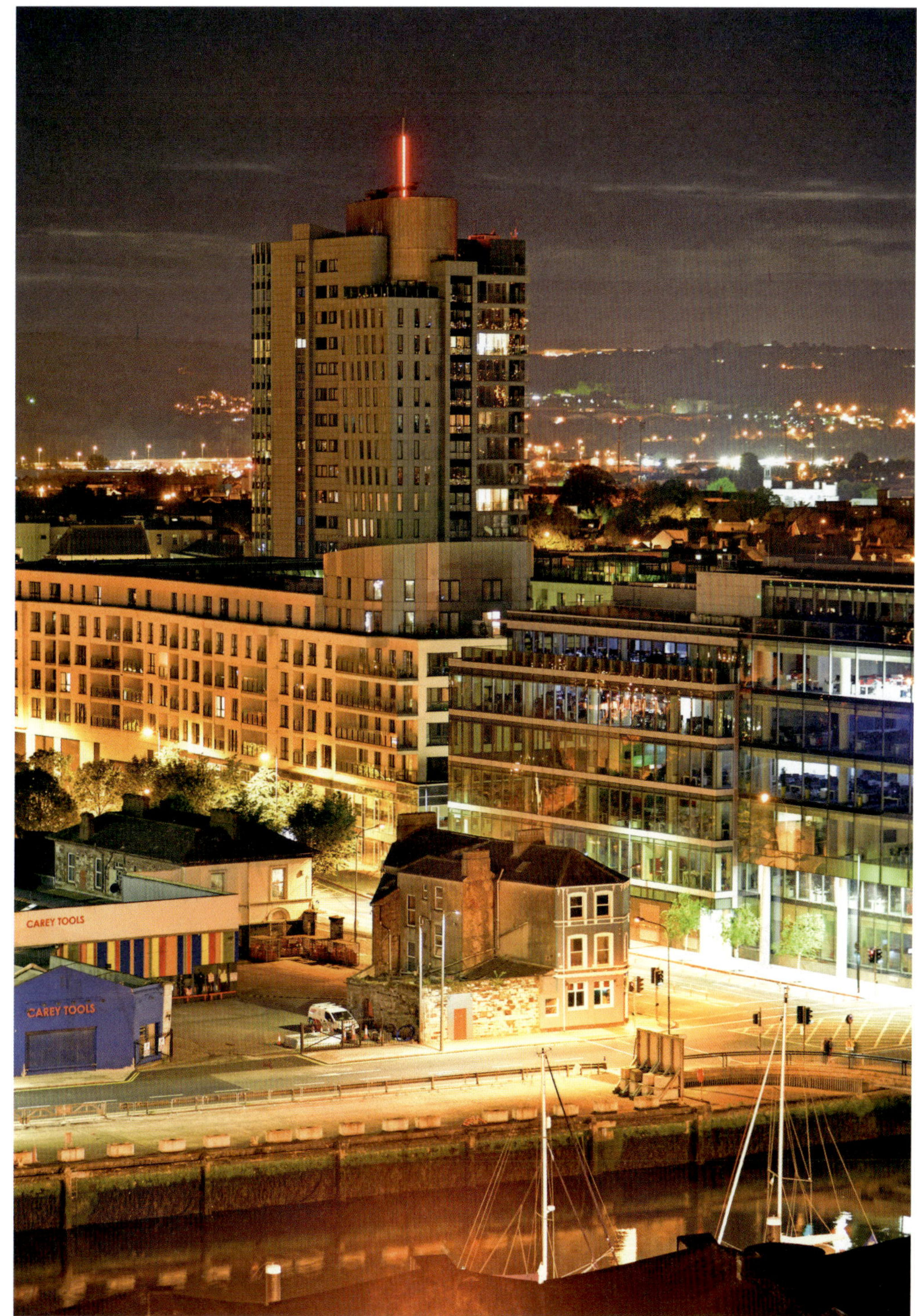

Opposite top: The moon over City Hall and the River Lee.

Opposite bottom: The Odlum's building. On the soon-to-be redeveloped docklands, this is one of the best-known buildings in Cork city.

Above: Modern apartments and offices on Cork's south side, with the Elysian in the background.

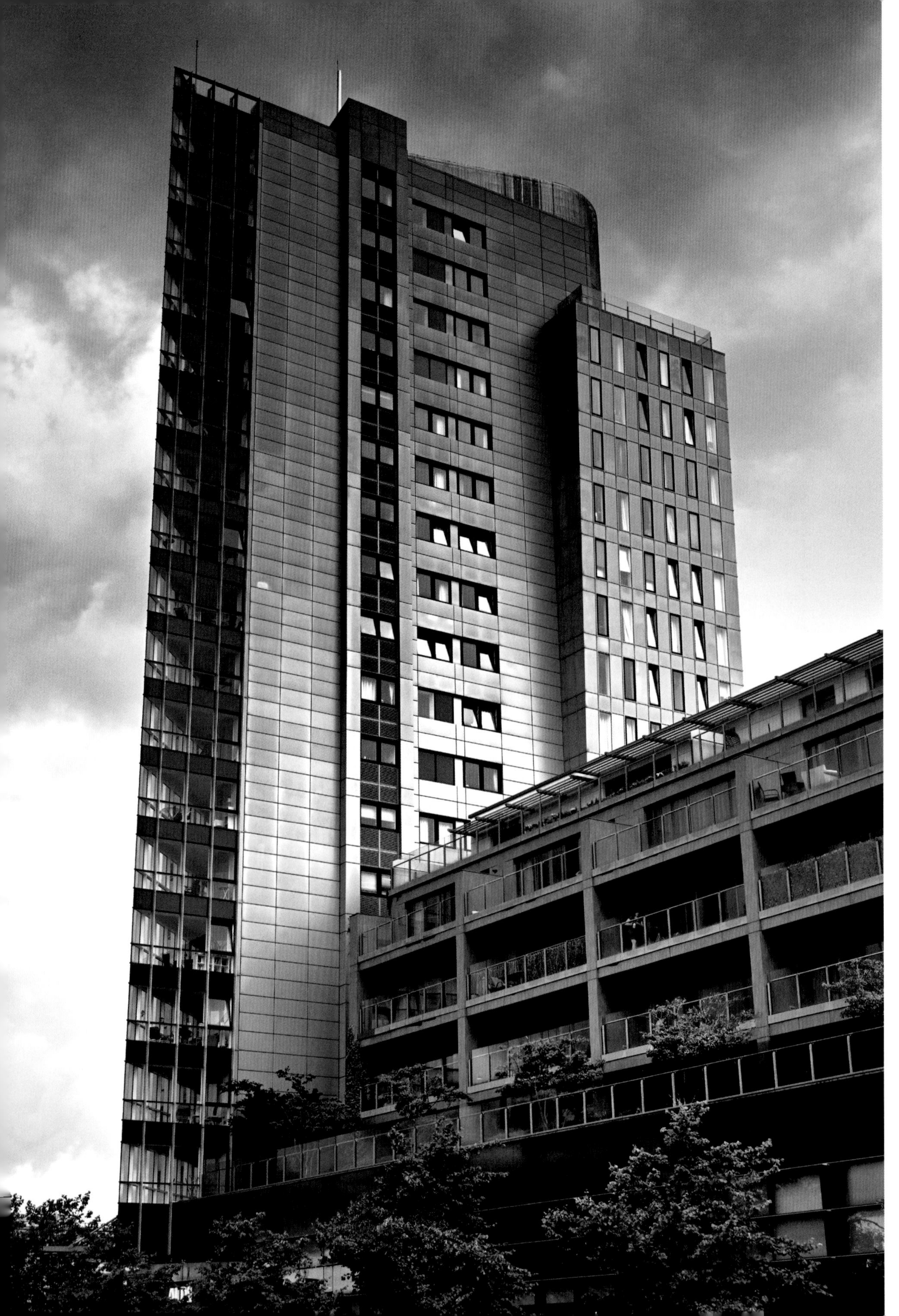

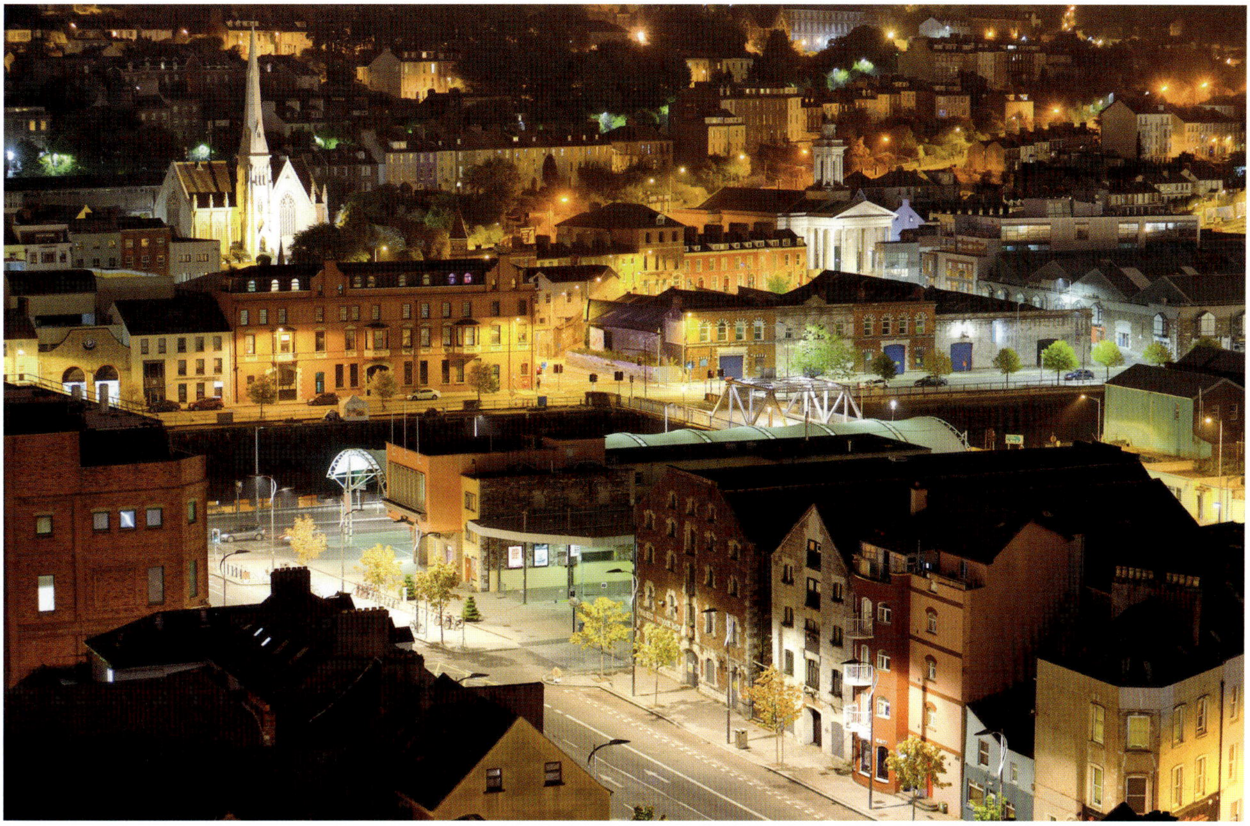

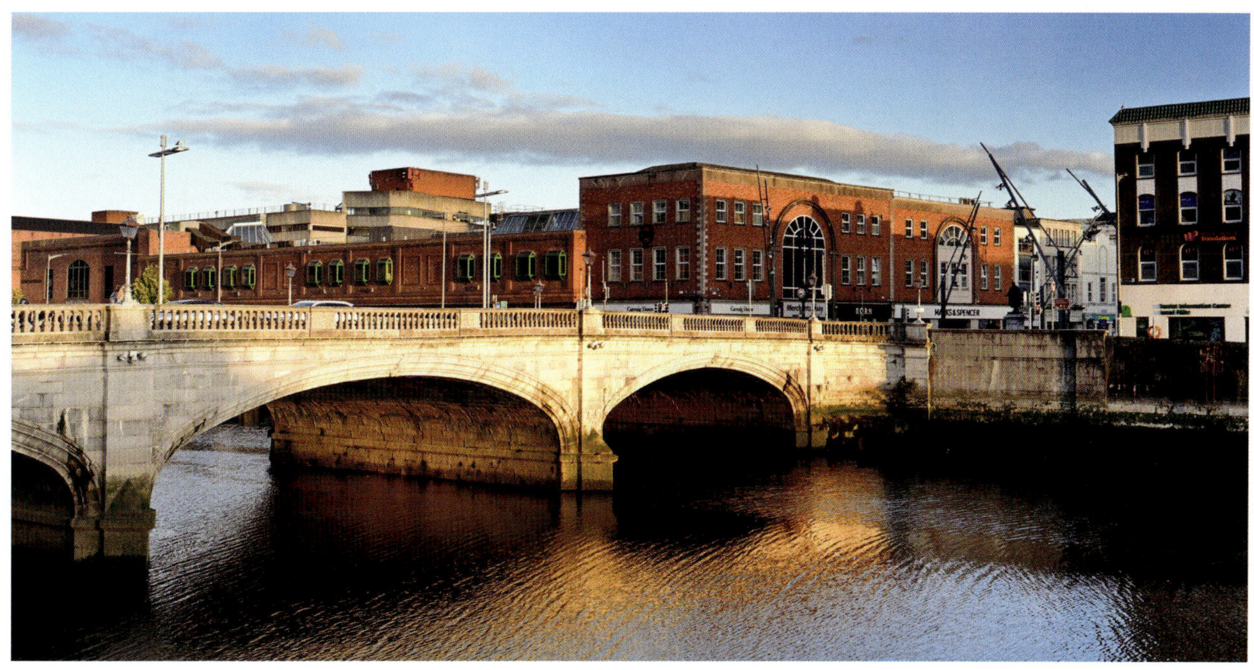

Opposite: The Elysian. Completed in 2008, it is Cork's tallest building and the third tallest in Ireland.

Above: Parnell Place at night near the bus station. Across the River Lee are the floodlit Trinity Presbyterian church (left) in the city's Victorian quarter, and St Patrick's Roman Catholic Church (right).

Below: Saint Patrick's Bridge. This triple-arch bridge links the north and south sides of Cork city.

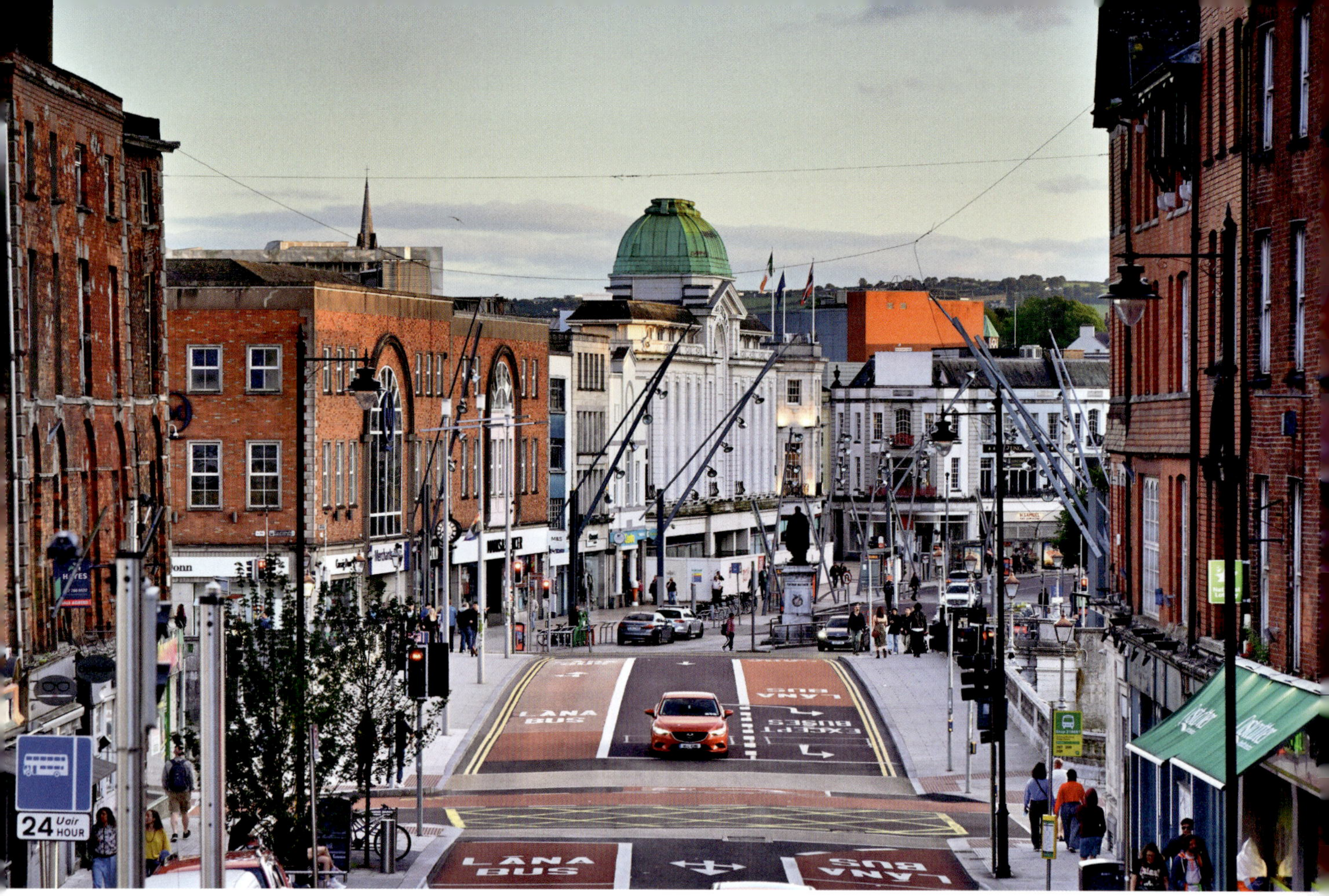
LÁNA
BUS
24 Uair
HOUR

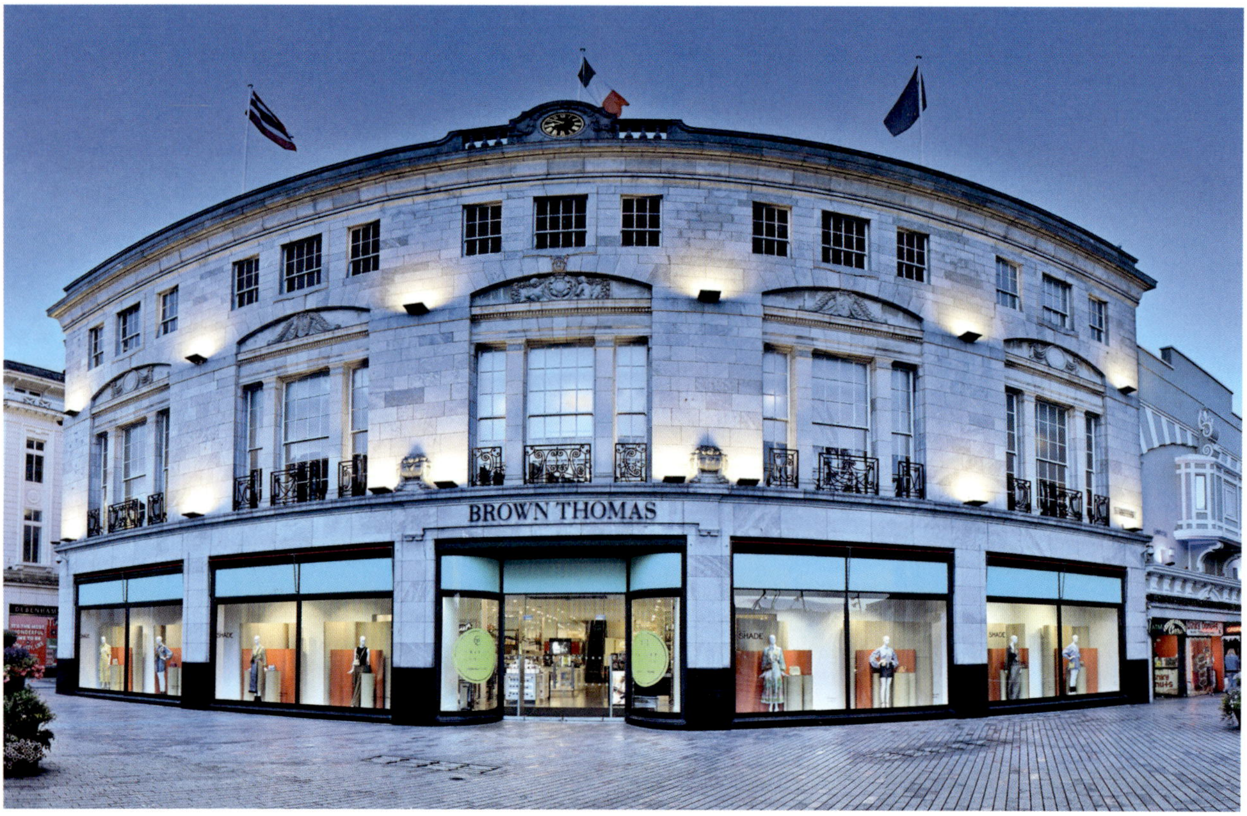
BROWN THOMAS

Opposite top: Looking down Saint Patrick's Street from Saint Patrick's Hill.

Opposite bottom: Brown Thomas, one of the iconic buildings on Saint Patrick's Street.

Below left: Saint Patrick's Bridge at night.

Below right: Mangan's clock on Saint Patrick's Street, a well-known meeting place.

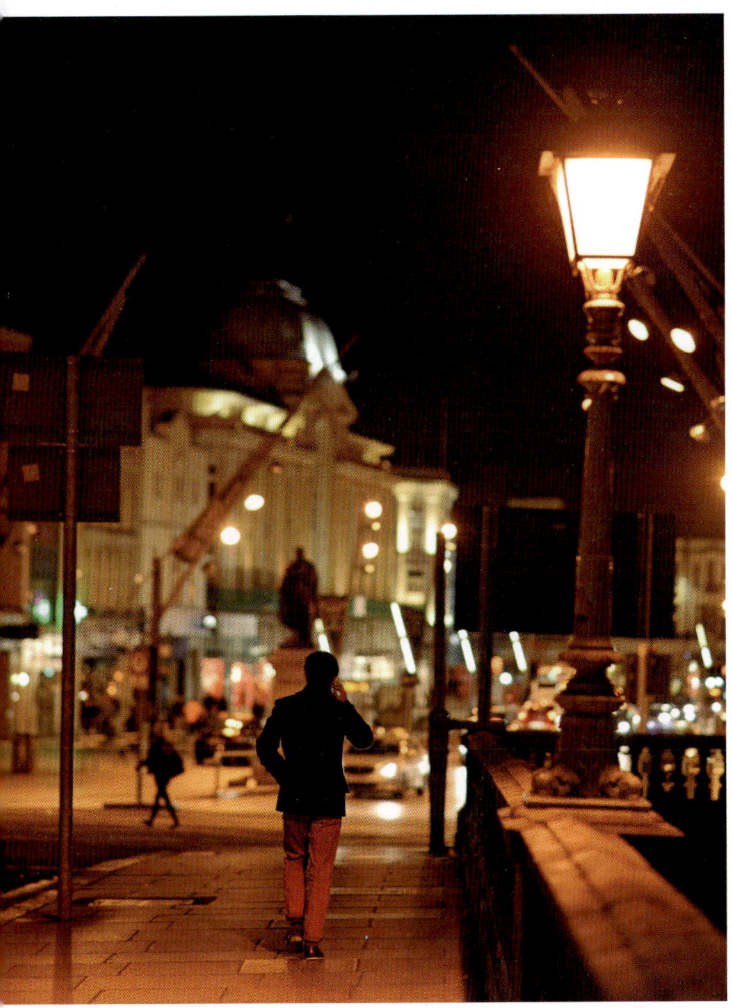

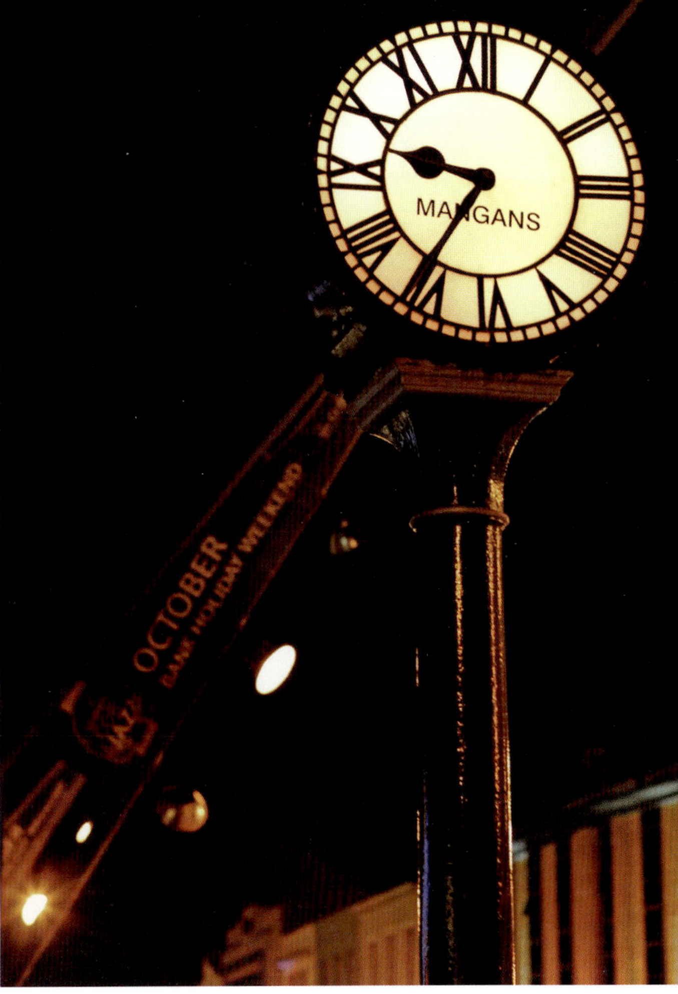

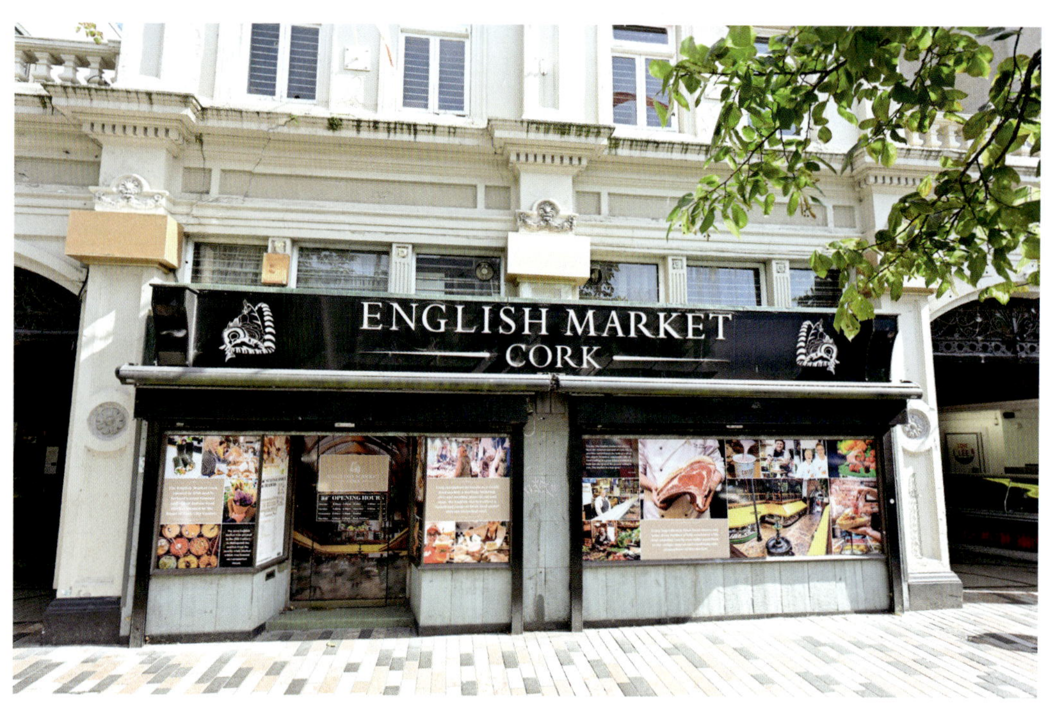

ENGLISH MARKET
CORK

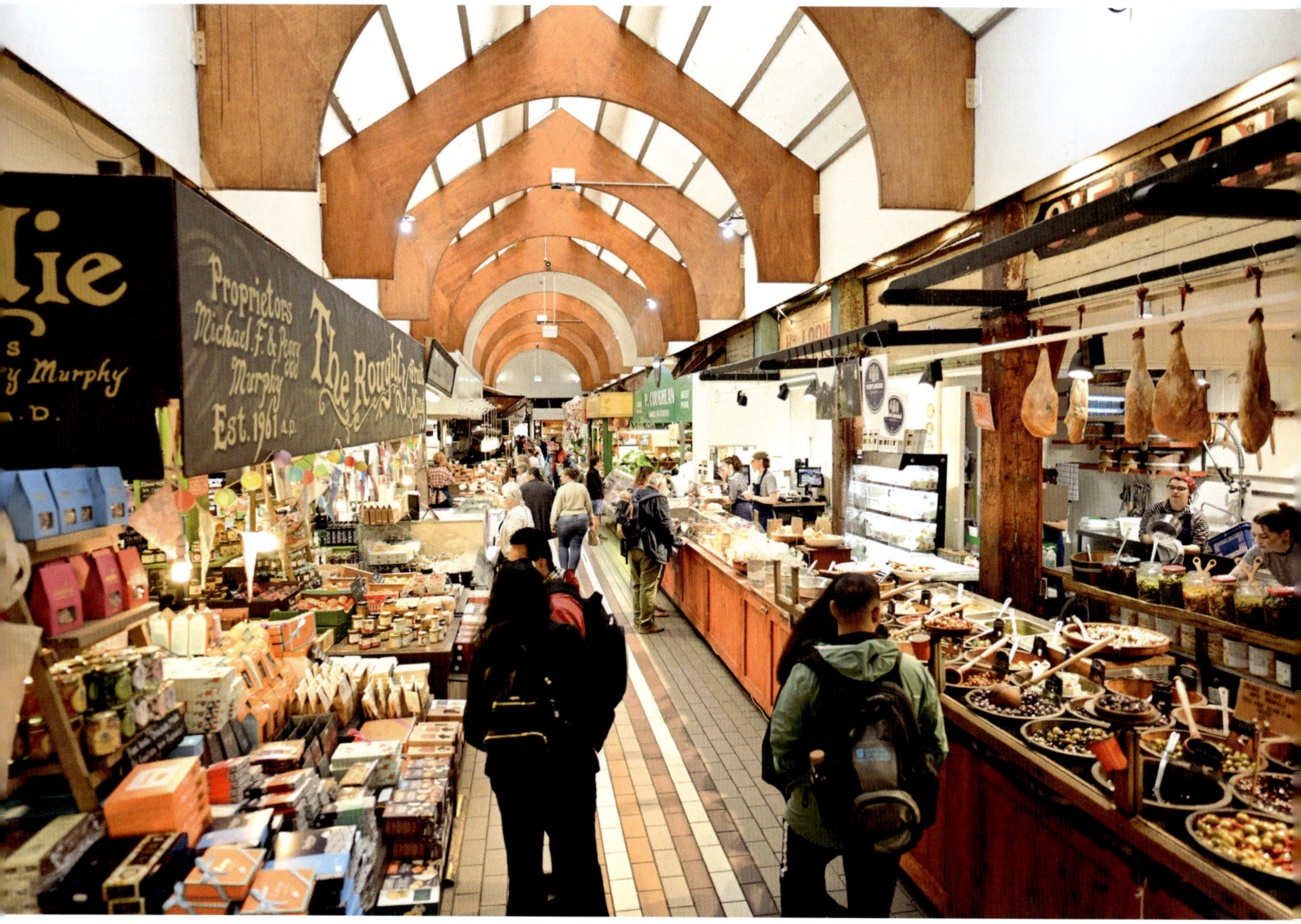

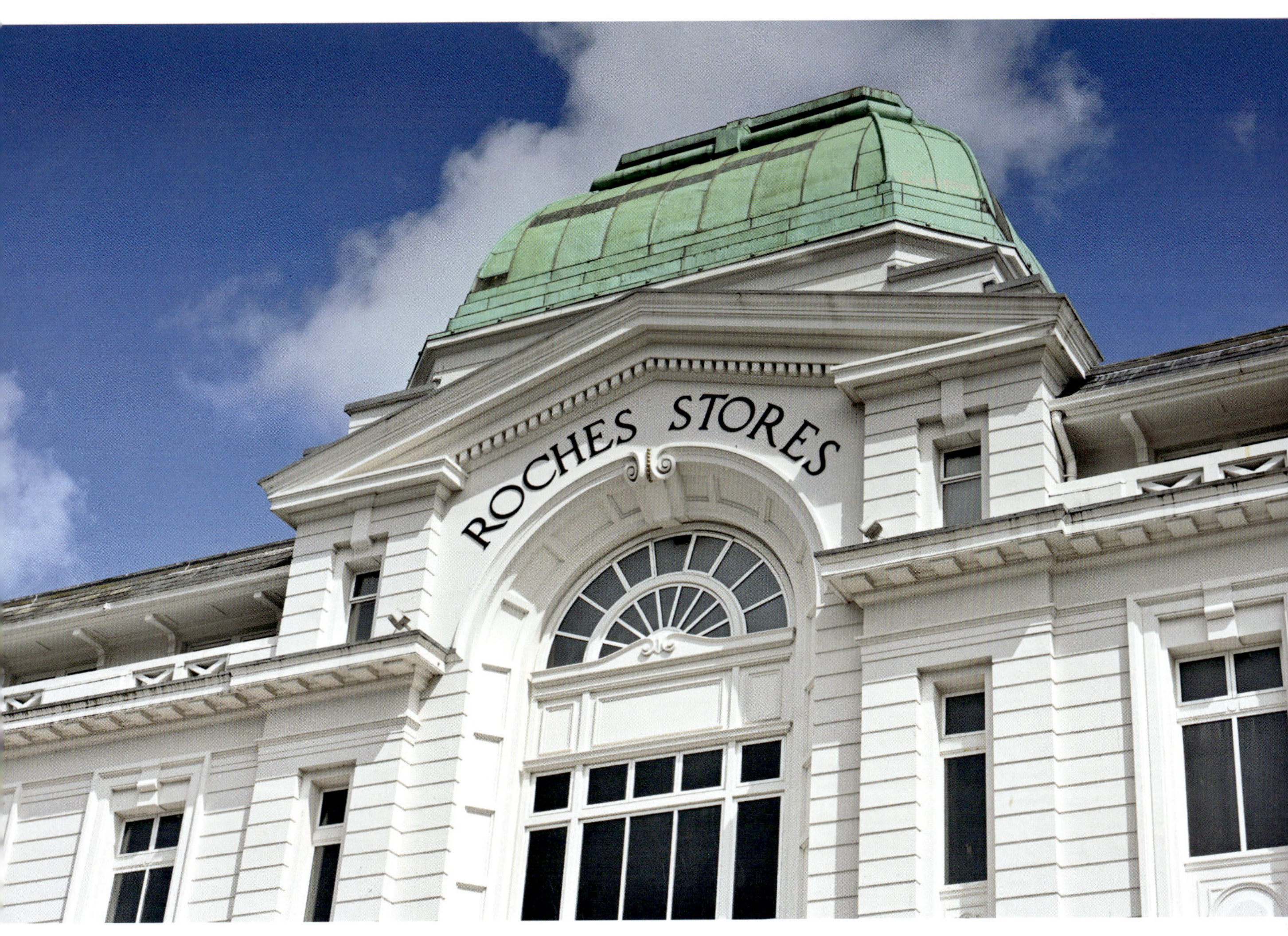

Opposite top: The English Market, Cork's famous food market.

Opposite bottom: Inside the English Market.

Above: The façade of Roches Stores on Saint Patrick's Street. Founded by William Roche in 1901, it began as a furniture shop and quickly turned into Cork's first department store. It closed in 2007.

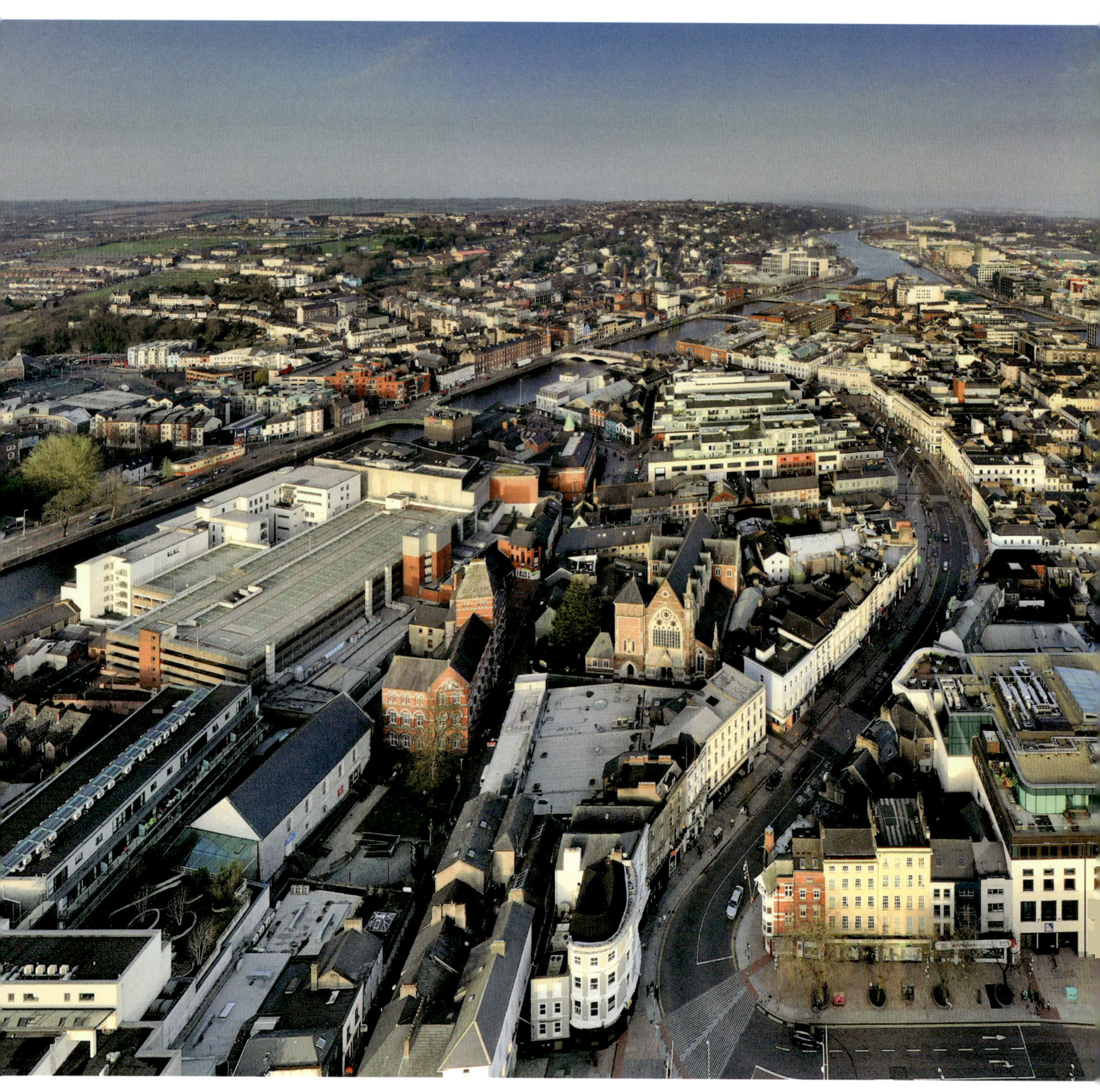

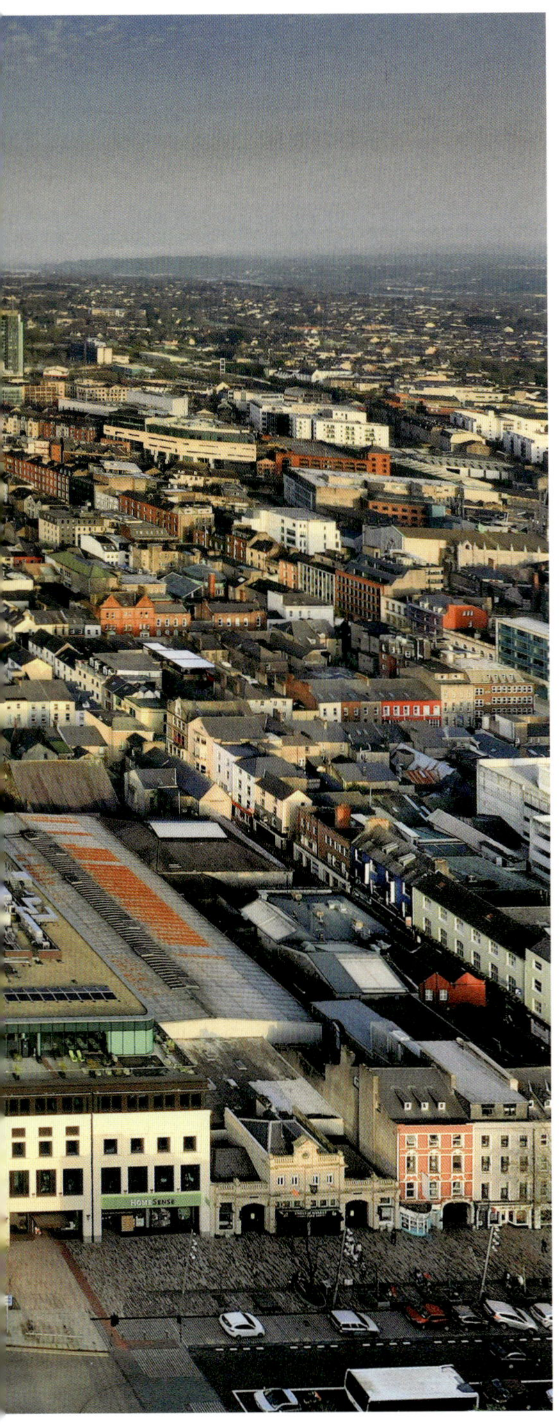

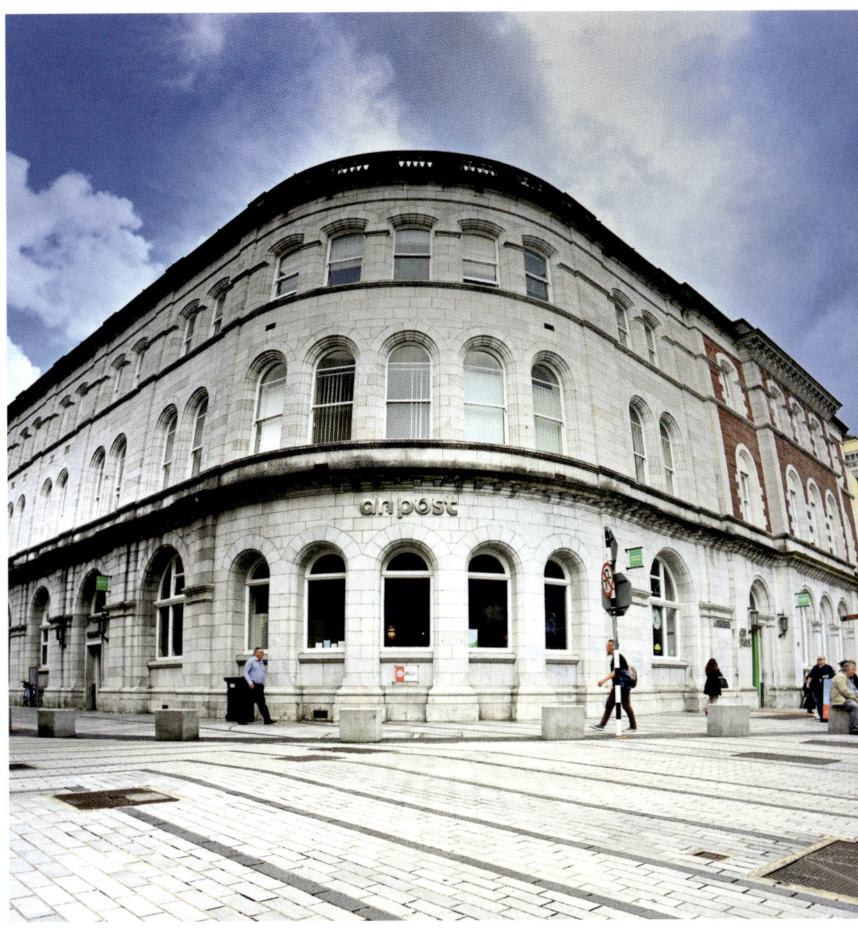

Left: An aerial view of Saint Patrick's Street.

Above: The limestone façade of Cork's General Post Office curves from Pembroke Street to Oliver Plunkett Street. Originally built as the George's Theatre in 1760, it was remodelled in the 1870s, after two fires damaged it substantially.

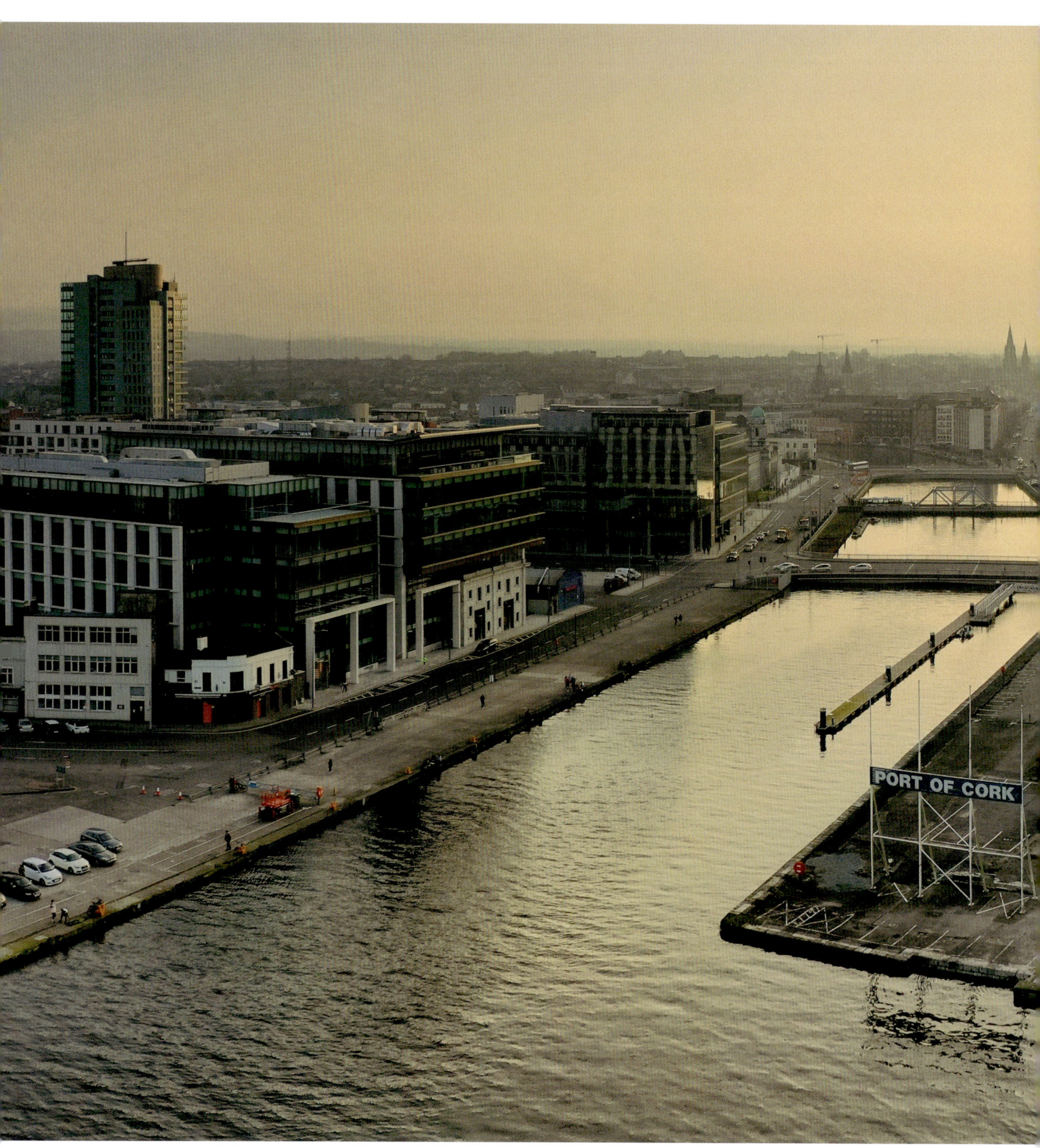

Custom House Quay on Lapp's Island with the River Lee branching on either side of it.

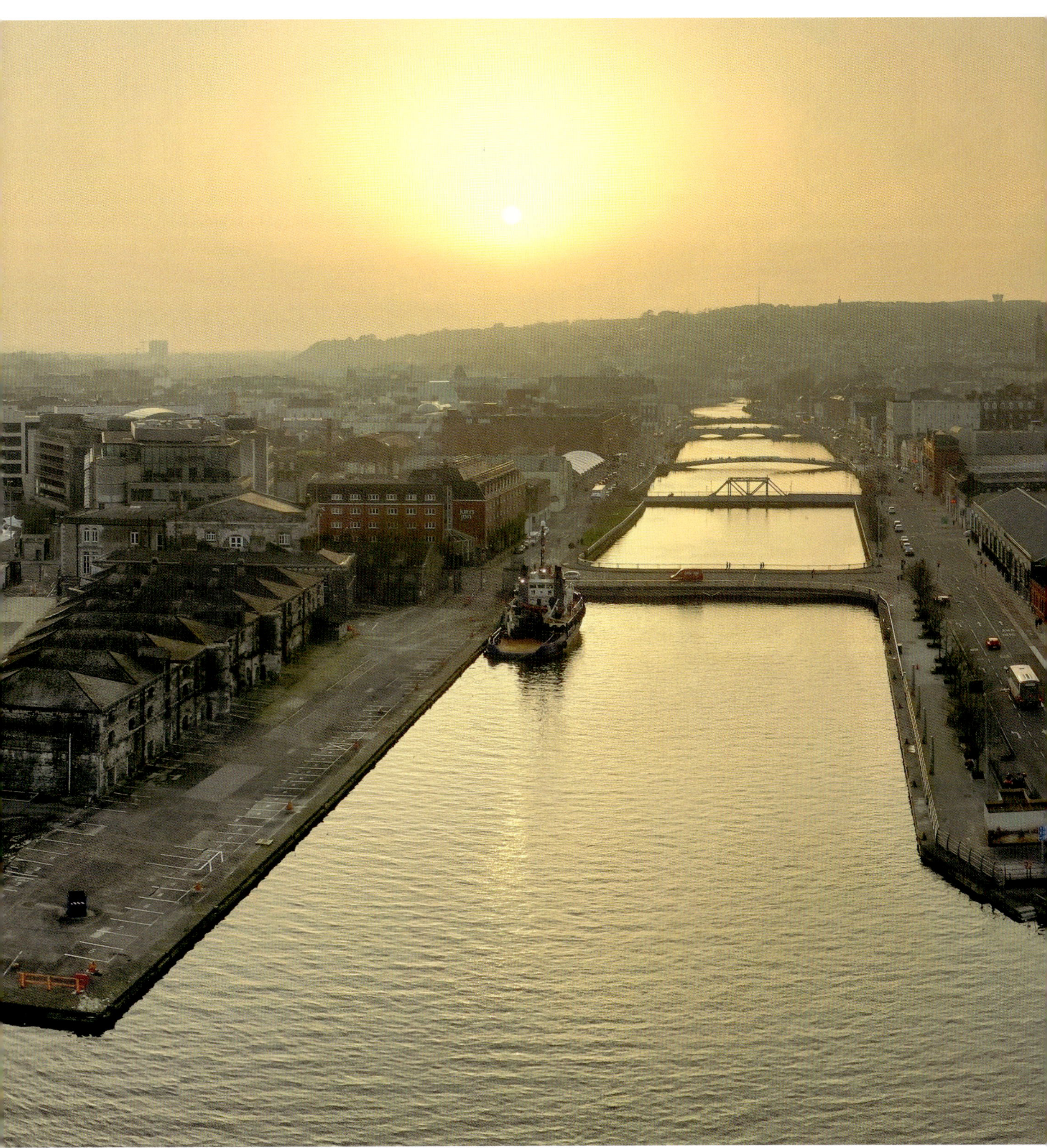

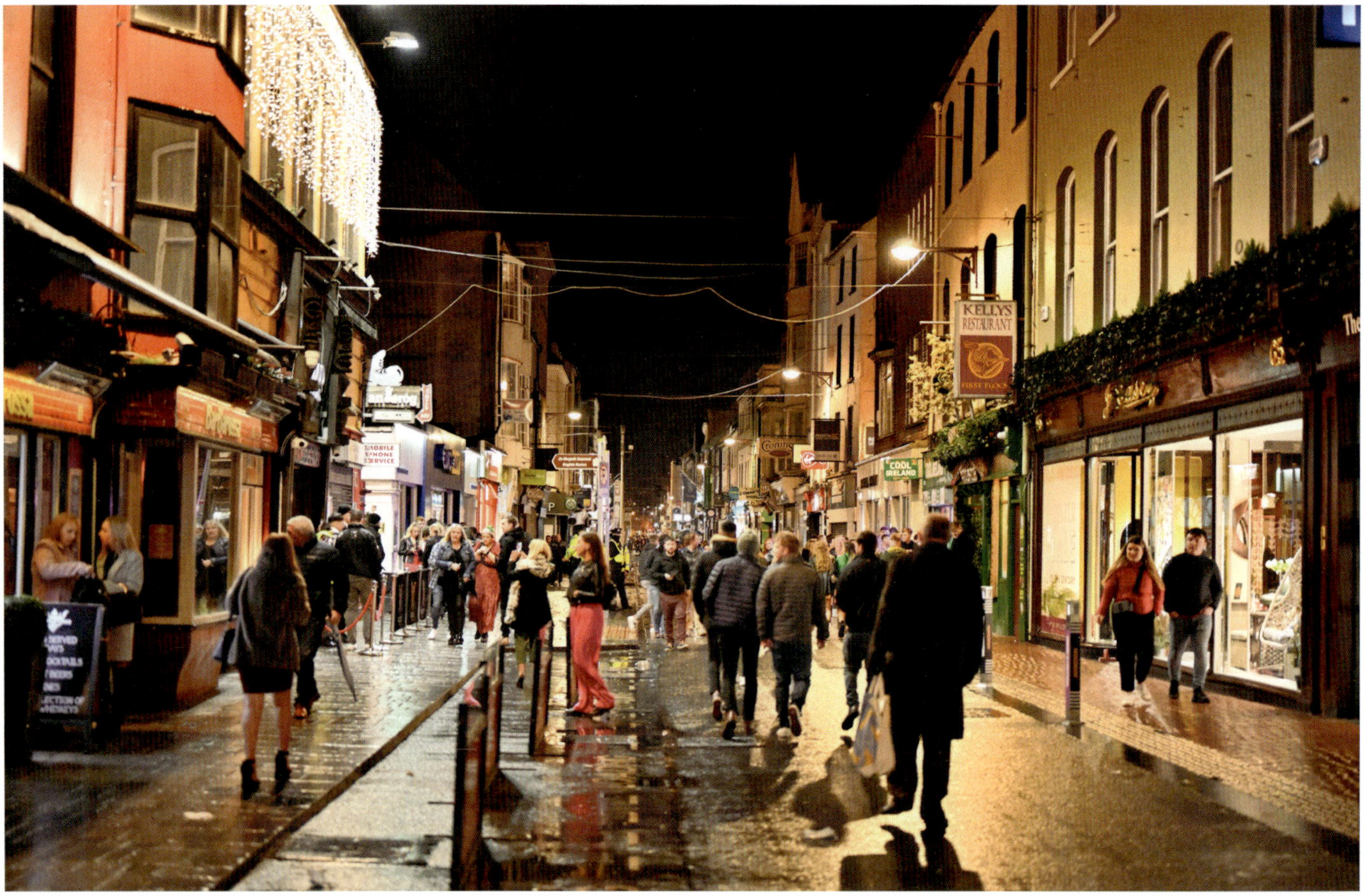

Above: Oliver Plunkett Street is a busy shopping area by day and a popular nightlife spot after sunset.

Right: A Beamish sign in the city centre. Since the establishment of the Beamish and Crawford Brewery in 1792, this stout has been synonymous with Cork.

Opposite: Daly's Bridge, better known as the Shakey Bridge because it bounces as you walk across, was built in 1926 and links Fitzgerald Park in the Mardyke to Sunday's Well.

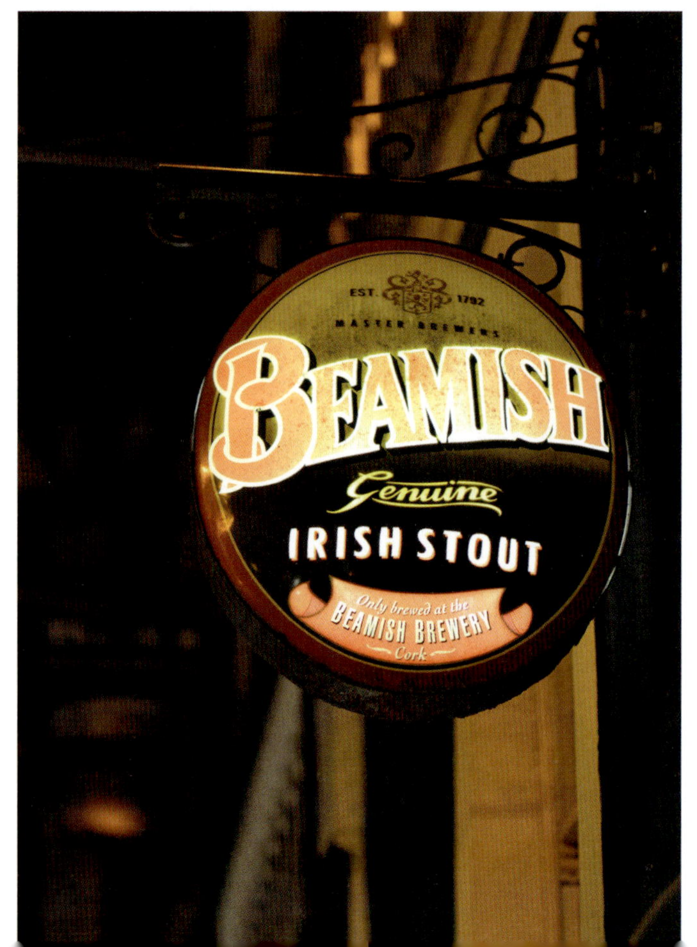

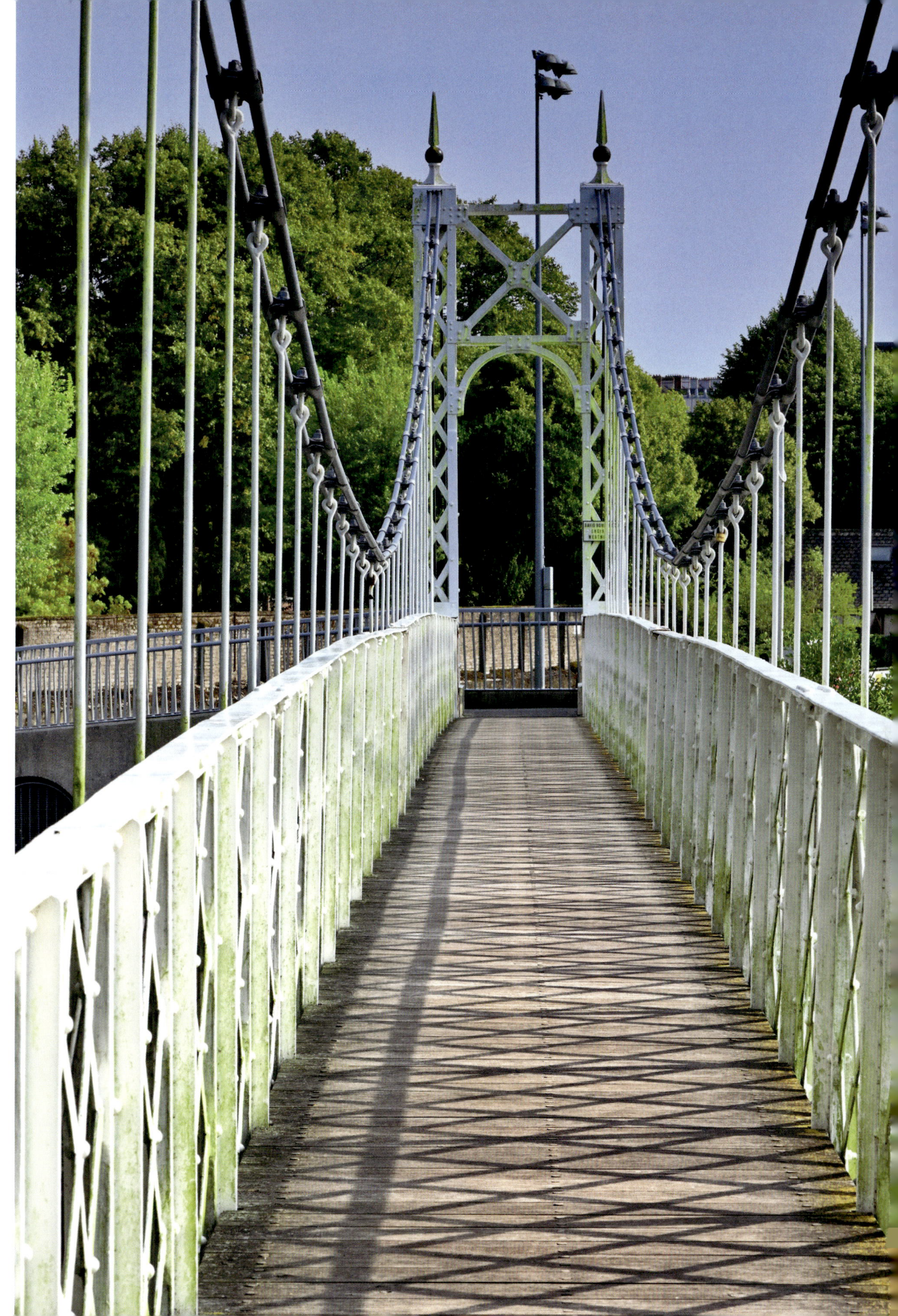

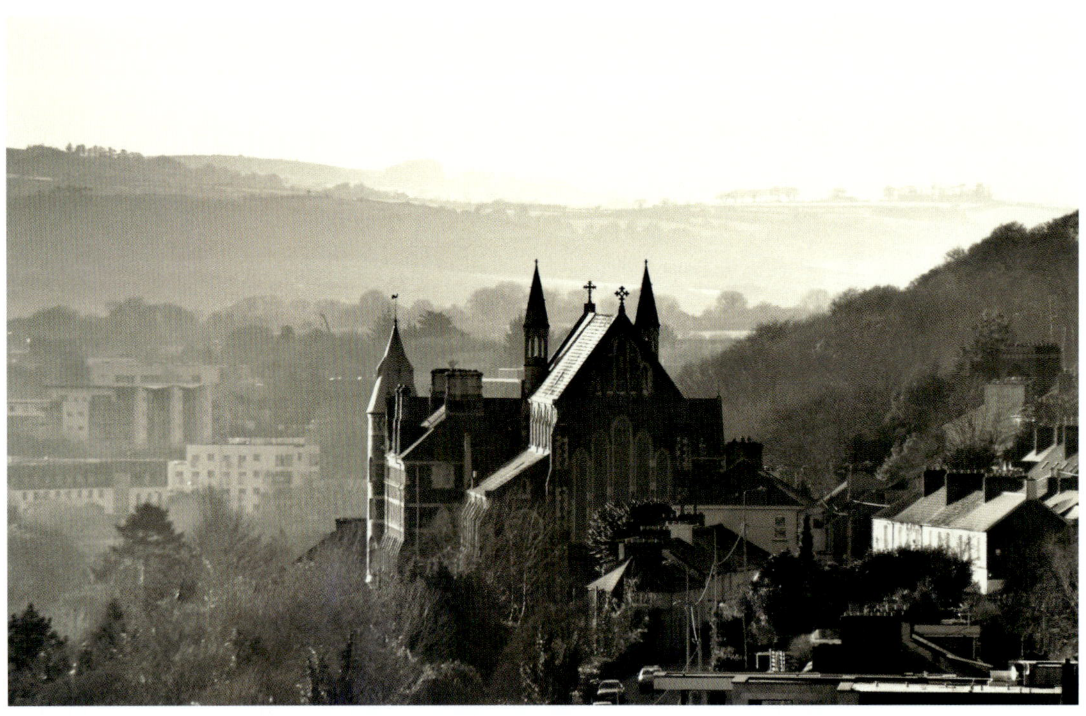

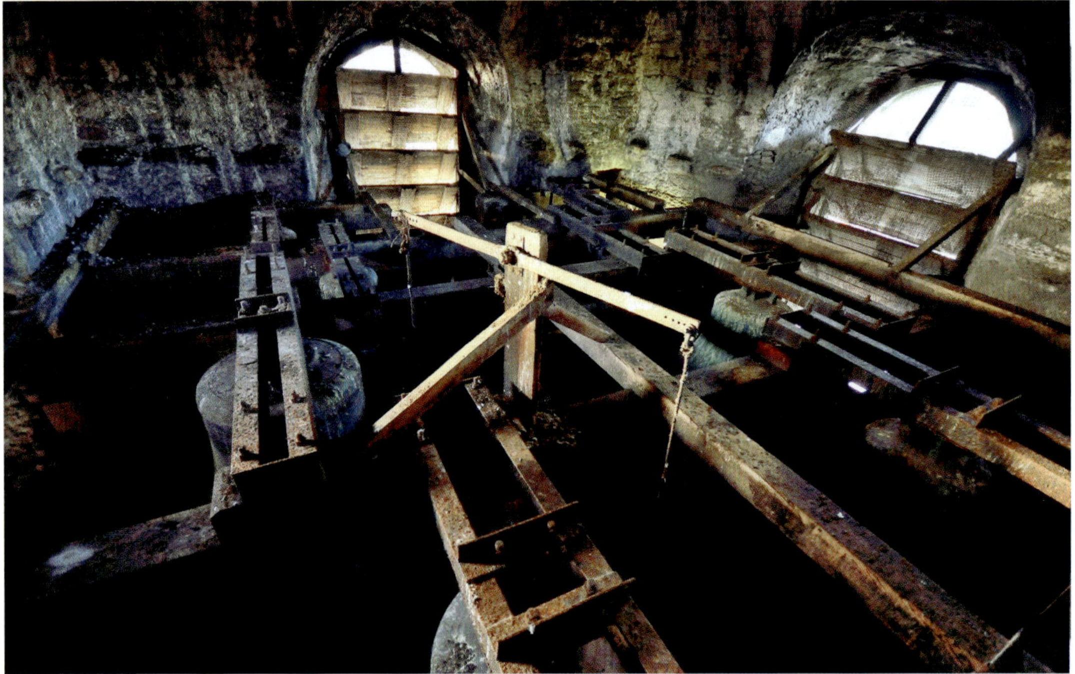

Top: Sunday's Well.

Above: The bells of St Anne's, famed in song as 'The Bells of Shandon'. Visitors are invited to ring them.

Opposite: The Church of St Anne in Shandon. Built in the 1720s, two of its facades are red sandstone and two are limestone, giving it a striking appearance.

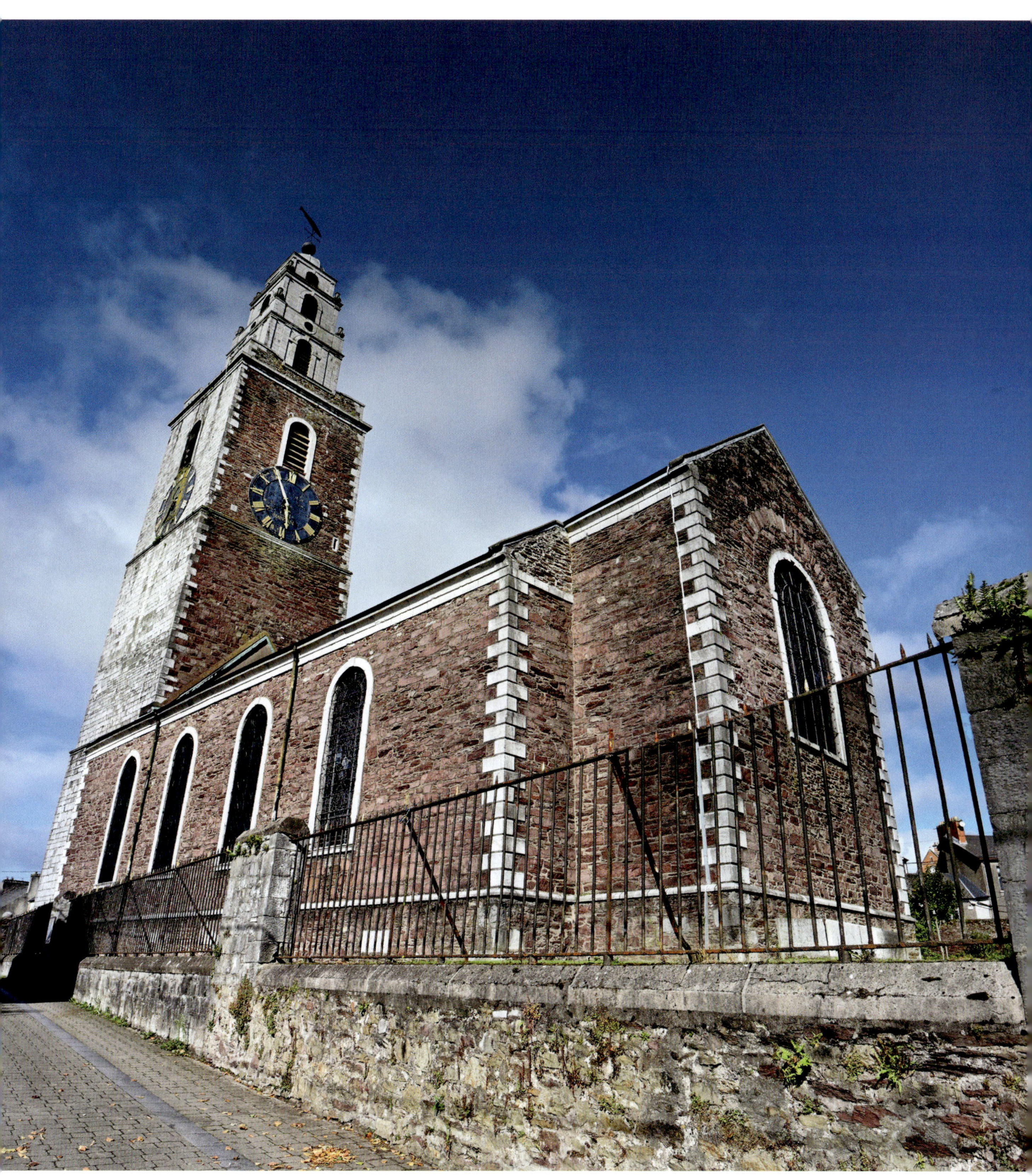

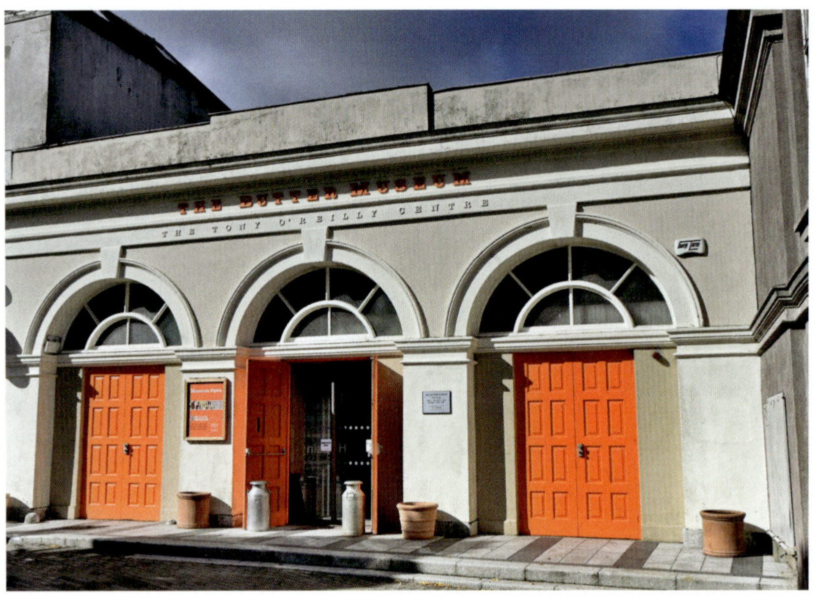

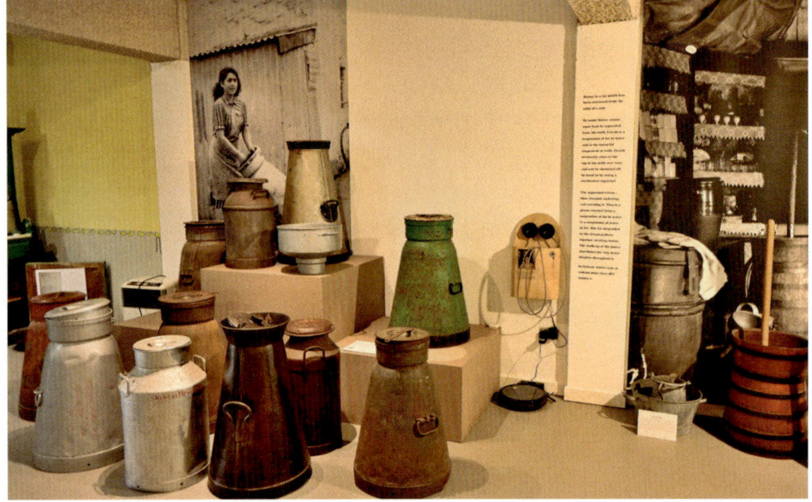

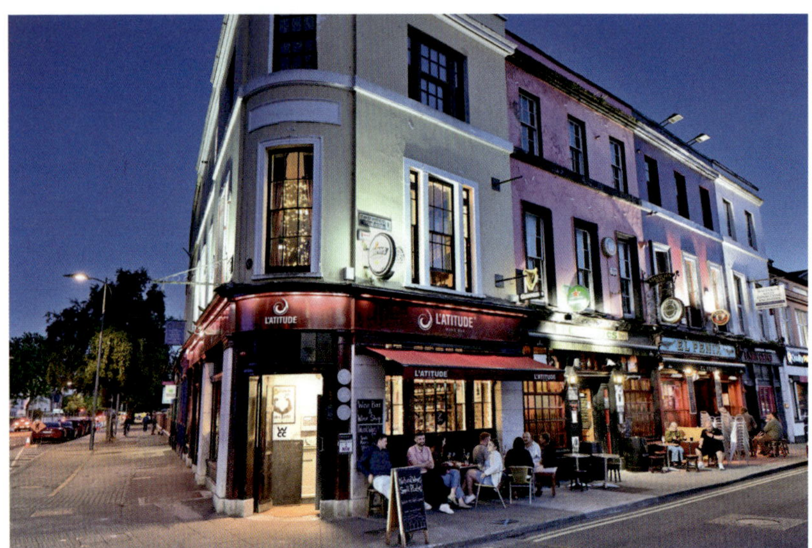

Left: Cork Butter Museum in Shandon. This handsome Neoclassical building housed the butter exchange in the nineteenth century, when Cork was the world's largest exporter of butter.

Middle: Butter churns at the Butter Museum.

Bottom: Relaxing after work with coffee and beer outside L'Atitude 51 at 1 Union Quay.

Opposite: The Gothic spire of Holy Trinity Church on Father Mathew Quay.

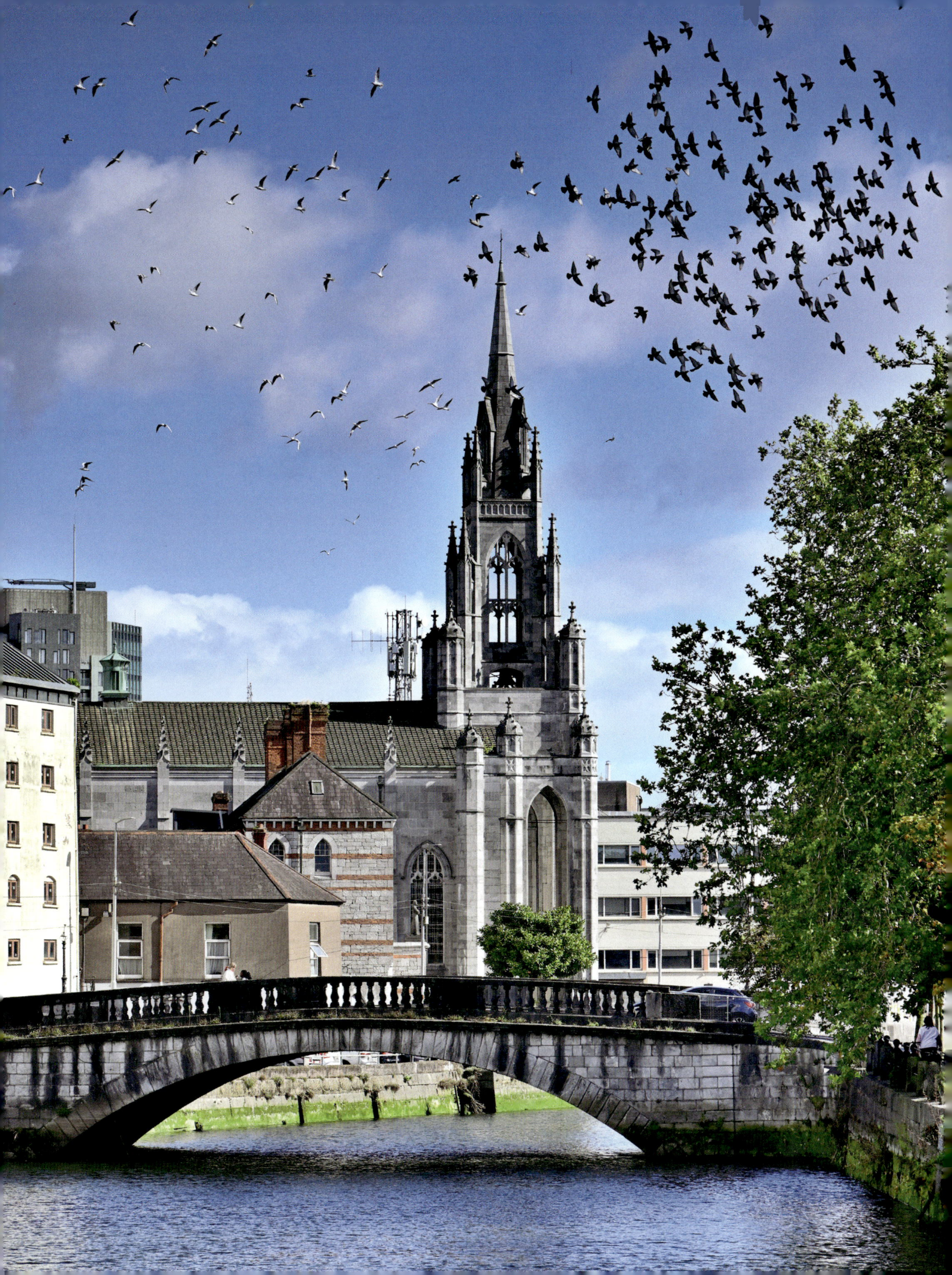

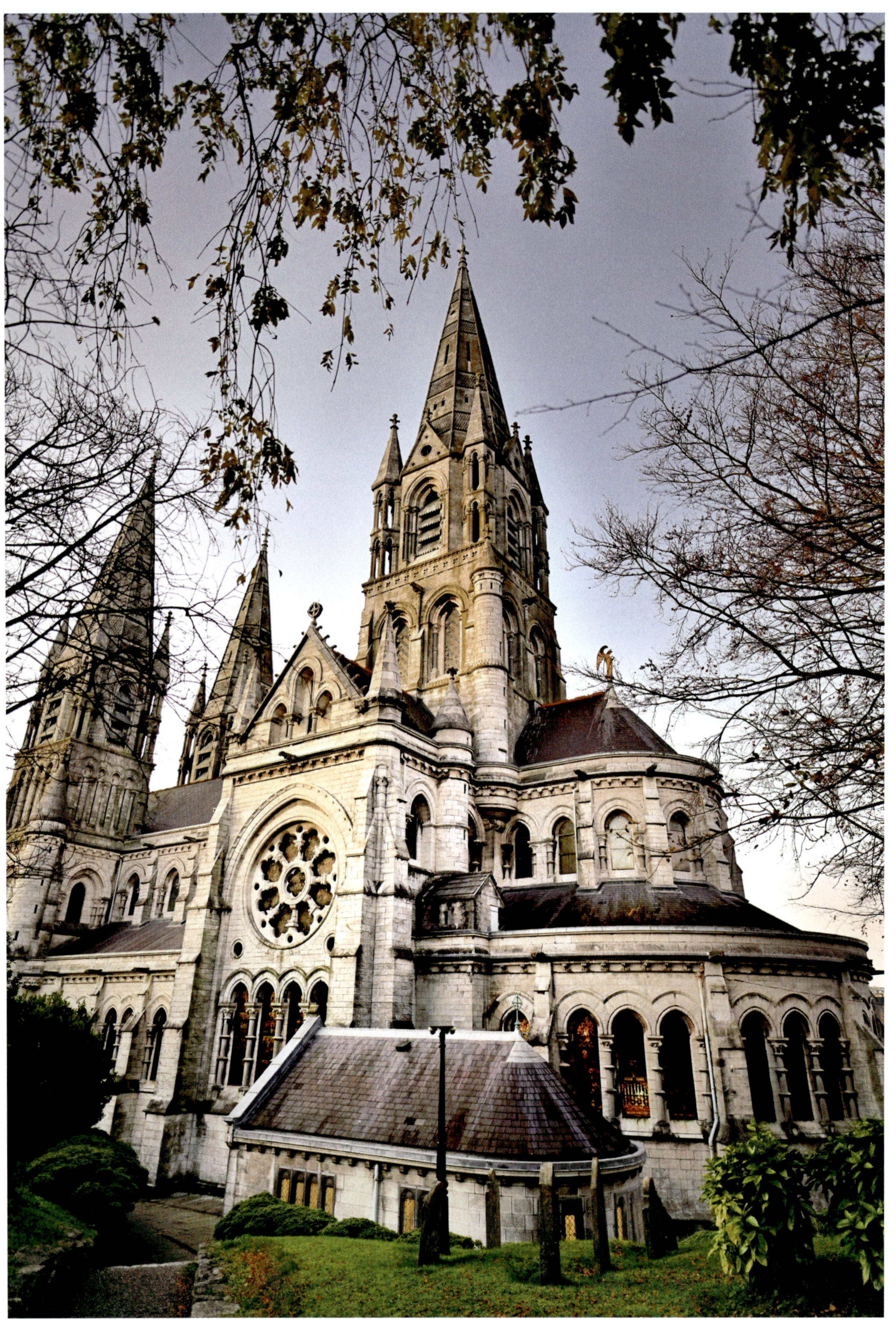

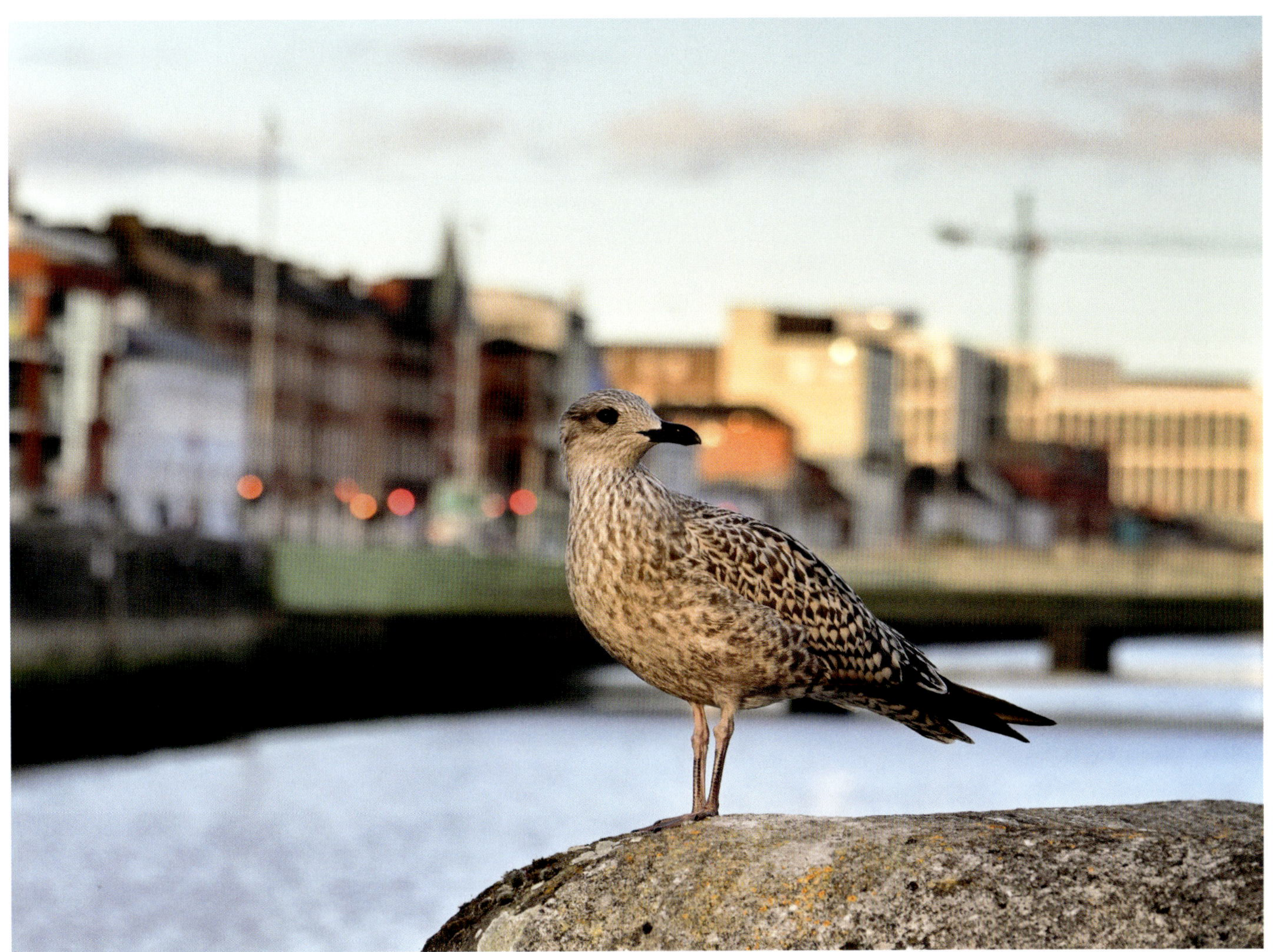

Opposite: St Fin Barre's Cathedral, constructed in the 1860s in the French Gothic style. With its three spires, it is one of Cork's most iconic landmarks.

Above: A young city seagull posing for a photo.

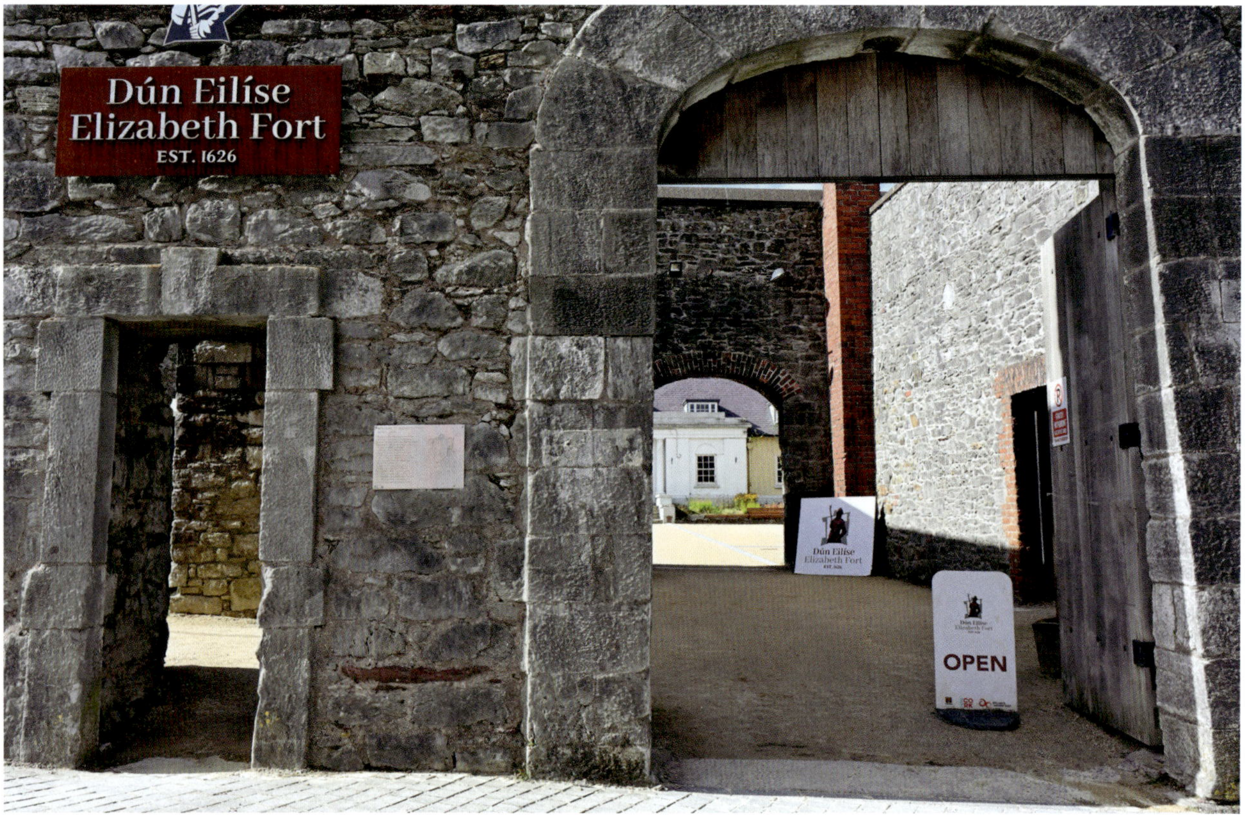
Dún Eilíse
Elizabeth Fort
EST. 1626
OPEN

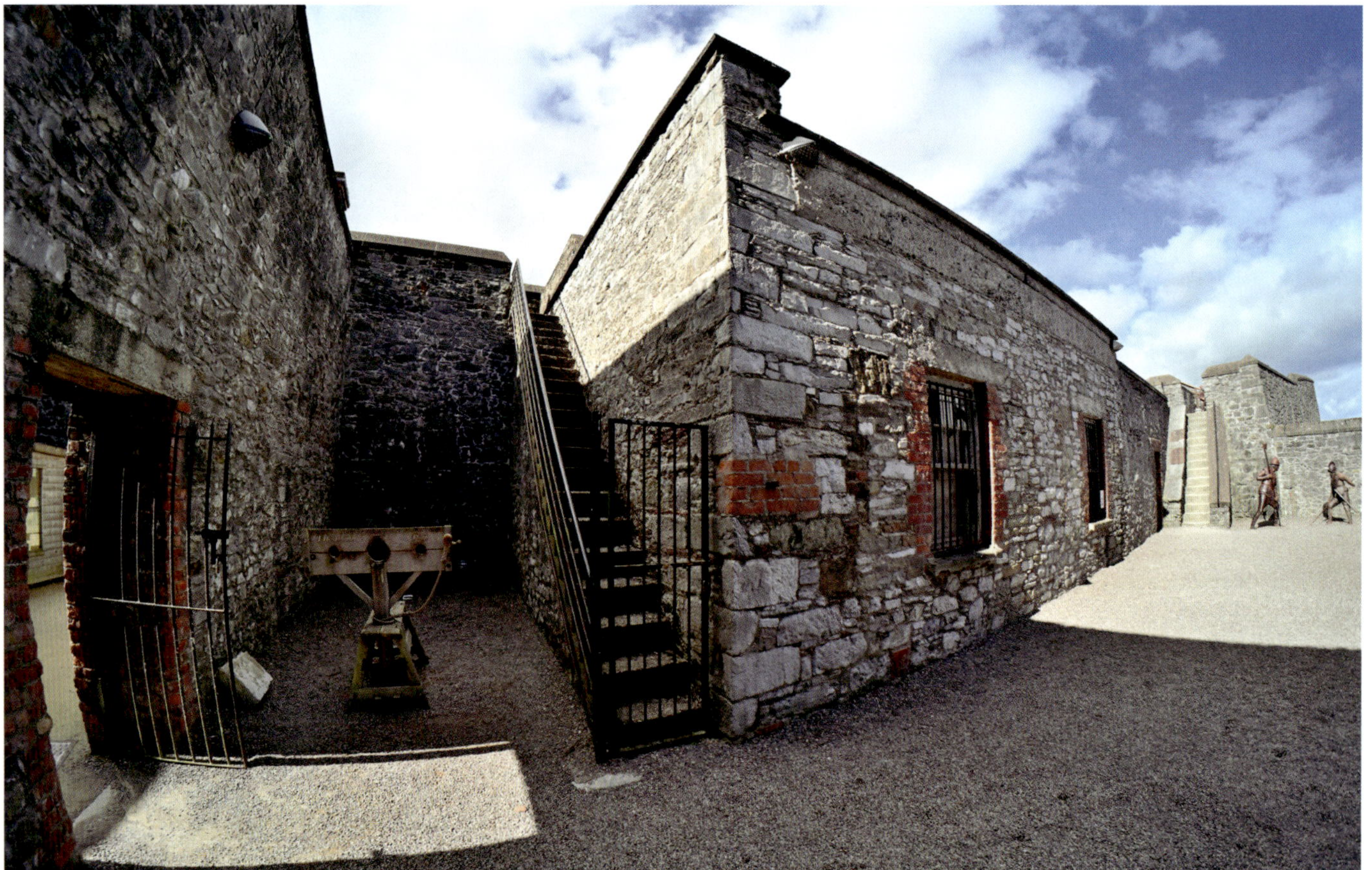

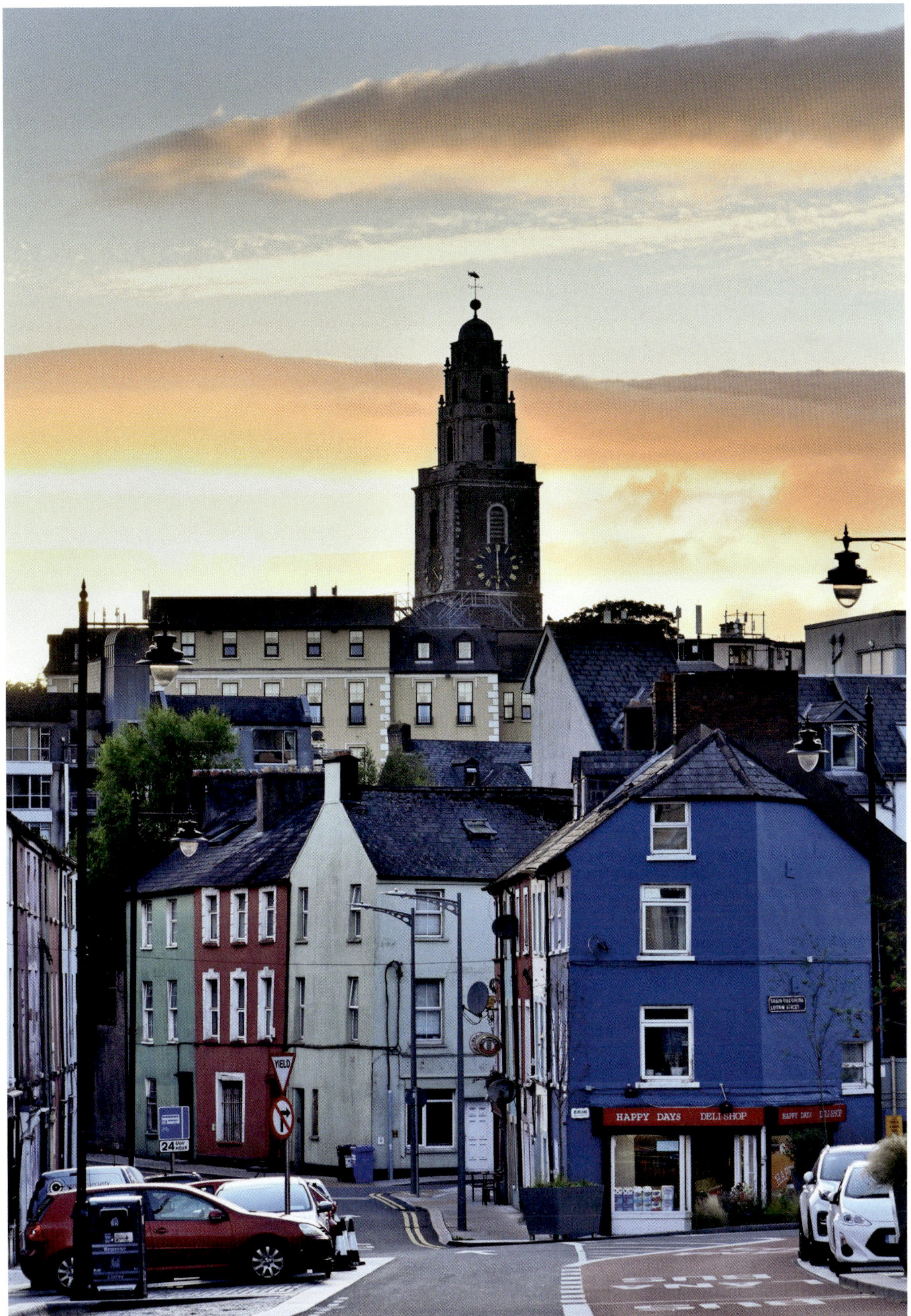

Opposite top: Elizabeth Fort. Built of earth and timber in 1601 and then rebuilt in stone in 1624, this hidden architectural gem in the city centre now houses a museum.

Opposite bottom: The stocks in Elizabeth Fort.

Above: Looking west along Coburg Street in Cork's Victorian Quarter towards the unmistakable tower of St Anne's Church in Shandon.

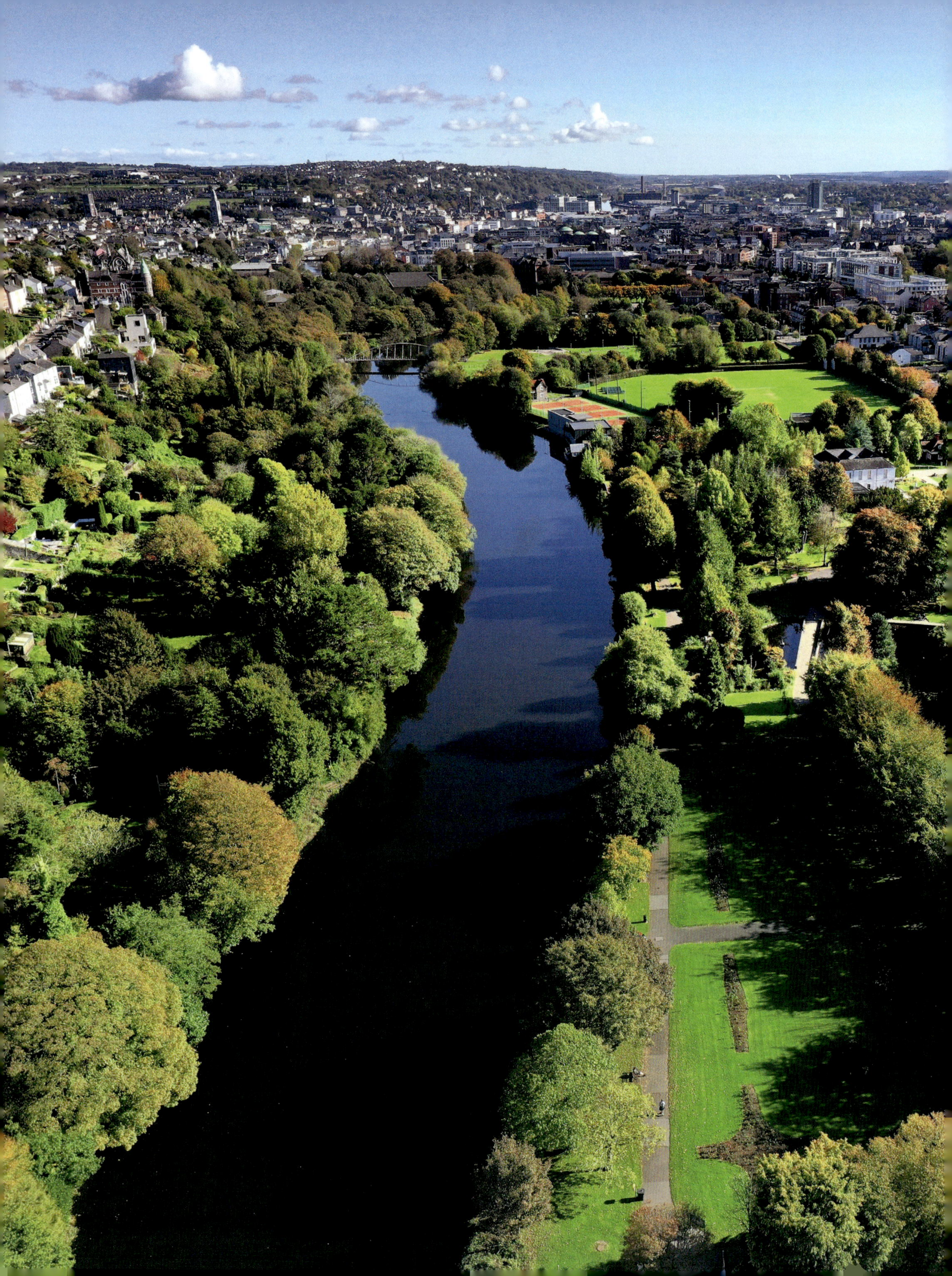

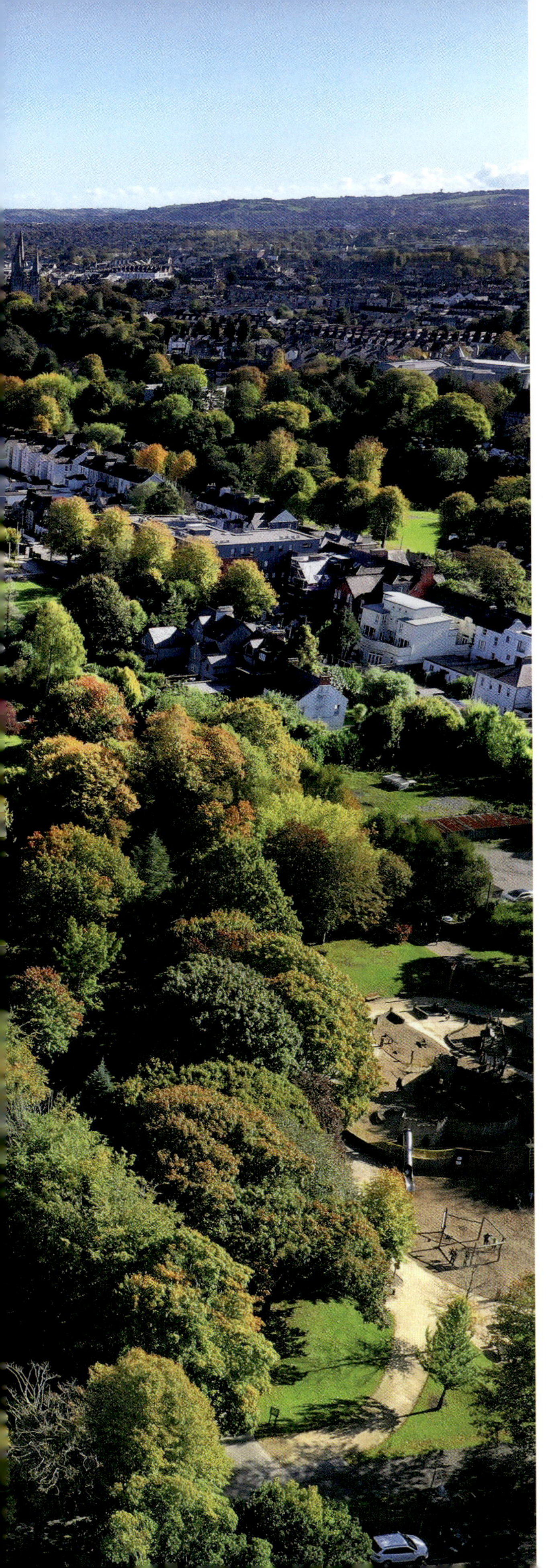

A tranquil River Lee and Fitzgerald Park in autumn. The Cork International Exhibition was held here in 1902 and afterwards, the twelve-acre park on the Mardyke was turned into a public park and named for the then Lord Mayor of Cork, Edward Fitzgerald.

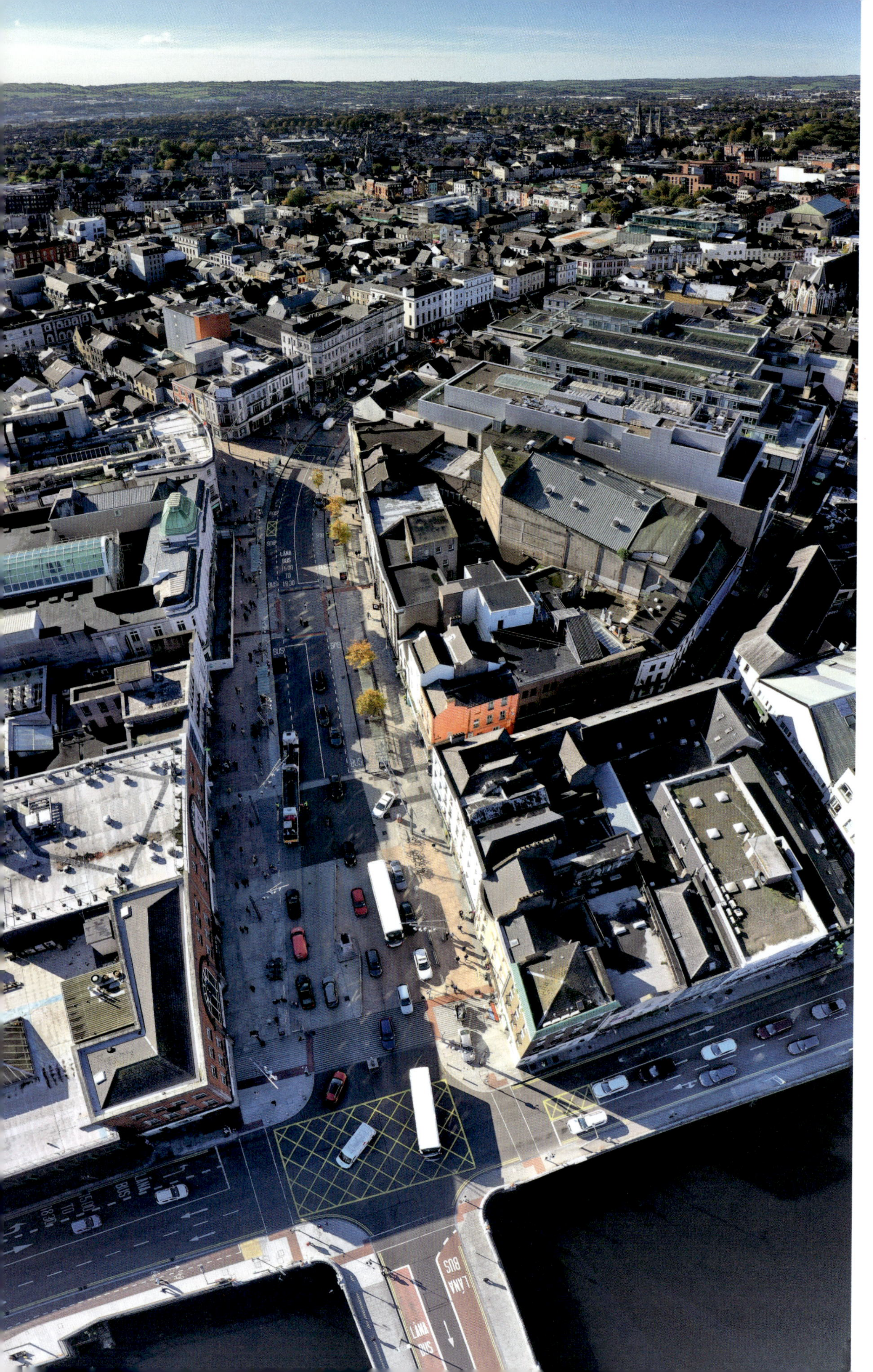

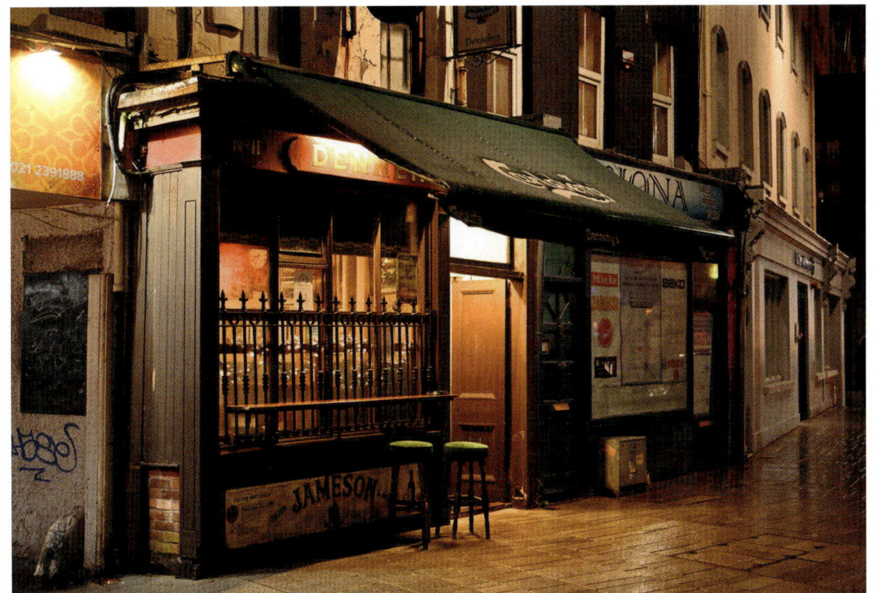

Opposite: An aerial view of Saint Patrick's Street.
Right: The Coal Quay at night.
Below: St Mary's Dominican Priory on Pope's Quay.

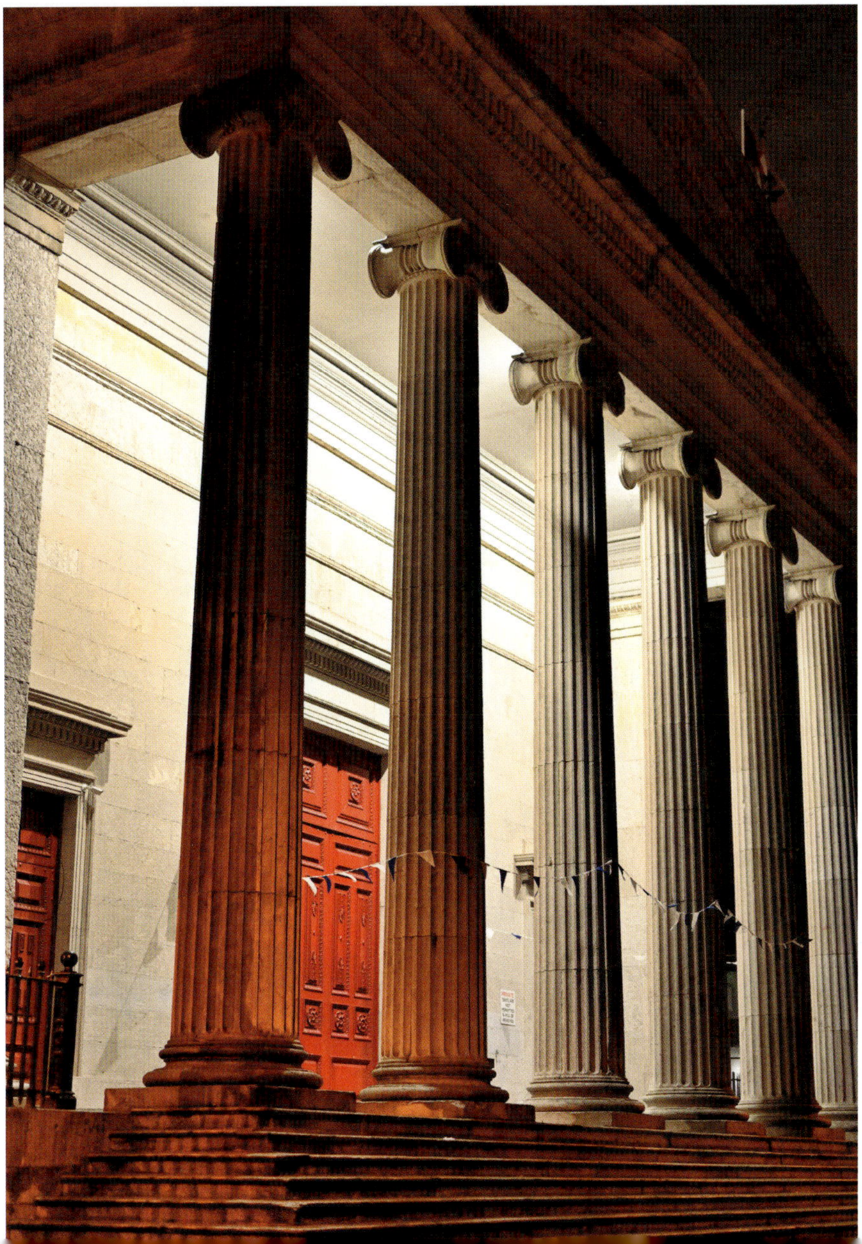

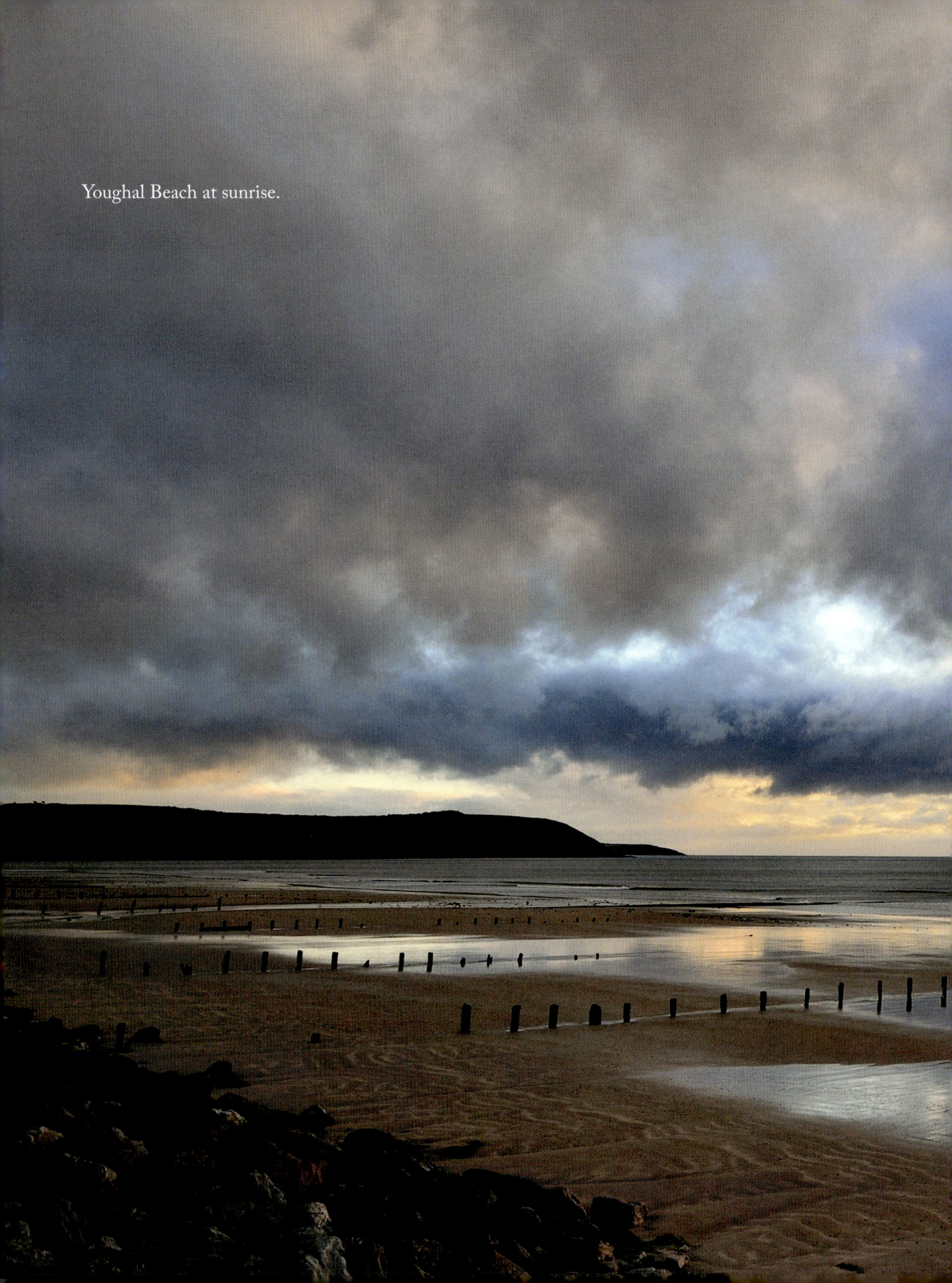
Youghal Beach at sunrise.

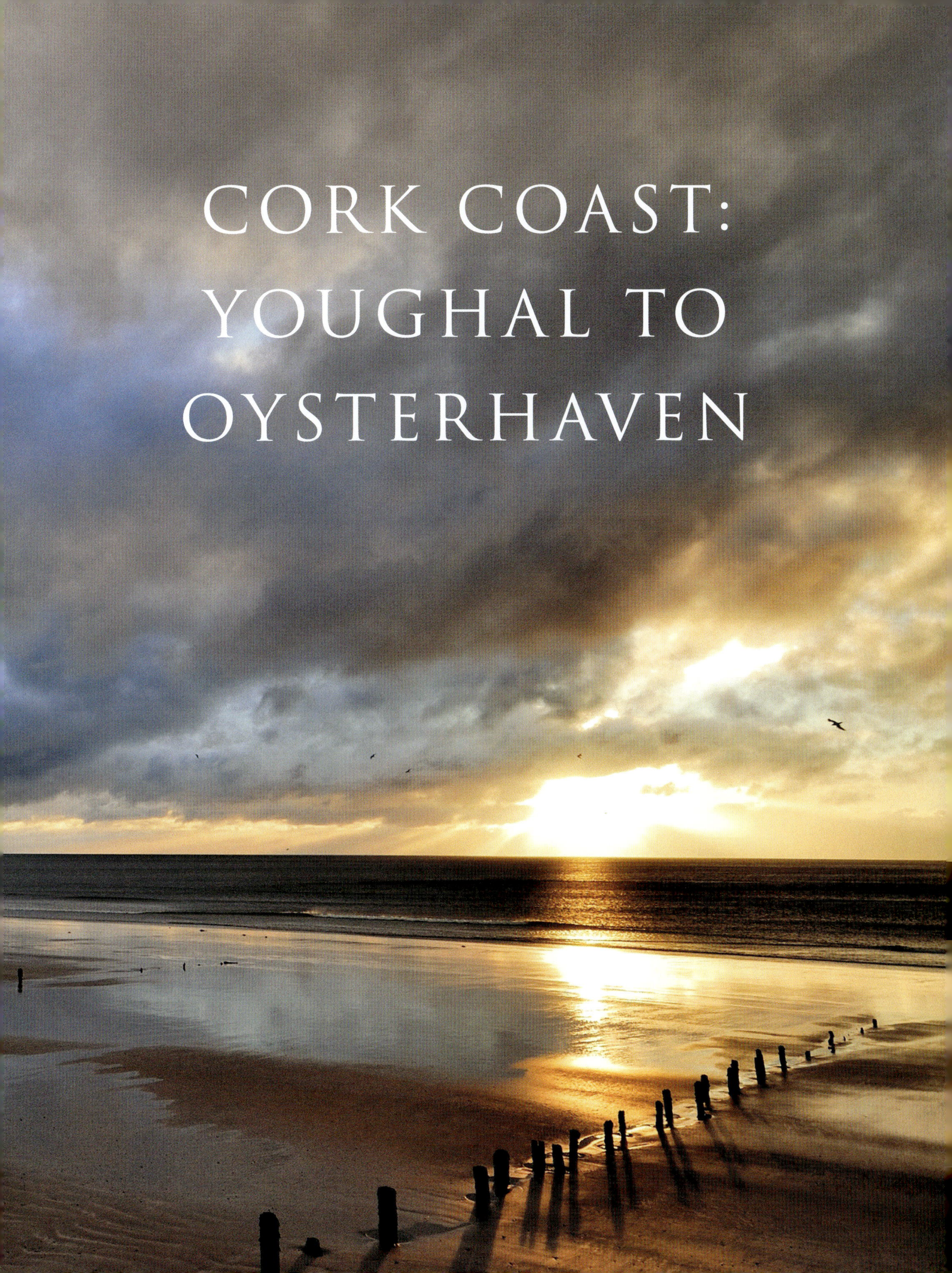

CORK COAST:
YOUGHAL TO
OYSTERHAVEN

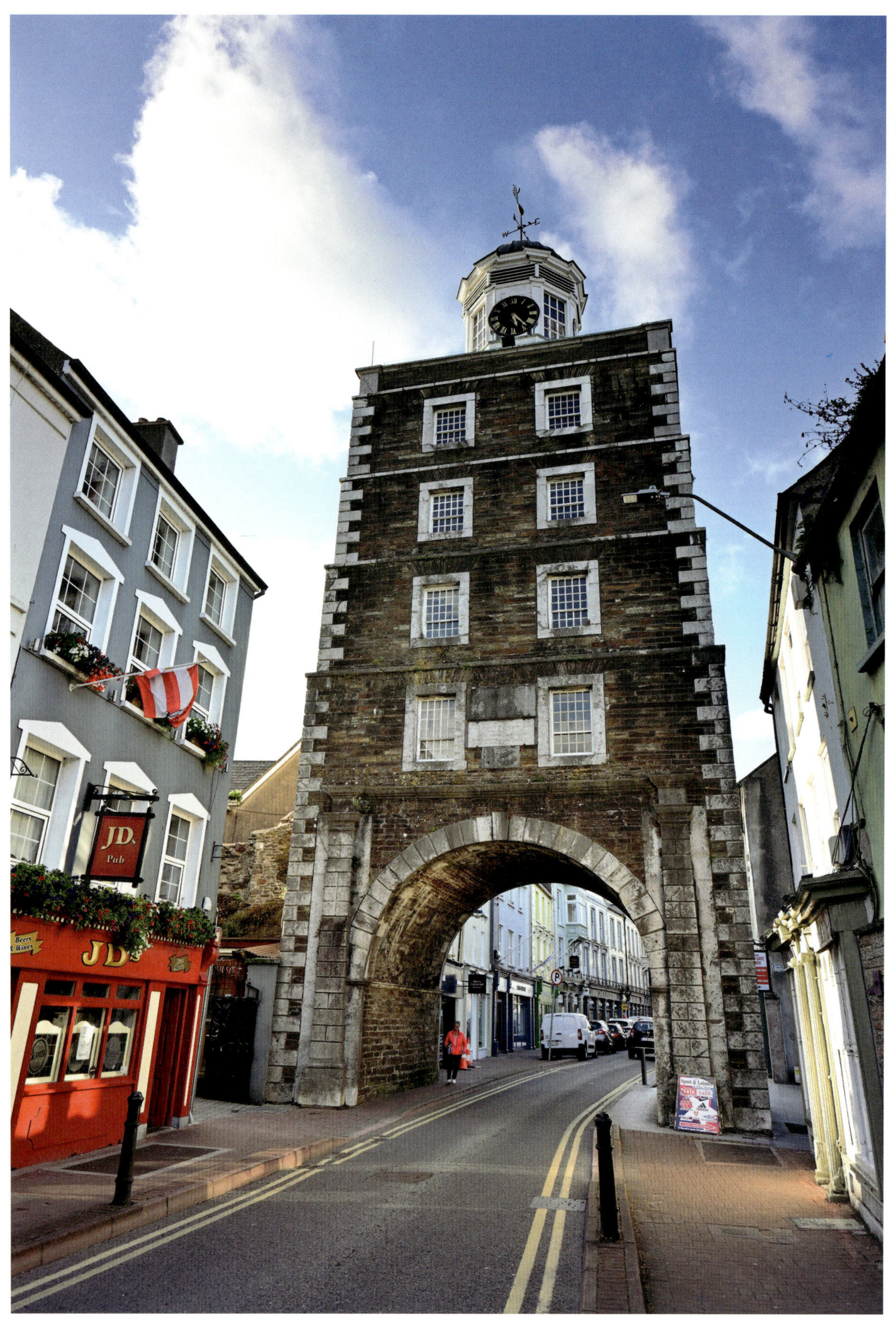

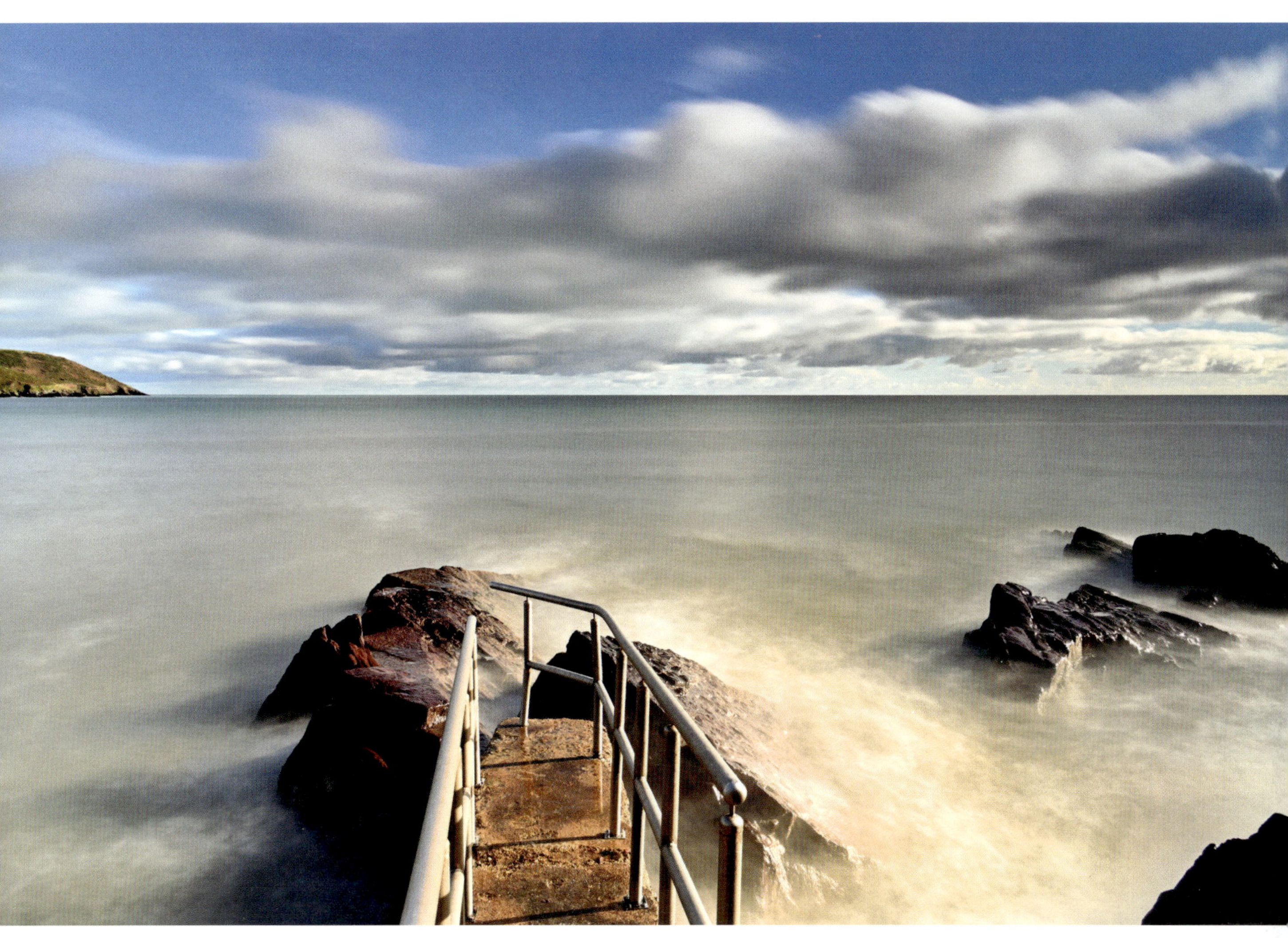

Opposite: Youghal Gate clock tower, built in 1777. This wonderful building is open to the public and boasts panoramic views of the beautiful seaside town.

Above: The swimming steps in Youghal. Just under the lighthouse, the steps are great for diving from at high tide and are popular with swimmers.

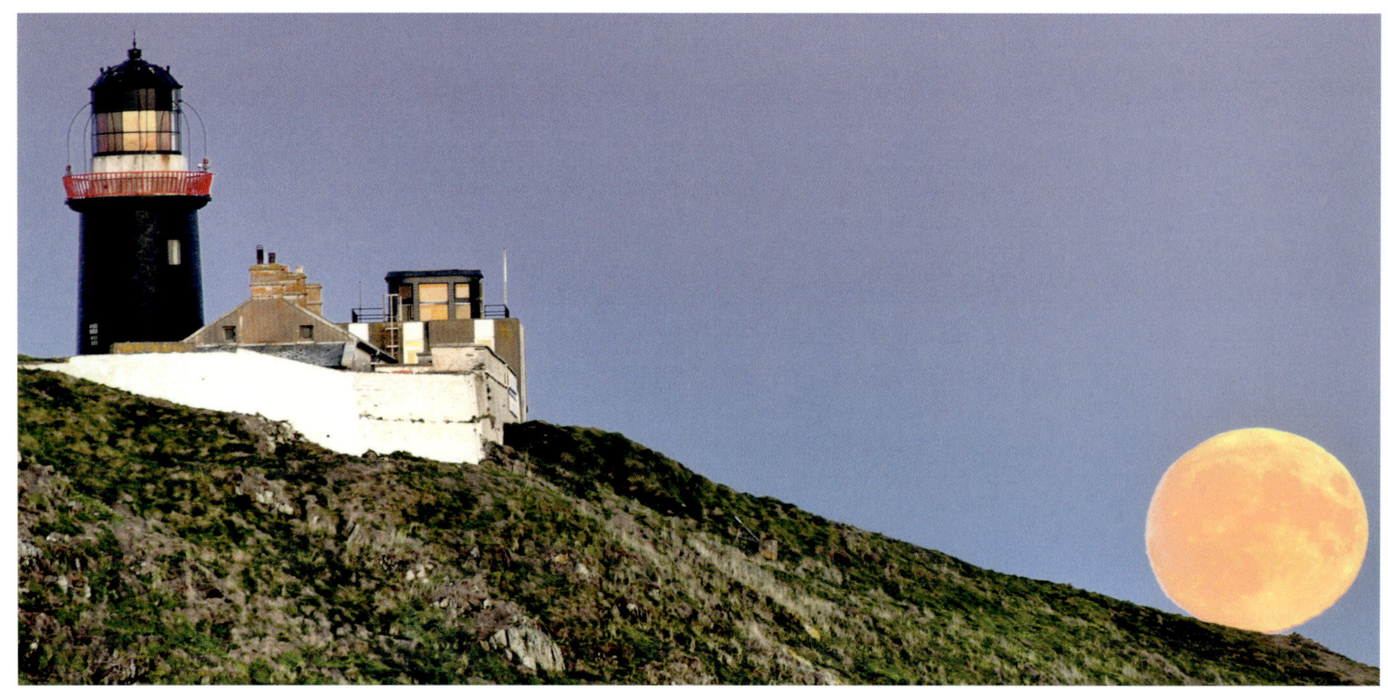

Above: A full moon rising behind Ballycotton lighthouse.

Below: Aerial view of Ballycotton island.

Opposite: The ghost ship *Alta* drifted across the Atlantic for eighteen months and spent about six weeks floating in Irish waters, unnoticed. It washed up on the east Cork coastline during a storm on 16 February 2020 when it was spotted by a jogger.

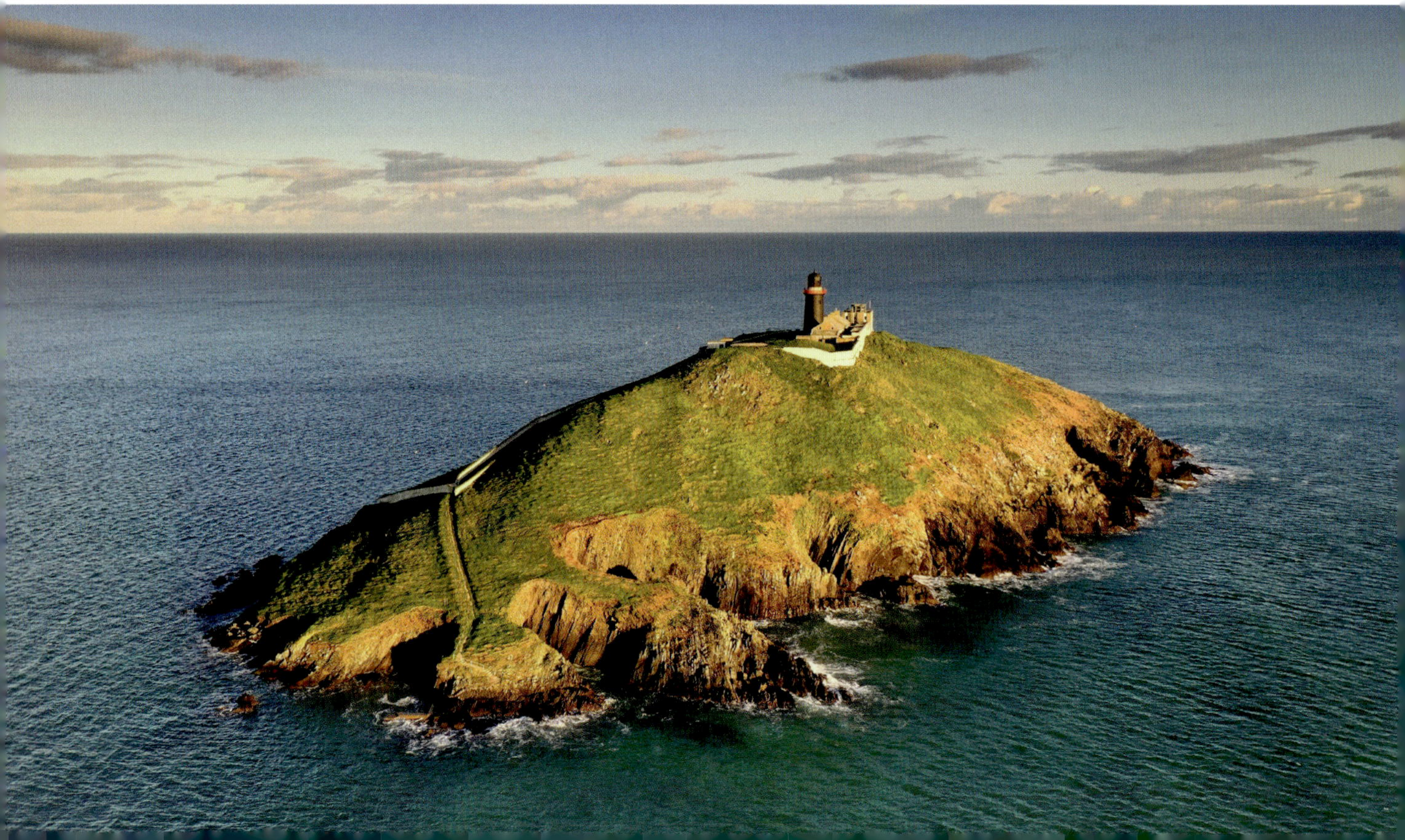

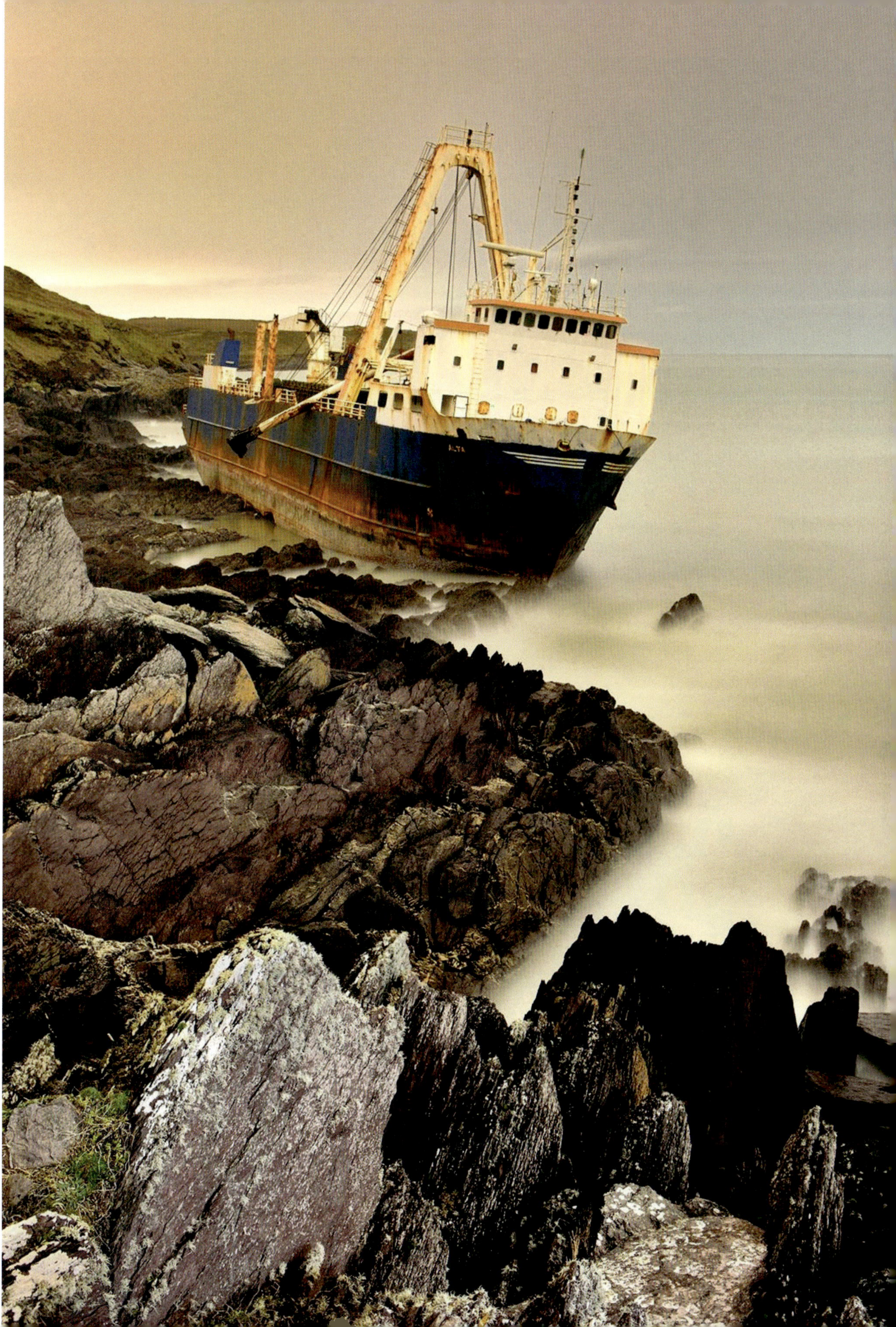

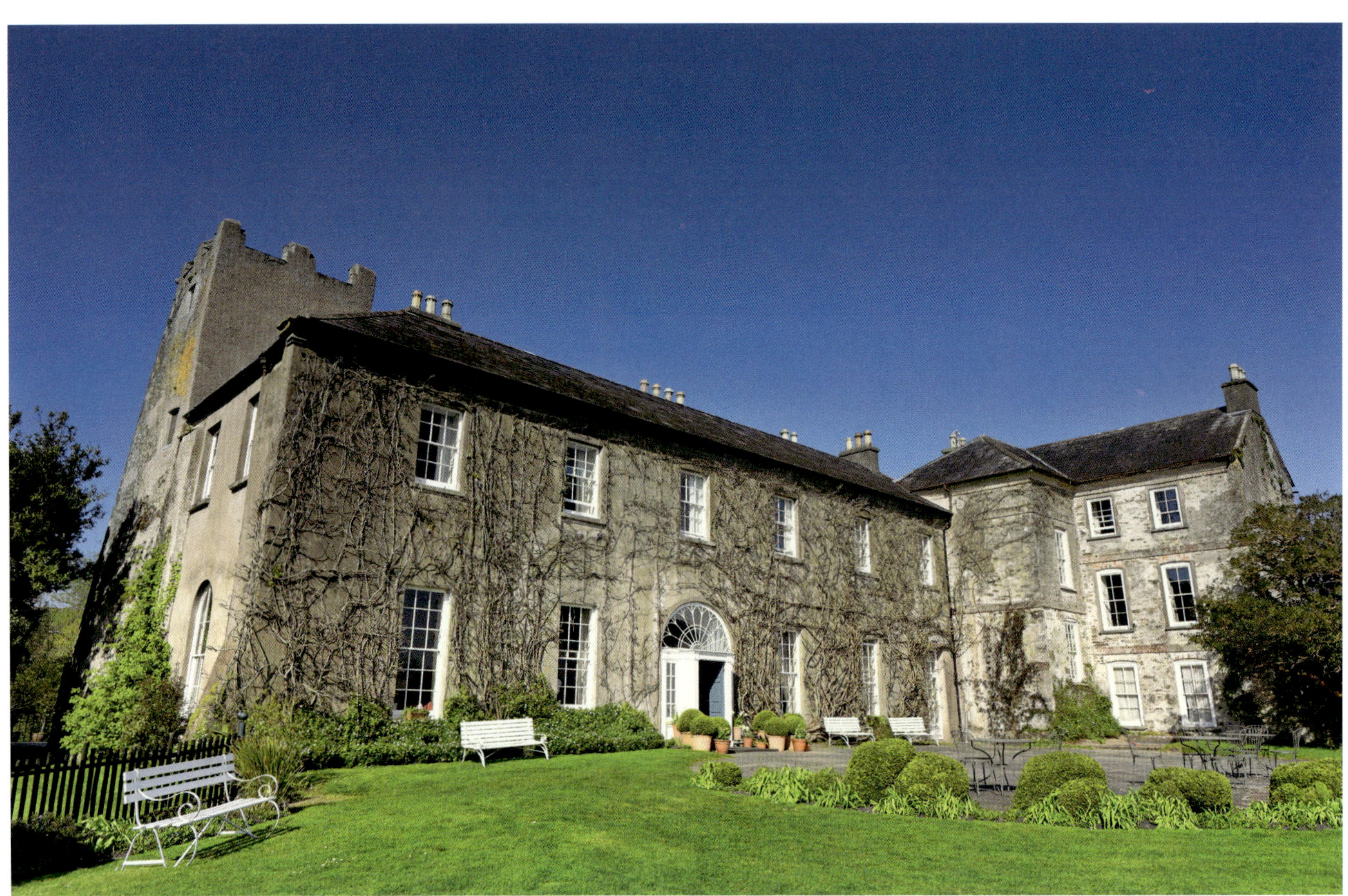

Above: Ballymaloe House is a charming Georgian building, which still retains one of its original sixteenth-century castle towers. The Allen family have lived here since the late 1940s, establishing the internationally renowned Ballymaloe Cookery School.

Below: The Old Midleton Distillery is home to the Jameson Experience. The building dates back to 1780, when John Jameson established his distillery in Midleton.

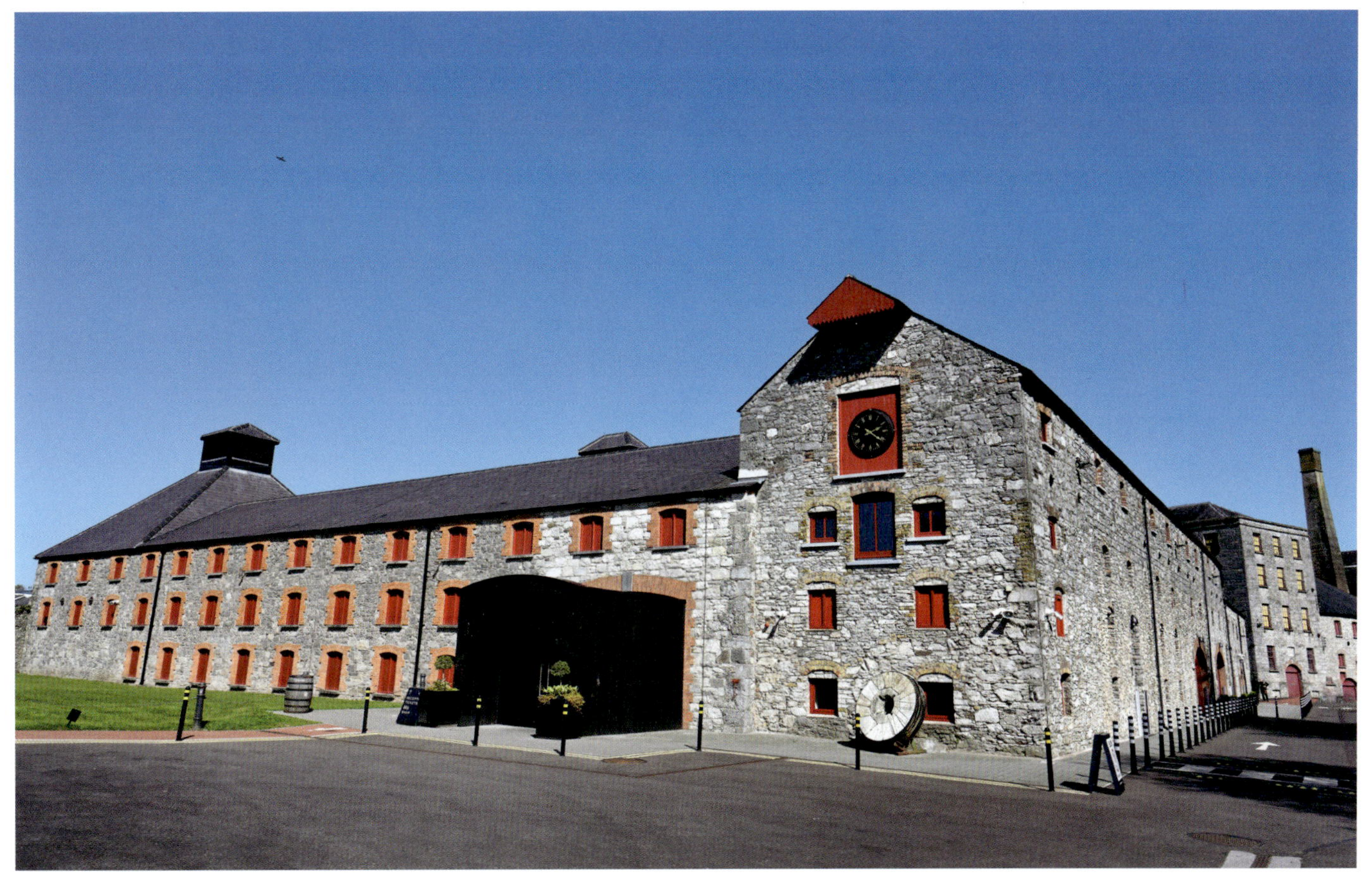

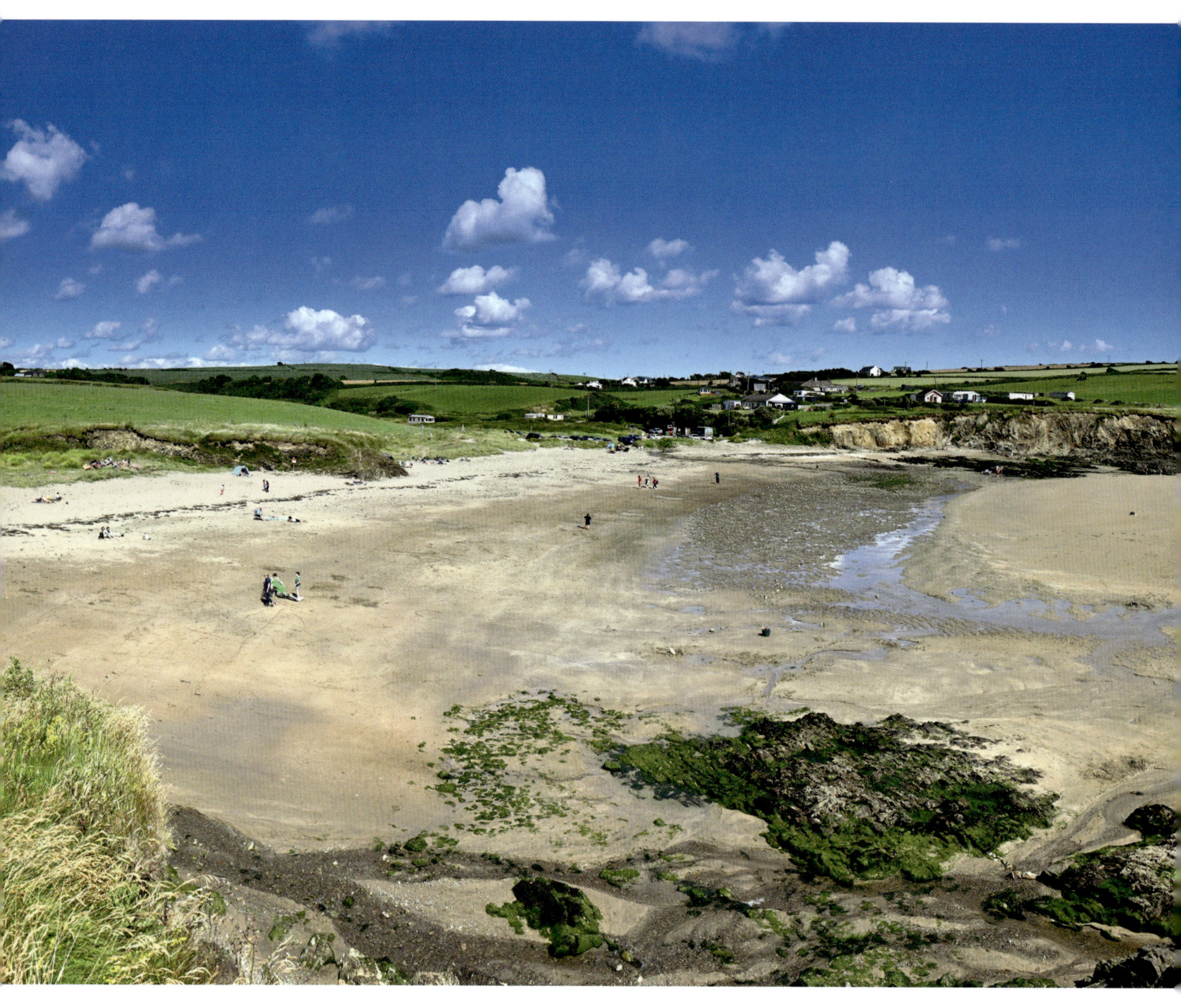

Inch Beach. Near Midleton, this family-friendly beach is very popular with east Corkonians.

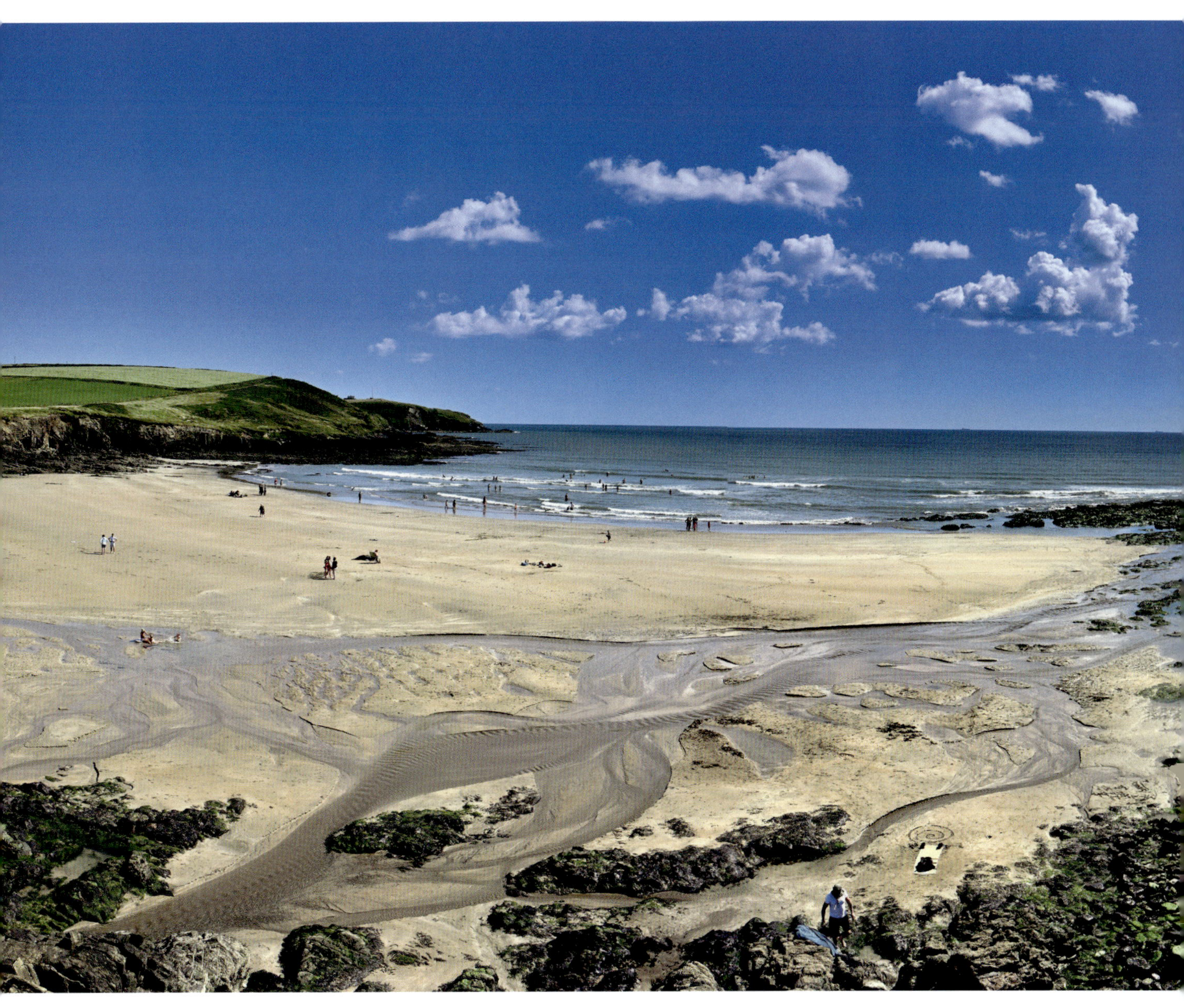

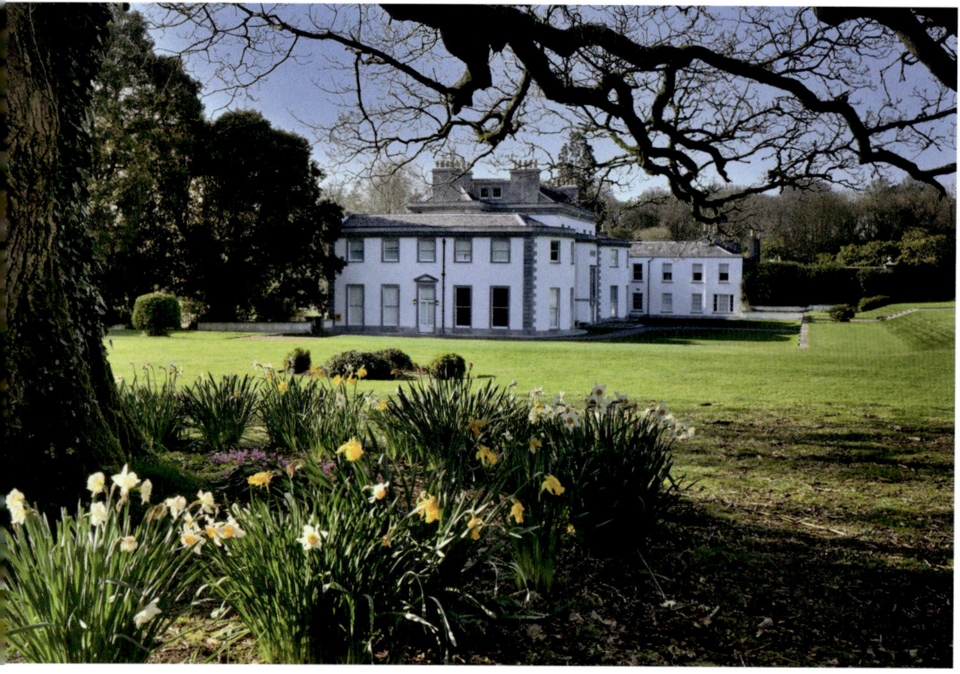

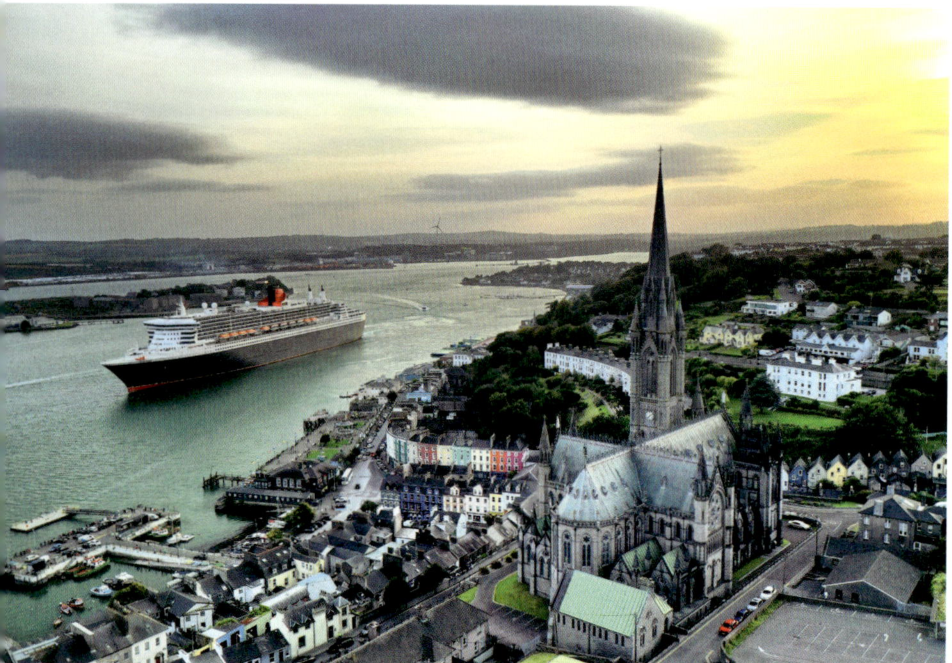

Top: Fota House and Gardens. This Regency house boasts an impressive Doric entrance portico. The gardens are open to the public and include a walled Italian garden and 280 hectares of parkland.

Bottom: Cobh at sunset. Cobh's deepwater quay hosts some of the world's largest cruise liners, including the *Queen Mary 2*, seen here departing, and was the last port of call for the ill-fated RMS *Titanic*.

Opposite: St Colman's Cathedral in Cobh. The line of houses beneath it is known as the deck of cards.

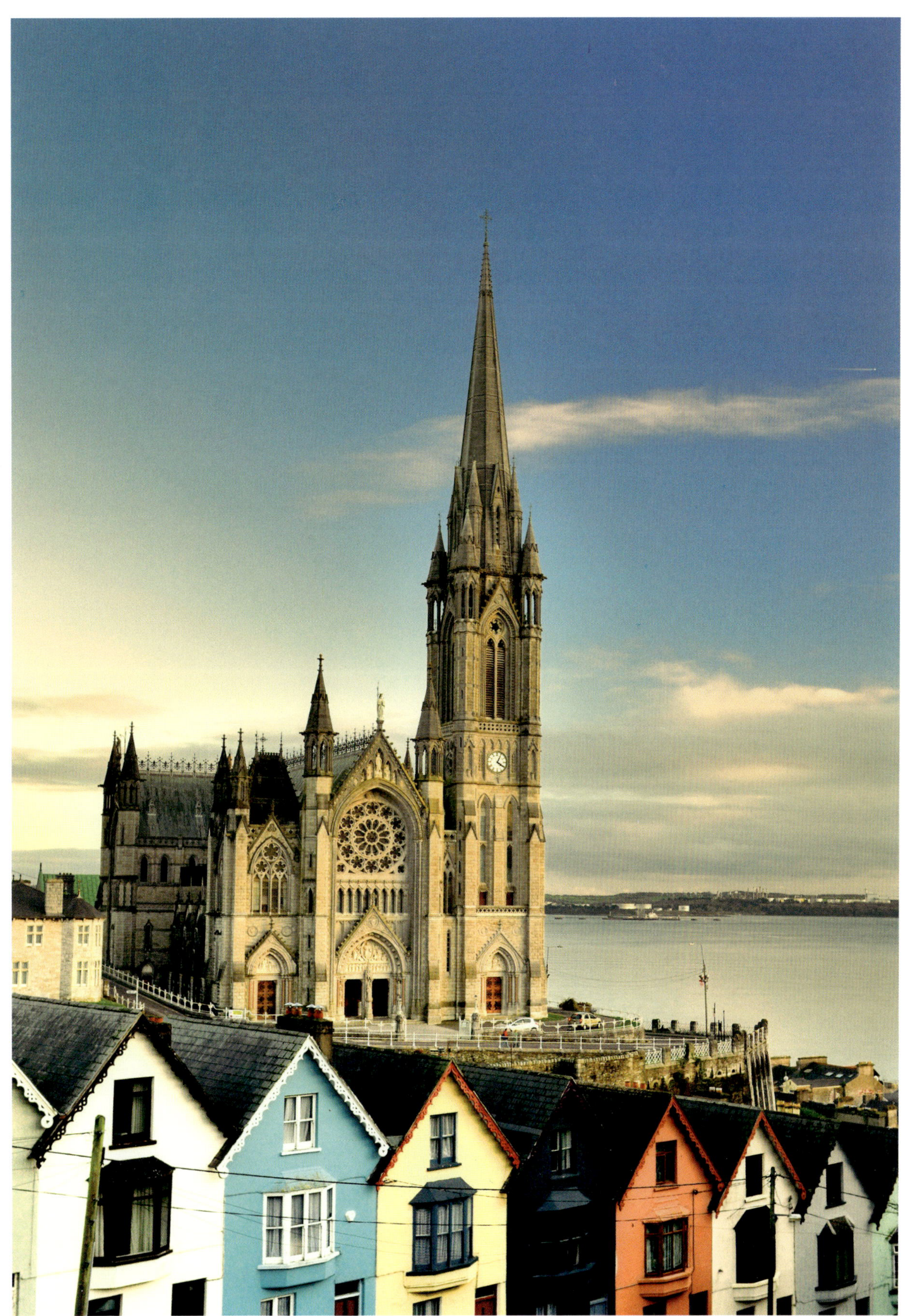

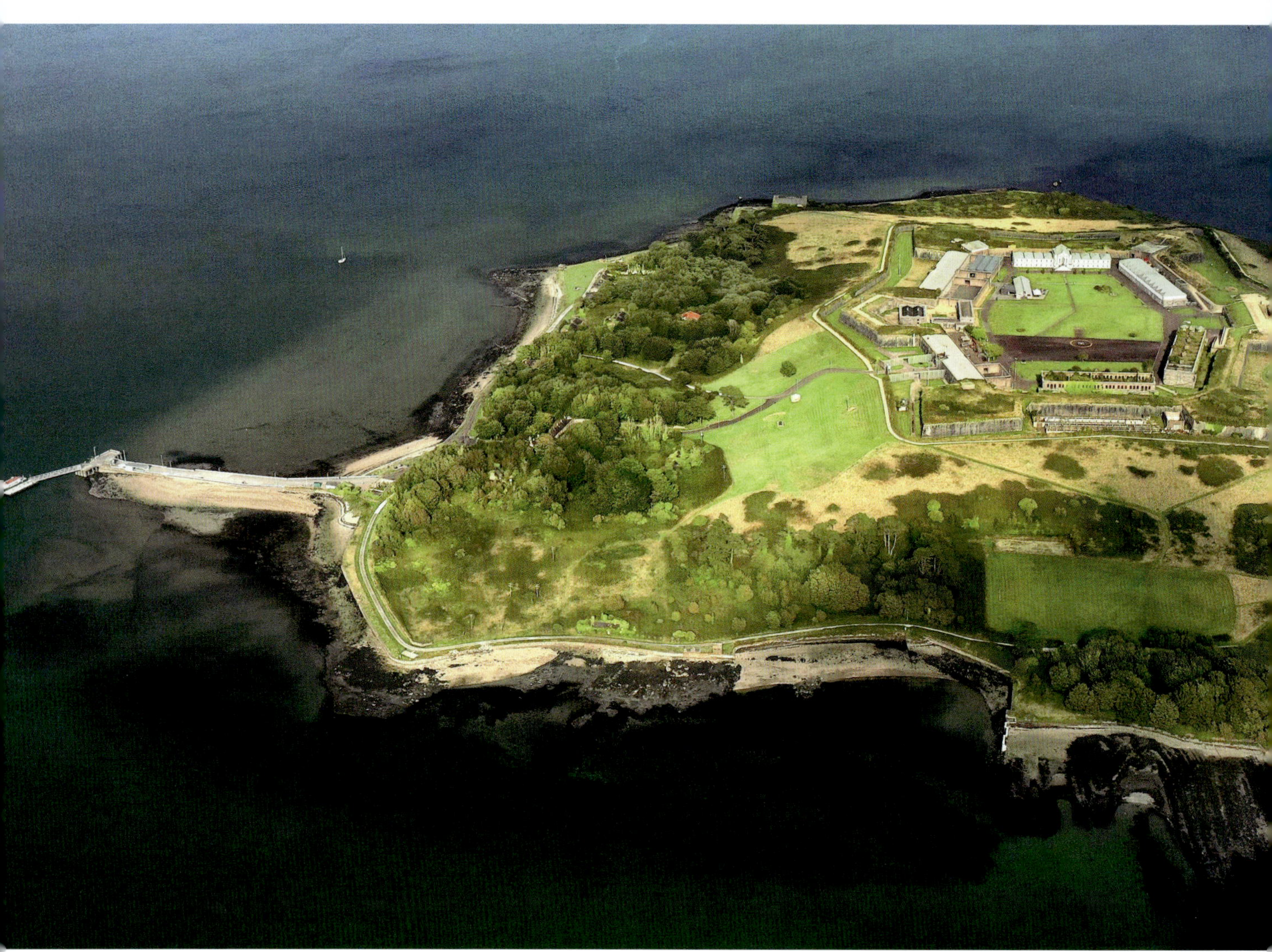

Above: Spike Island. Known as Ireland's Alcatraz, it became a prison in the 1600s but its history goes back many hundreds of years. There was an Early Christian monastery on the island, which was plundered by Vikings in the ninth century. Today, it is one of Europe's top tourist attractions.

Opposite top: Haulbowline, home to the Irish navy.

Opposite bottom: Blackrock Castle. Built in the sixteenth century as defence for Cork's upper harbour, it now houses an observatory and astronomy centre and is open to the public.

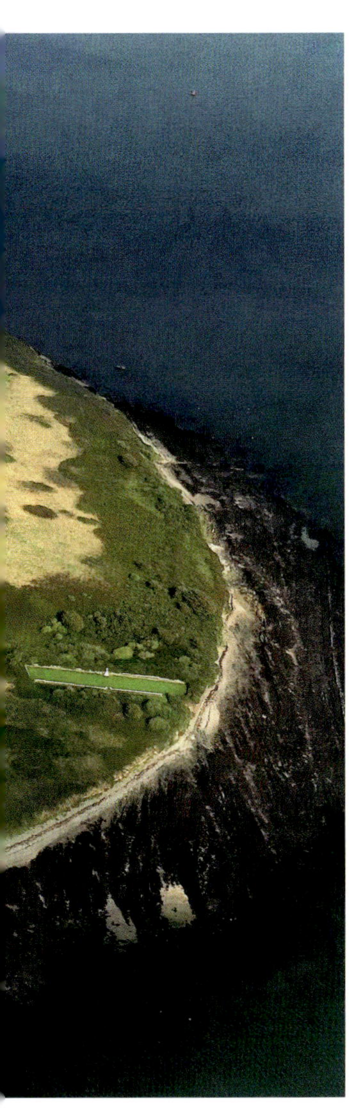

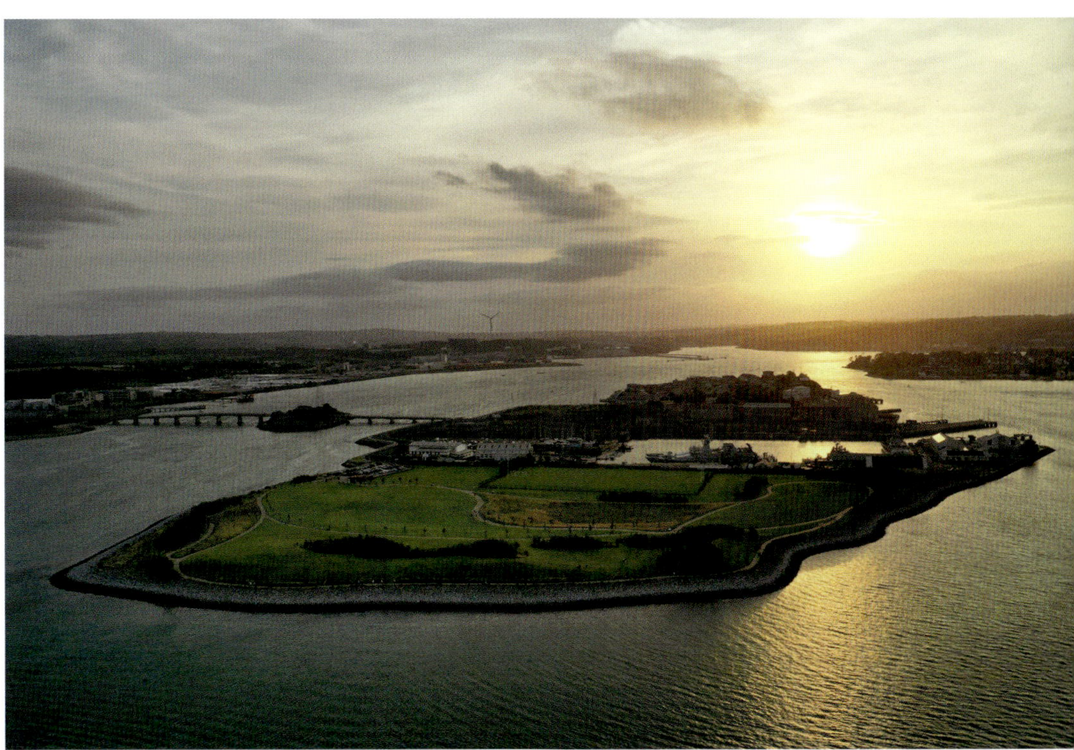

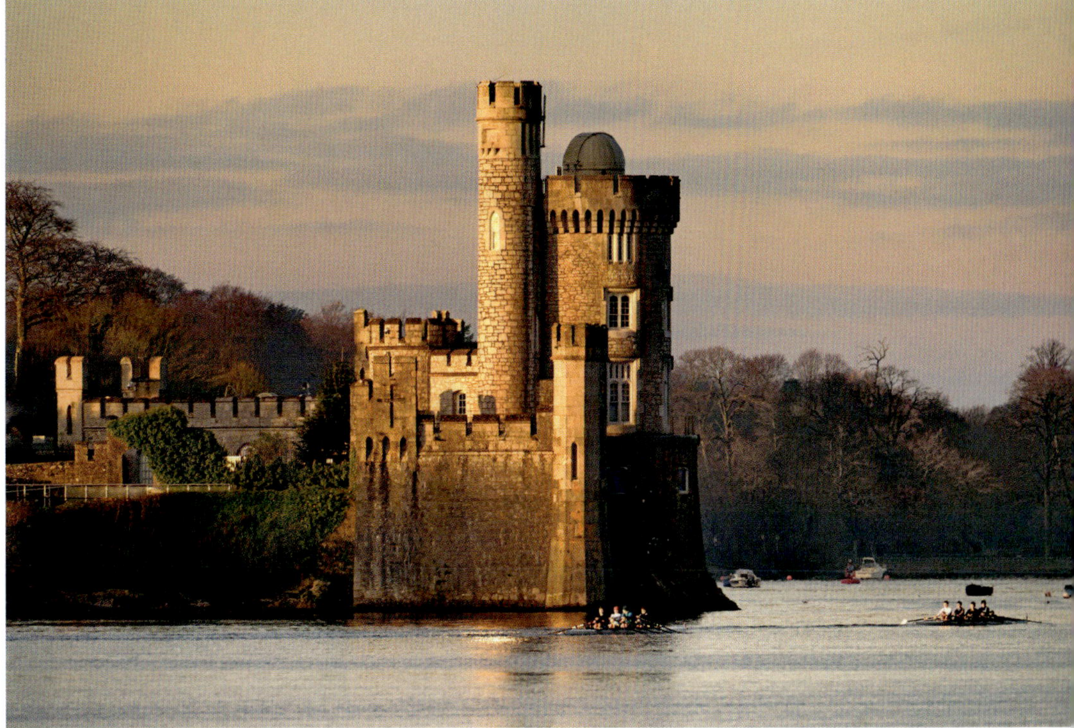

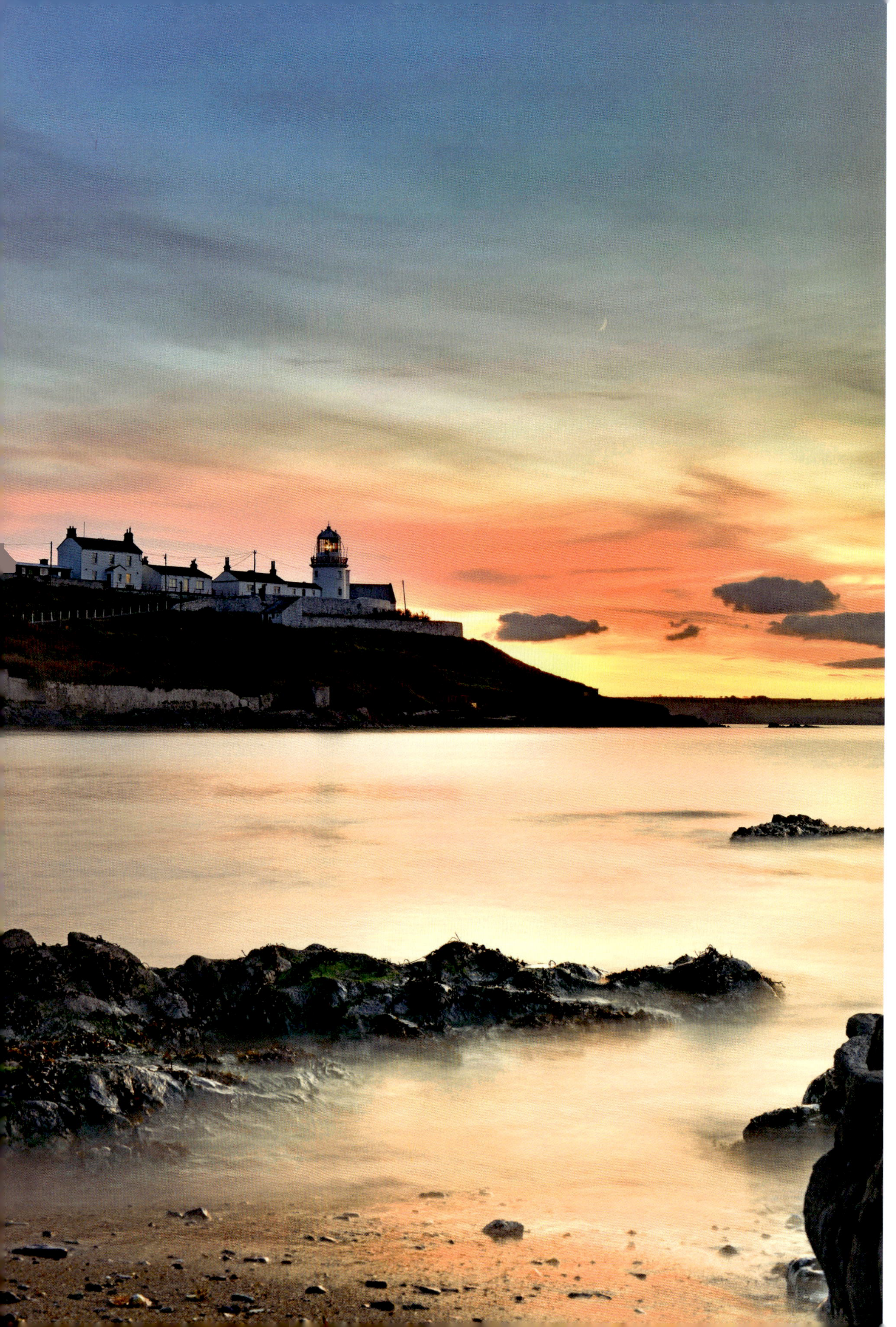

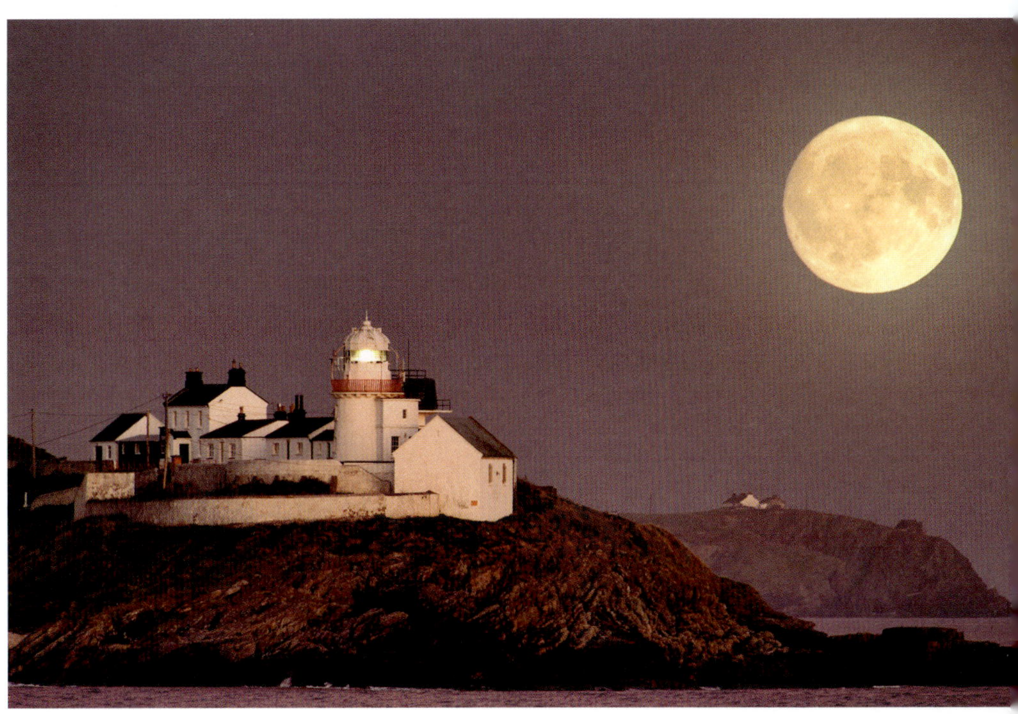

Opposite: A winter sunset viewed from White Bay Beach.
Right: The full moon rising behind Roche's Point lighthouse.
Below: Sunset at Ringabella.

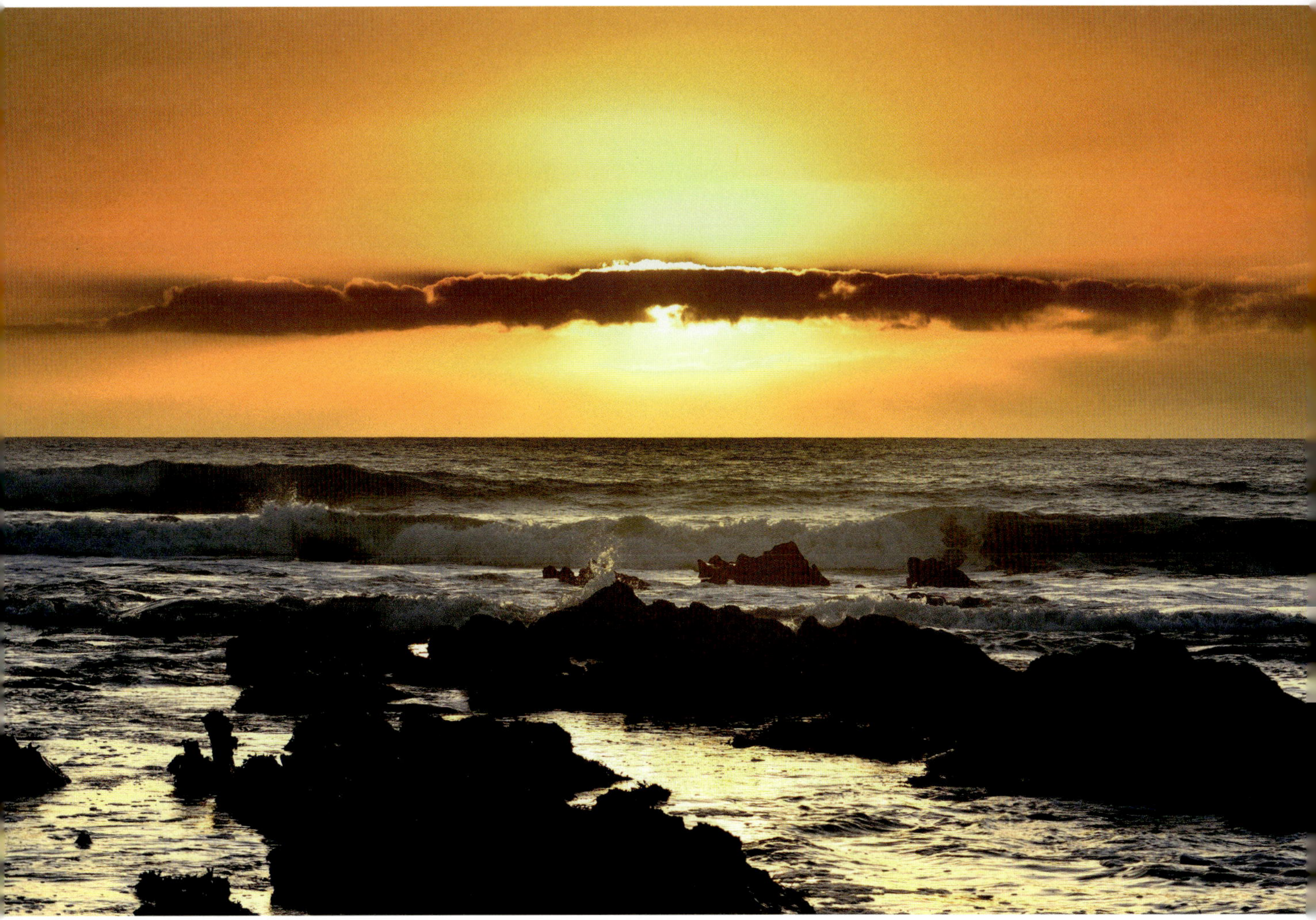

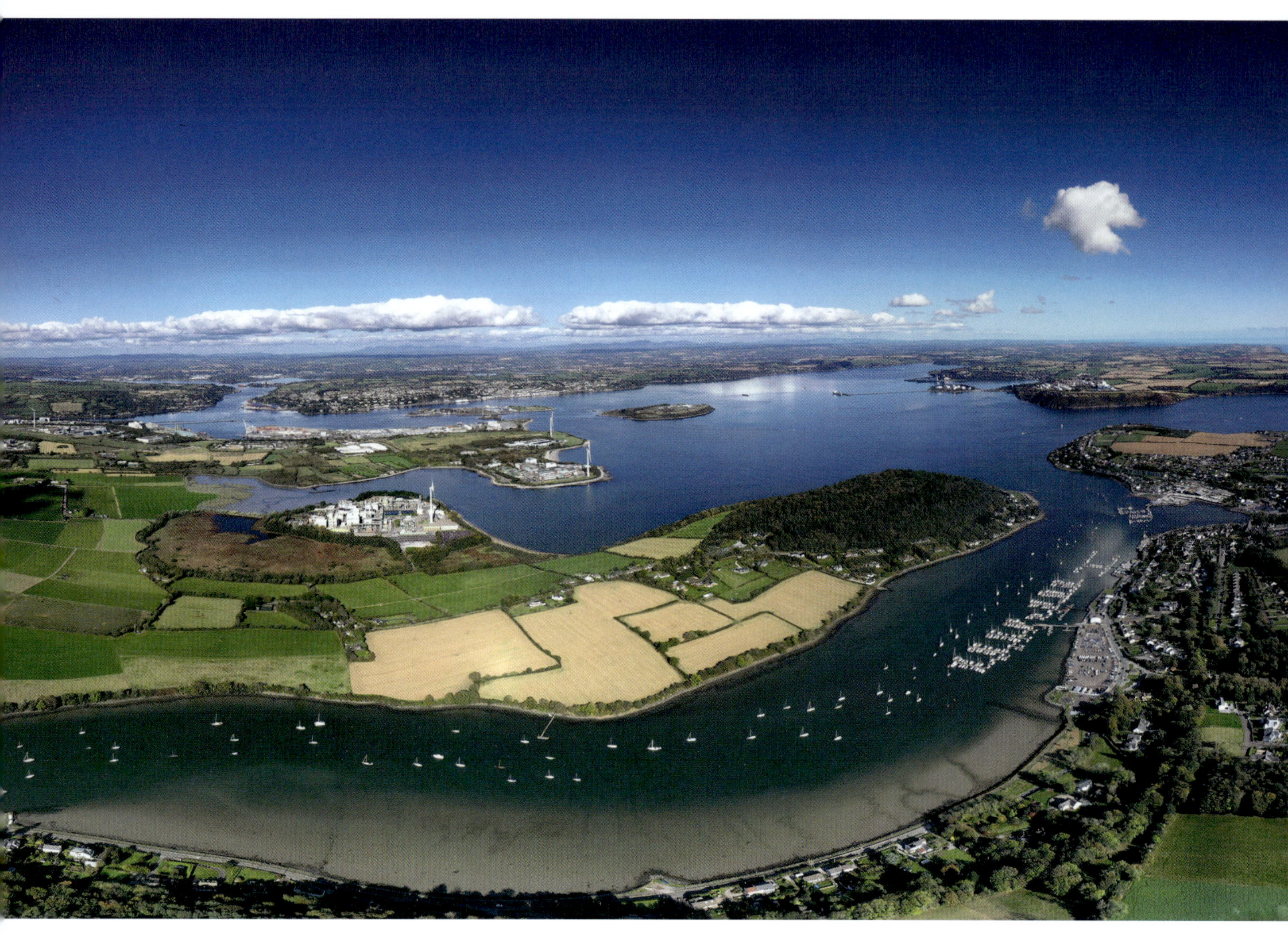

Above: Ringaskiddy and Cork Harbour from the air.

Opposite top: The Chetwynd Viaduct on the West Cork railway line near Bishopstown was built in 1849. Now disused, it is soon to become part of the West Cork Greenway.

Opposite bottom: The picturesque village of Robert's Cove at low tide.

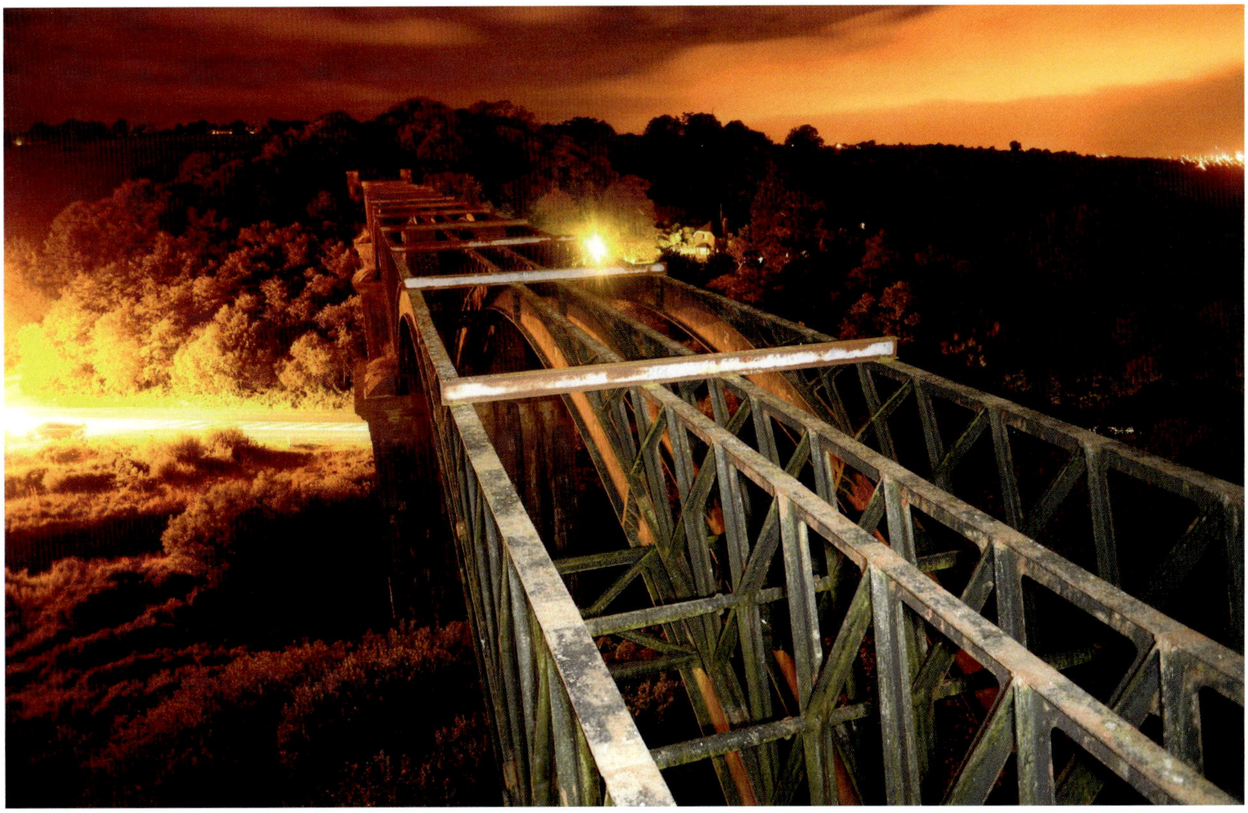

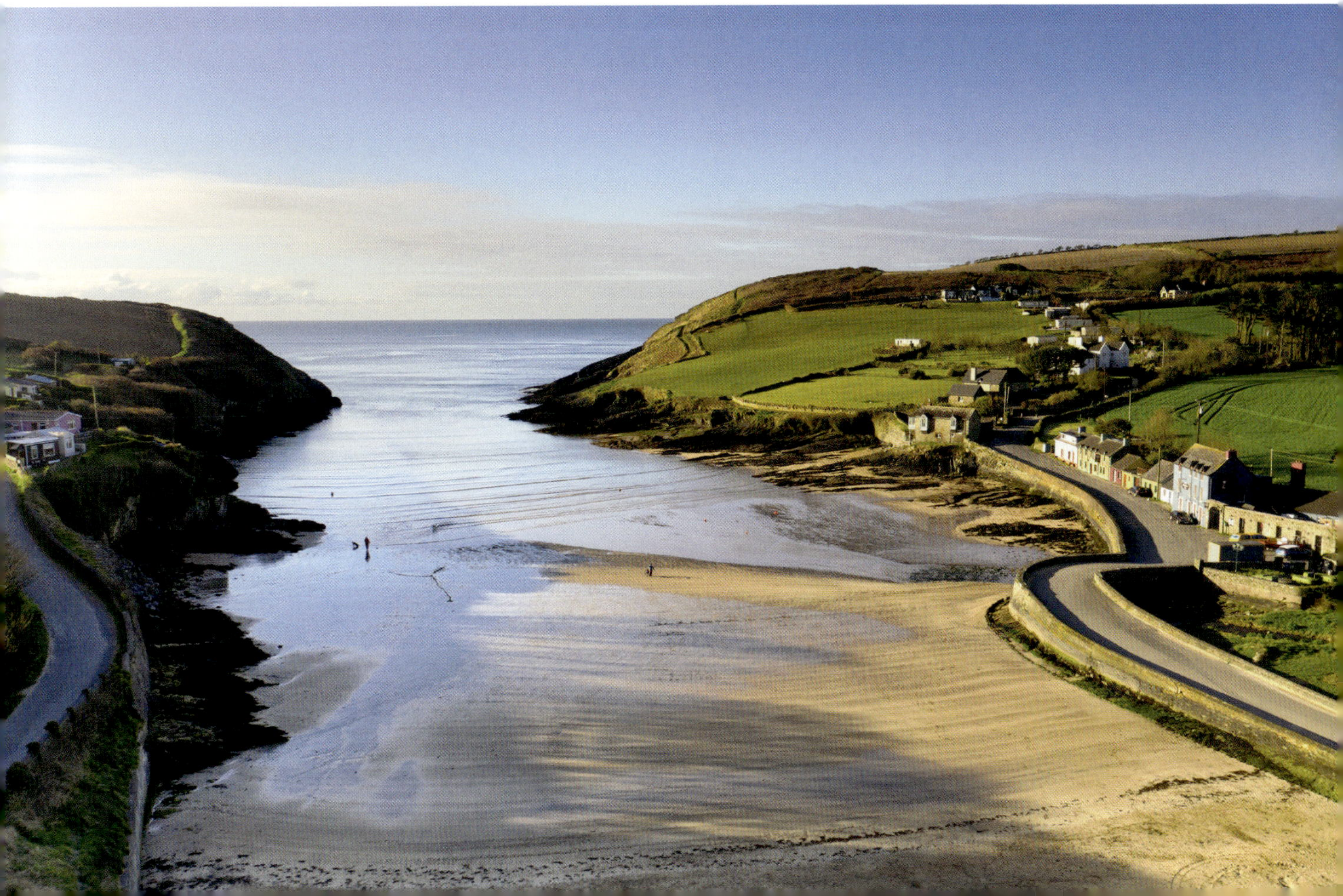

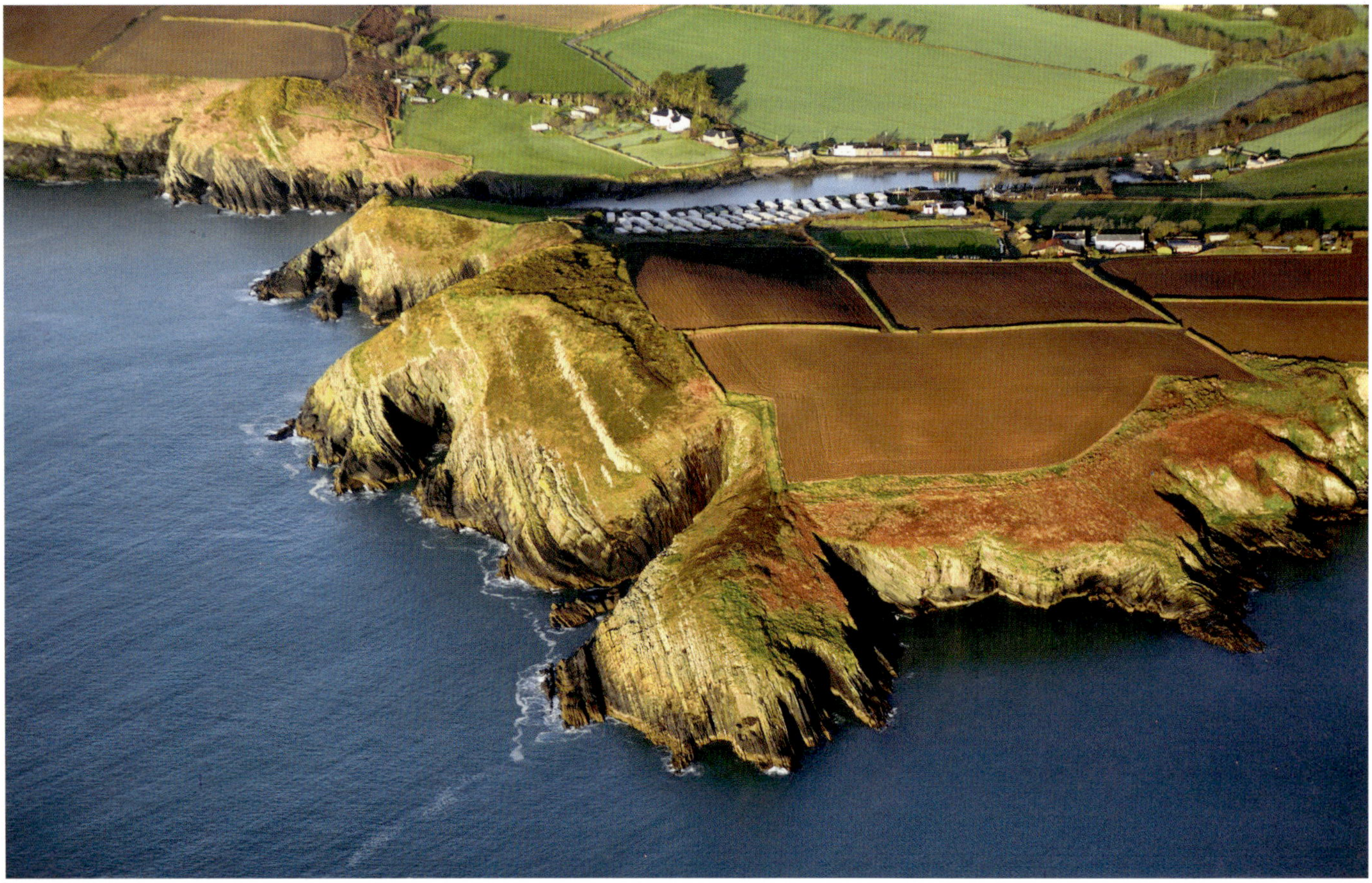

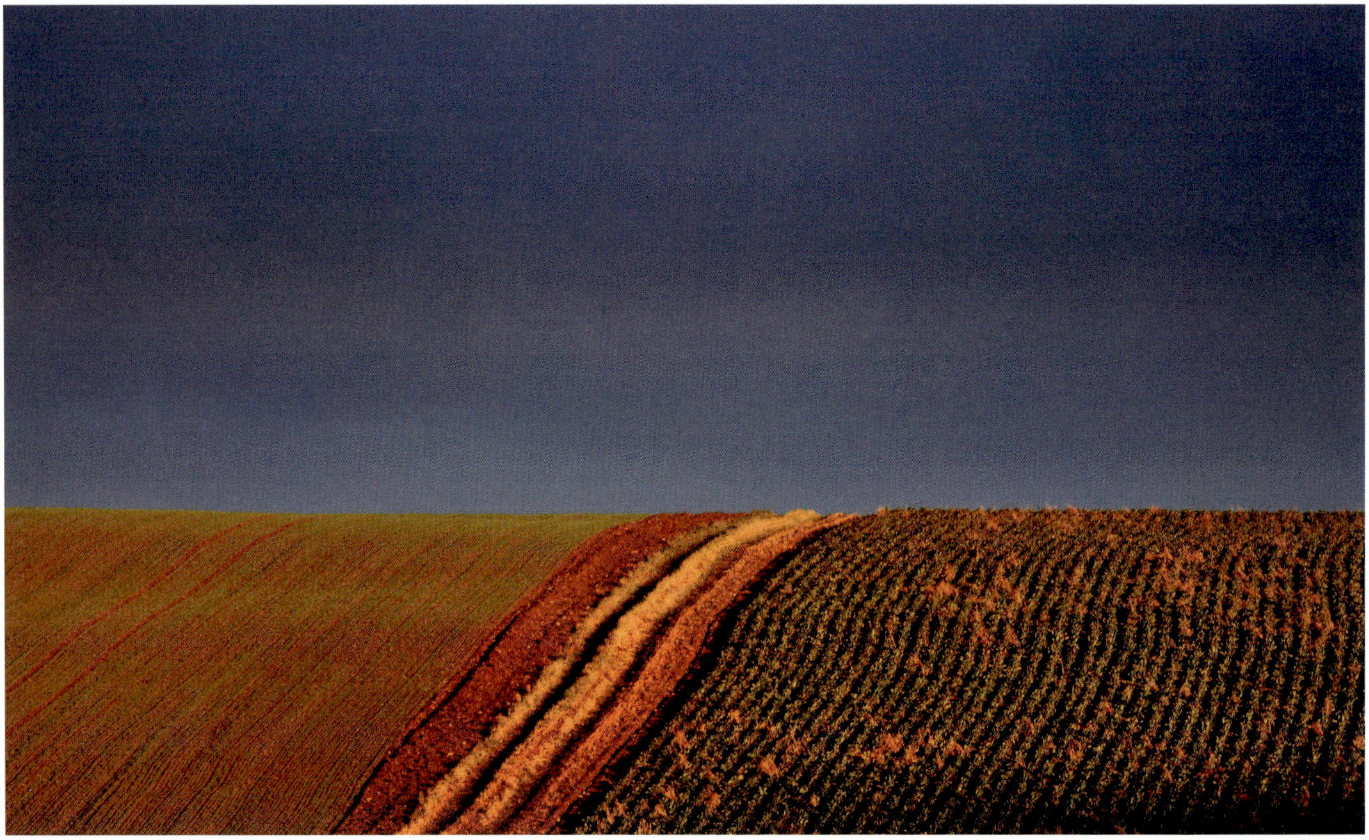

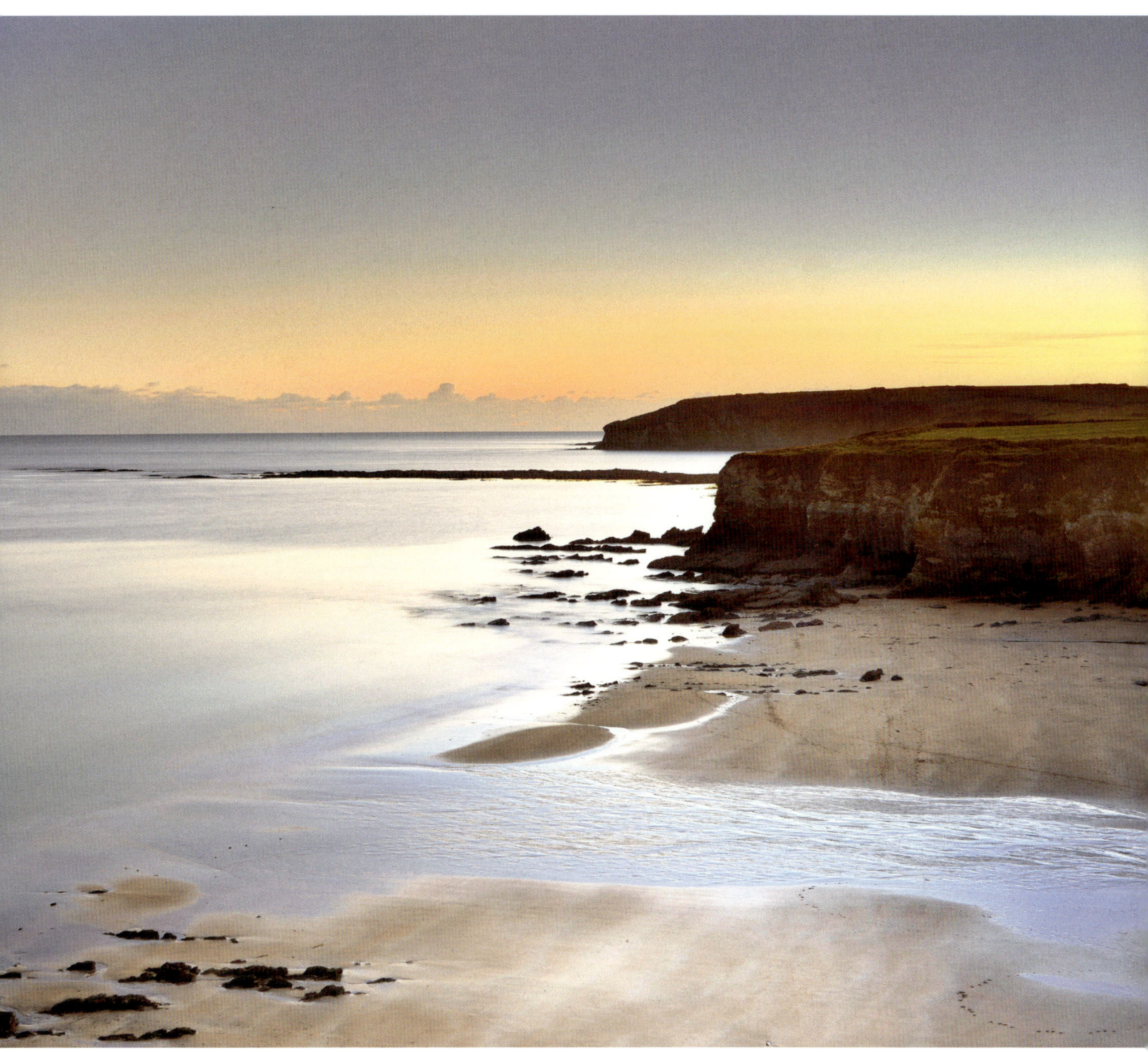

Opposite top: The tiny peninsula of Cork Head in early morning sunshine.

Opposite left: A colourful field with seedlings breaking through the iron-rich soil.

Above: Rocky Bay after sunset. Not far from Minane Bridge, this sandy beach, with exposed Devonian cliffs, is popular with locals.

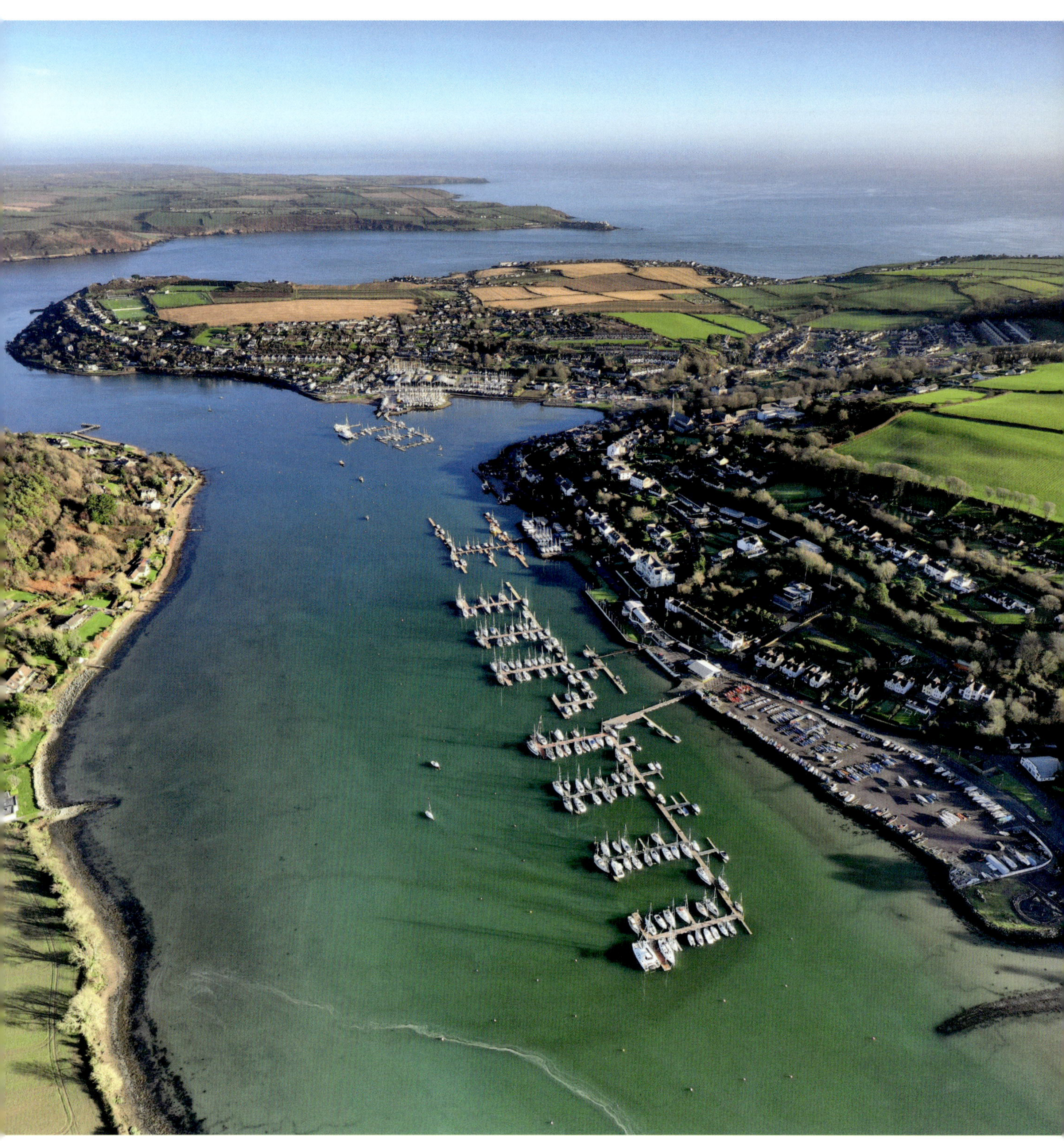

Opposite: An aerial view of Crosshaven and the Royal Cork Yacht Club. Founded in 1720, it is the world's oldest yacht club.

Below: The holiday village of Fountainstown in winter with Cork Harbour in the distance.

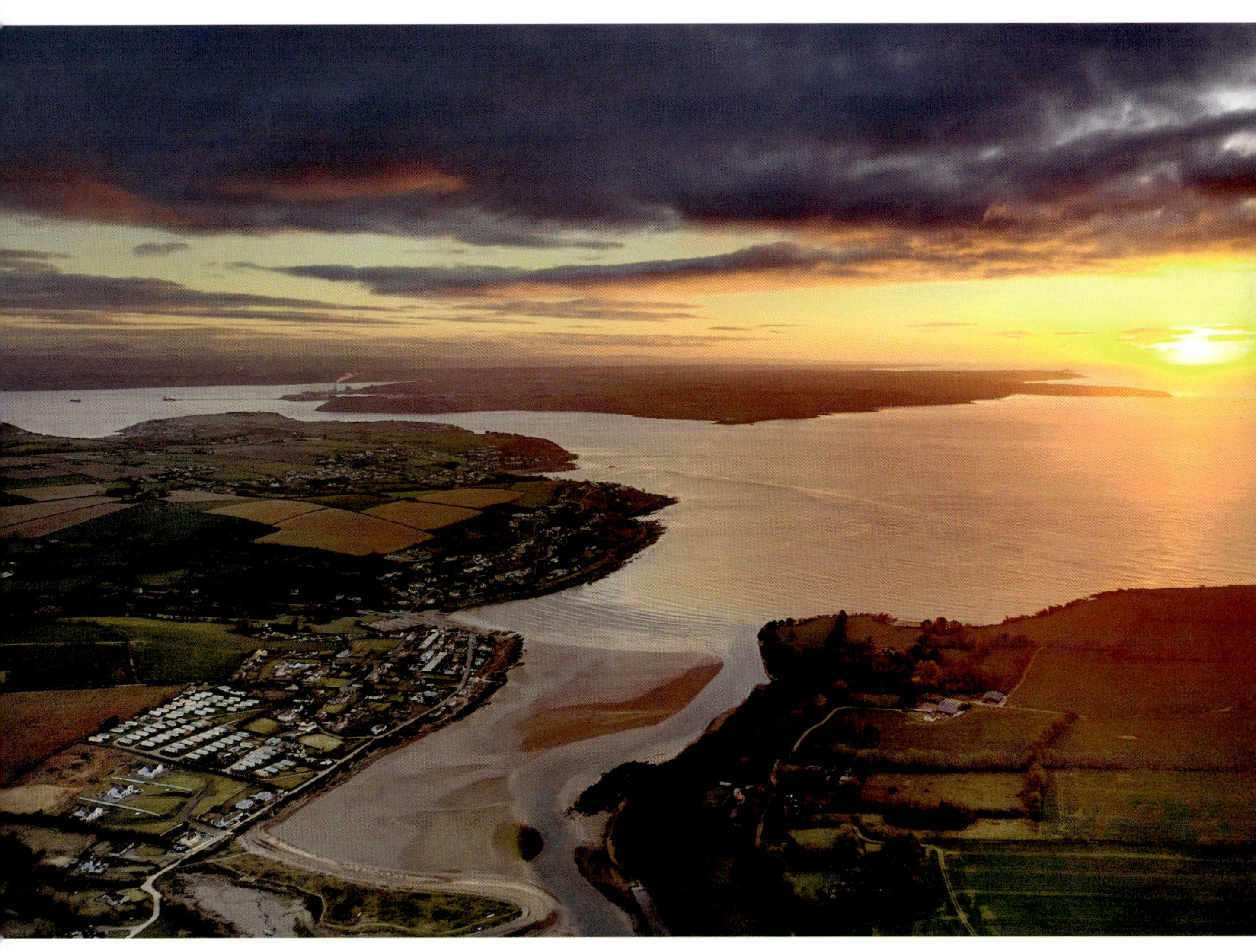

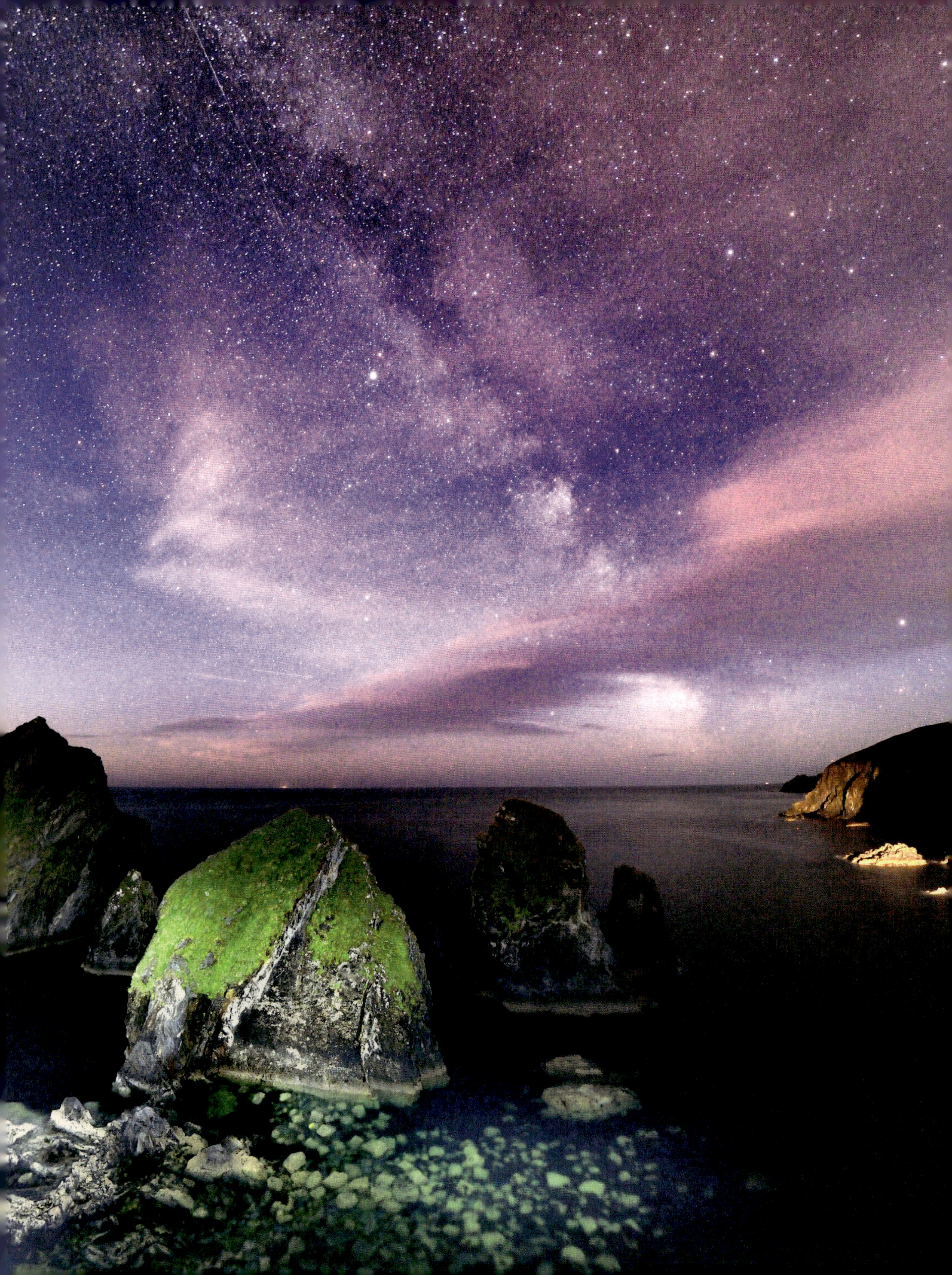

Opposite: The Milky Way over Nohoval Cove.
Right: Hay bales in September sunshine.
Below: *Astrid* at dawn the morning after it sank. The Dutch sail-training vessel ran aground in July 2013 but all hands were saved.

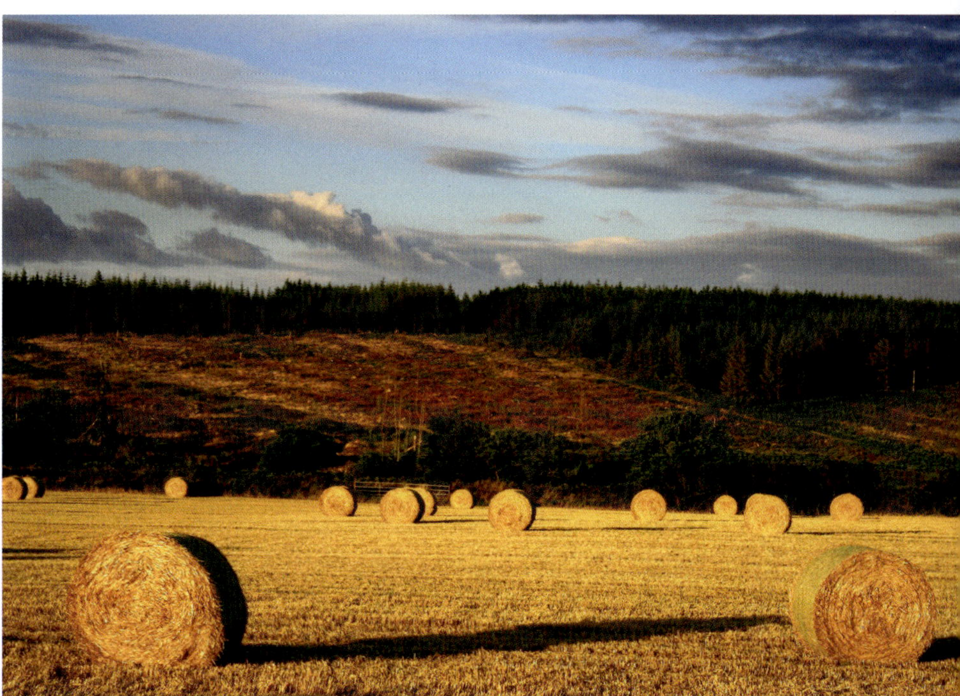

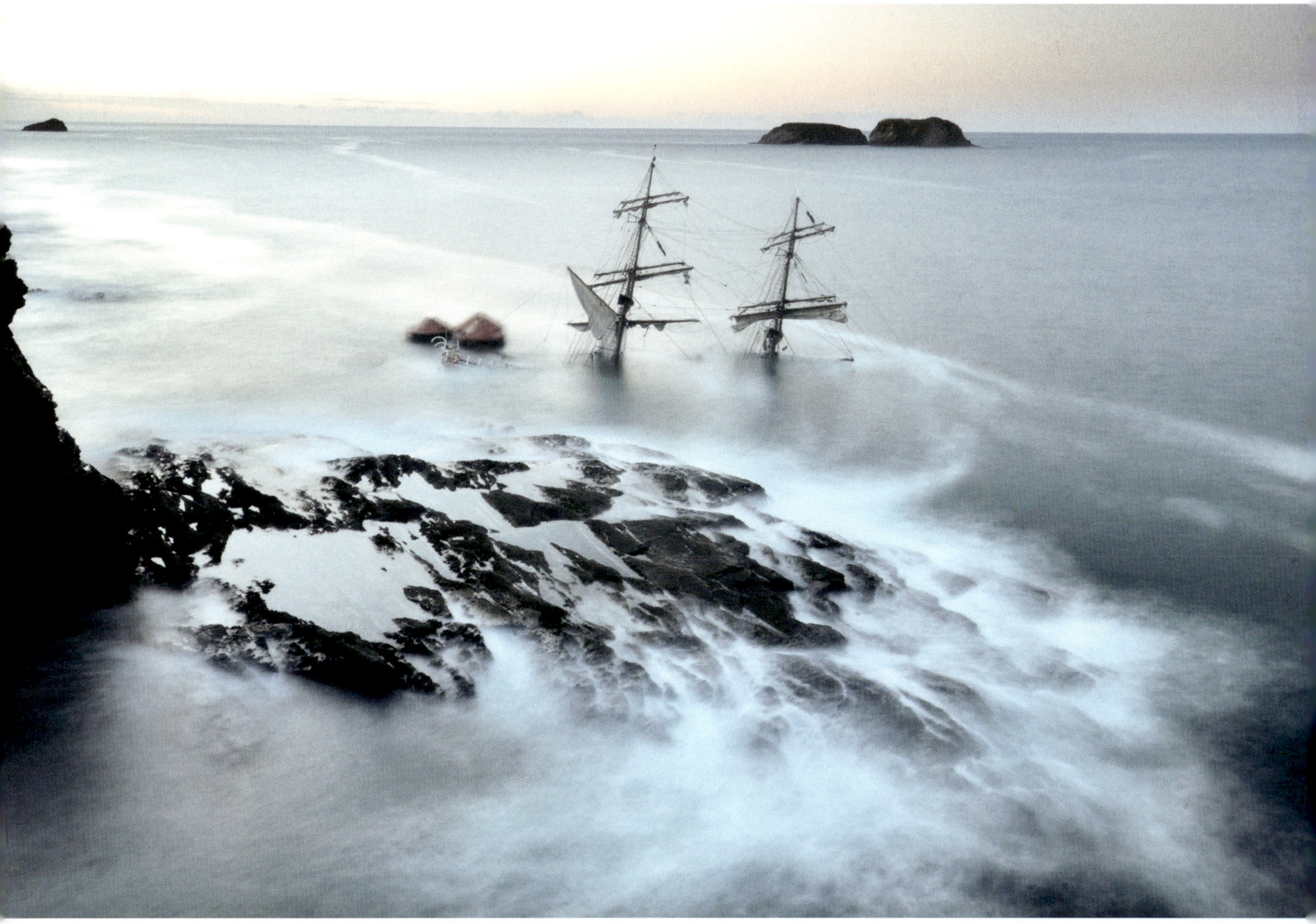

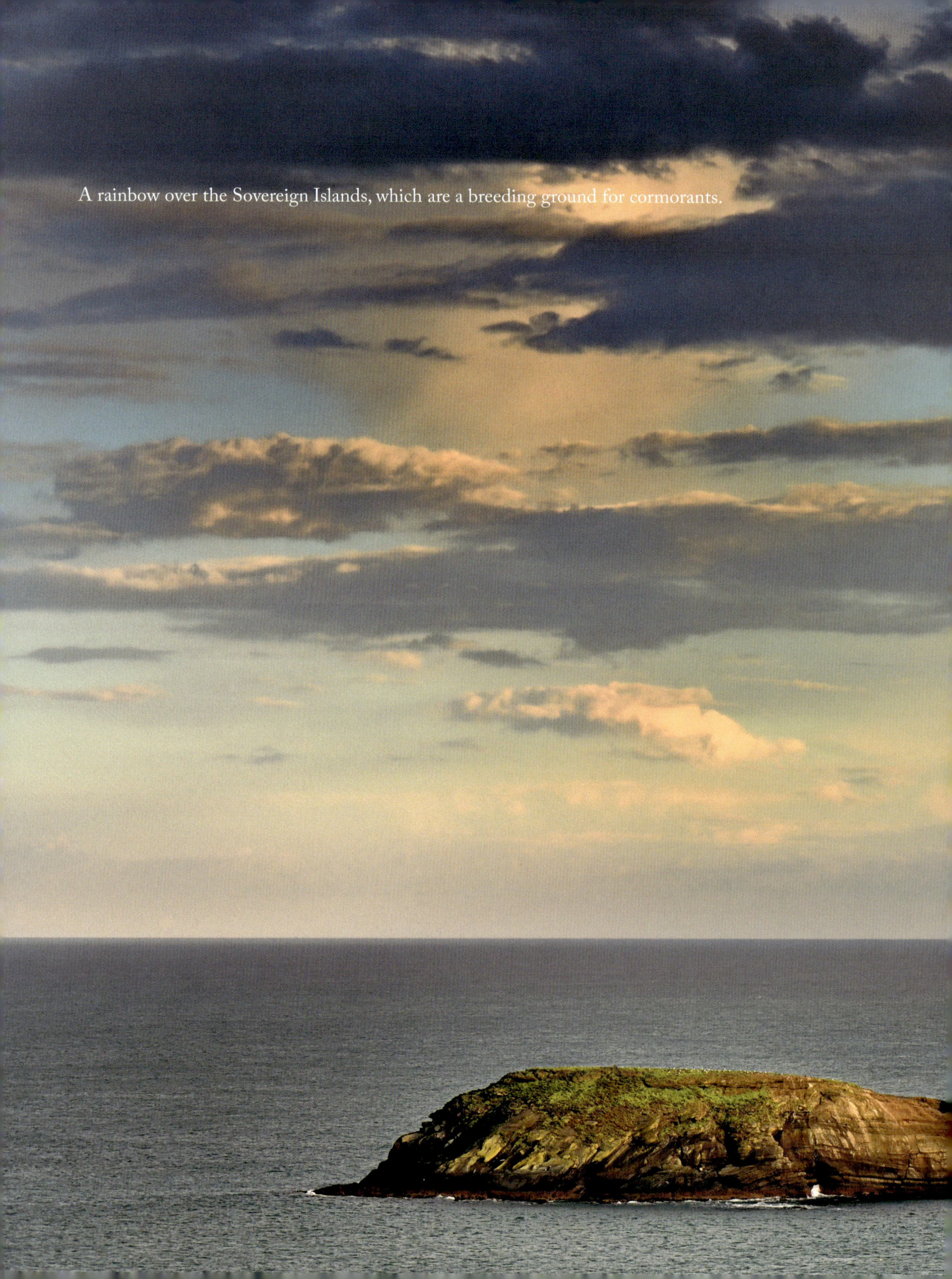
A rainbow over the Sovereign Islands, which are a breeding ground for cormorants.

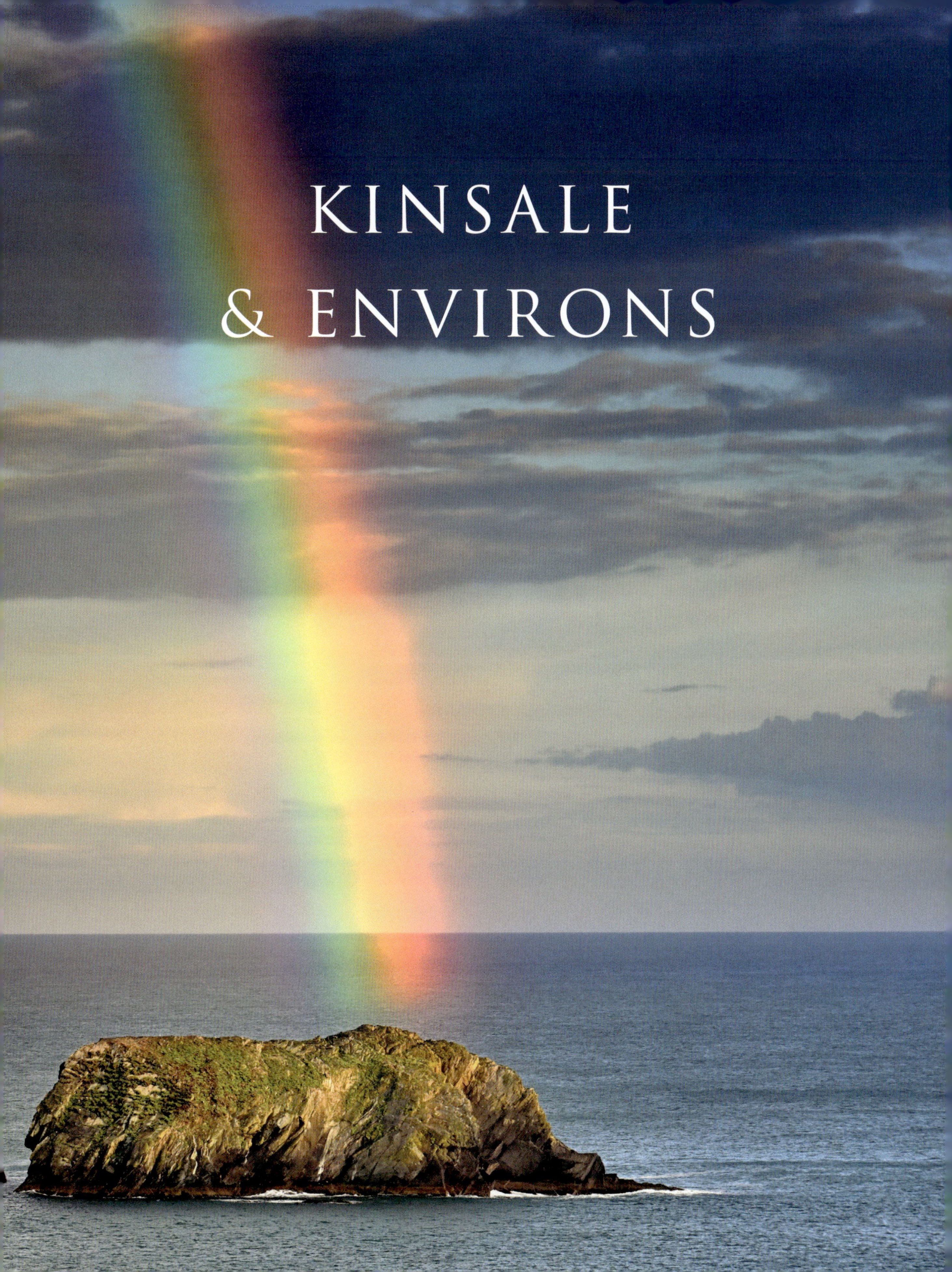
KINSALE
& ENVIRONS

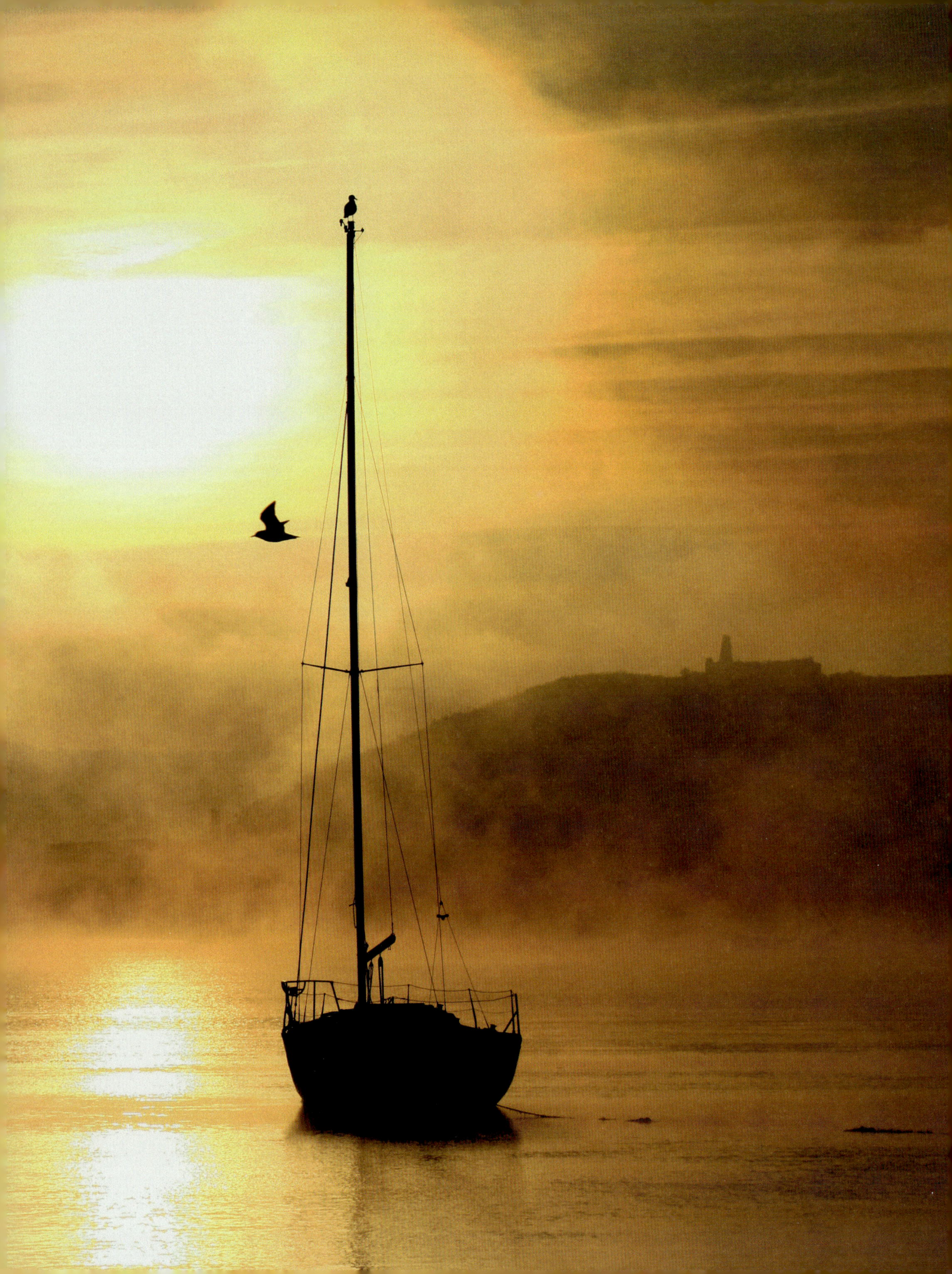

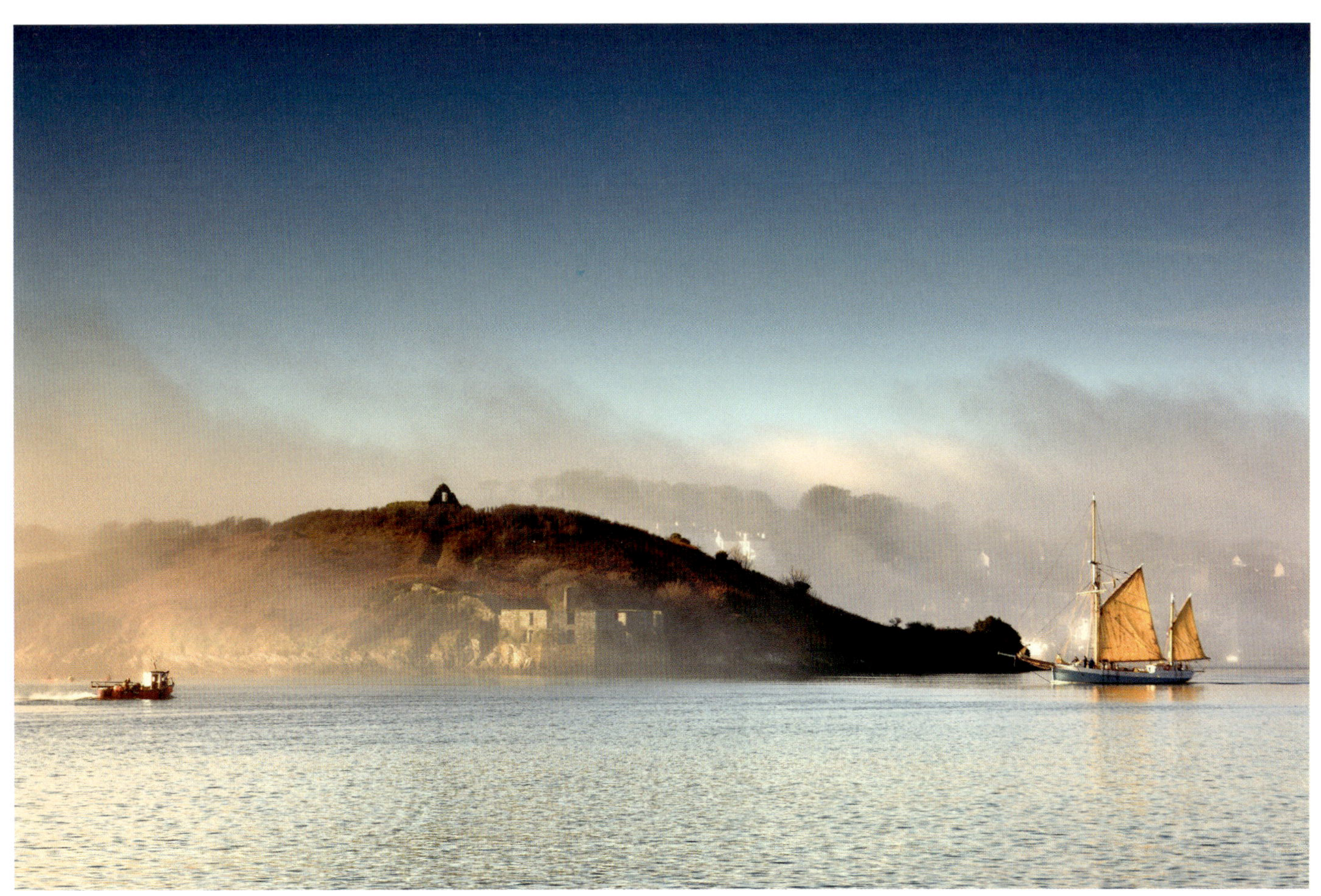

Opposite: Sailboat at sunrise with James Fort in the background. The fort was built between 1602 and 1607, following the Battle of Kinsale.

Above: Misty morning with the sailing boat *Ilen* passing James Fort. Designed by Limerick man Conor O'Brien and built in Baltimore in 1926, the *Ilen* spent seventy years in the Falklands before returning home. It has been rebuilt and now serves as a sail-training boat.

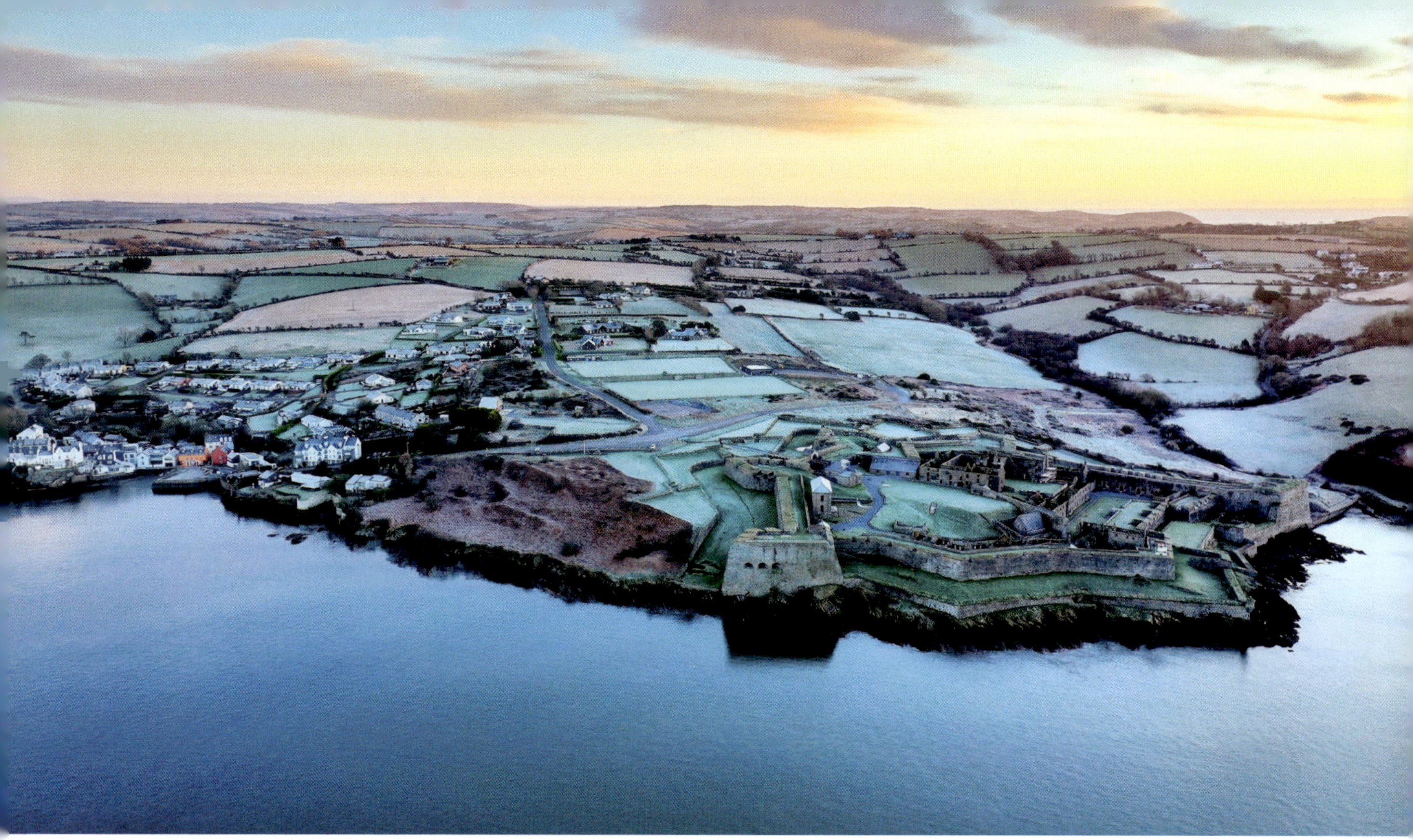

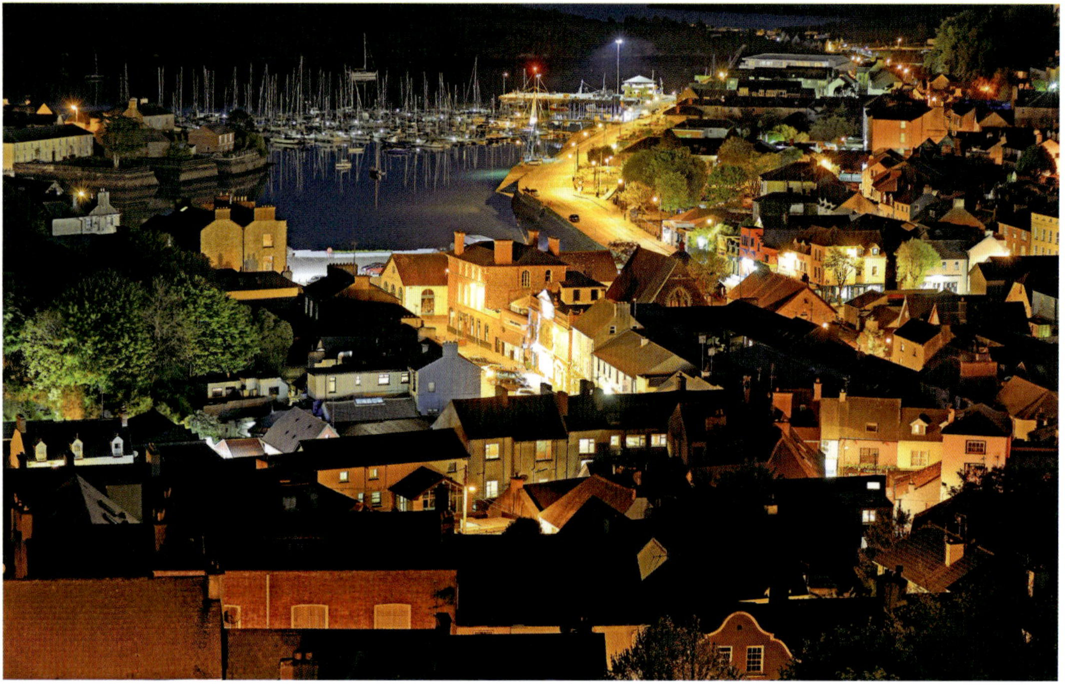

Top: Charles Fort and Summercove in Kinsale on a frosty morning. Charles Fort was built in around 1677, and sits directly across the estuary of the River Bandon from the older James Fort.

Above: Kinsale at night.

Opposite: Sunrise from the viewing mast at the pier in Kinsale.

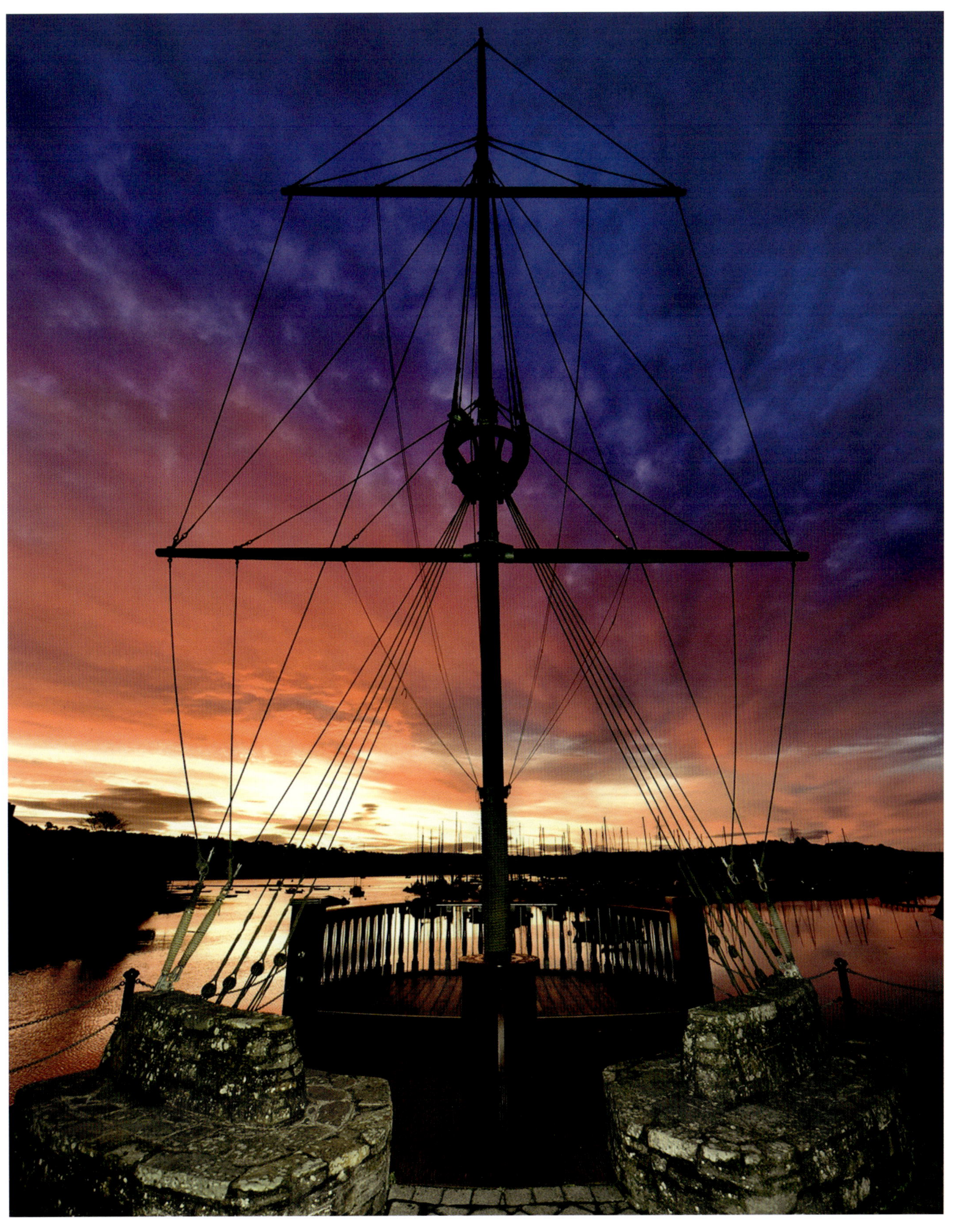

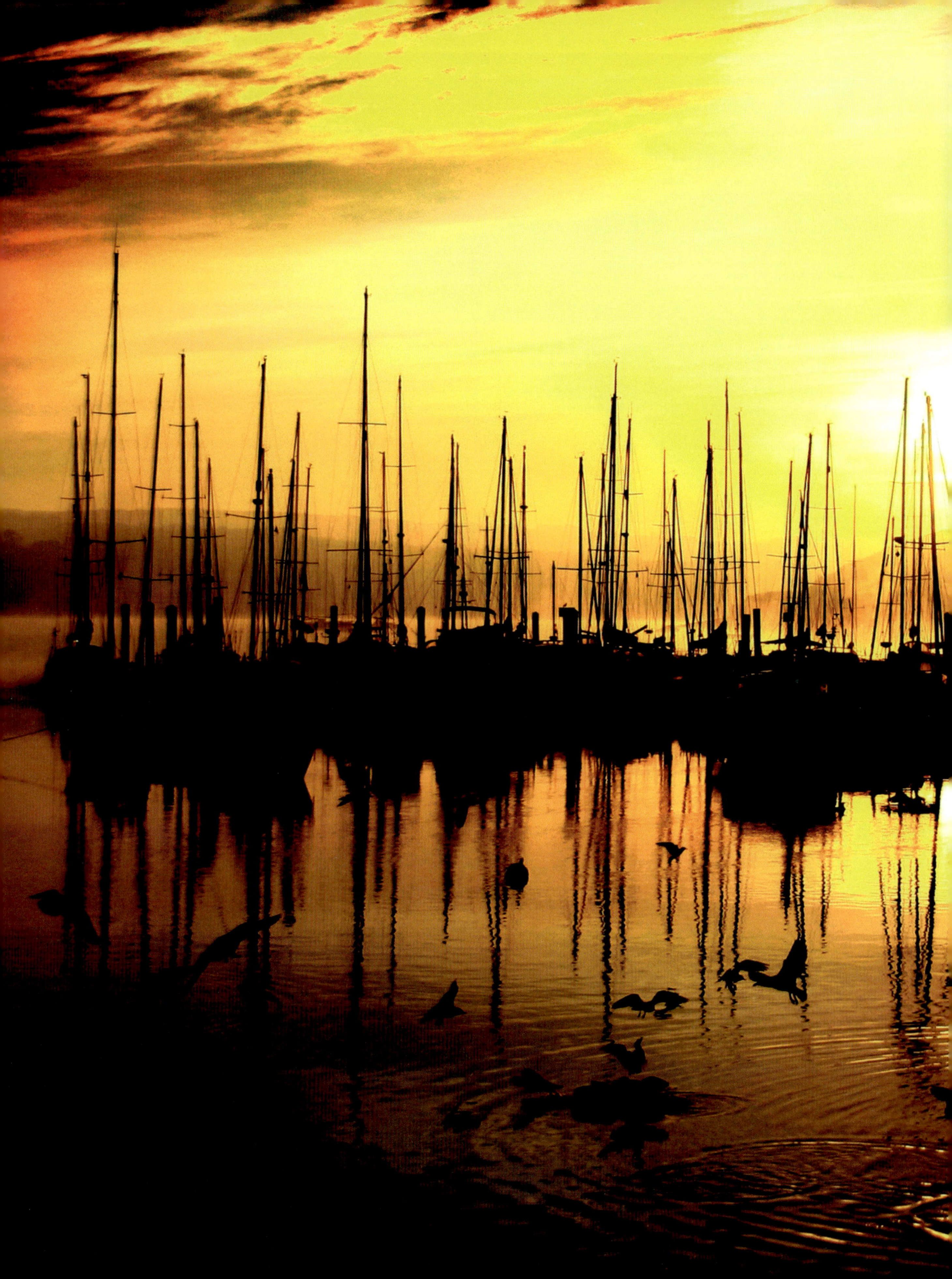

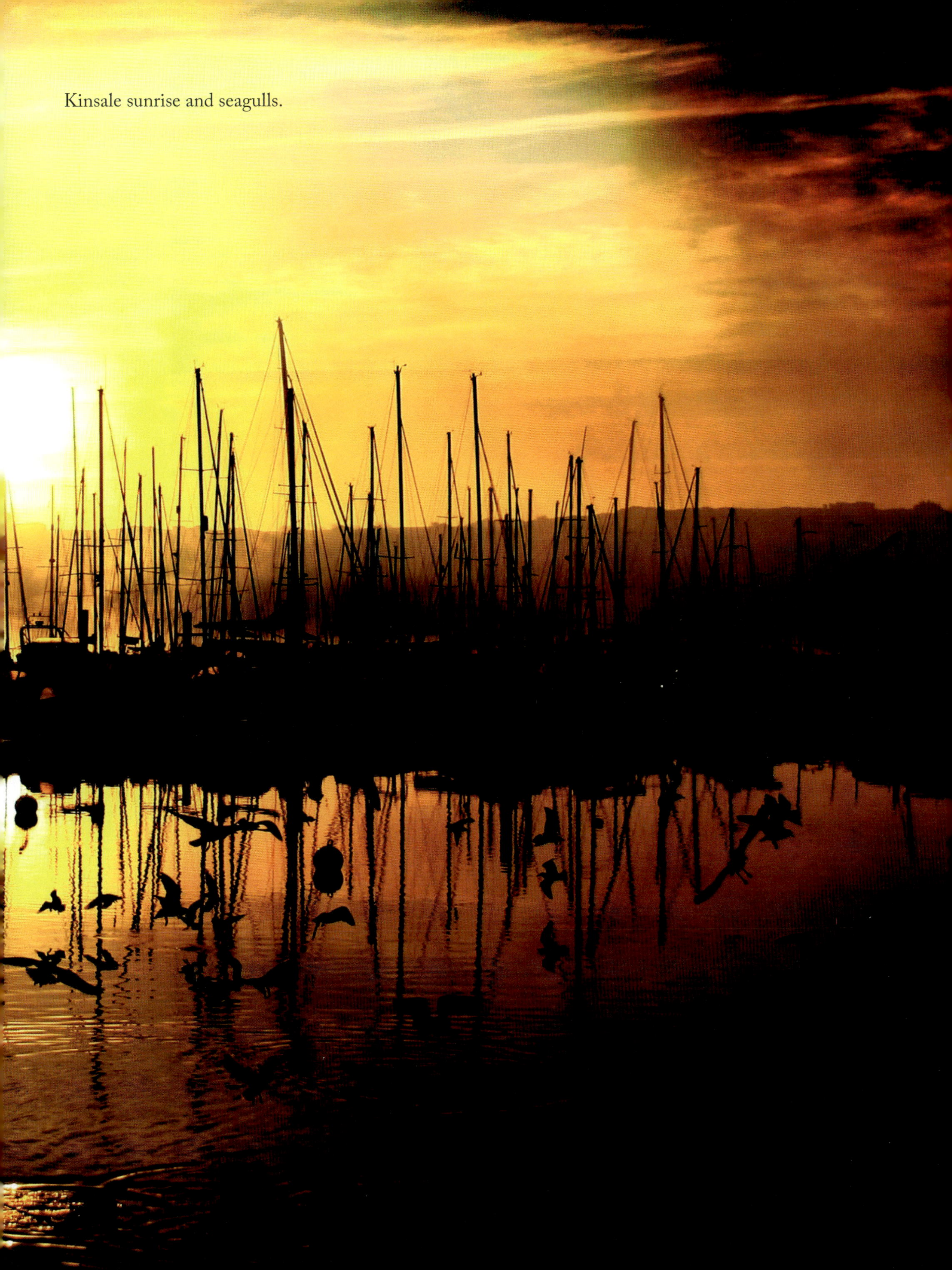

Kinsale sunrise and seagulls.

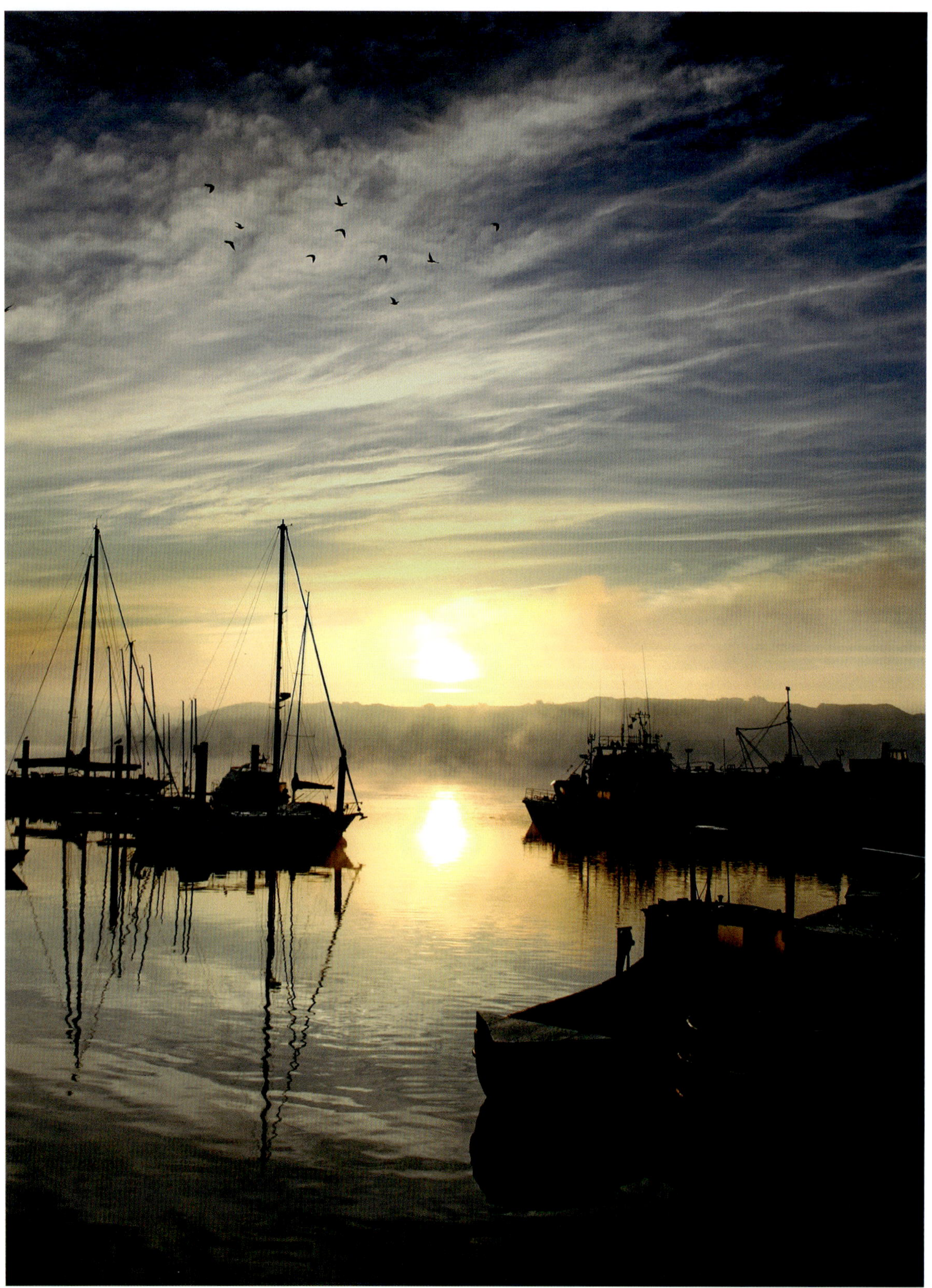

Above: Kinsale Harbour. This medieval town with its narrow winding streets, deep-water port and two marinas is very popular with sailors and fishermen. It has some of the best restaurants in the country, earning Kinsale a reputation as Ireland's gourmet capital.

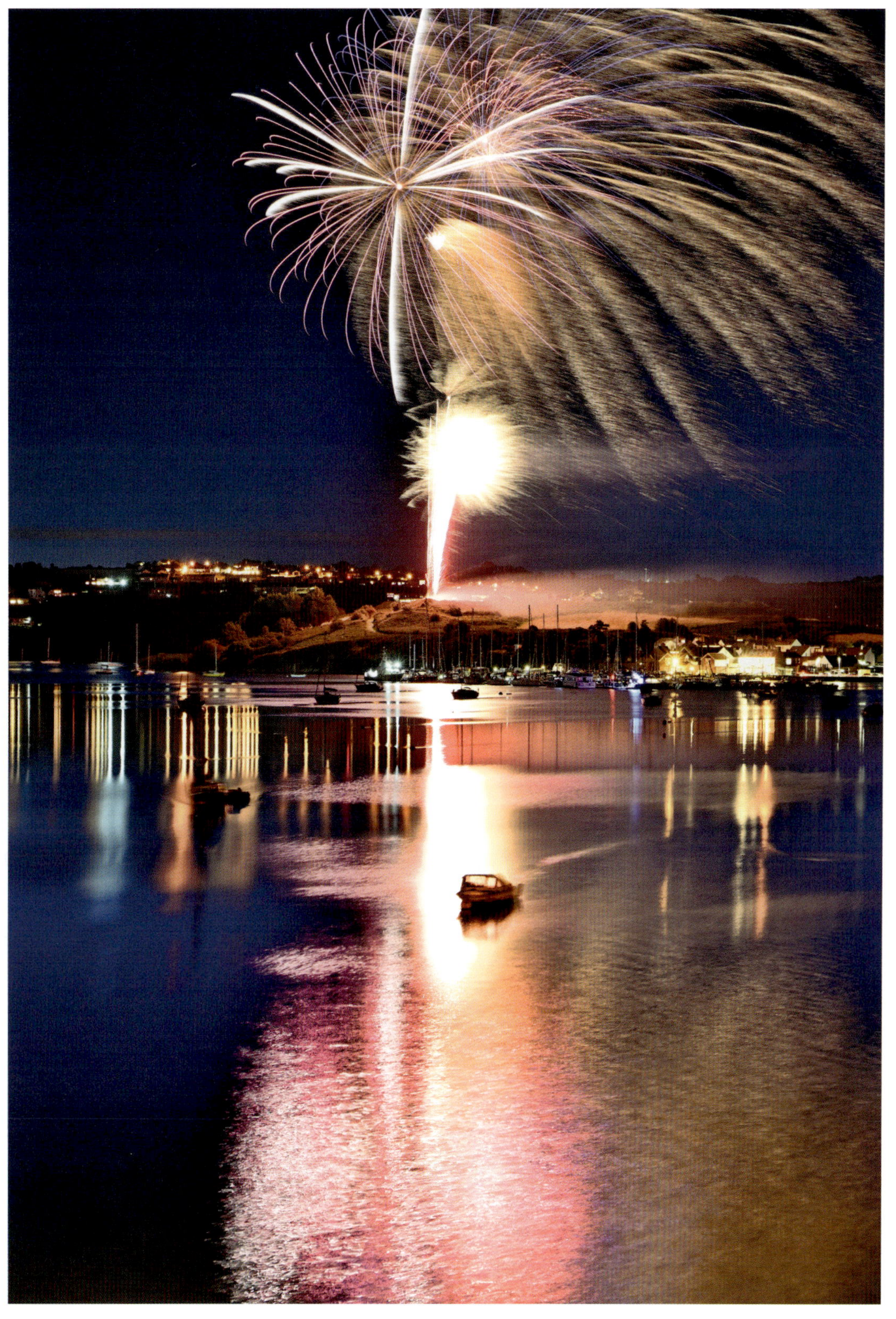

Above: Fireworks at the Kinsale Regatta, which is held every August bank holiday weekend.

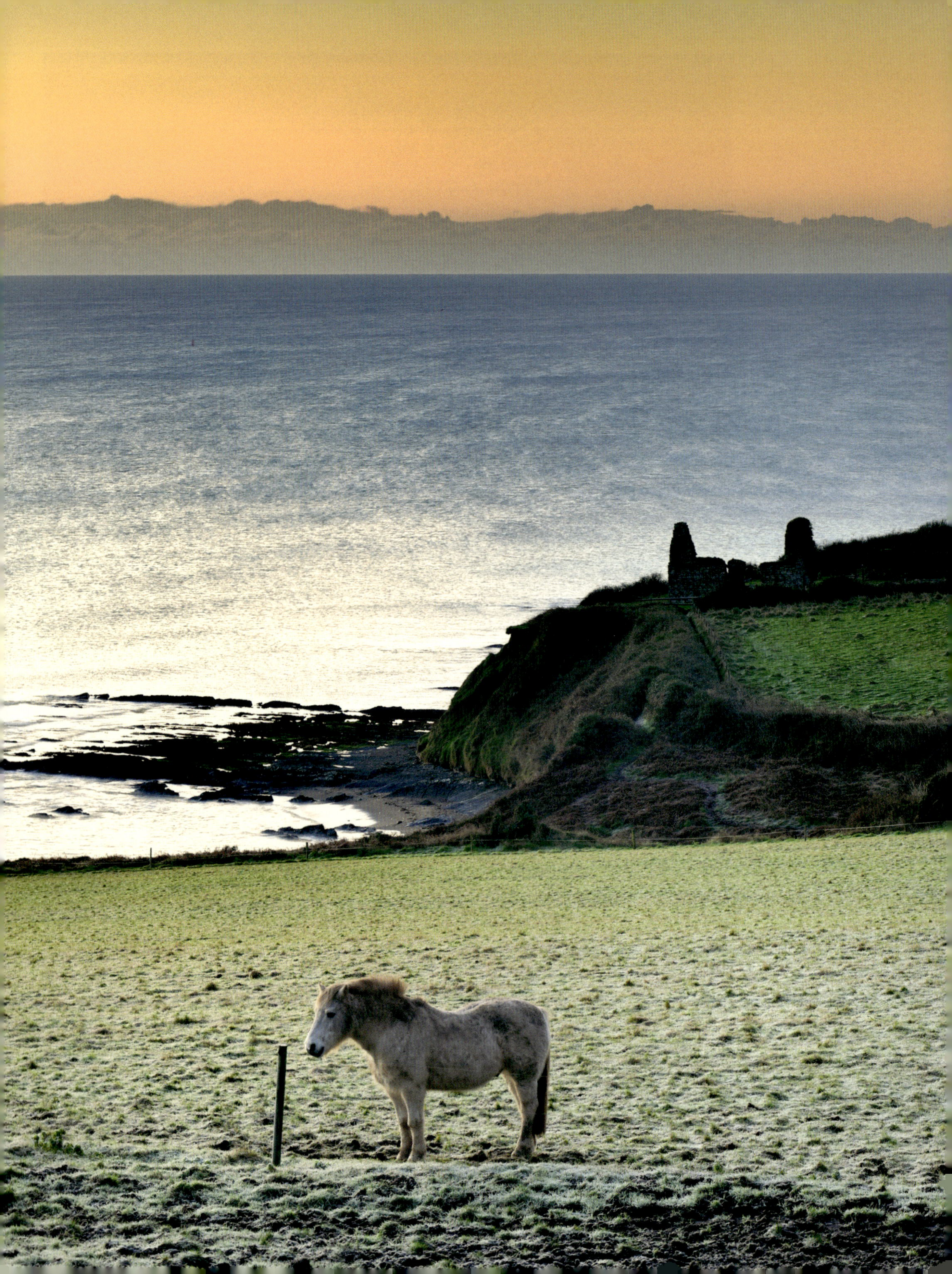

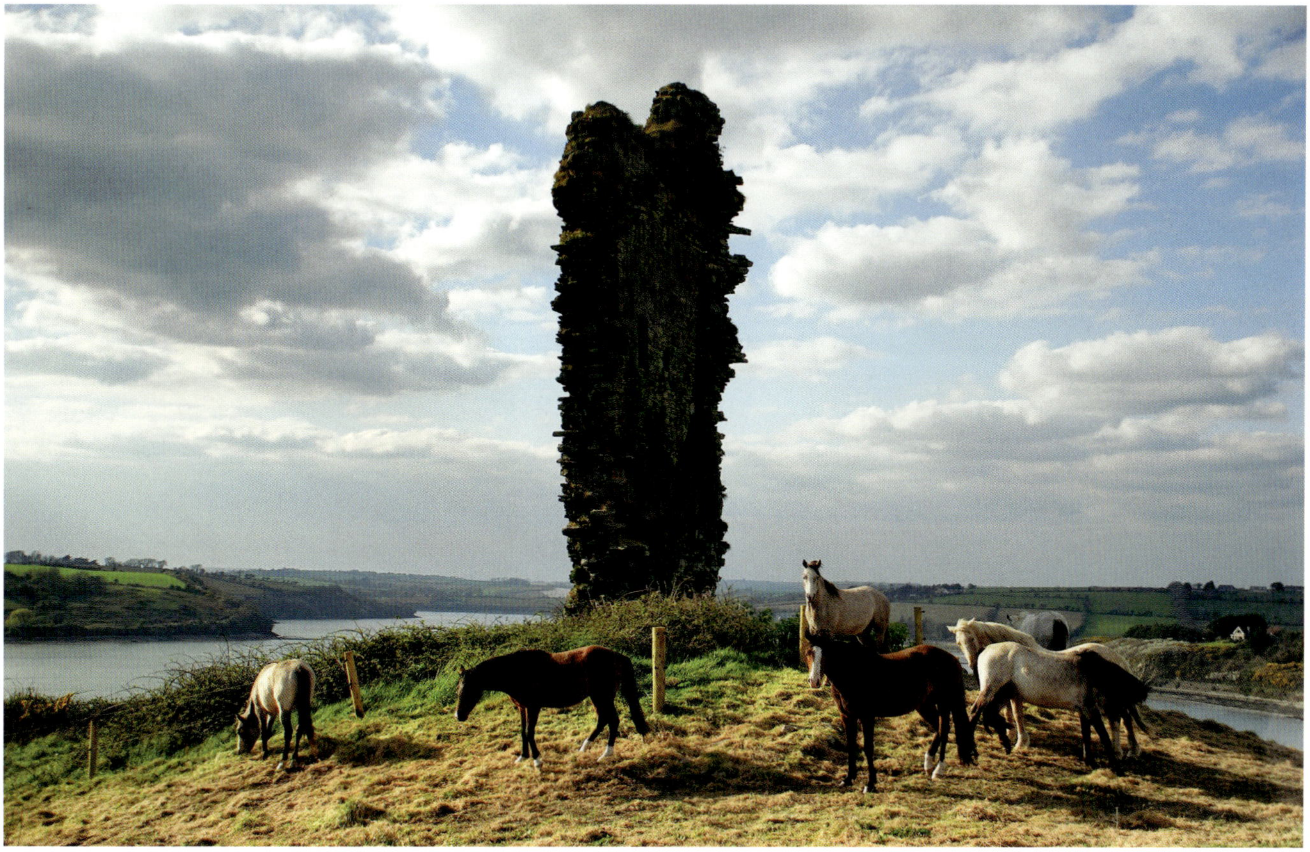

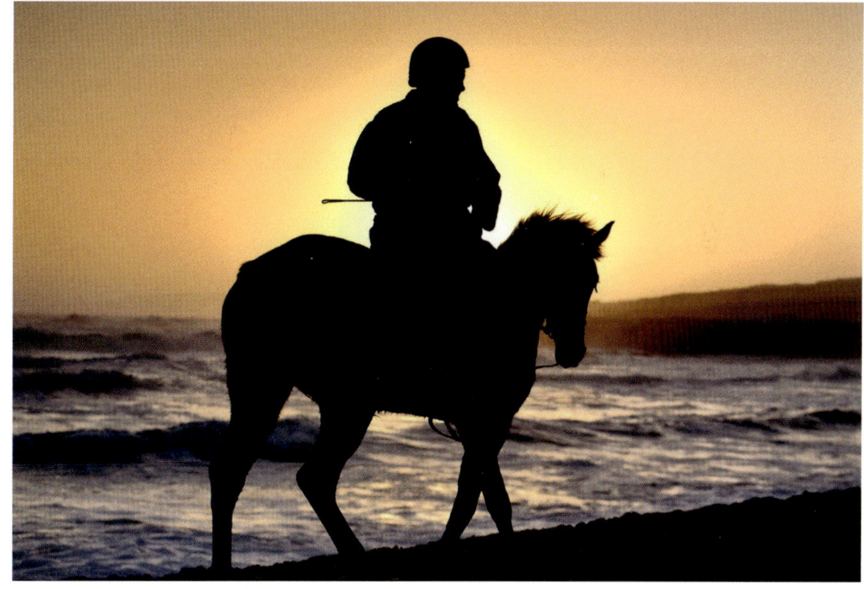

Above: Horses graze beside the ruin of Ringrone Castle, which dates to the twelfth or thirteenth century.

Left: A frosty morning at Courtaparteen.

Right: Horse riding at sunset at Bullens Bay.

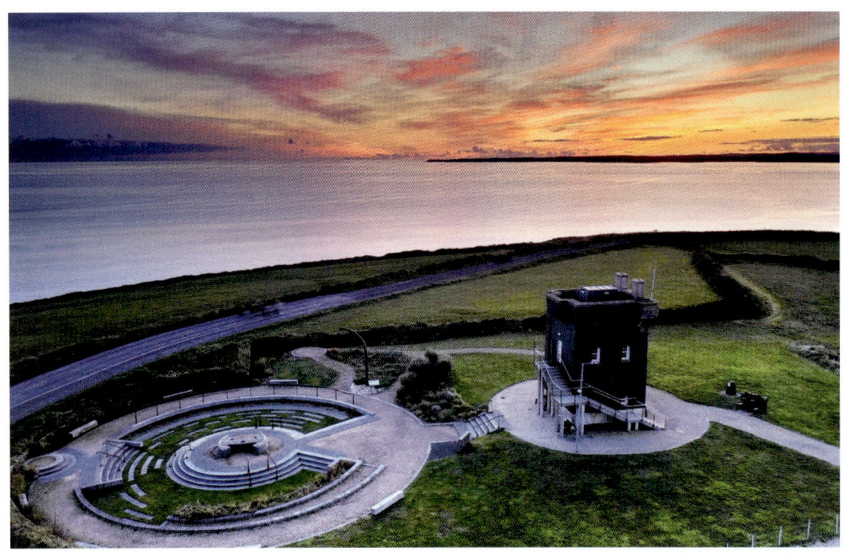

Left: The *Lusitania* museum and signal tower on the Old Head of Kinsale. RMS *Lusitania* was a merchant vessel sunk by Germany on 7 May 1915, an action which drew the US into the First World War. Among the 1,197 who died was Hugh Lane, who established the Municipal Gallery of Modern Art in Dublin.

Below: Paragliding over the cliffs of the Old Head of Kinsale.

Opposite: An aerial view of the Dock Beach with Kinsale in the background.

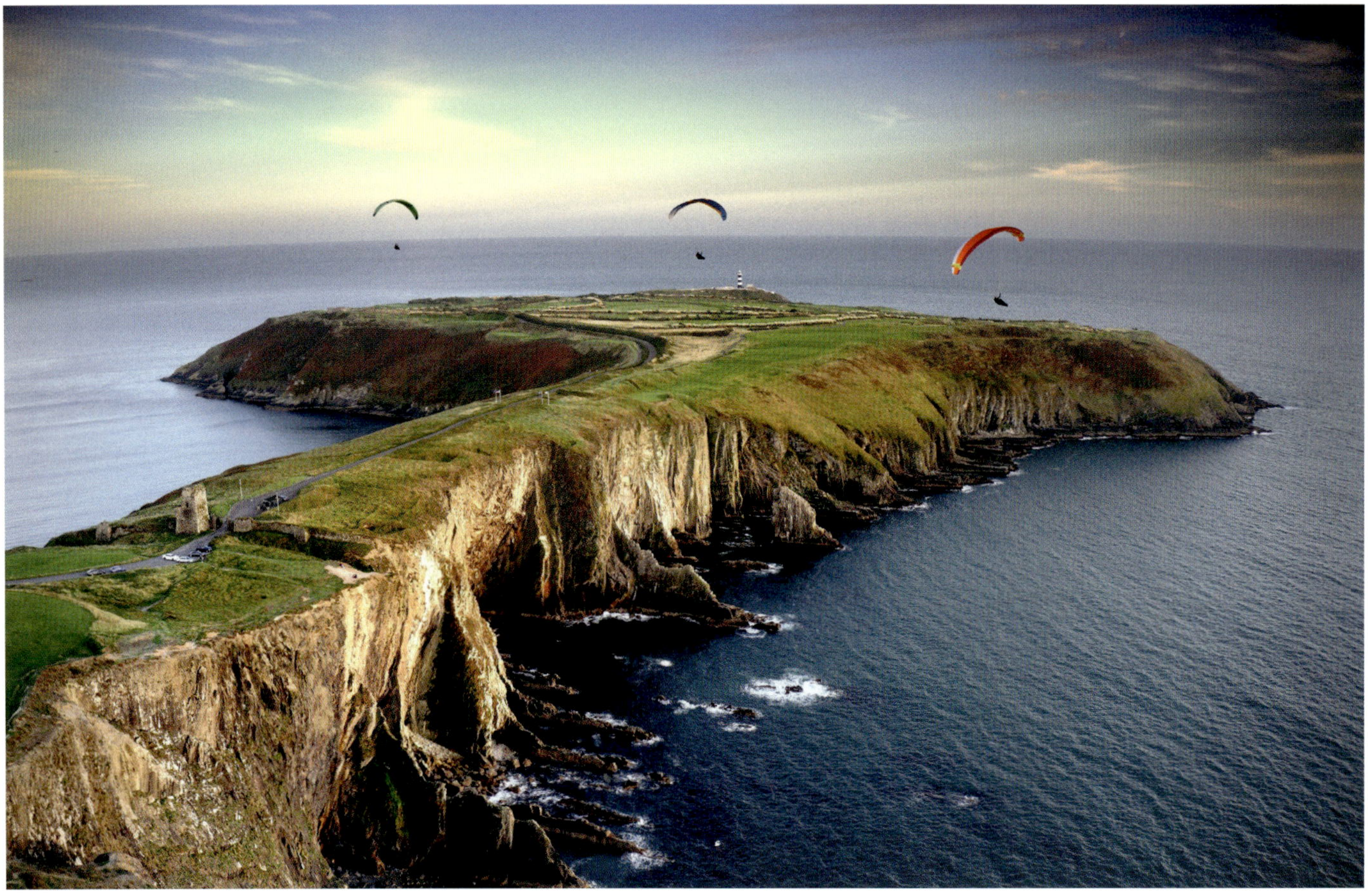

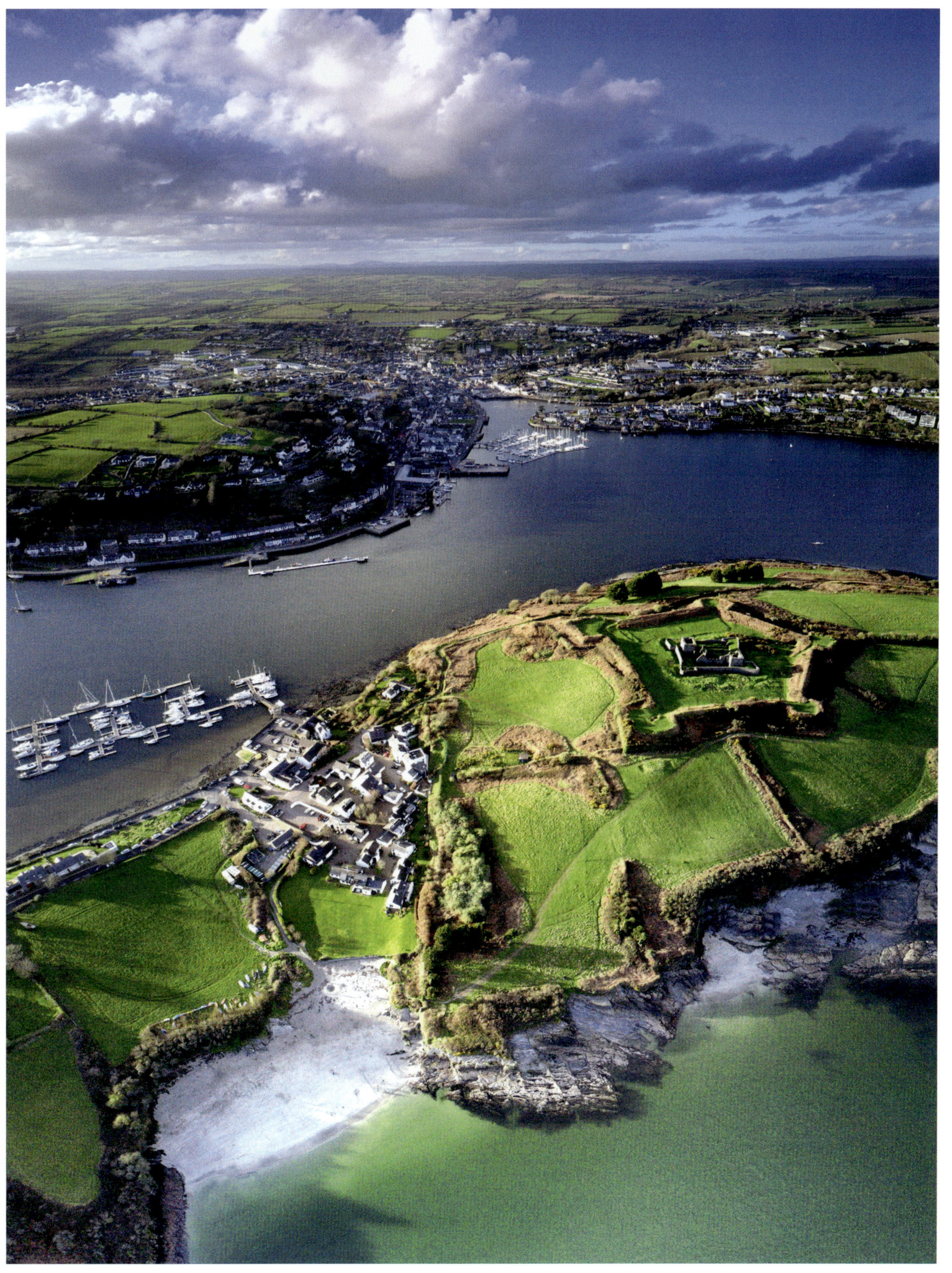

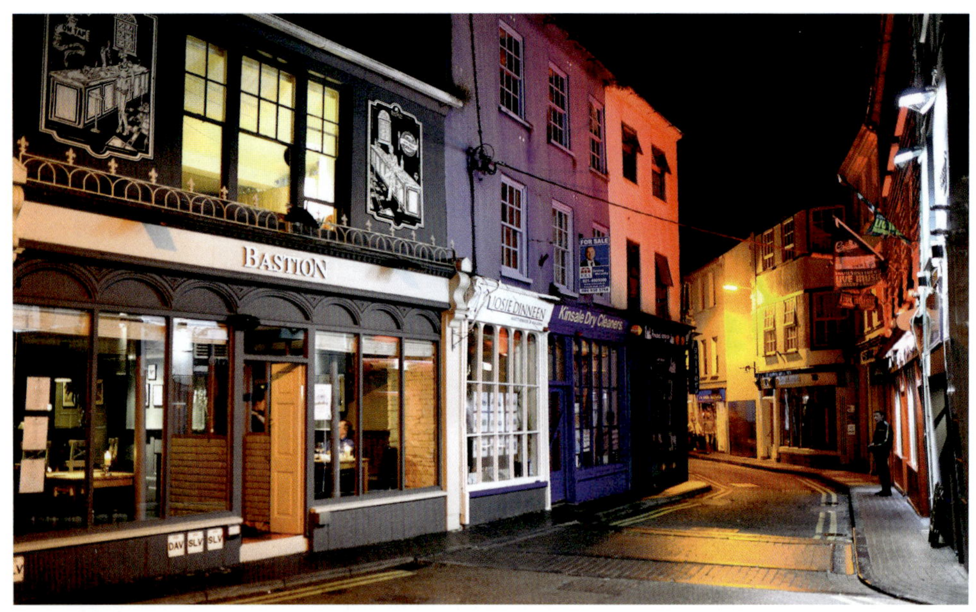

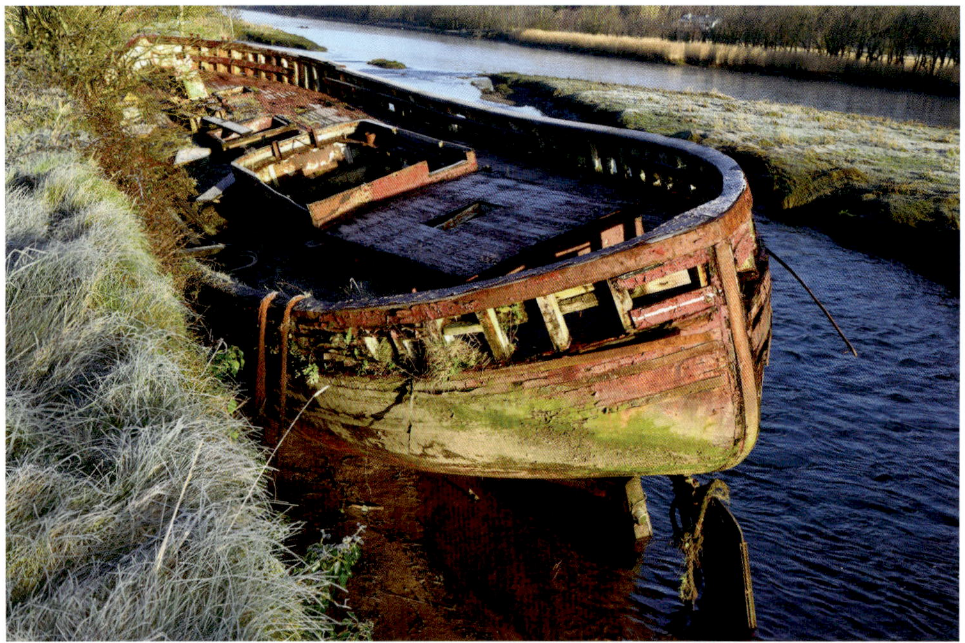

Top: Kinsale by night.

Above: A retired fishing boat on the banks of the River Bandon.

Opposite top: Garrylucas on a hazy sunny evening.

Opposite bottom: A misty evening at Nun's Cove, near White Strand.

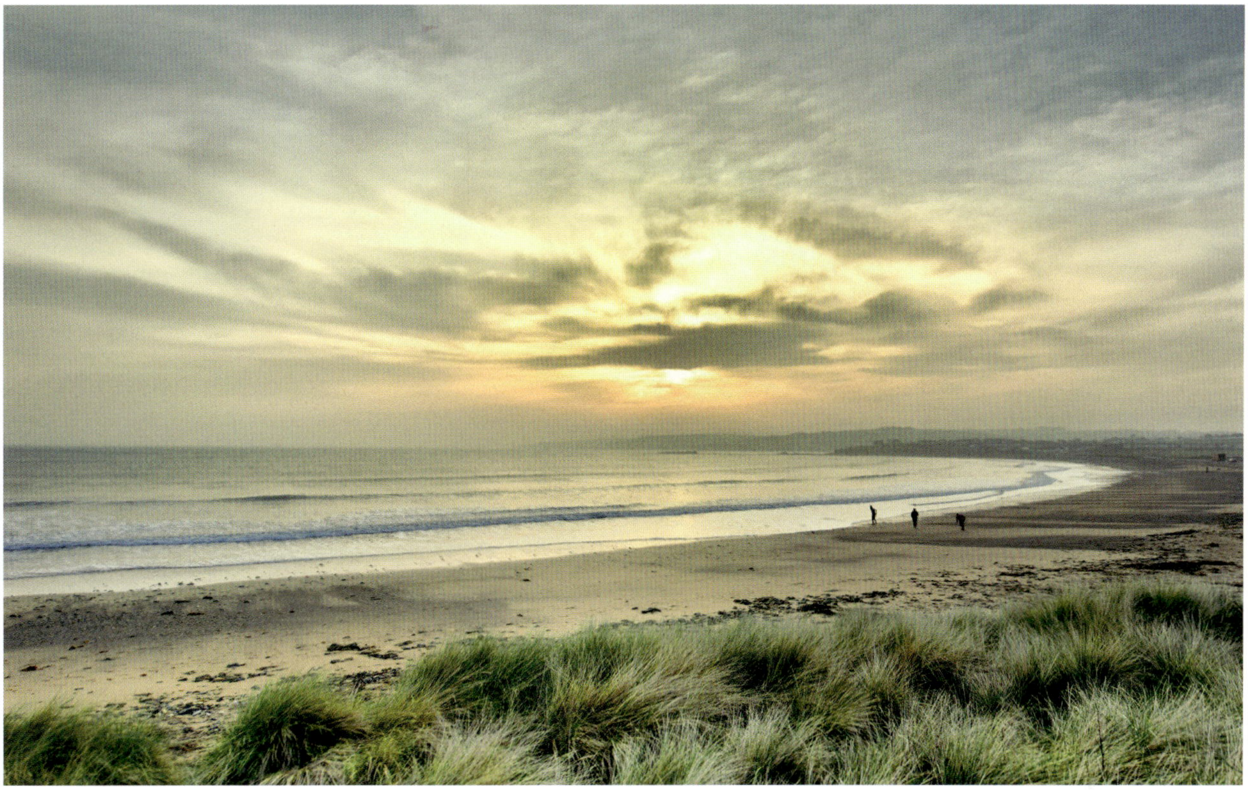

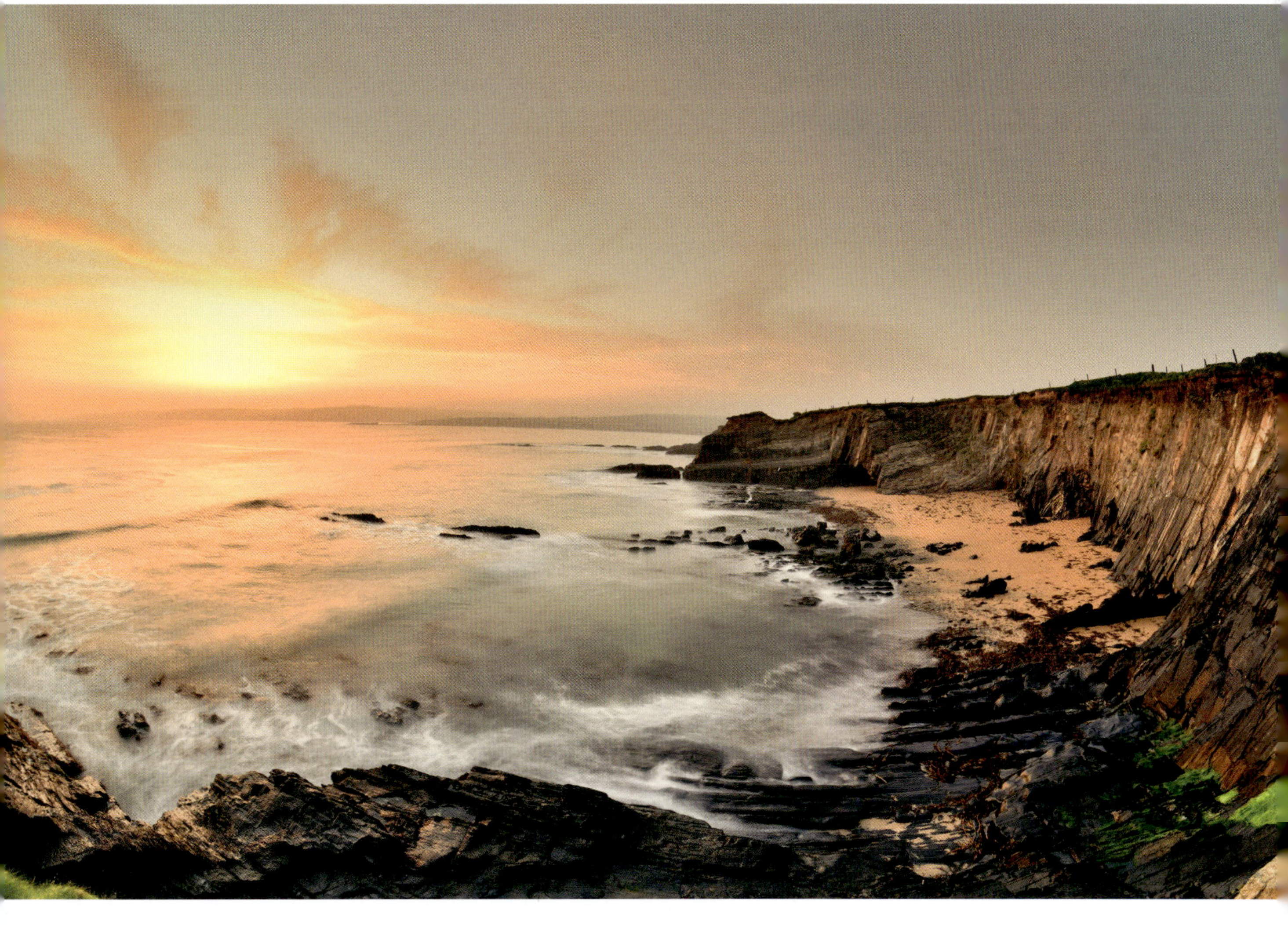

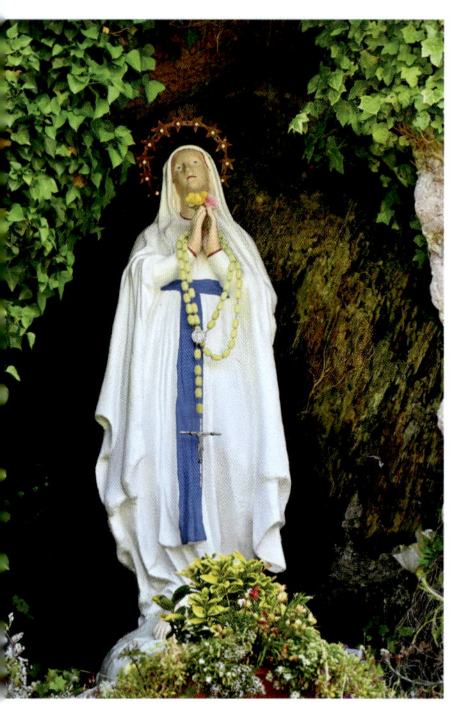

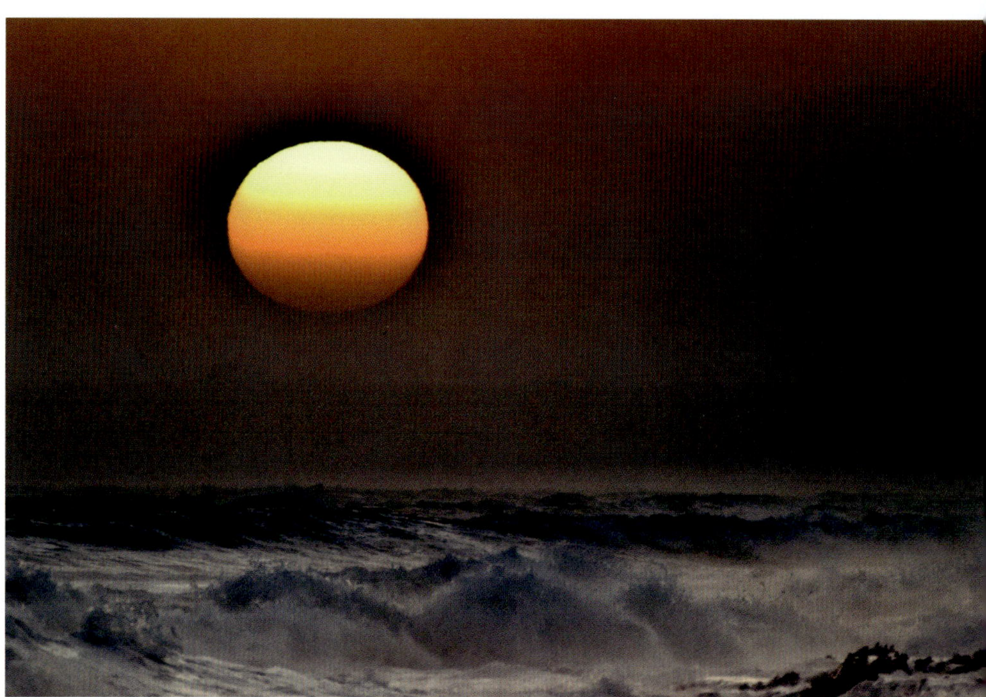

Above left: Religious statue at Ballinspittle. In 1985, people claimed to see this statue of Our Lady move. The story drew crowds of over one hundred thousand, with visitors still coming today.

Above right: The sun setting into a stormy sea.

Opposite top: Getting soaked at Garrettstown.

Right: Moonrise and sunset at Garrettstown.

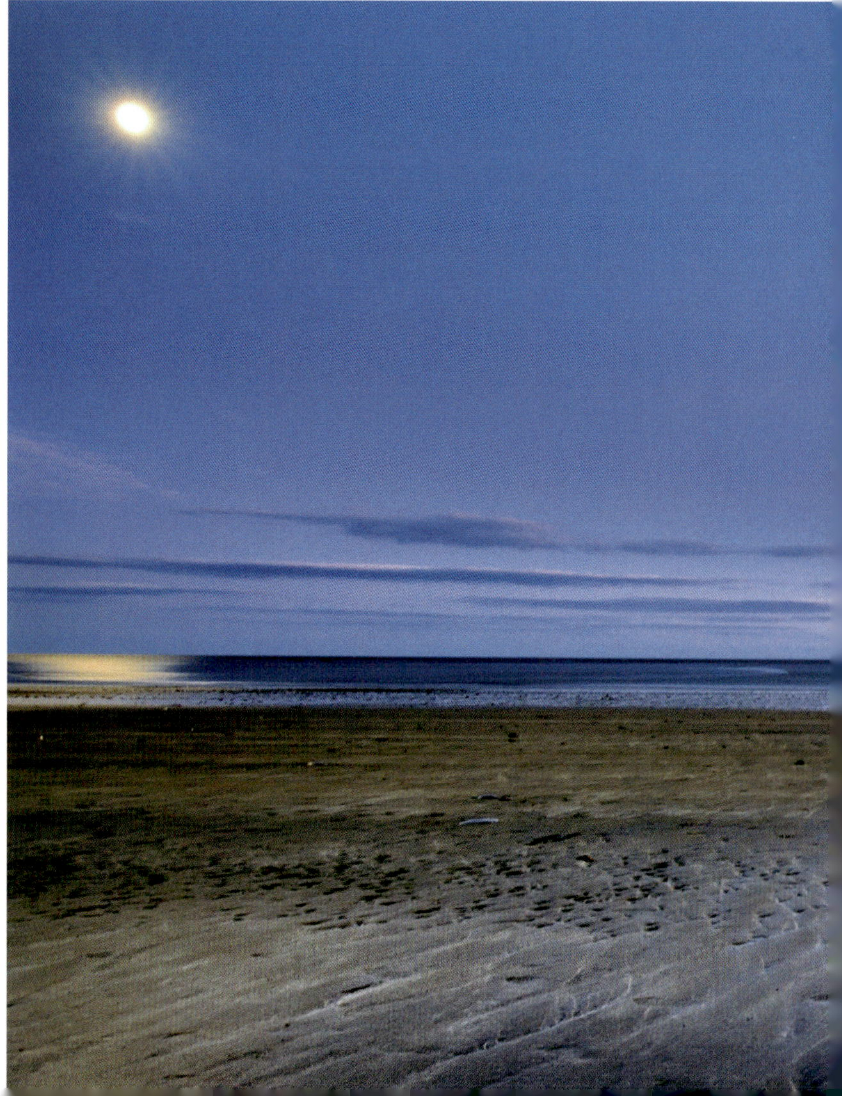

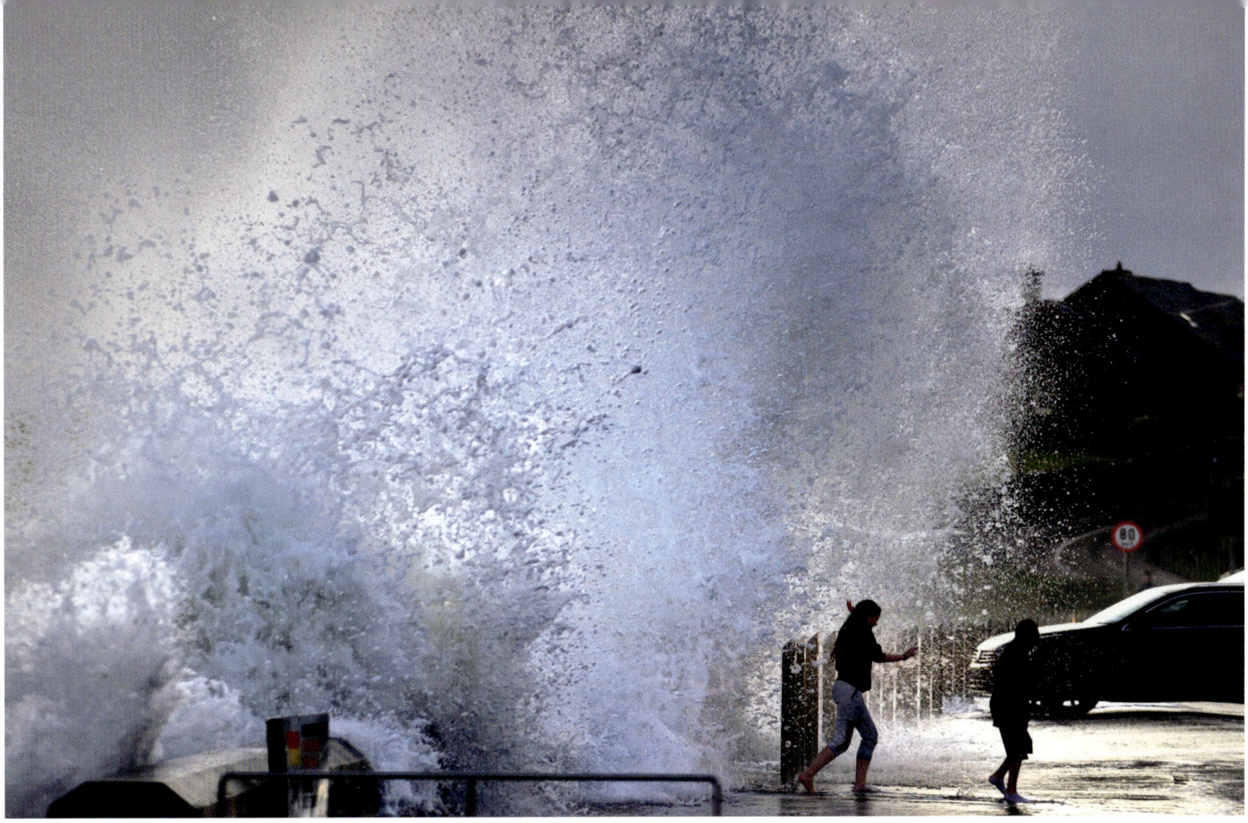

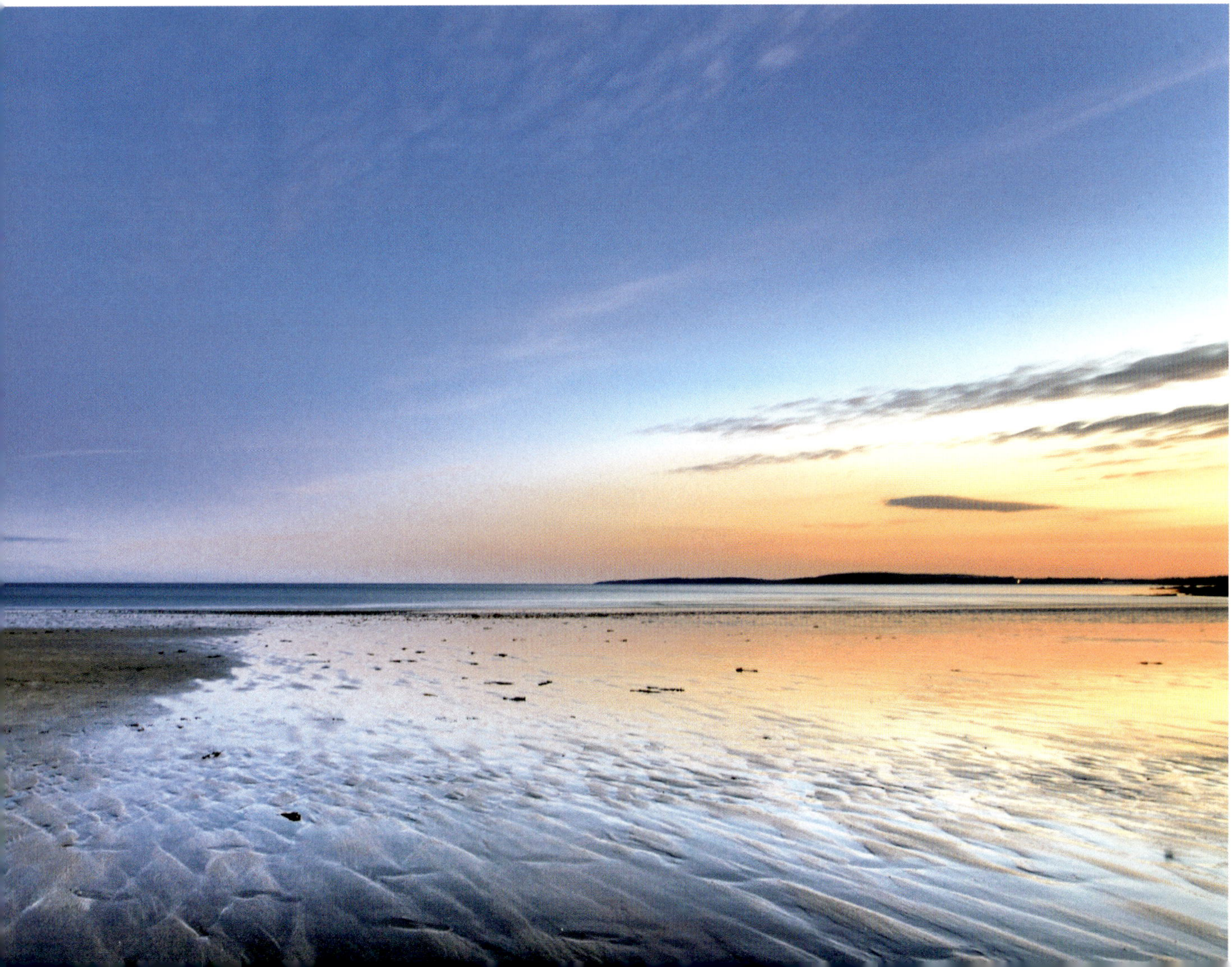

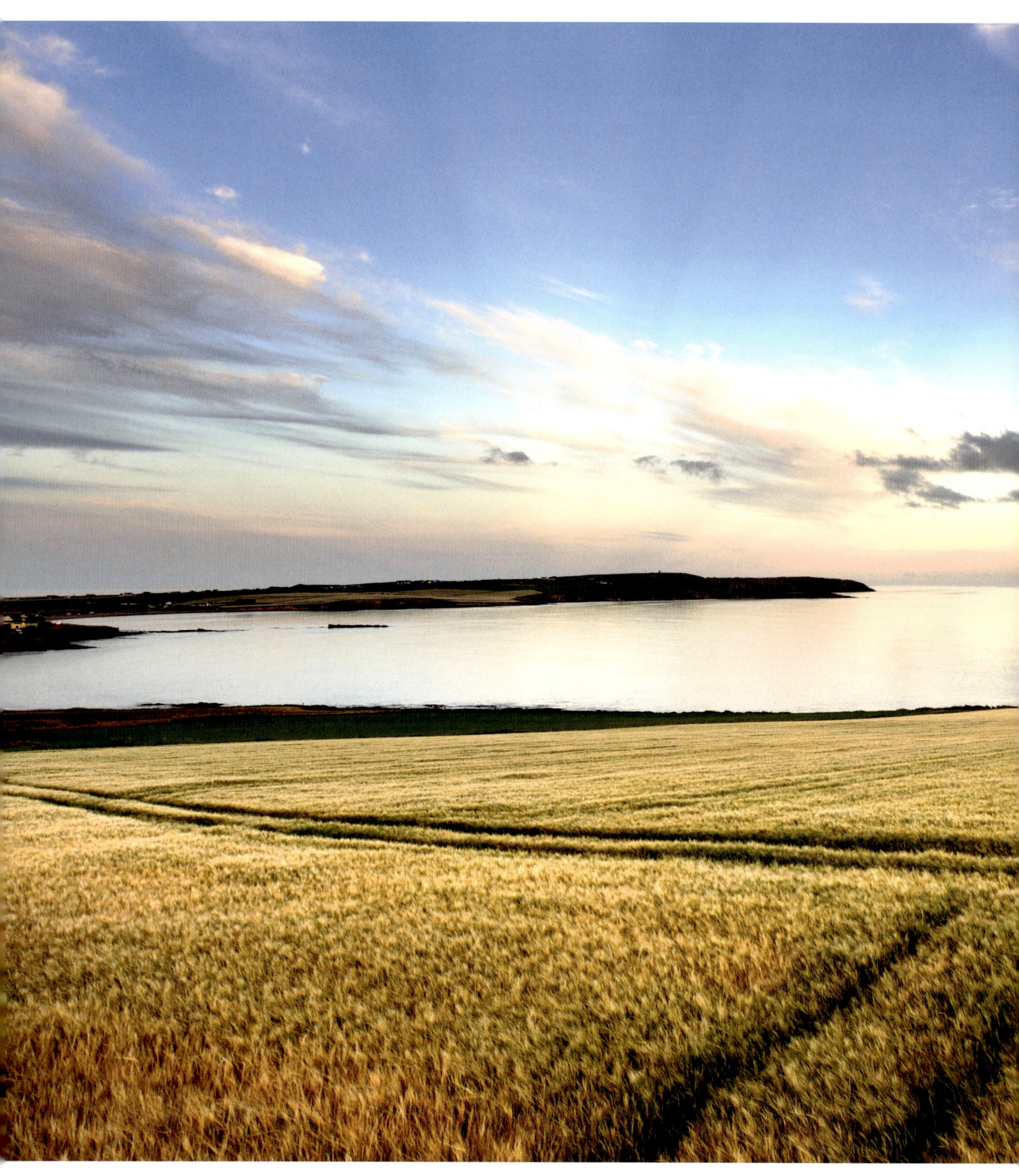

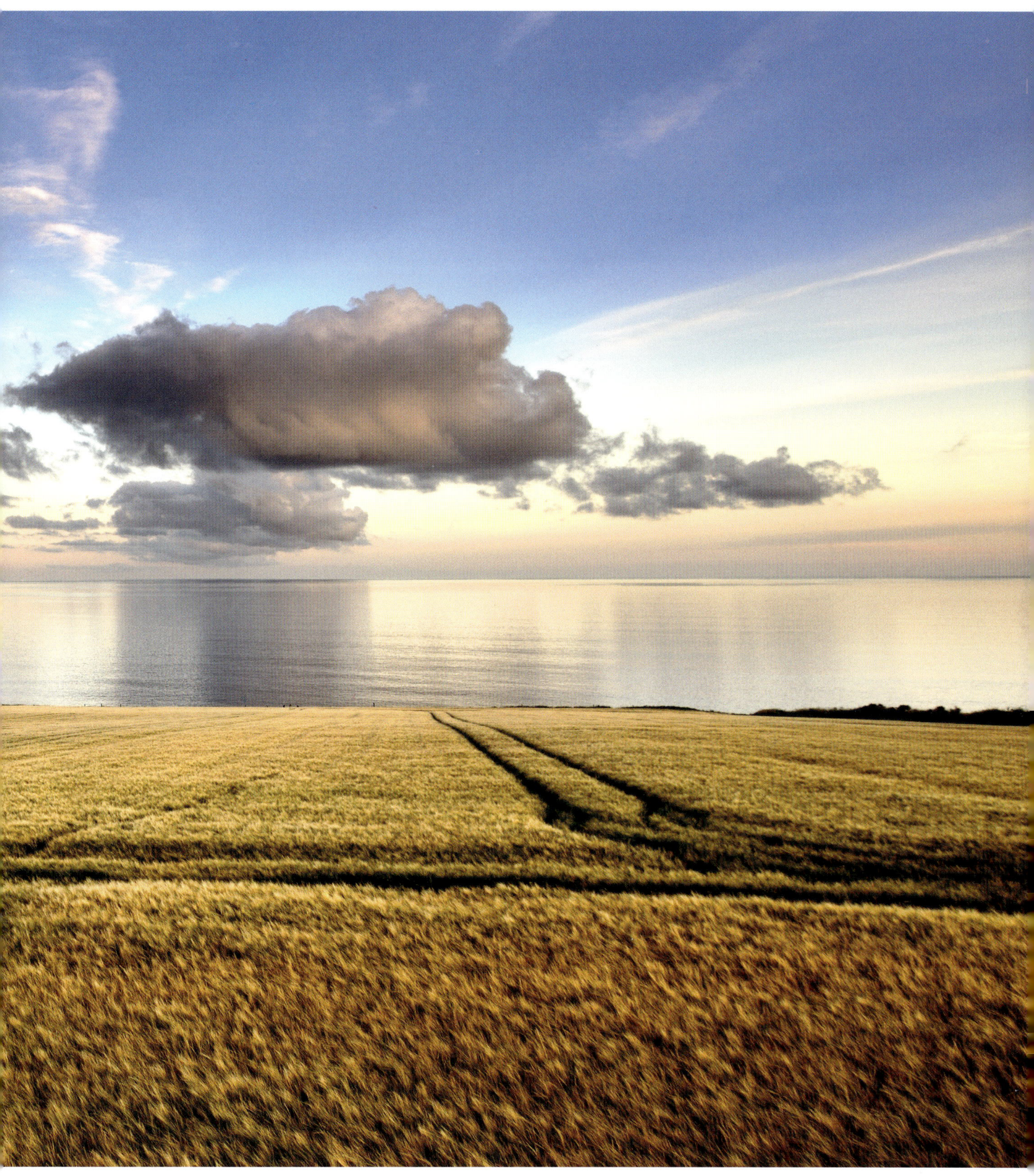

Harvest sunset.

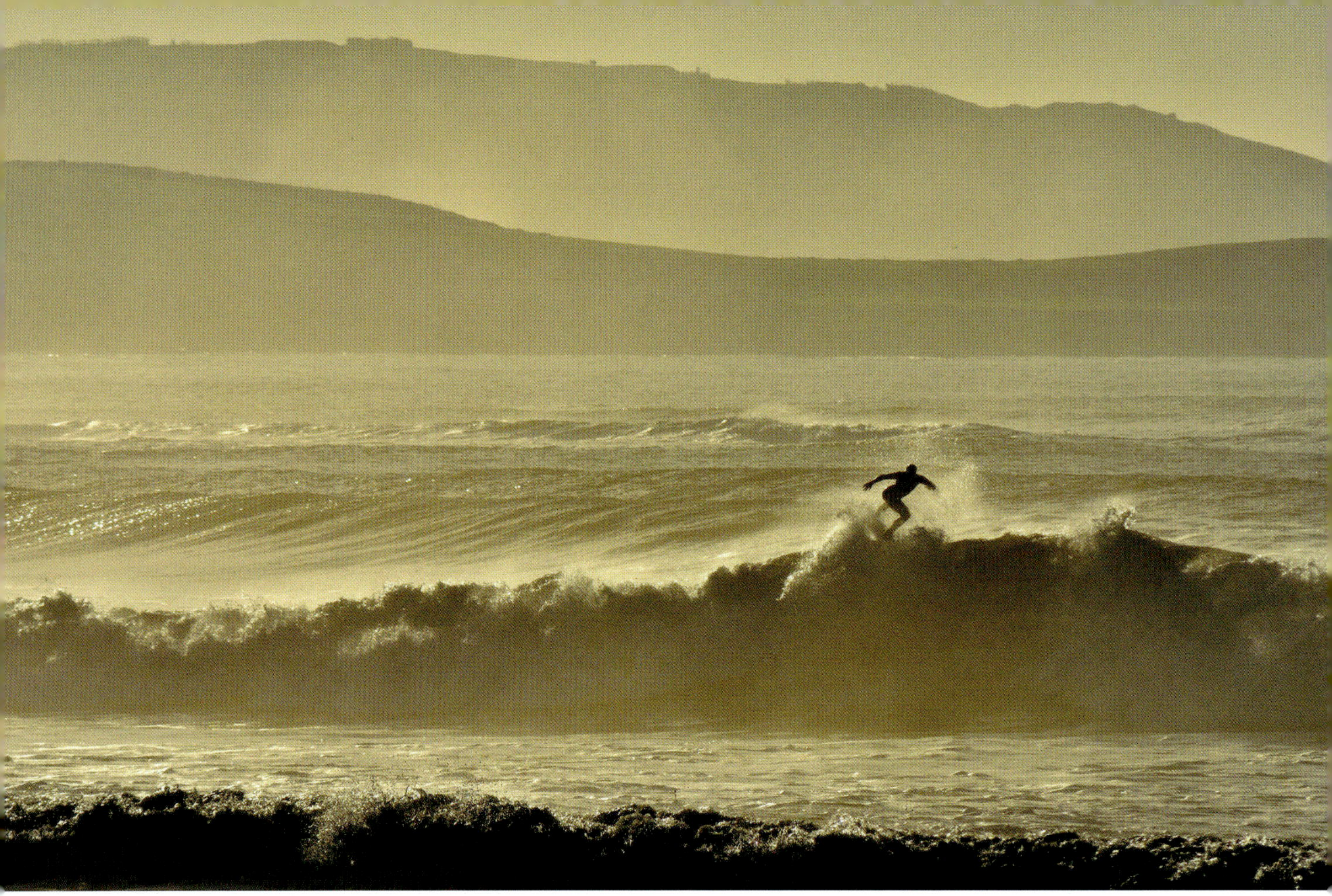

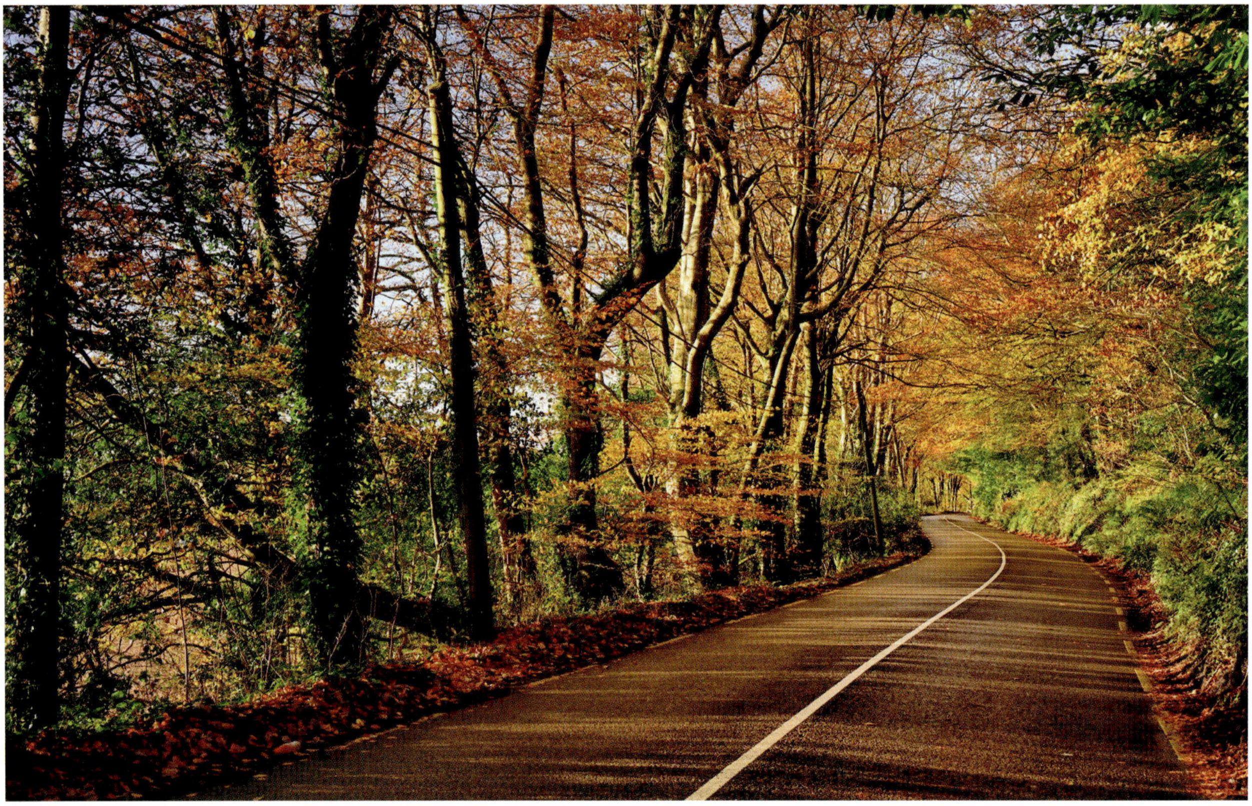

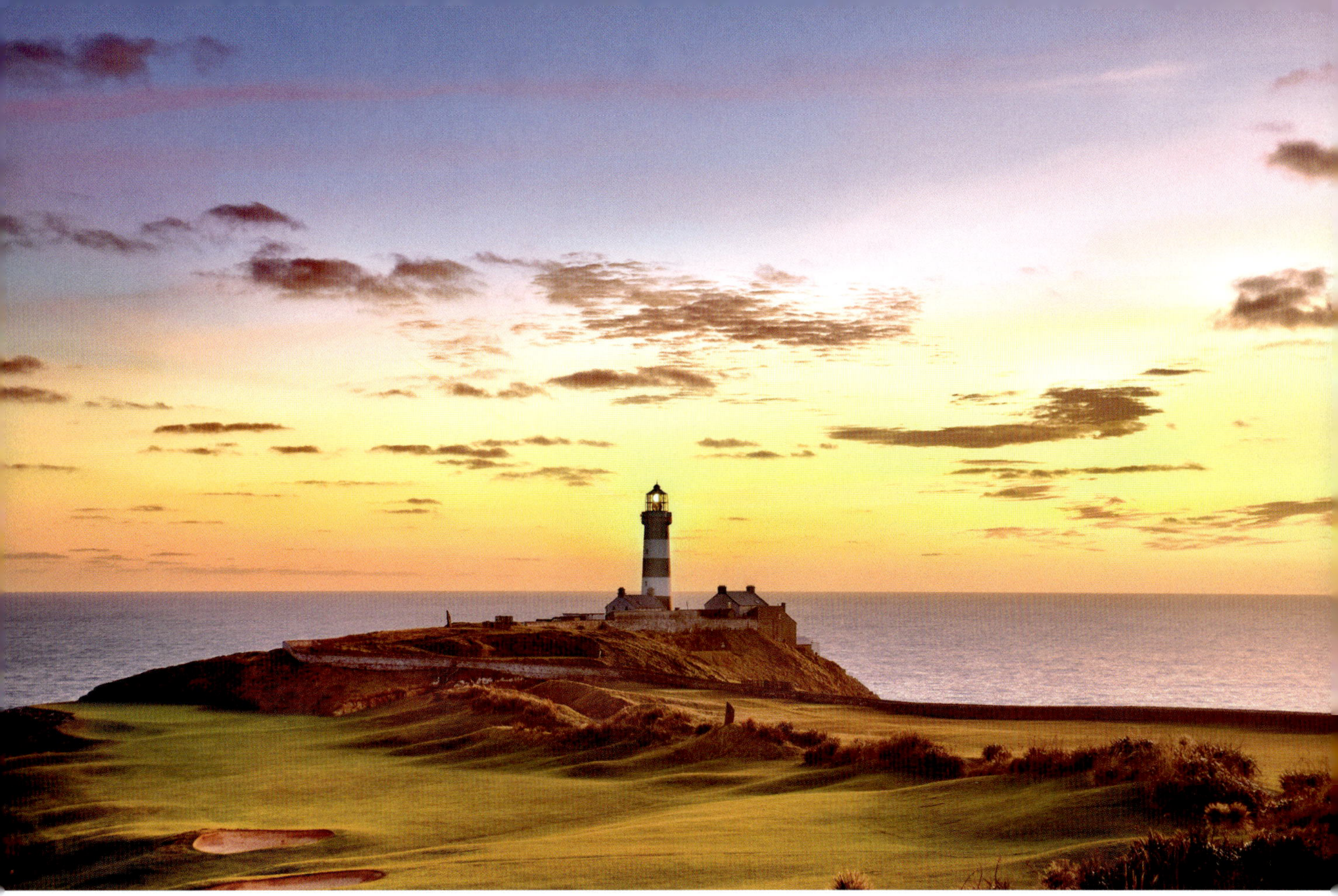

Opposite left: Braving the winter cold to surf at Garrettstown.

Left: Autumn colours at Shippool Woods, south of Innishannon.

Above: New year's sunset at the Old Head of Kinsale Lighthouse.

Right: Sea pinks in full bloom at the Old Head of Kinsale cliffs.

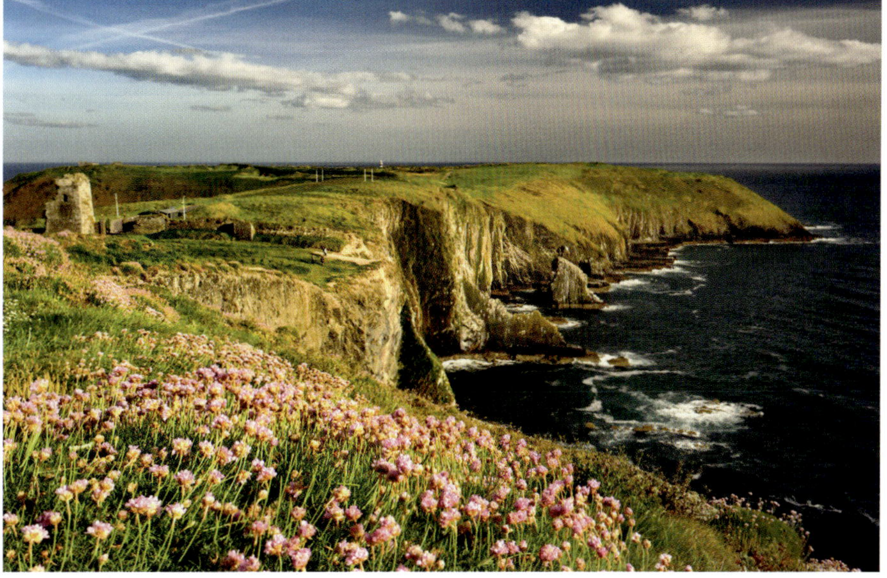

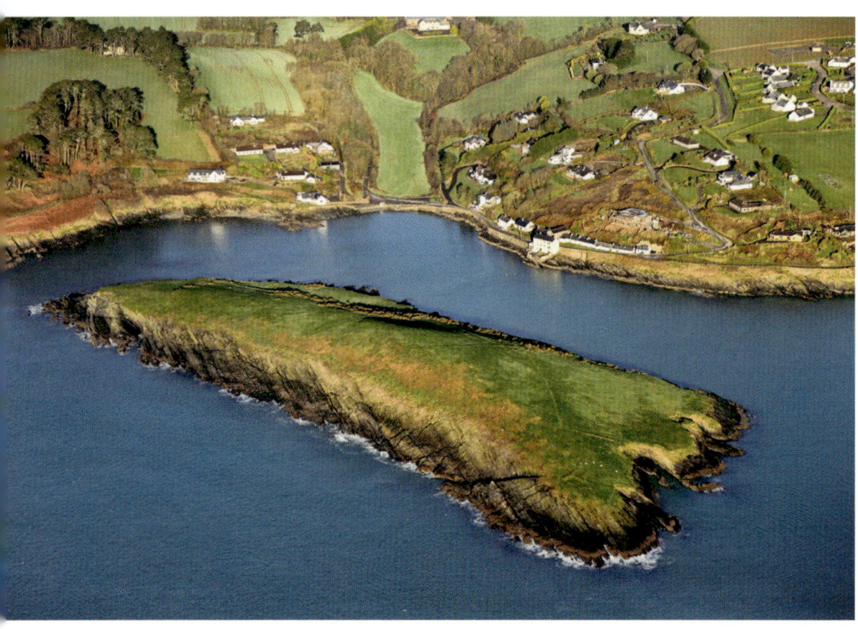

Left: Sandycove island. The annual Sandycove Island Challenge, a 1.8km swim around the island, is held in September.

Below: The Old Head of Kinsale Lighthouse facing the rising sun.

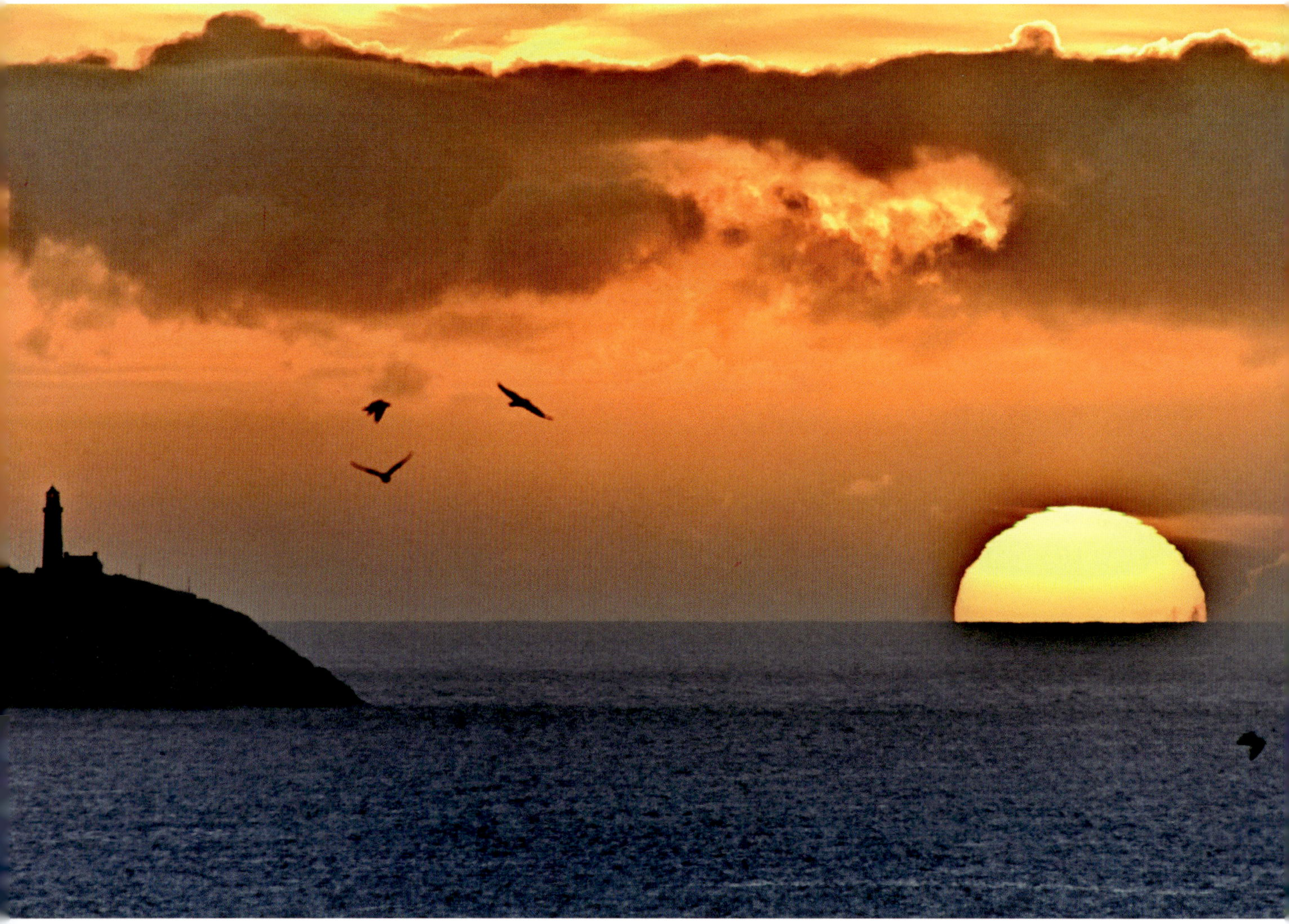

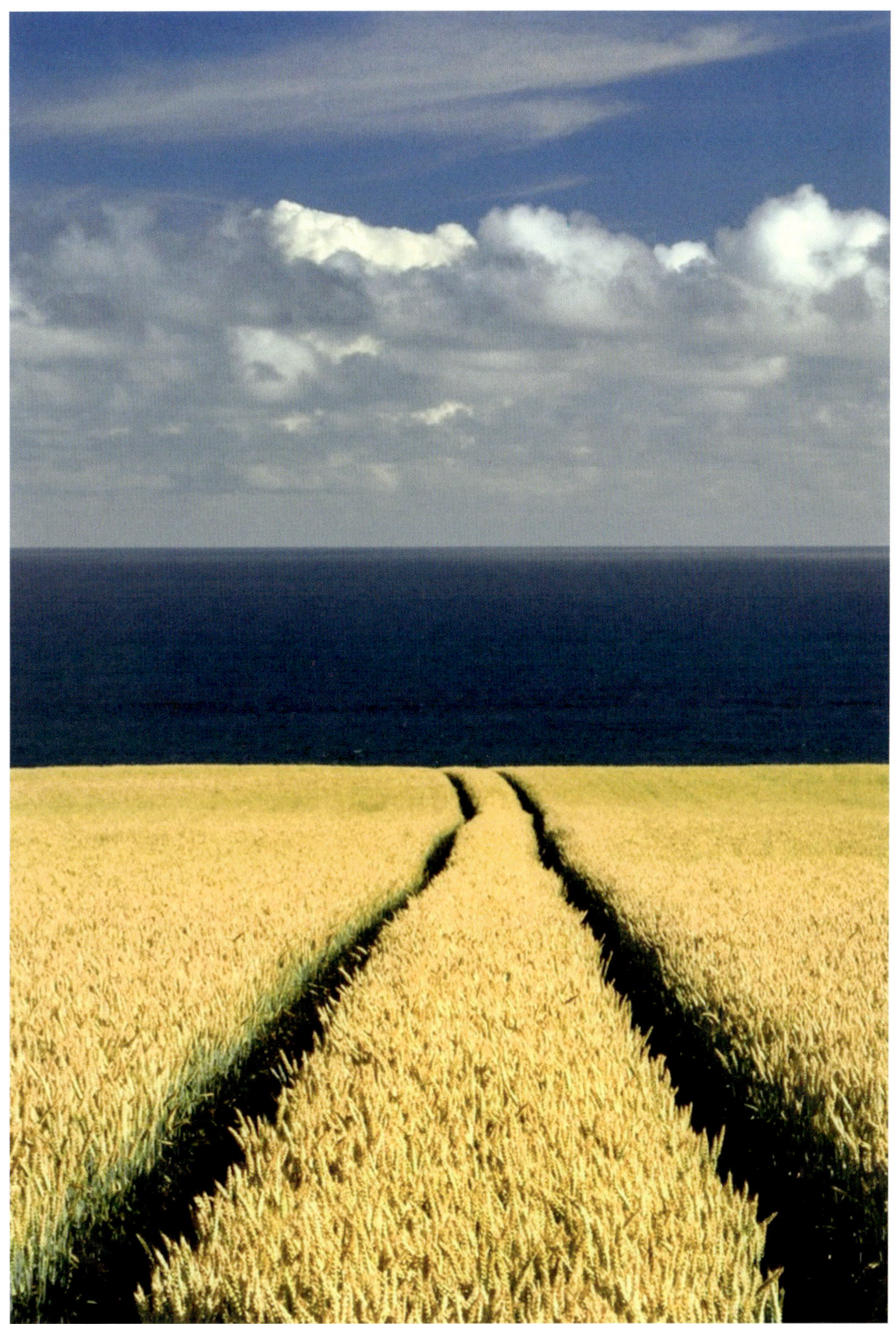

Tractor tracks leading down to the sea.

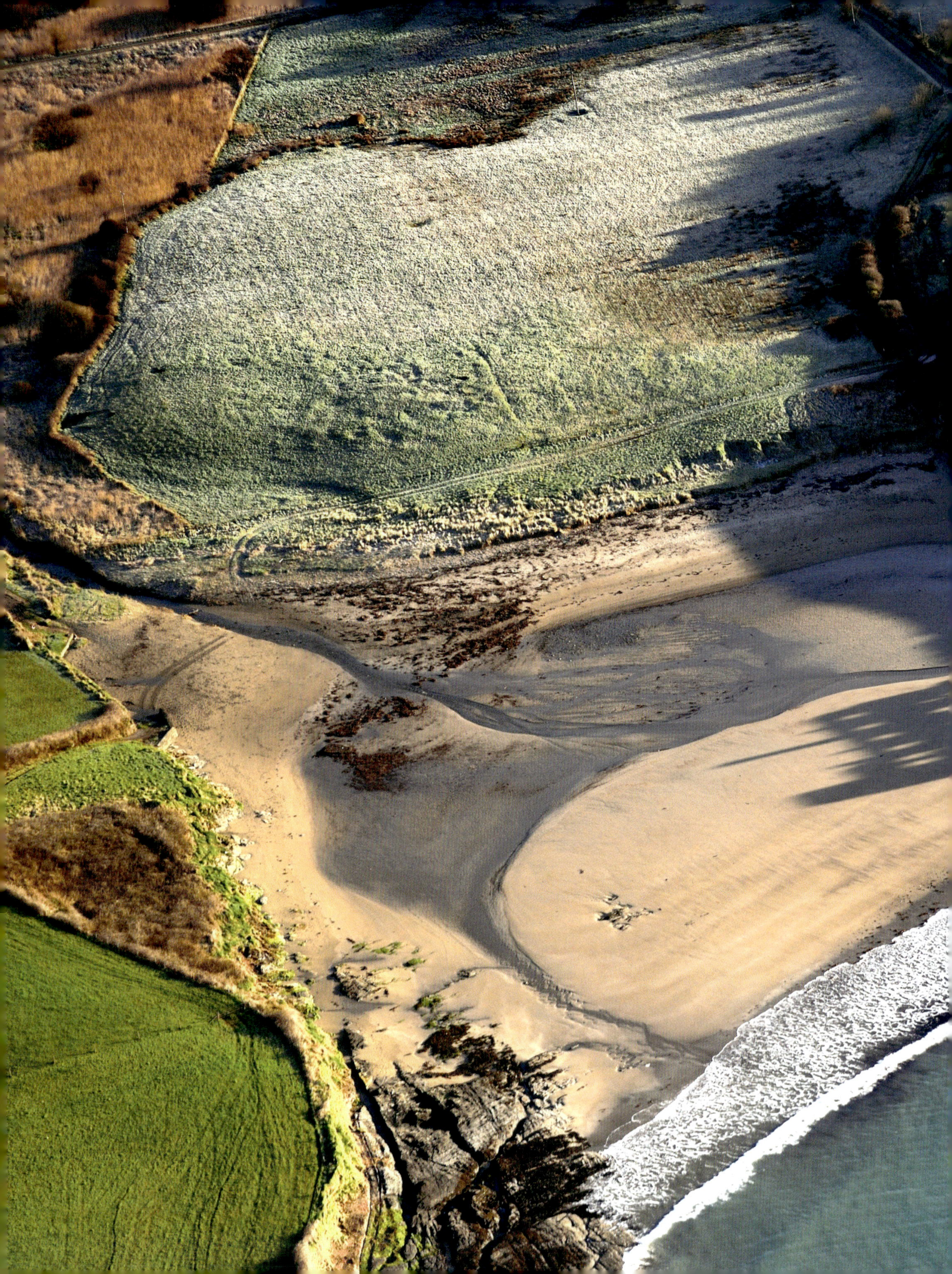

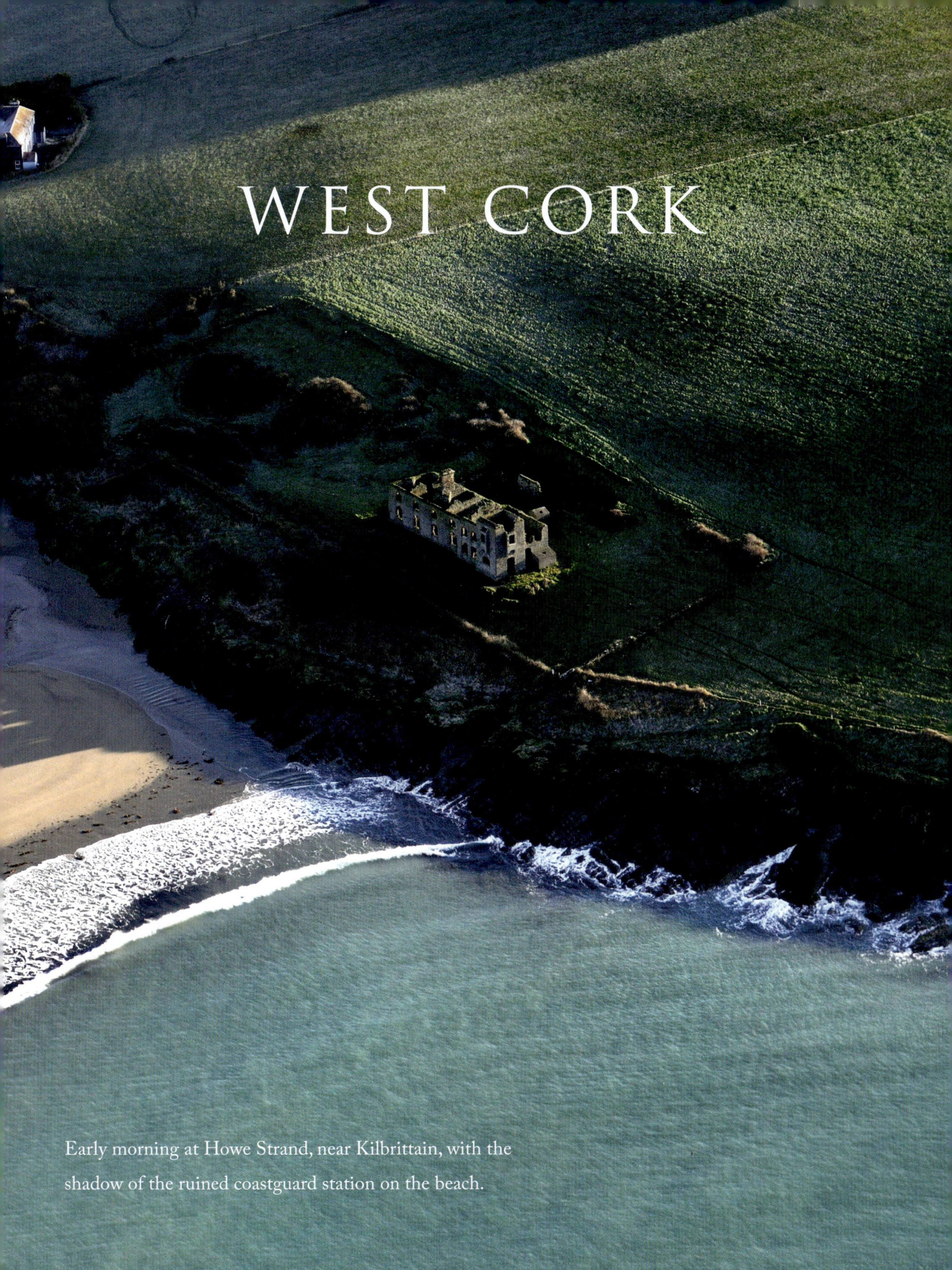

WEST CORK

Early morning at Howe Strand, near Kilbrittain, with the
shadow of the ruined coastguard station on the beach.

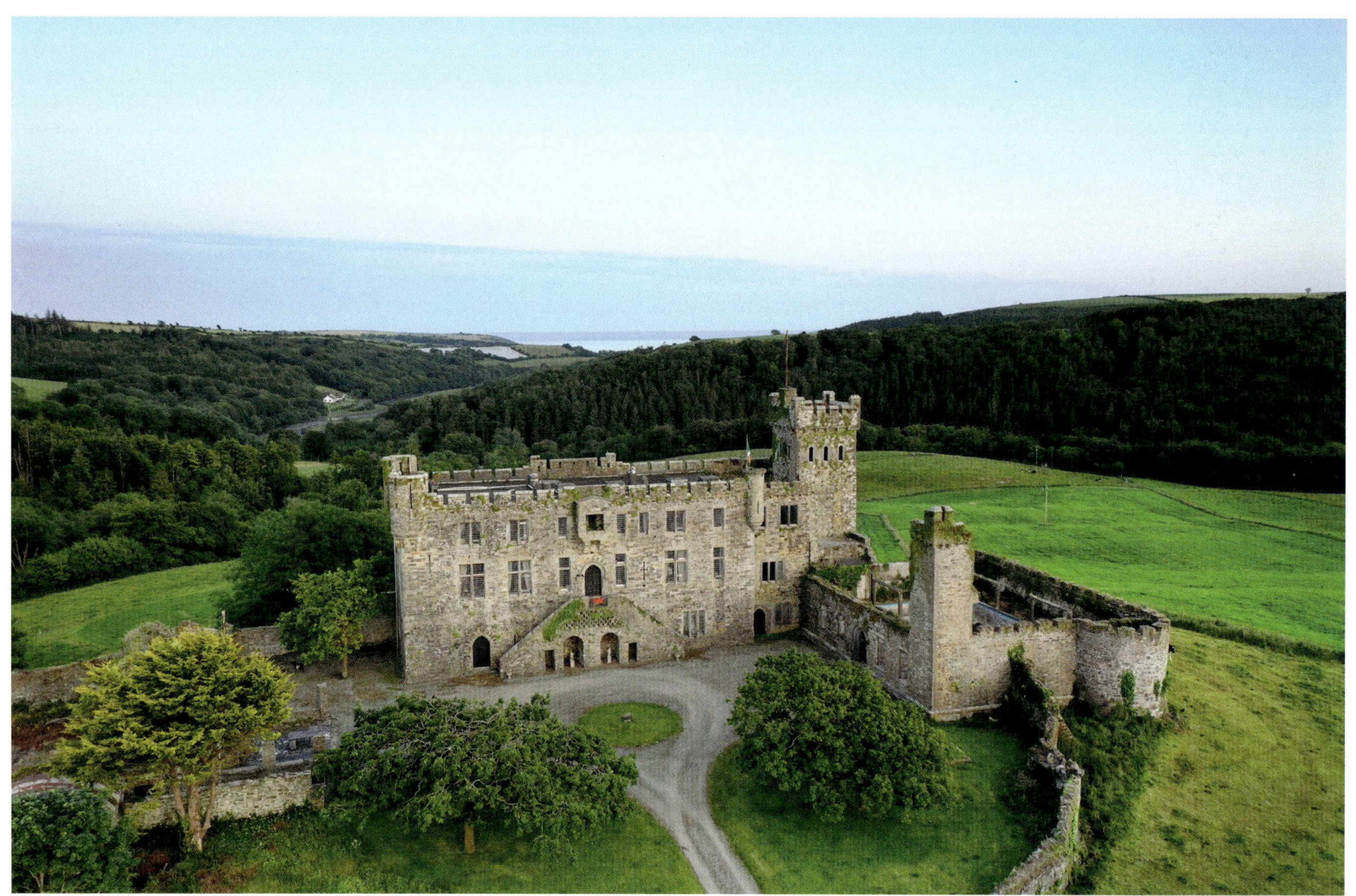

Above: Kilbrittain Castle. Built around 1035, it is one of Ireland's oldest inhabited castles.

Right: Bandon weir after heavy rain. The River Bandon is renowned for its game angling and leaping salmon can be seen, especially when water levels are high.

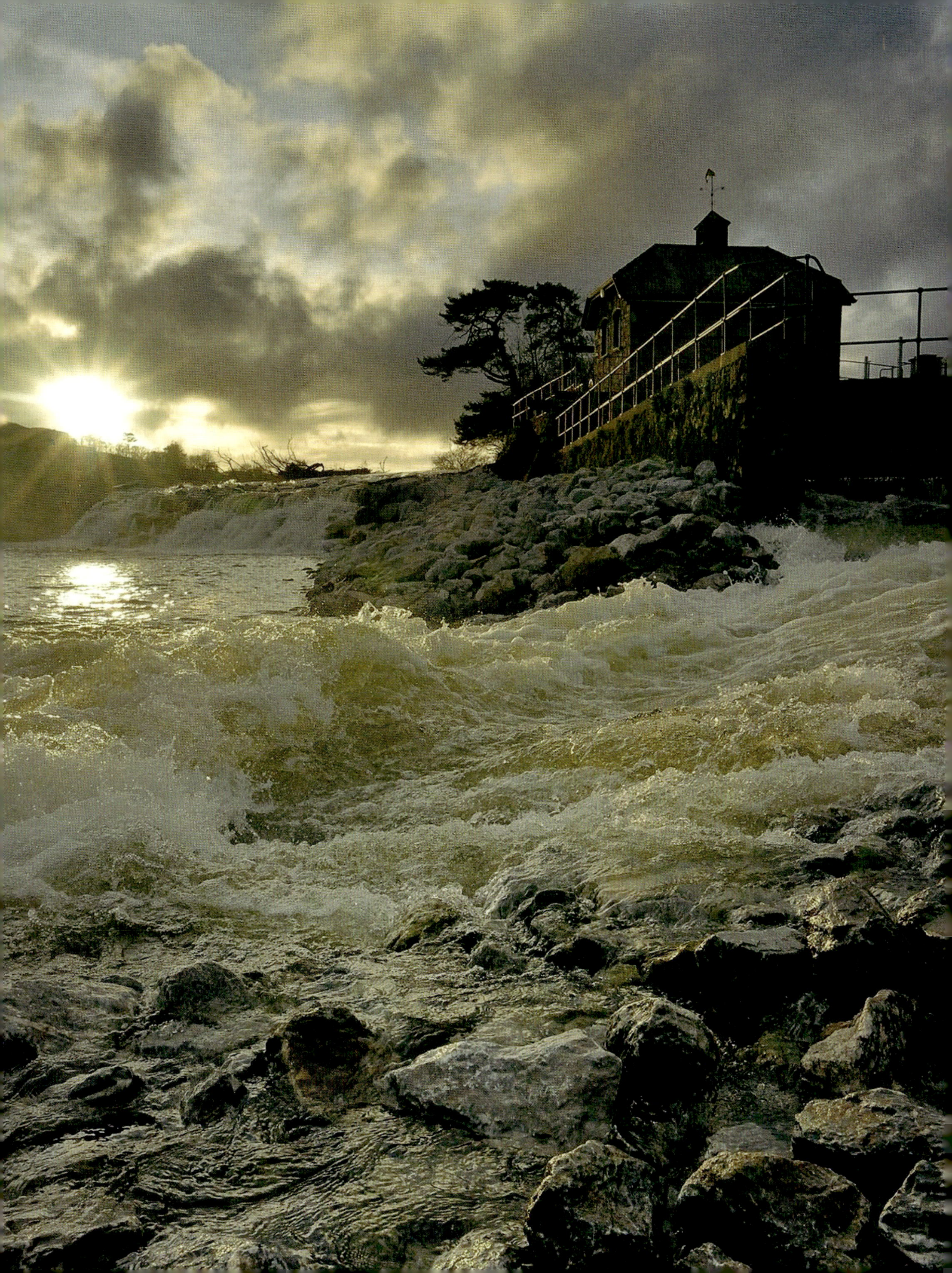

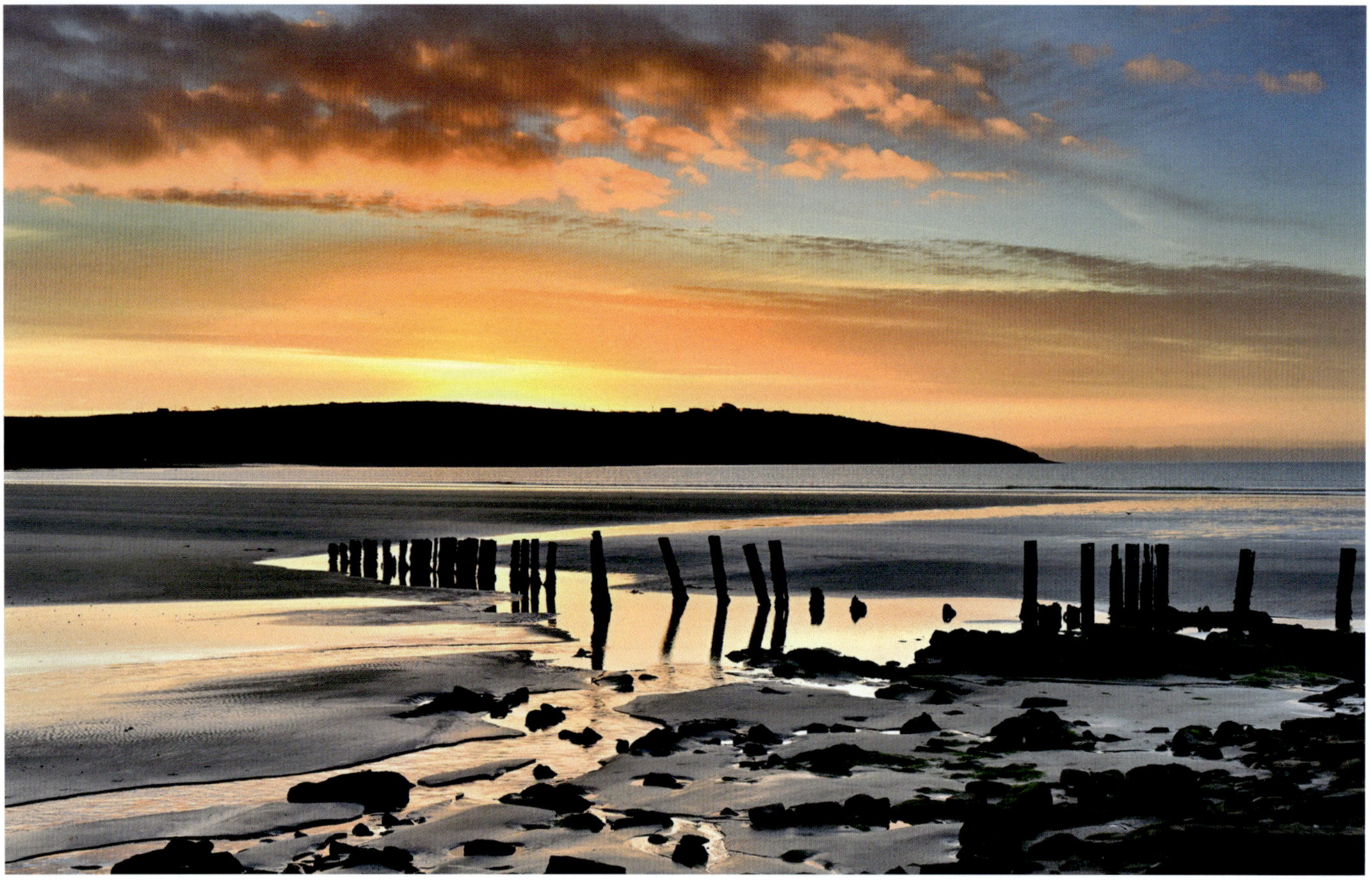

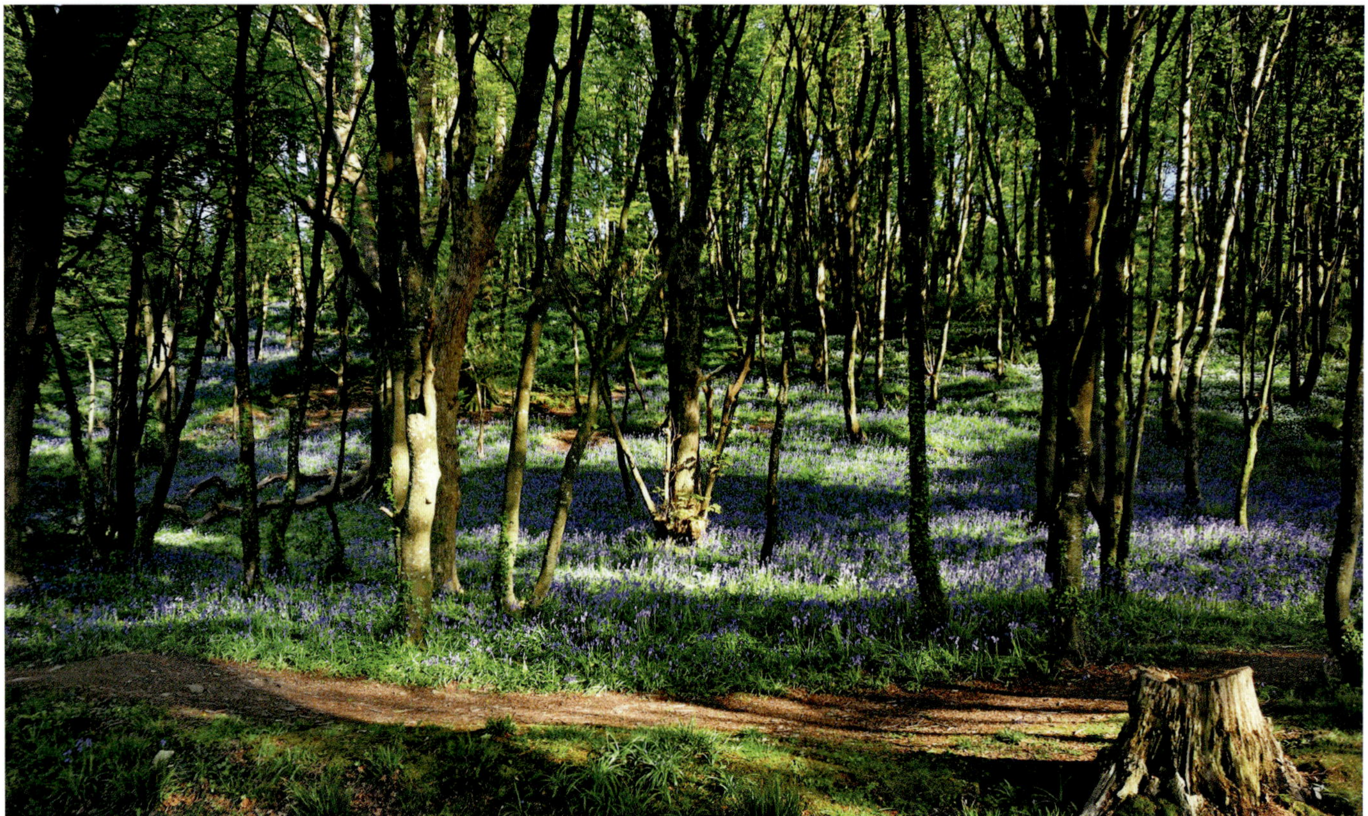

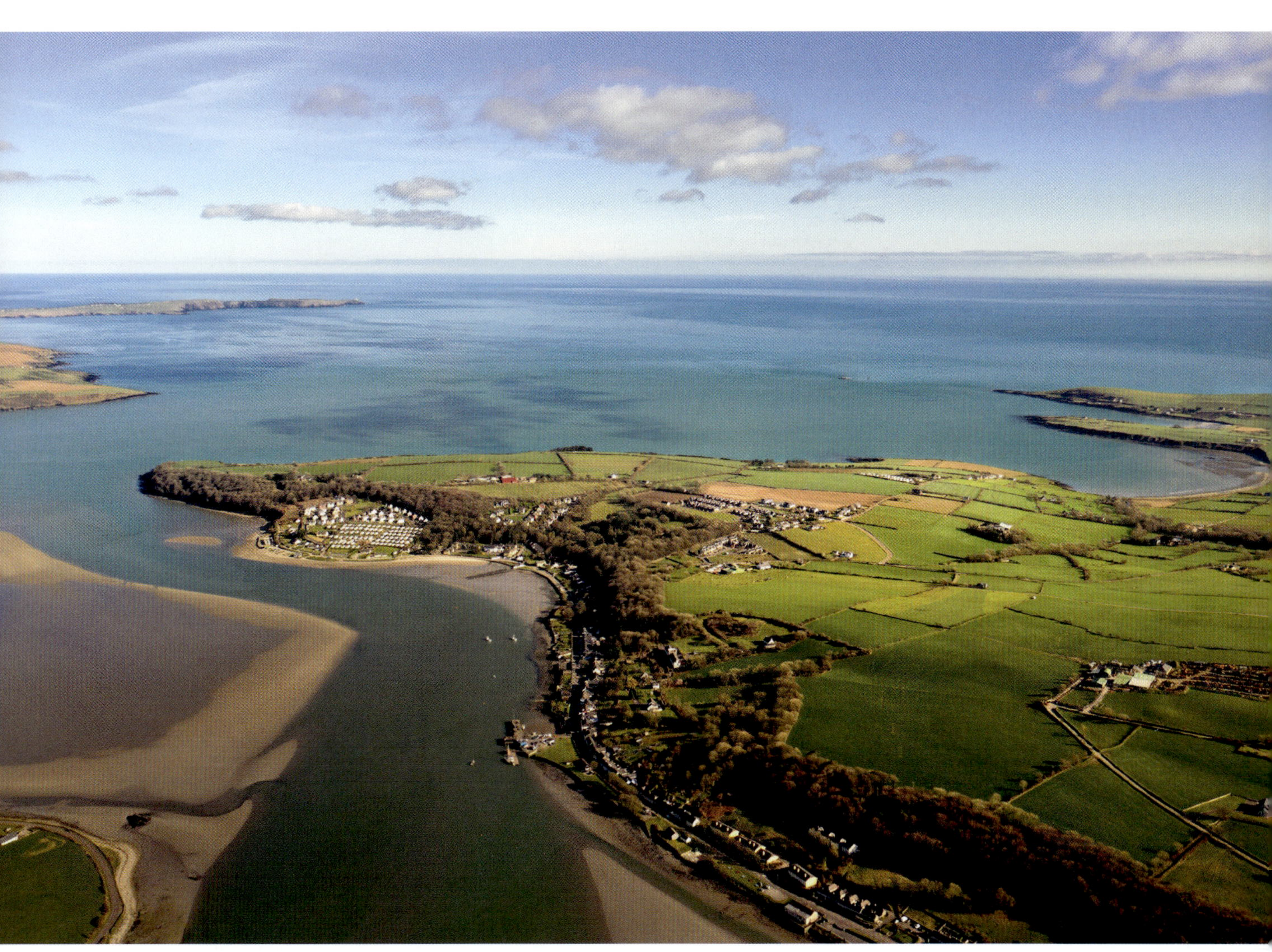

Opposite top: Sunrise at Coolmain Beach.

Opposite bottom: Bluebells in Courtmacsherry Woods in May give this little forest

in the tranquil village of Courtmacsherry a fairytale appearance.

Above: An aerial view of Courtmacsherry Bay at low tide.

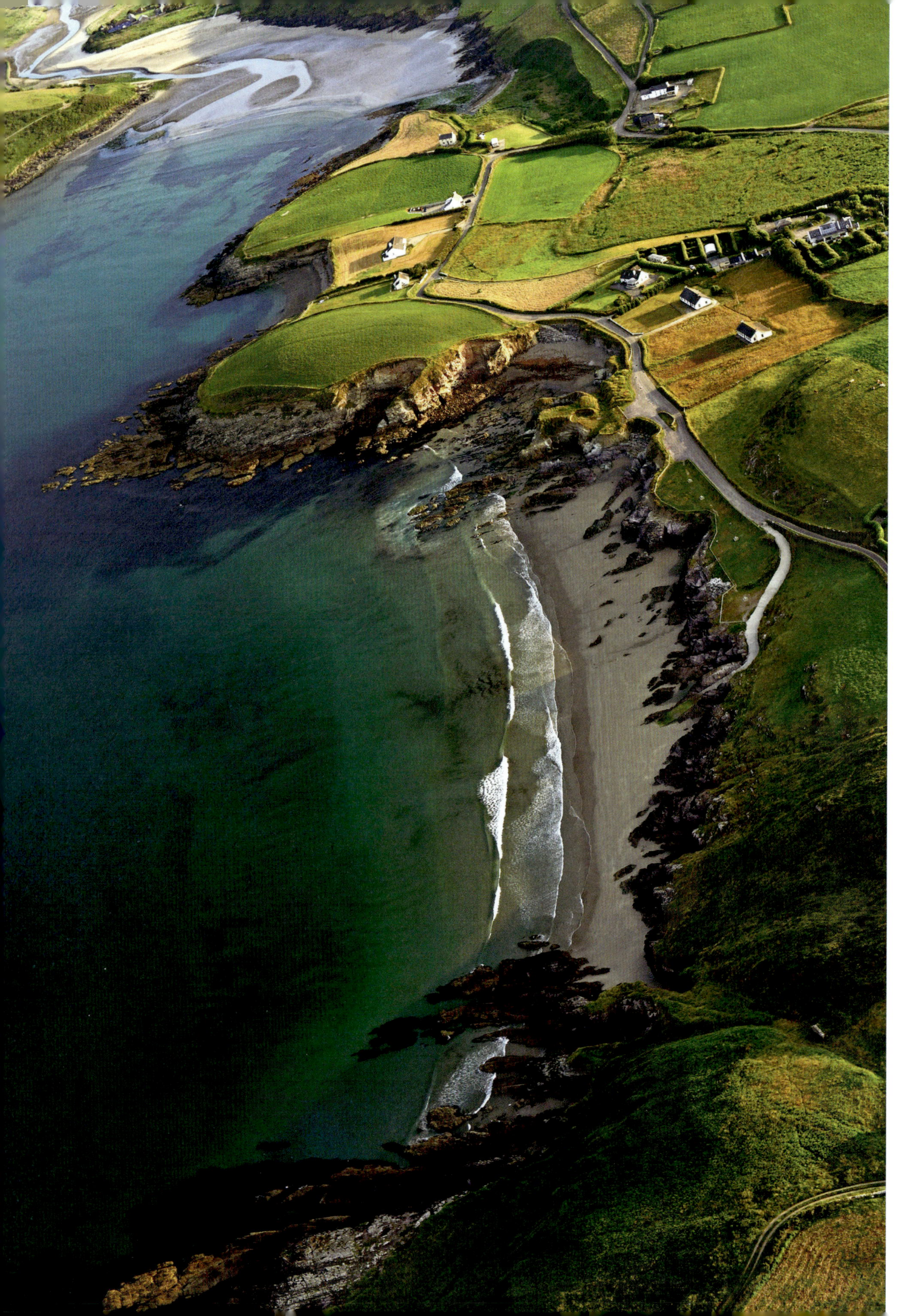

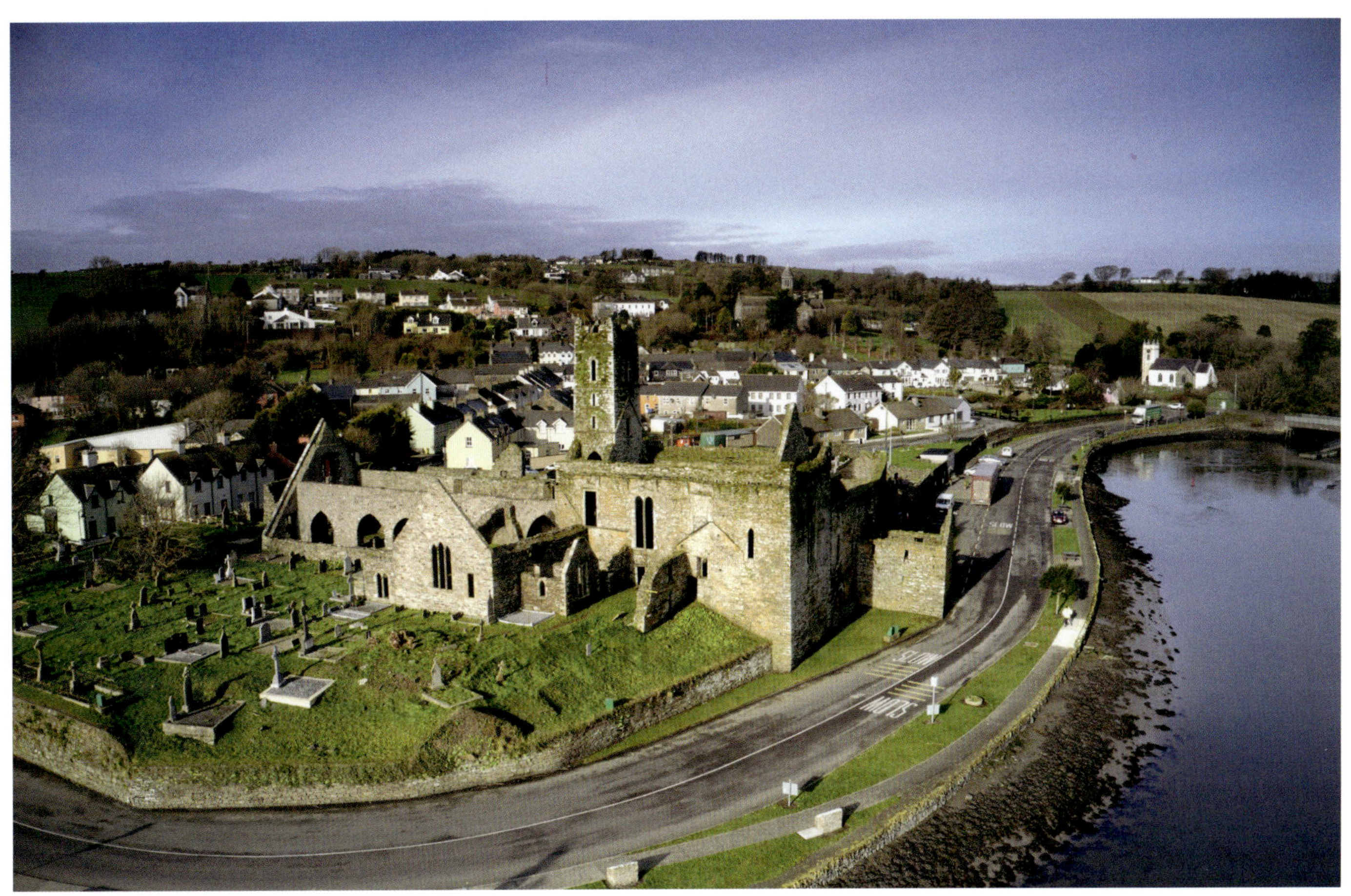

Opposite: The beaches at Dunworly, south of Courtmacsherry, viewed from the air.

Above: On the banks of the Argideen River in the picturesque village of Timoleague is a ruined Franciscan friary, built in the early fourteenth century. The bell tower was added in 1510.

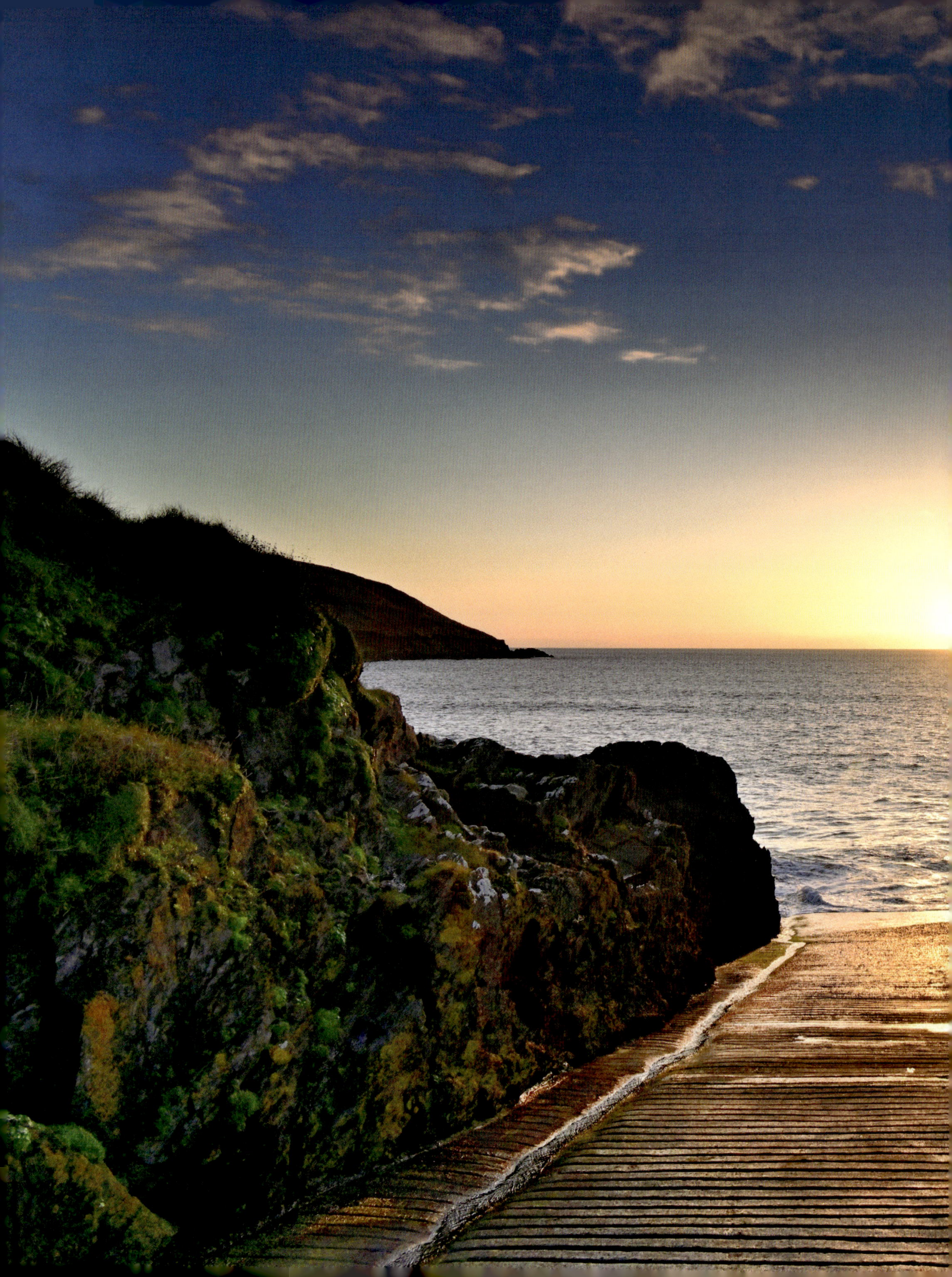

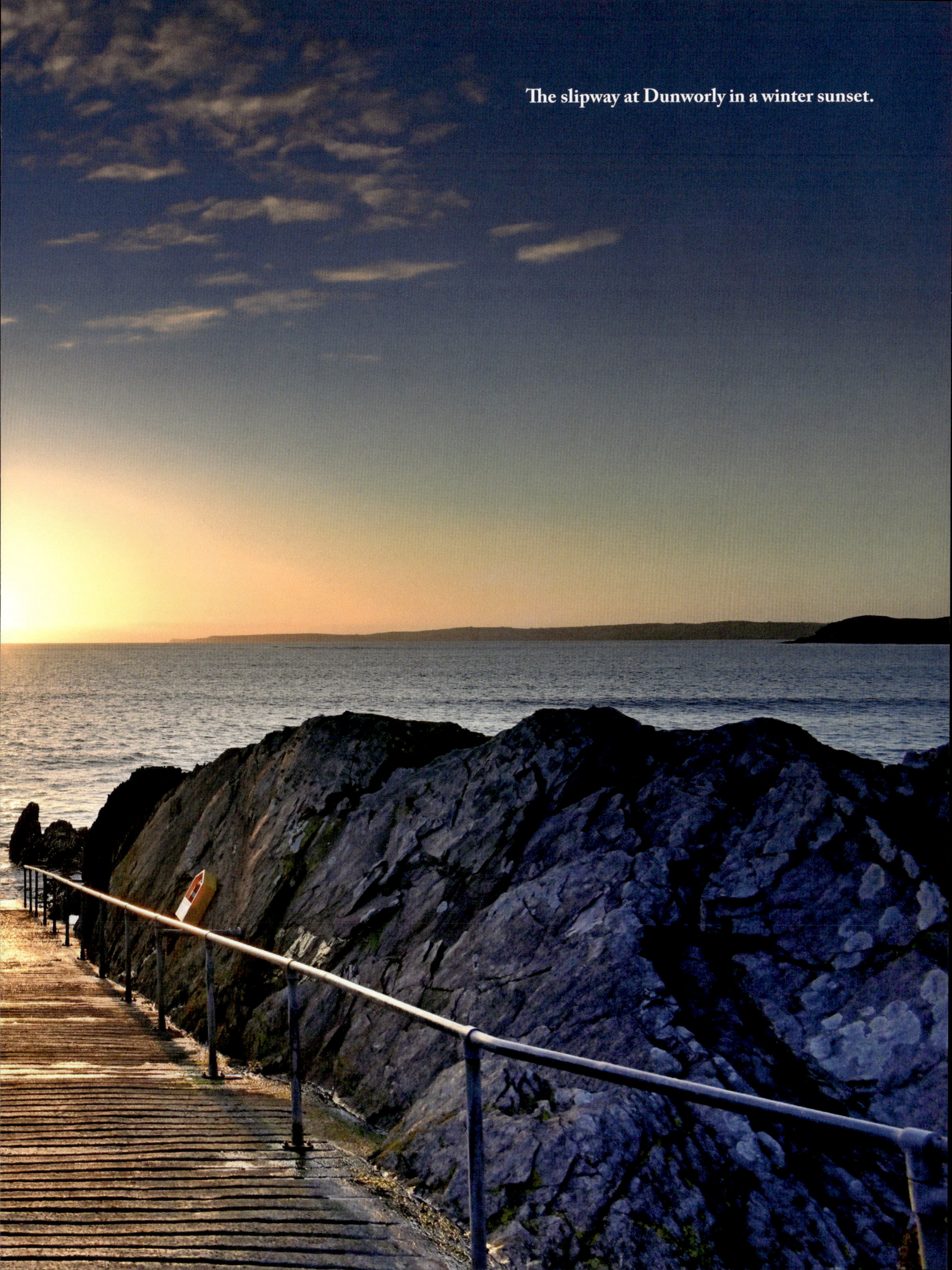
The slipway at Dunworly in a winter sunset.

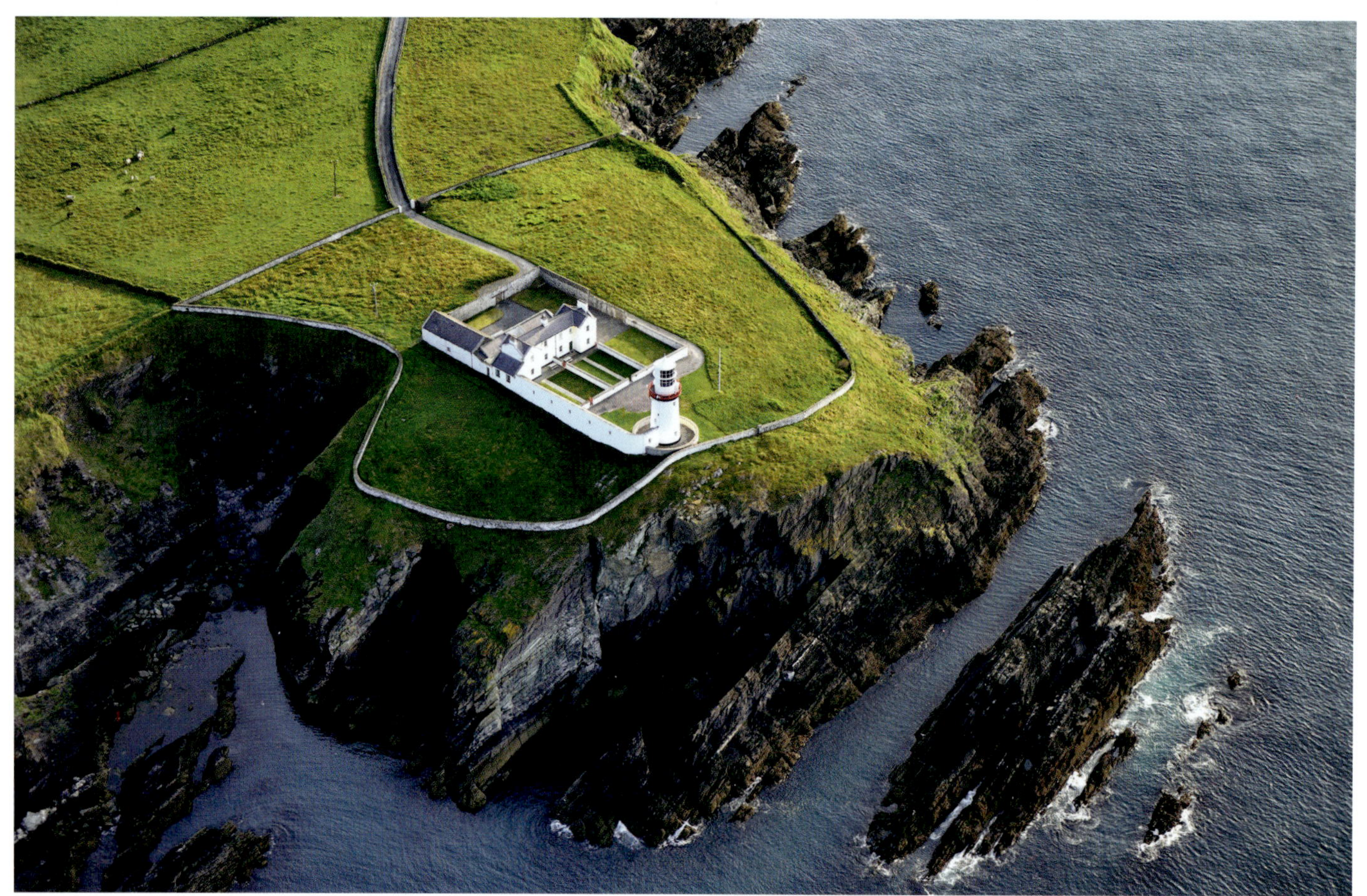

Above: Galley Head lighthouse. Just outside Clonakilty, the 53-metre-tall lighthouse was built in 1875. The lightkeepers' cottages are owned by the Irish Landmark Trust and available to rent.

Opposite: An aerial view of Inchydoney Beach.

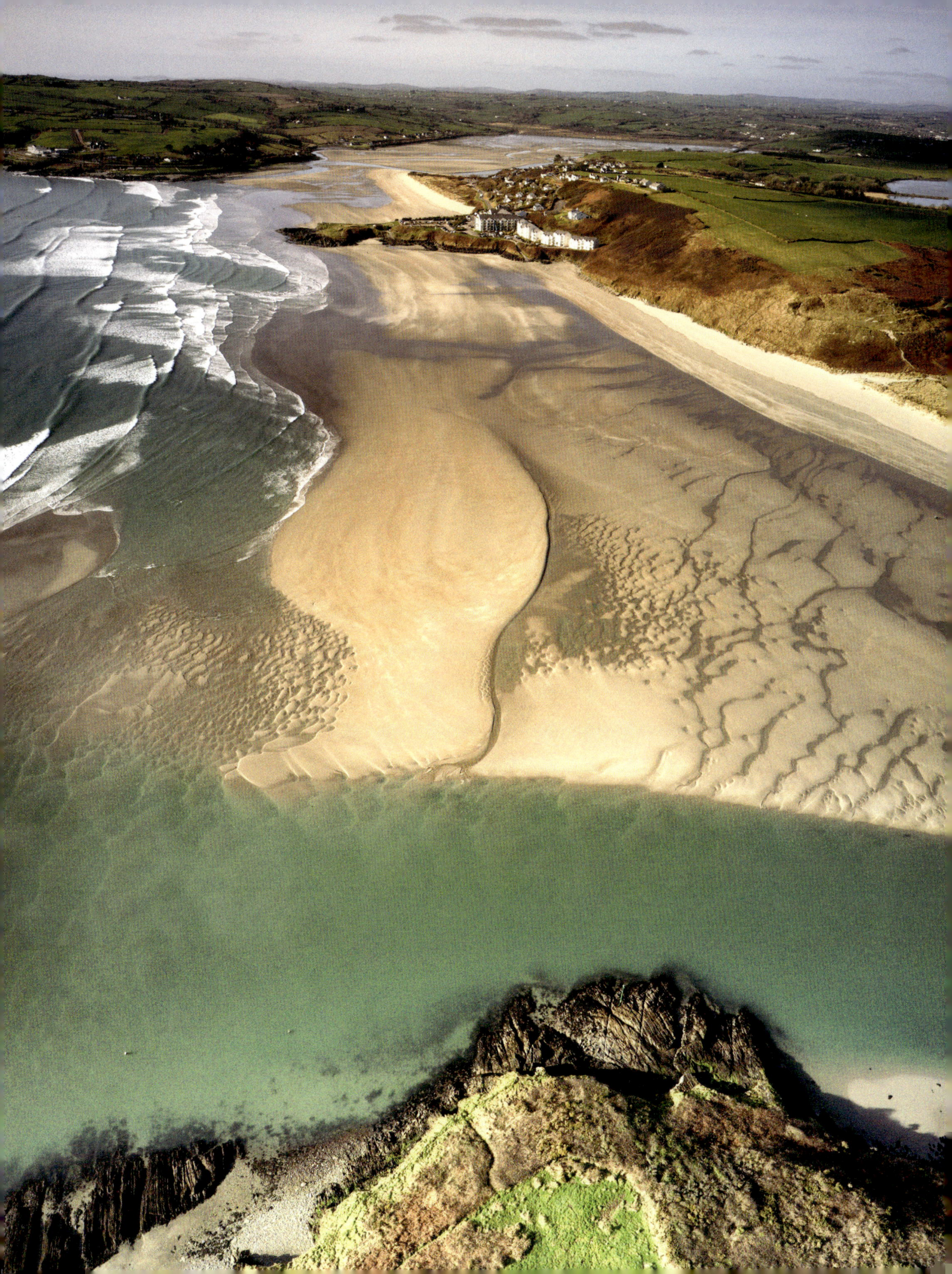

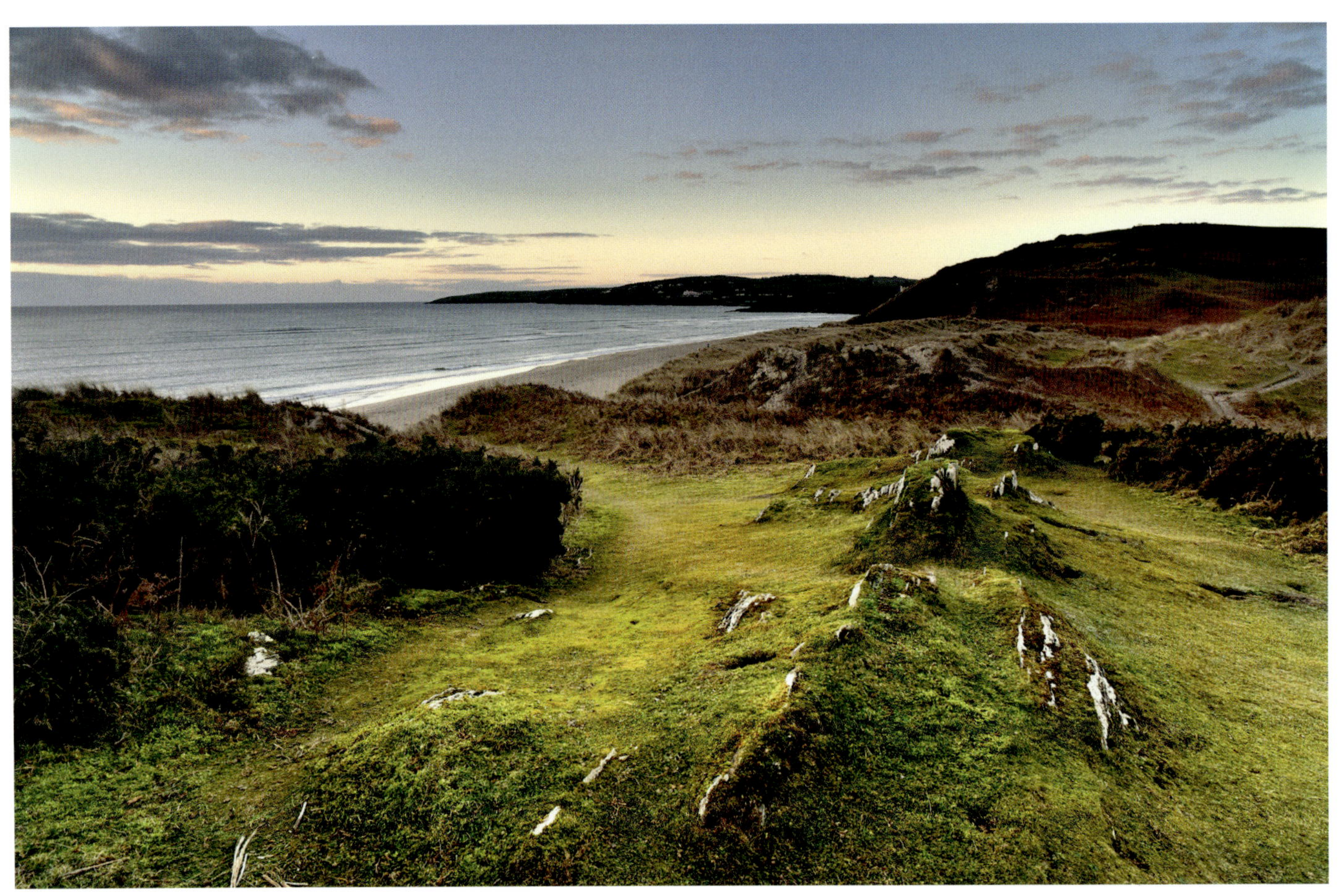

Above: The east beach at Inchydoney.

Below: Looking west to Owenahincha on a perfect spring evening.

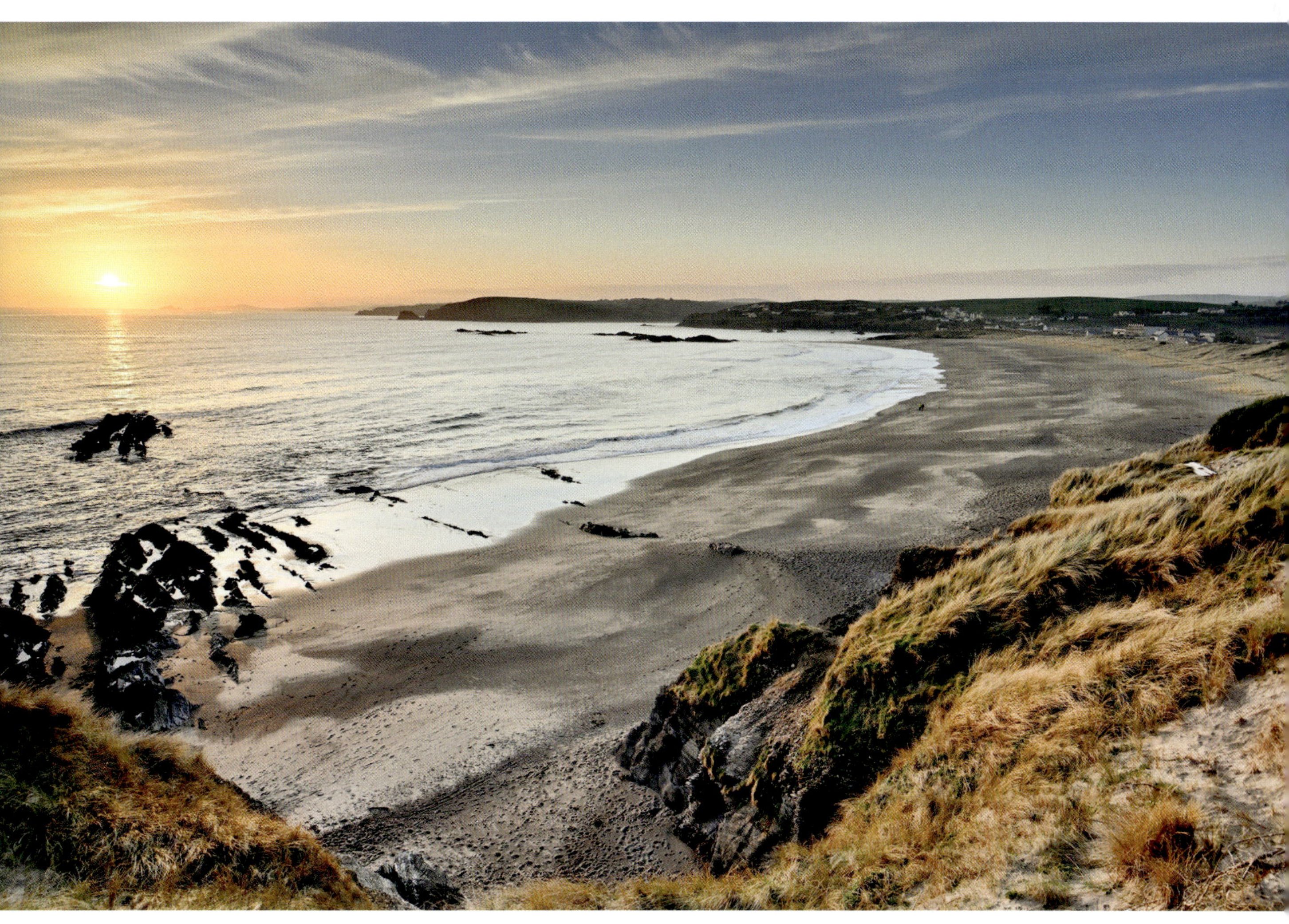

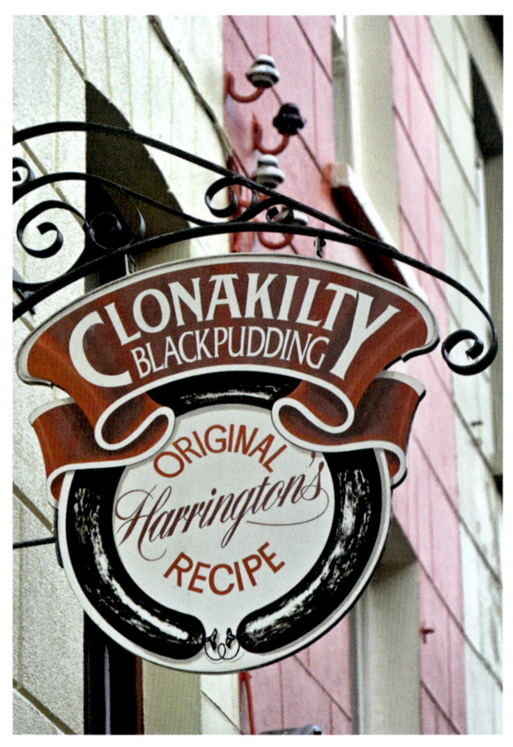

Right: Clonakilty is famous for its black pudding, which features on the menus of some of Ireland's finest restaurants.

Below: The two-kilometre stretch of Long Strand near Clonakilty.

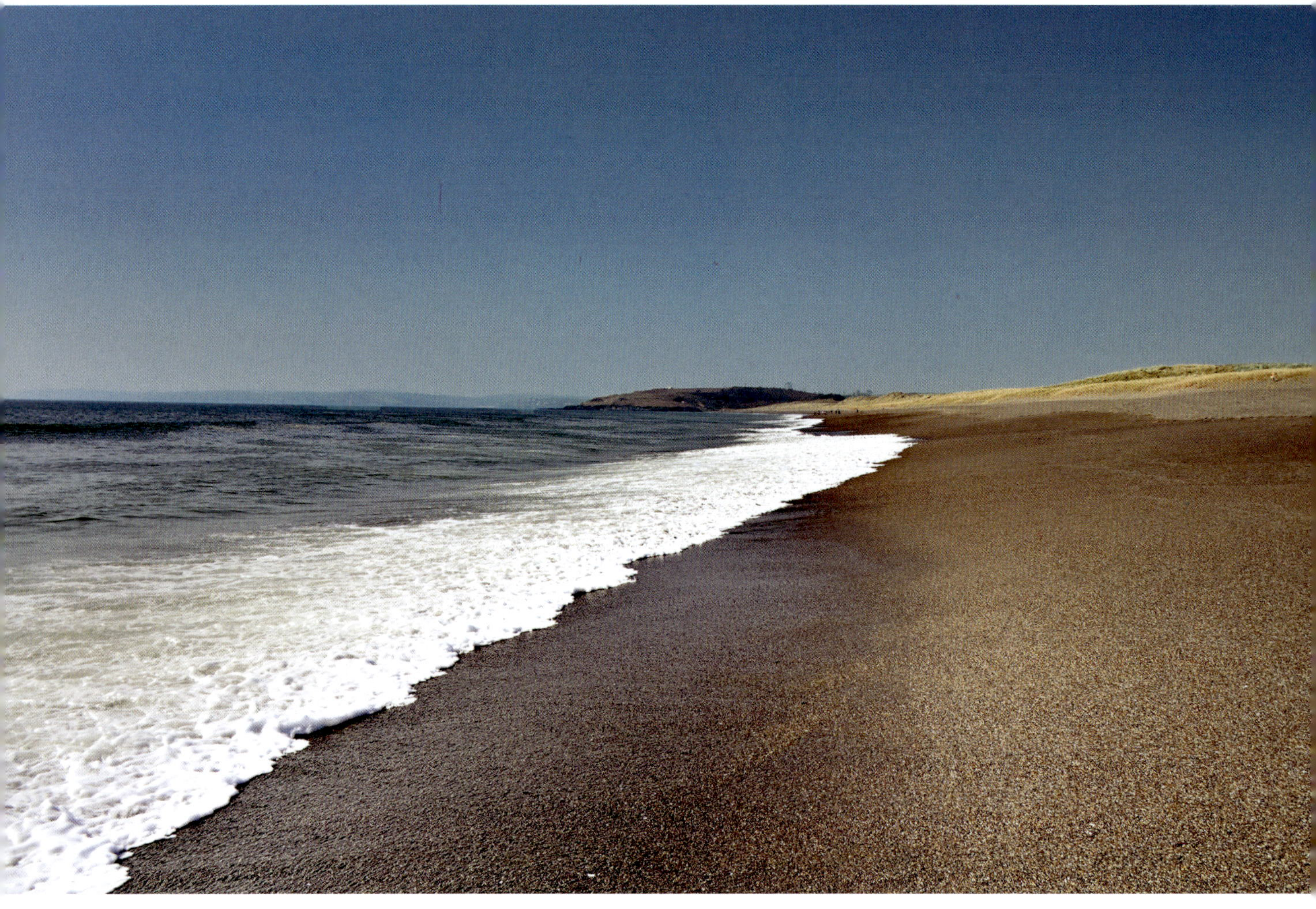

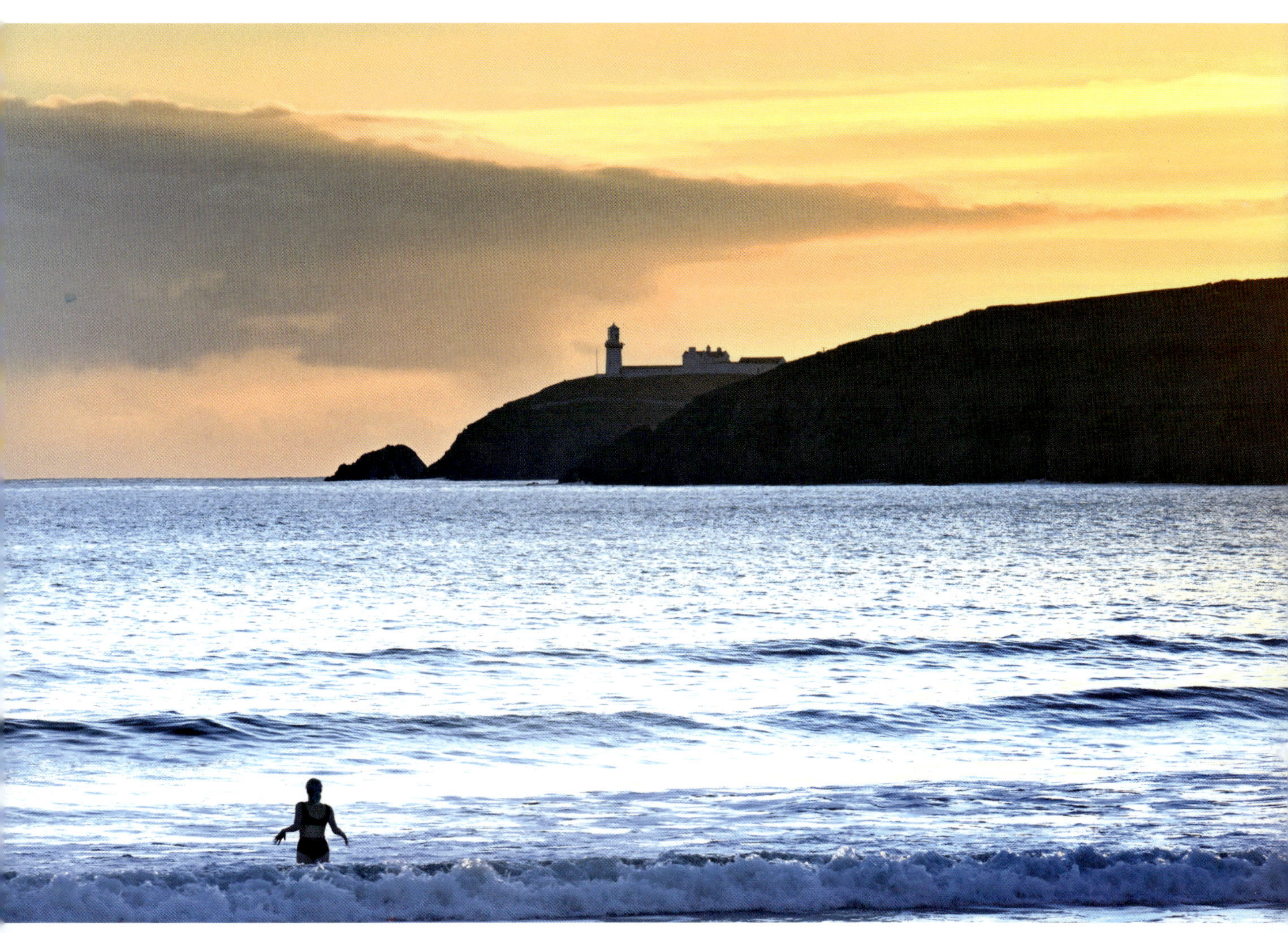

Above: Winter swimming at Red Strand, with Galley Head lighthouse in the distance.

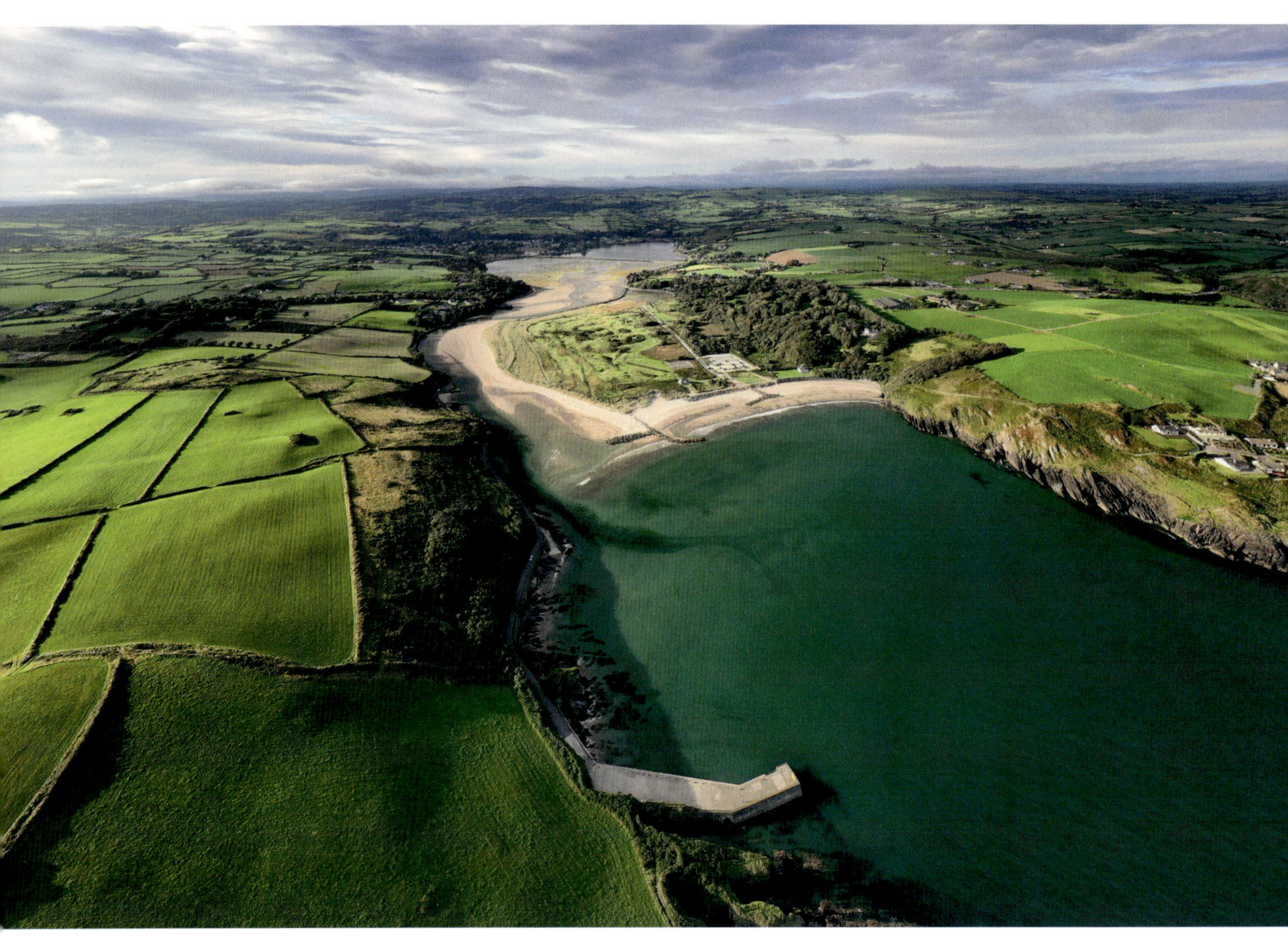

Above: Warren Beach. This beautiful beach is a birdwatching paradise, at the mouth of the Rosscarbery River.

Opposite: Drombeg stone circle is one of the most visited megalithic sites in the country. Built in the Bronze Age, approximately three thousand years ago, it is aligned with the setting sun of the midwinter solstice (21 December). One megalith lies on its side and is known as the 'Druid's Altar'.

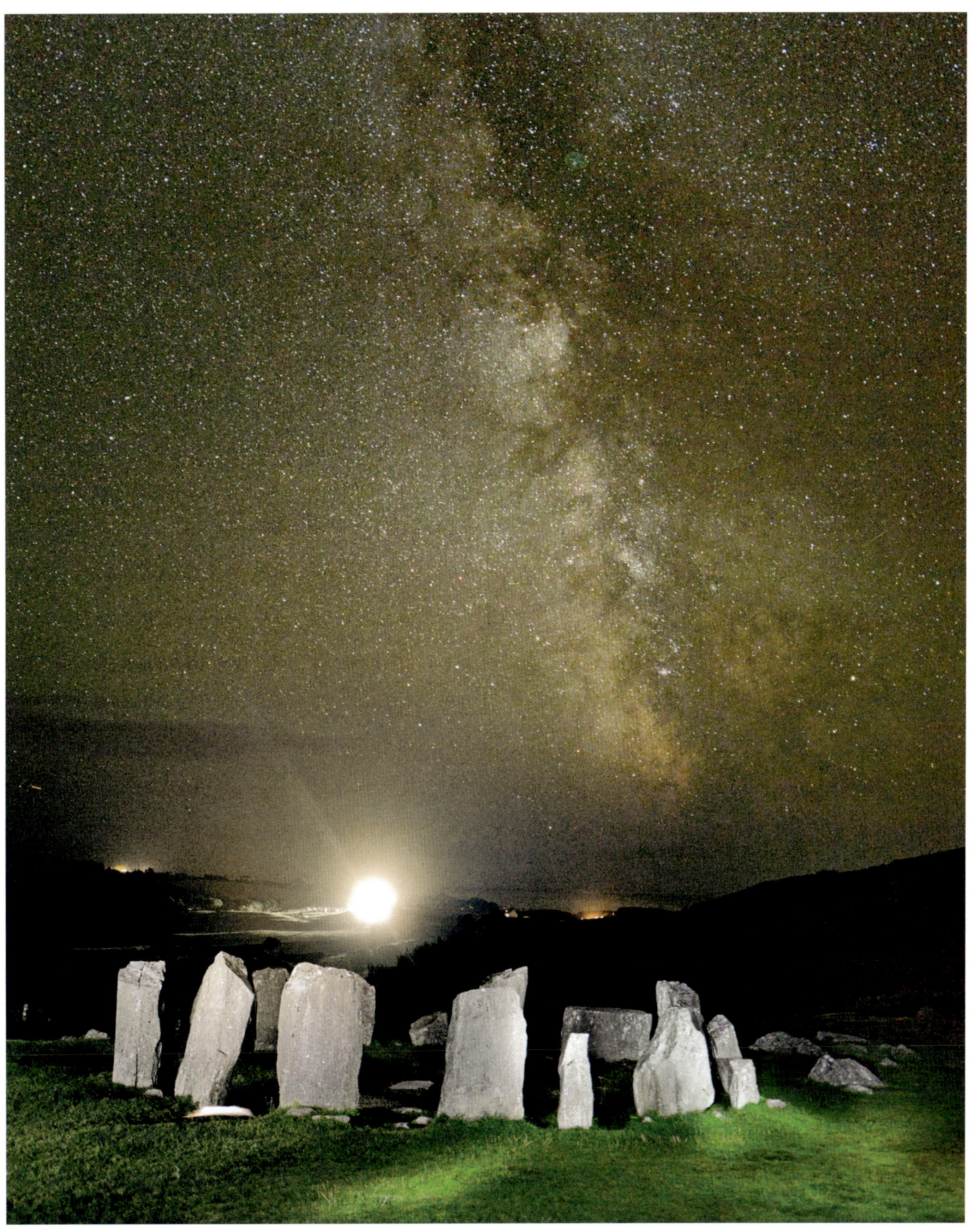

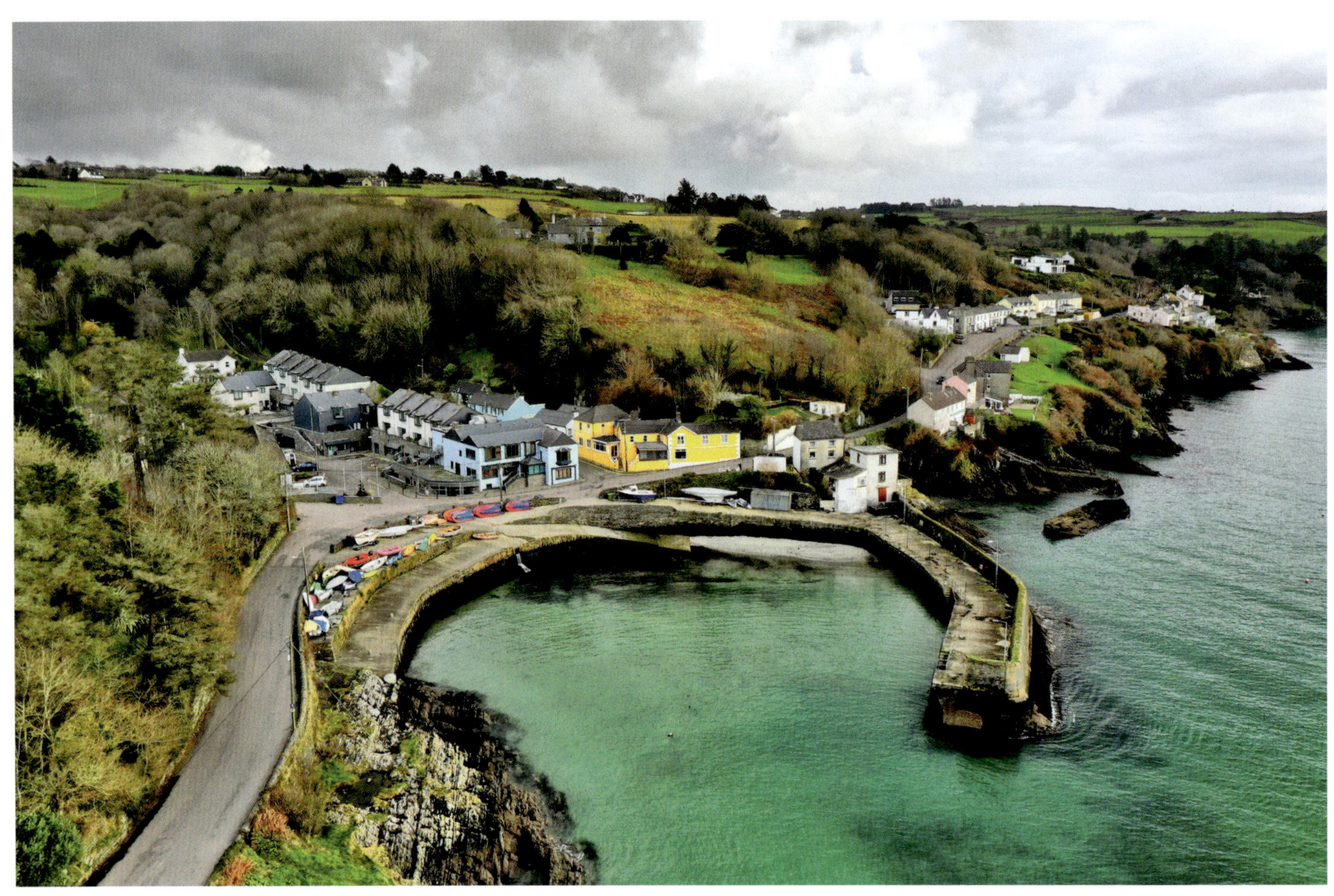

Above: The quiet village of Glandore on a winter's evening.

Opposite: Two tiny islands, called Adam and Eve, guard the entrance of Glandore Harbour.

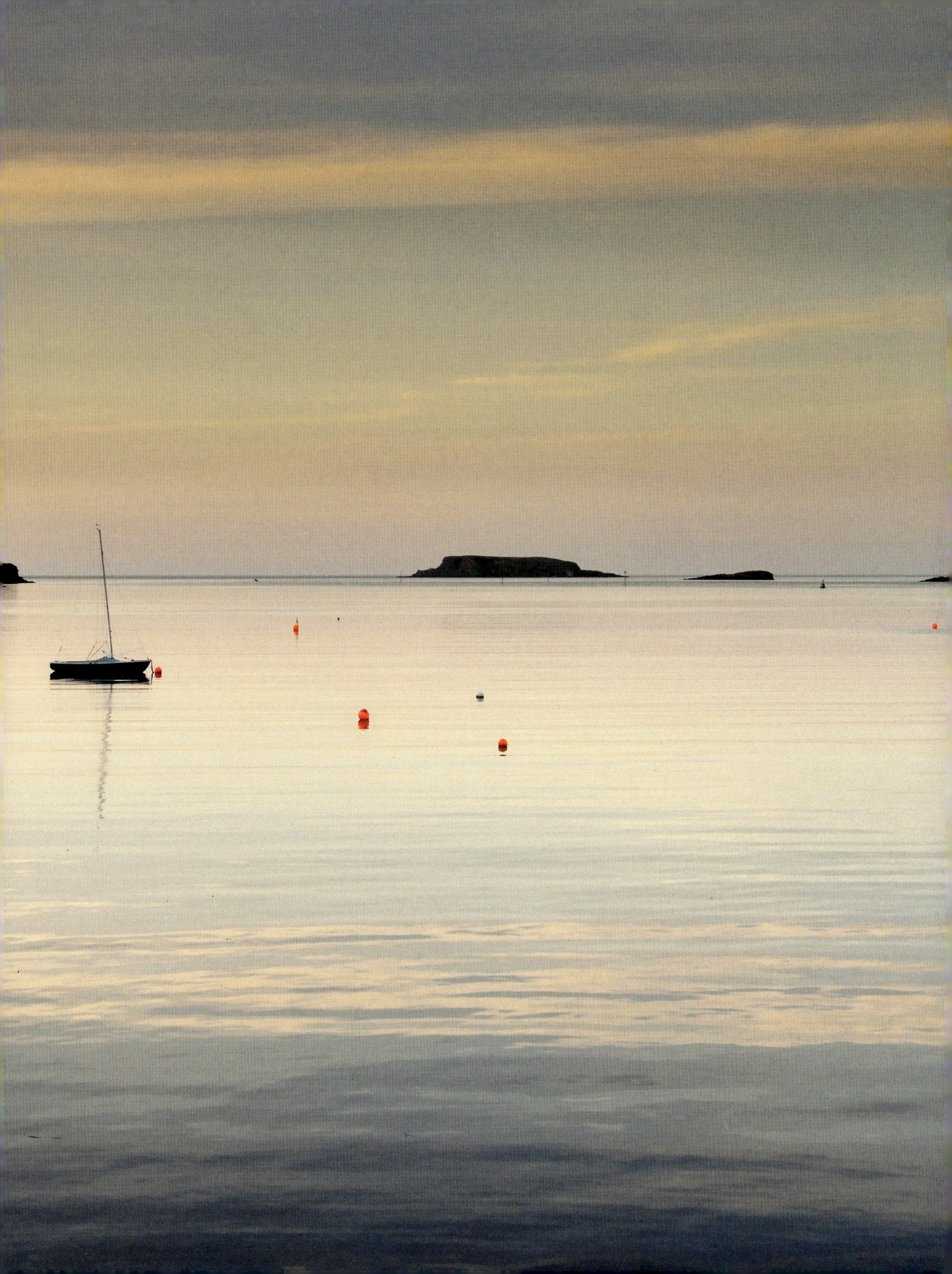

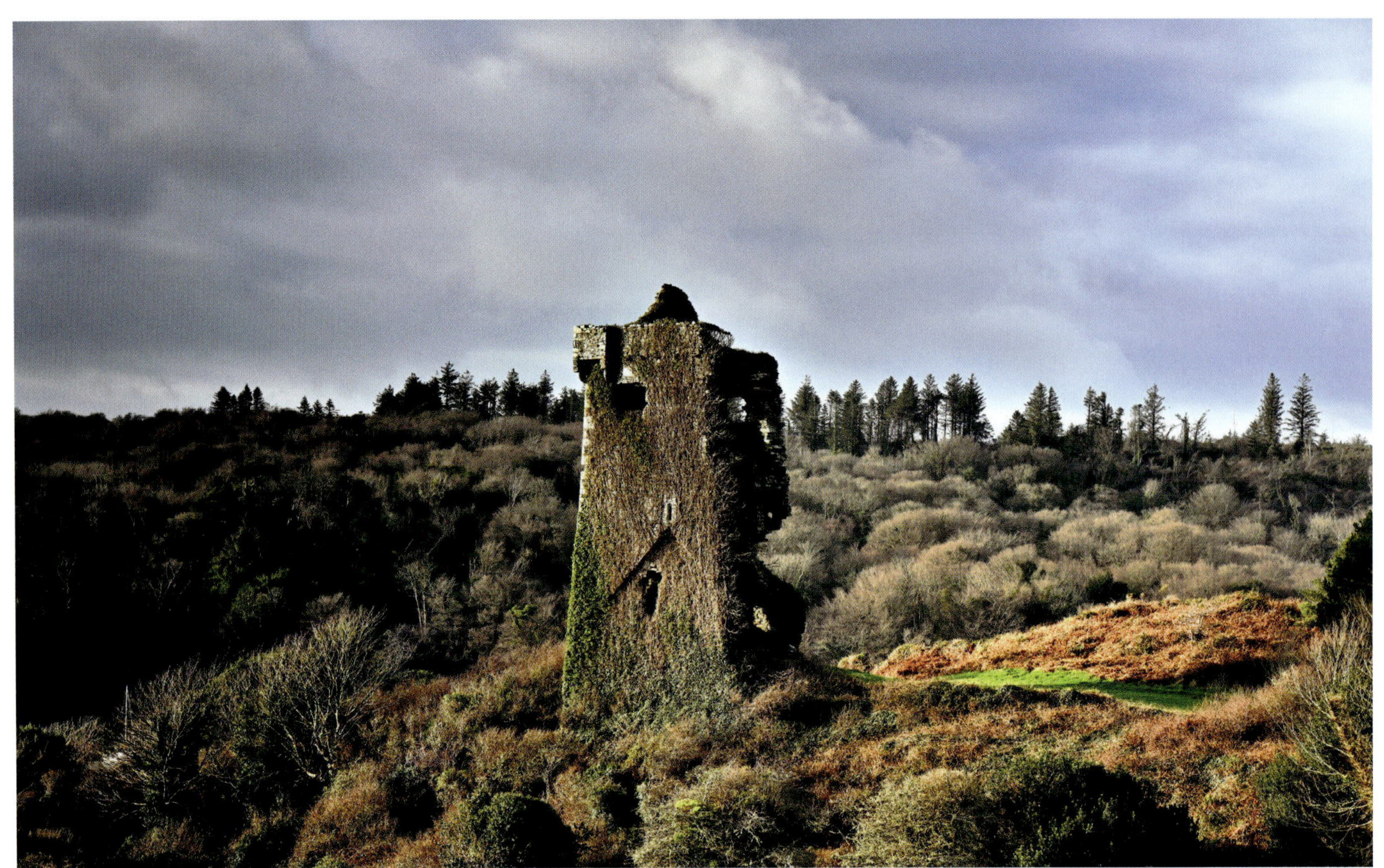

Above: The ruined Raheen tower house near Unionhall. Built in 1560 by the O'Donovan clan, it survived less than a century: Cromwell's troops destroyed it in 1649.

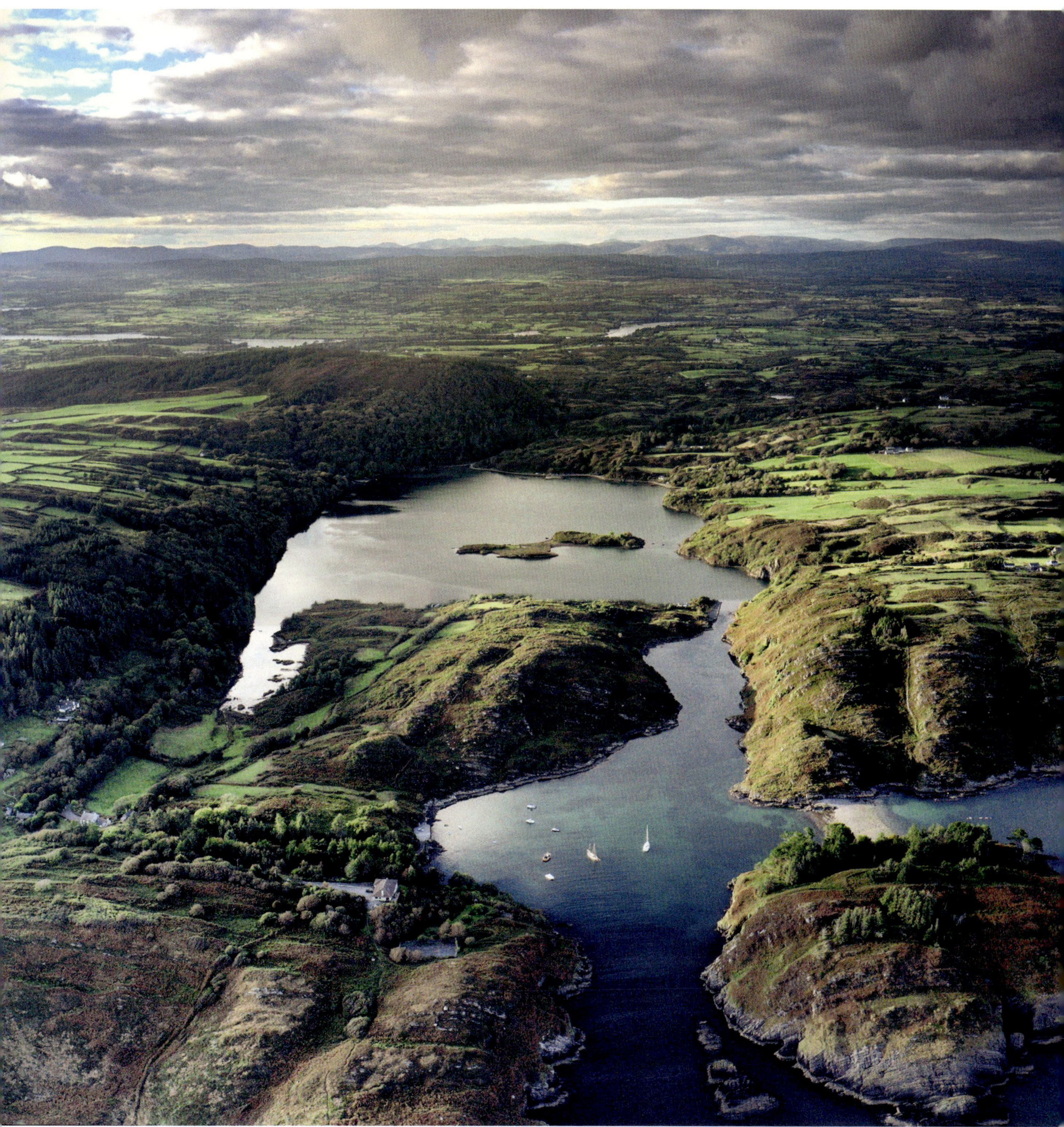

Above: Looking down on Lough Hyne, Ireland's first marine nature reserve.

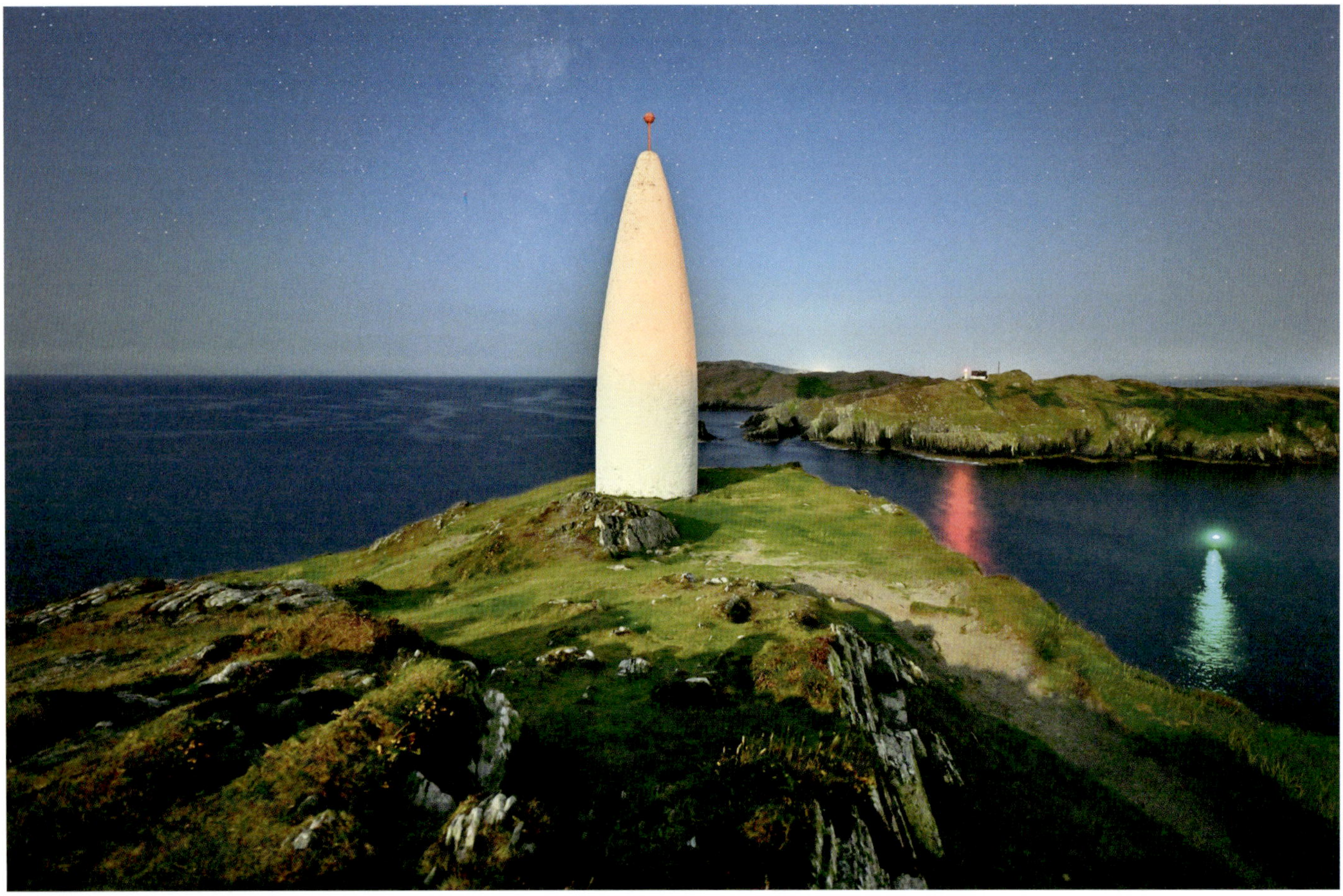

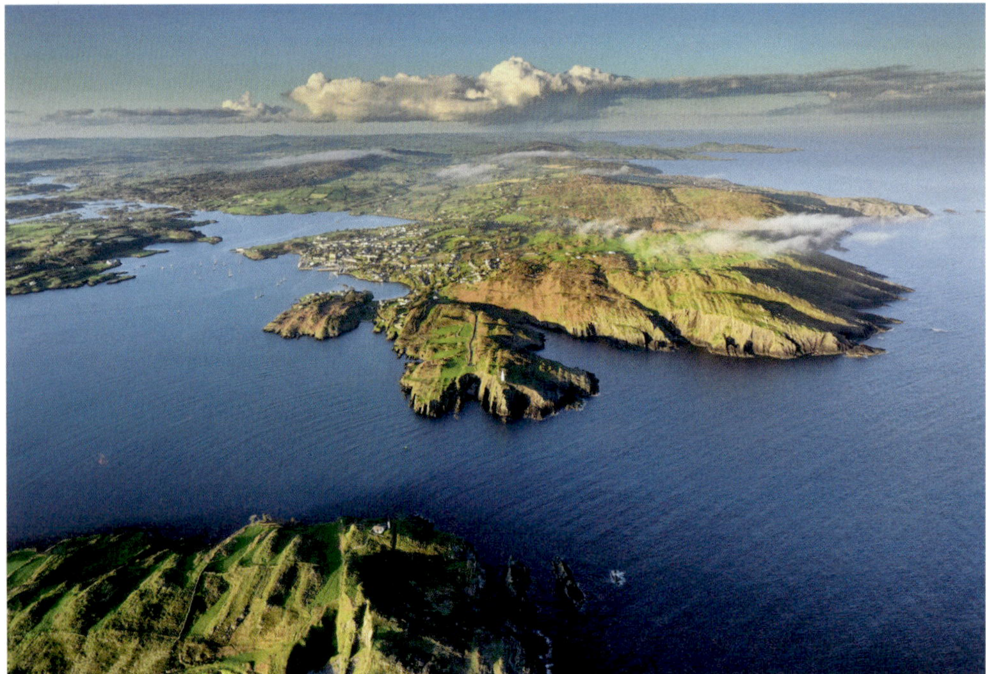

Above: Baltimore Beacon. This navigation mark, dating back to the 1800s, overlooks the mouth of Baltimore Harbour.

Left: Baltimore and Roaringwater Bay from the air.

Opposite: Late evening sunshine lights up the beaches of Sherkin Island.

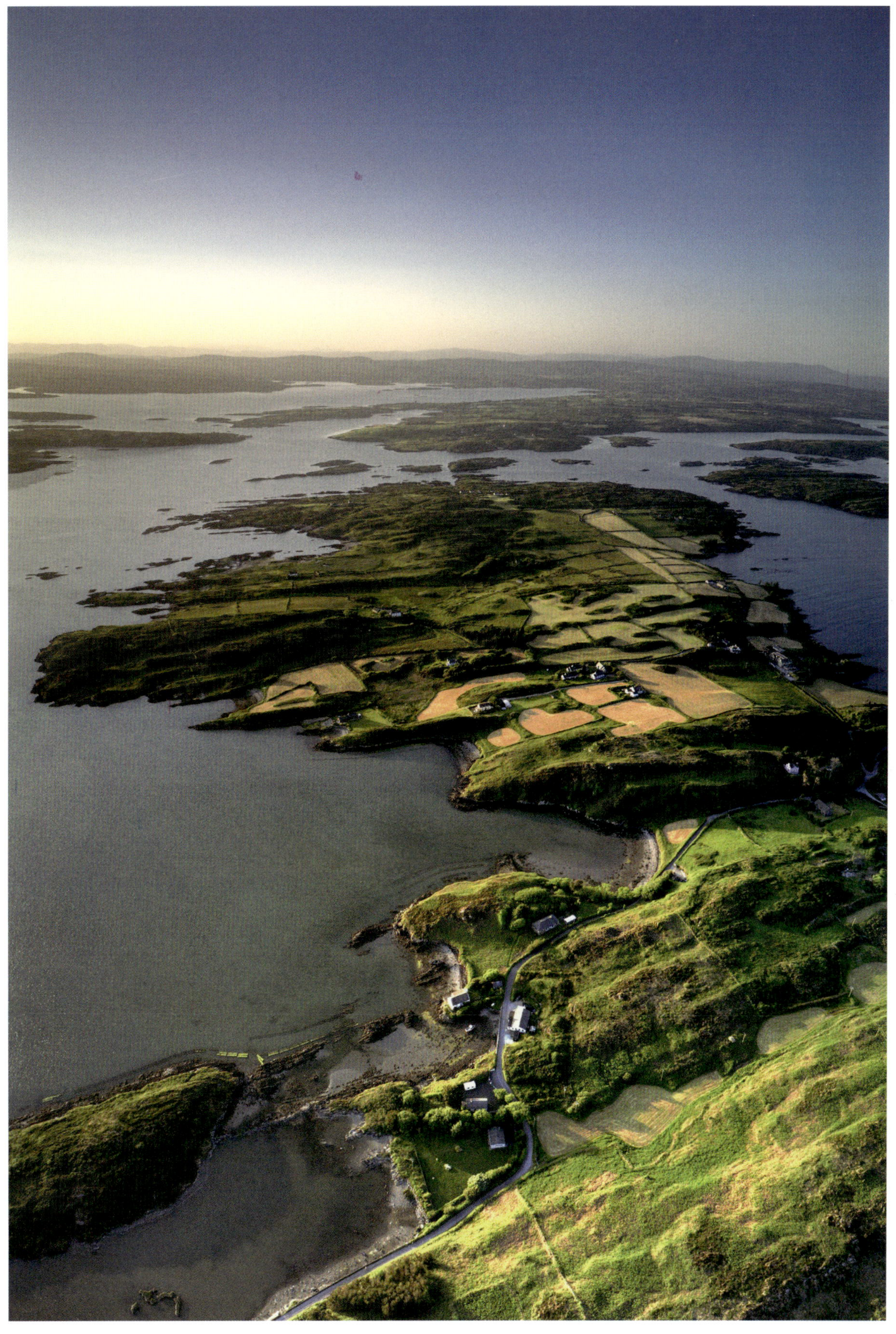

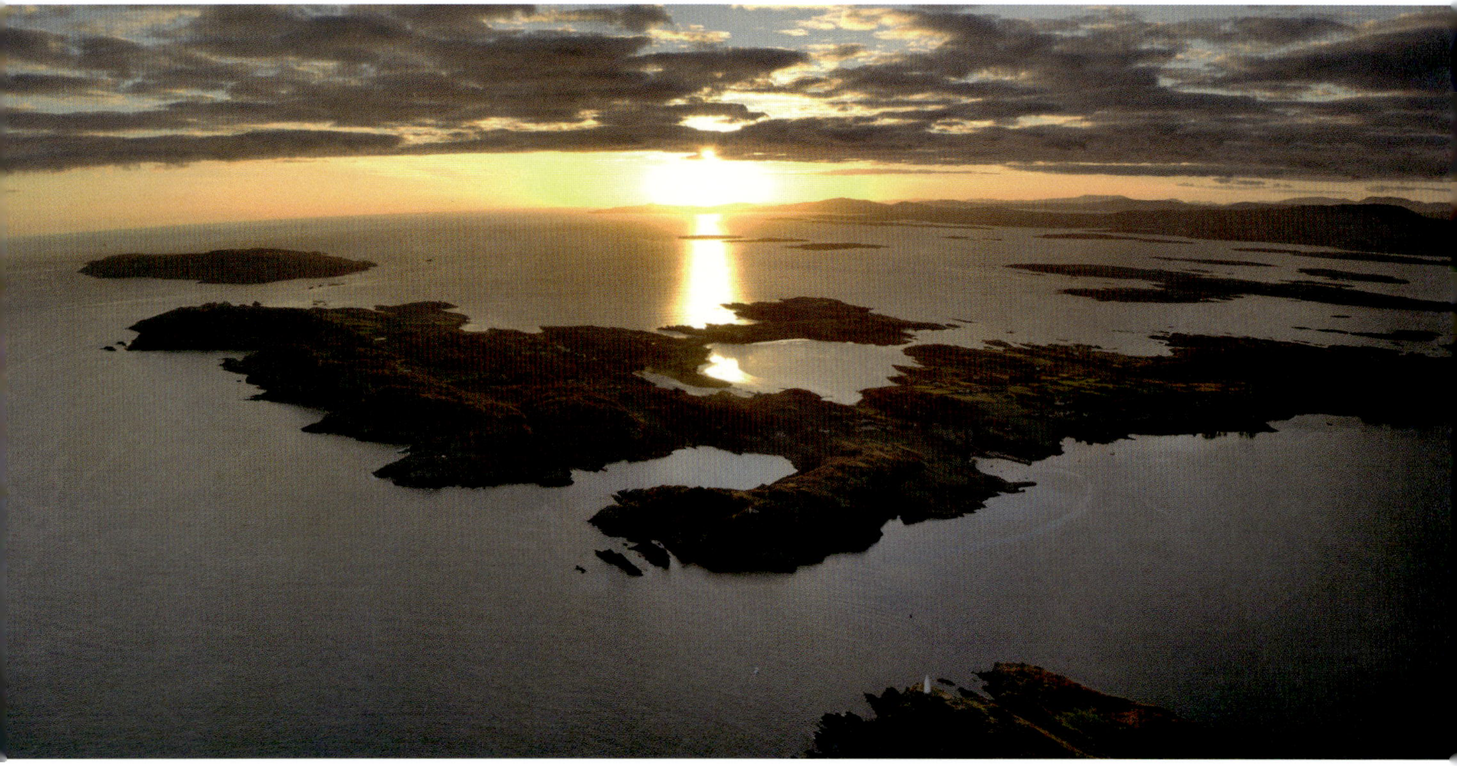

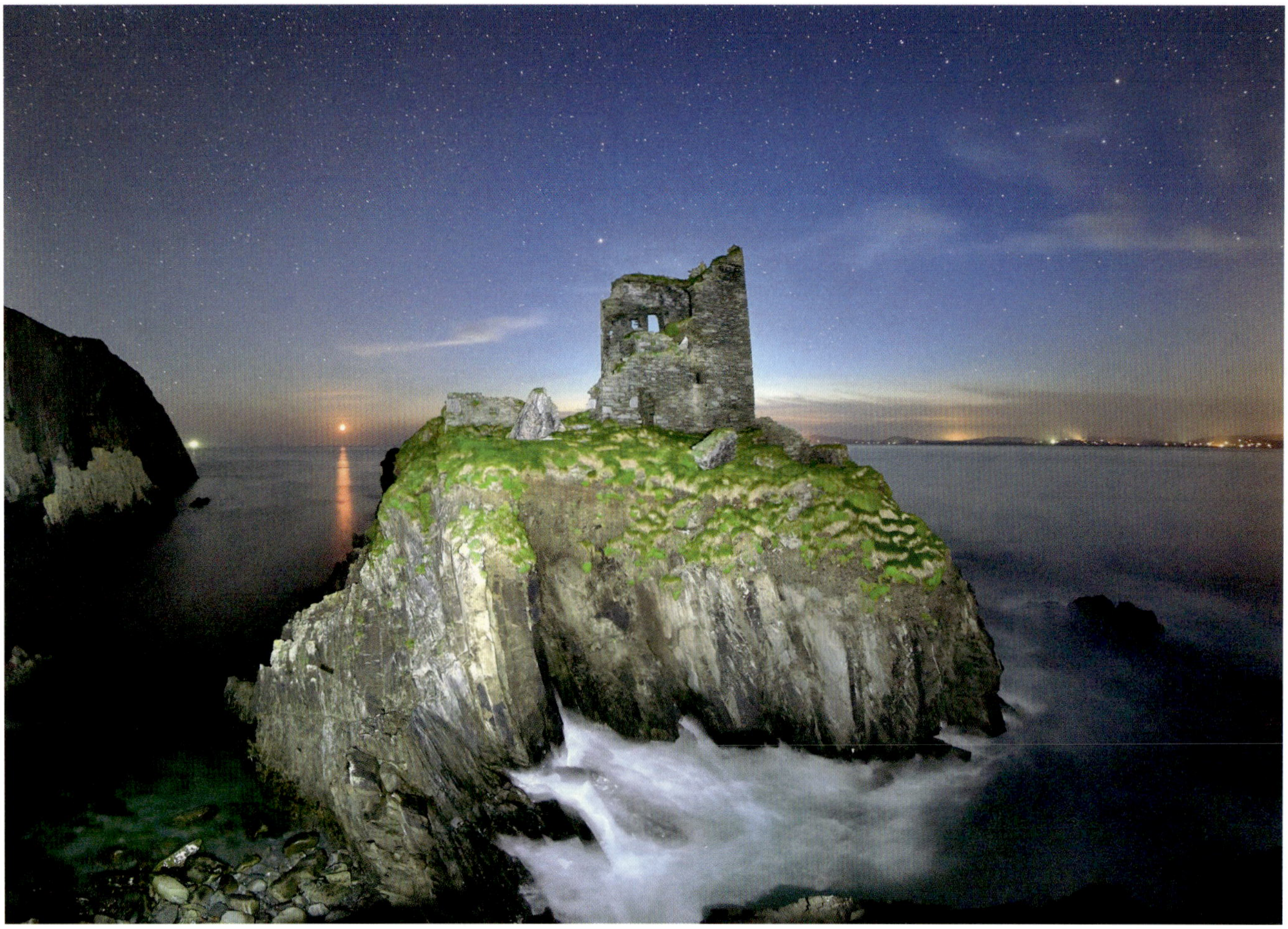

Opposite top: Sunset over Sherkin Island with the mountains of west Cork in the distance. A short ferry trip from Baltimore, Sherkin was the ancestral home of the O'Driscoll clan.

Opposite bottom: The ruined Dún an Óir ('fort of gold') on Cape Clear Island is one of the O'Driscoll castles built in the mid-sixteenth century.

Below: Ballydehob's twelve-arch bridge. This imposing structure was built in 1886 as part of the West Cork Railway.

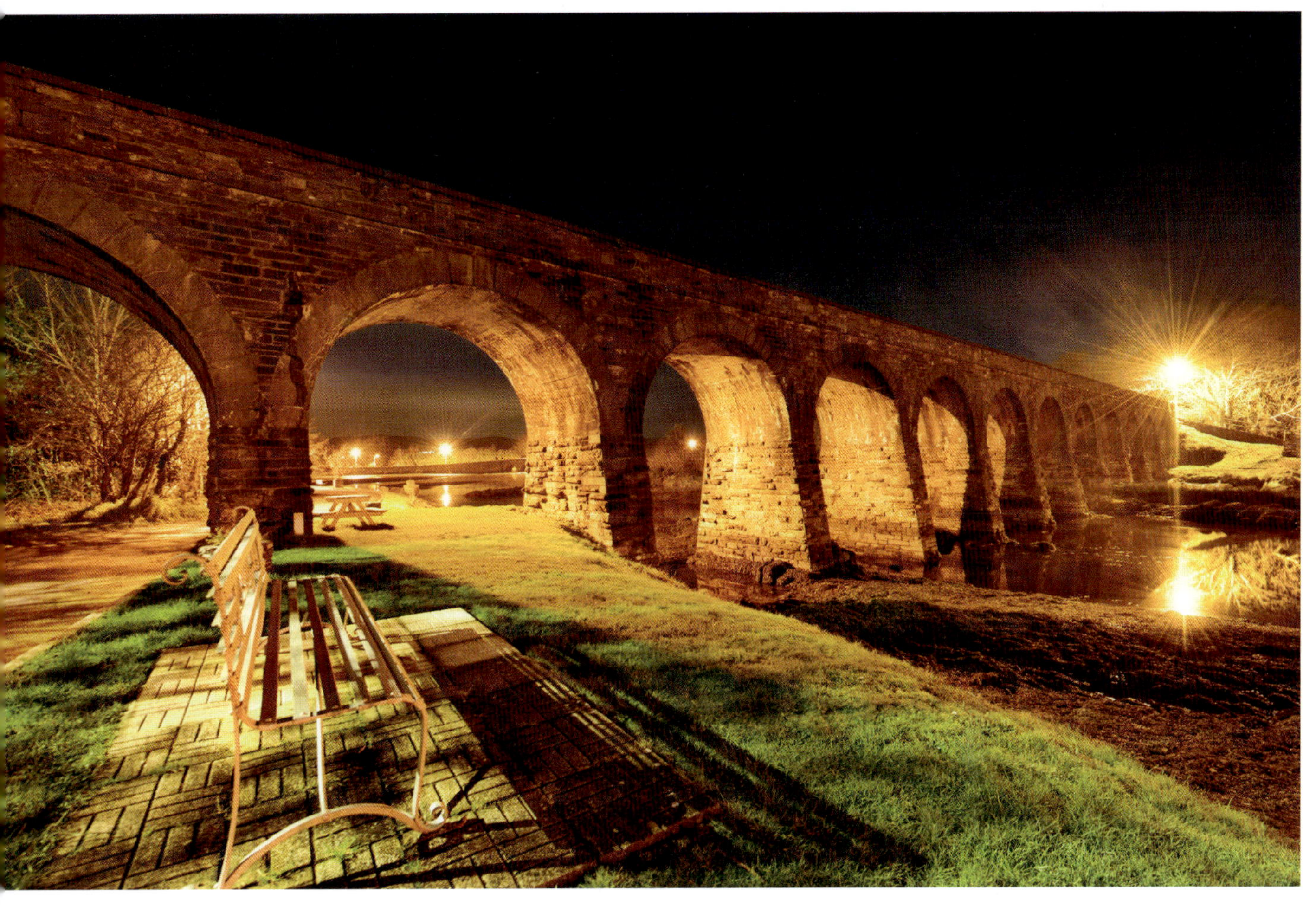

The Fastnet, Ireland's
most iconic lighthouse,
is 54 metres tall.
Situated 13km off the
mainland, it is Ireland's
most southerly point.

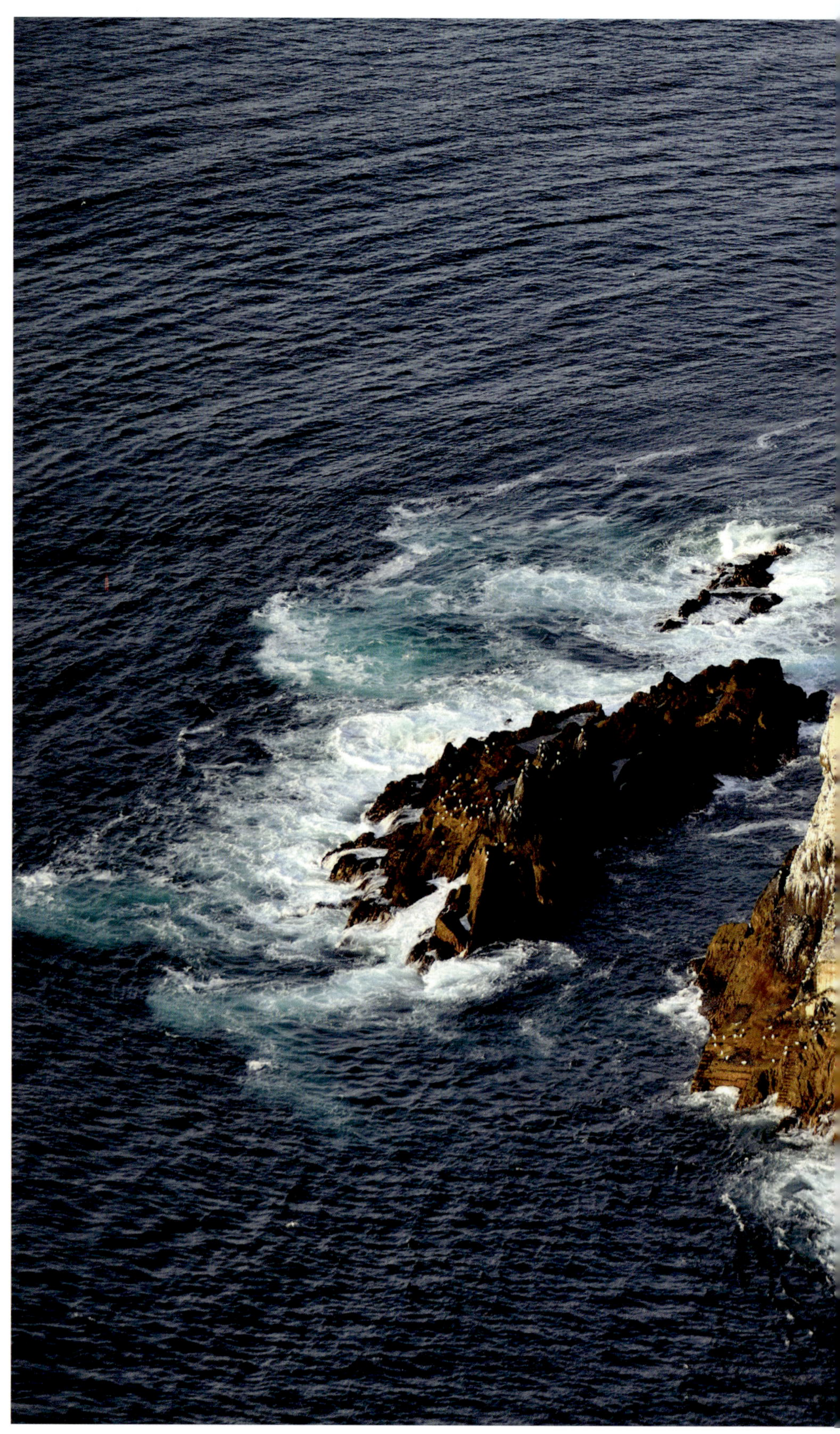

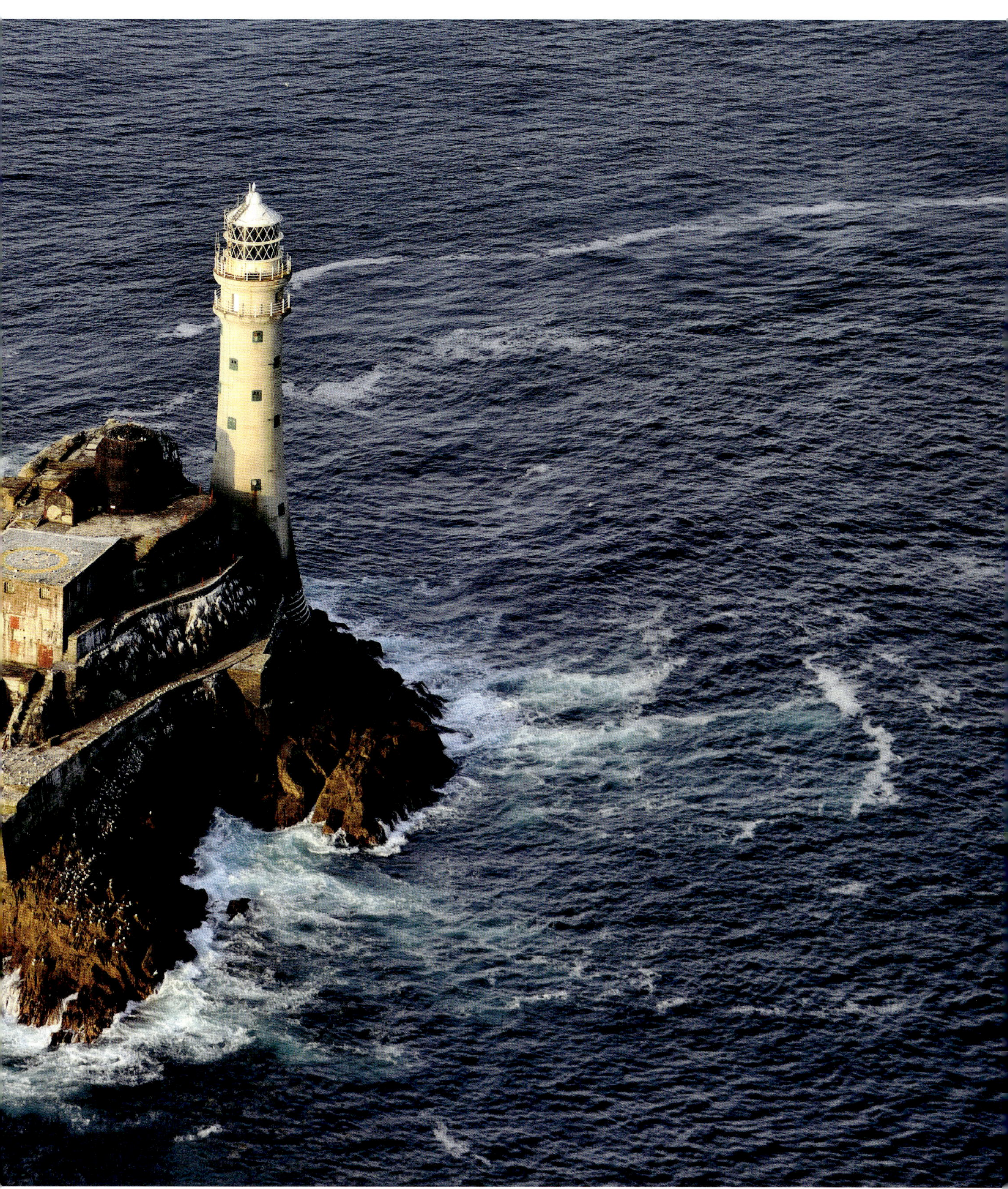

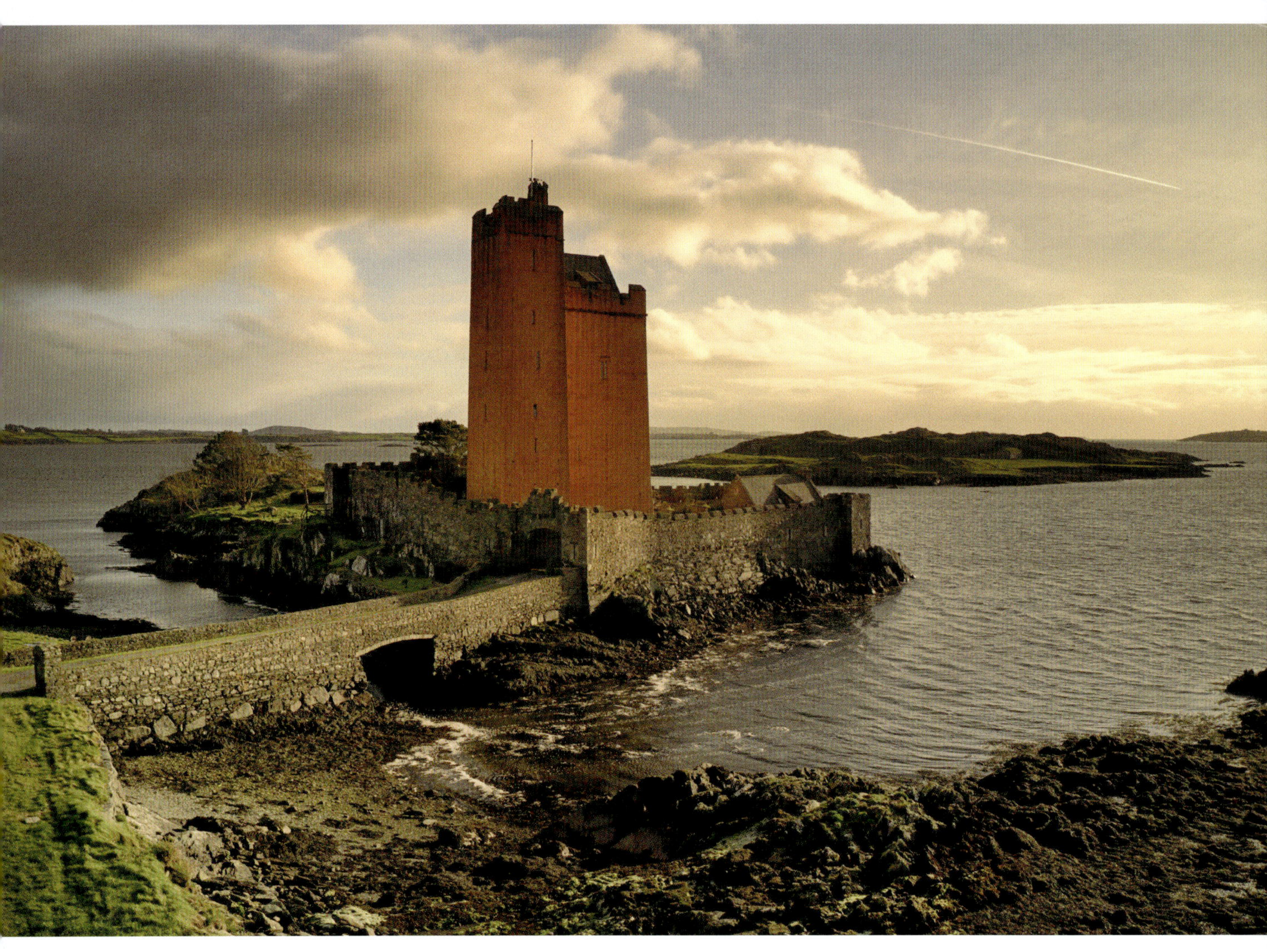

The fifteenth-century Kilcoe Castle, one of the many restored castles in west Cork, is famously owned by renowned actor Jeremy Irons.

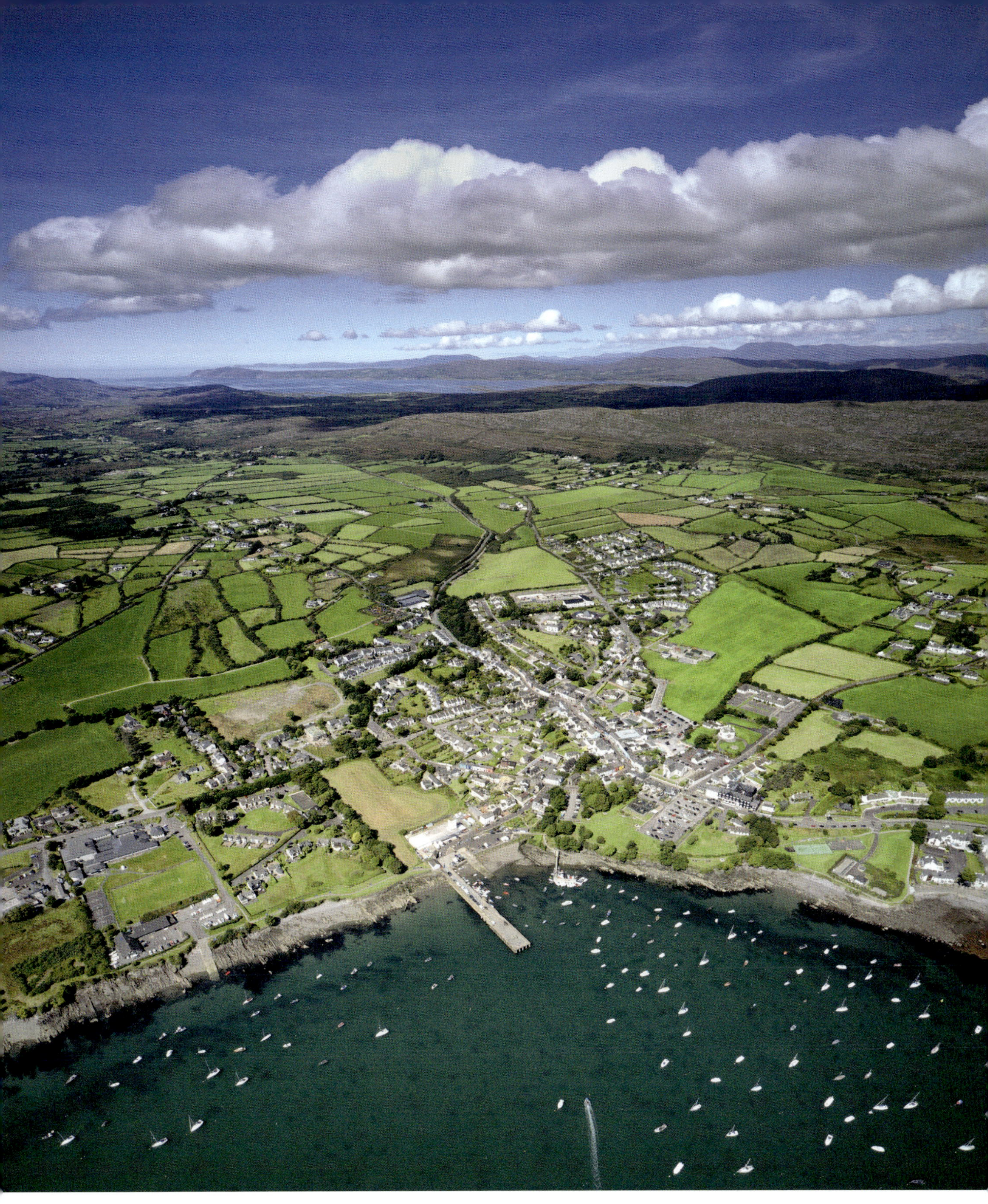

Above: An aerial view of the sailing village of Schull.

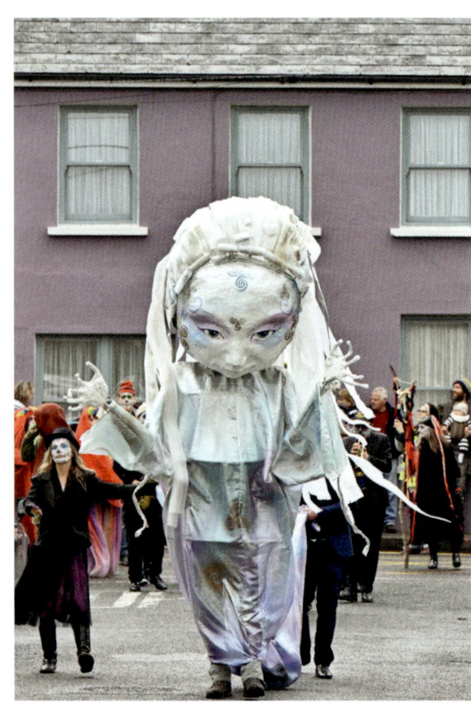

Left: The Ballydehob Jazz Festival takes place on the May bank holiday each year and features a lively parade.

Below: Brow Head, with the Sheep's Head and Beara Peninsulas in the background. Brow Head is the southernmost point on the island of Ireland.

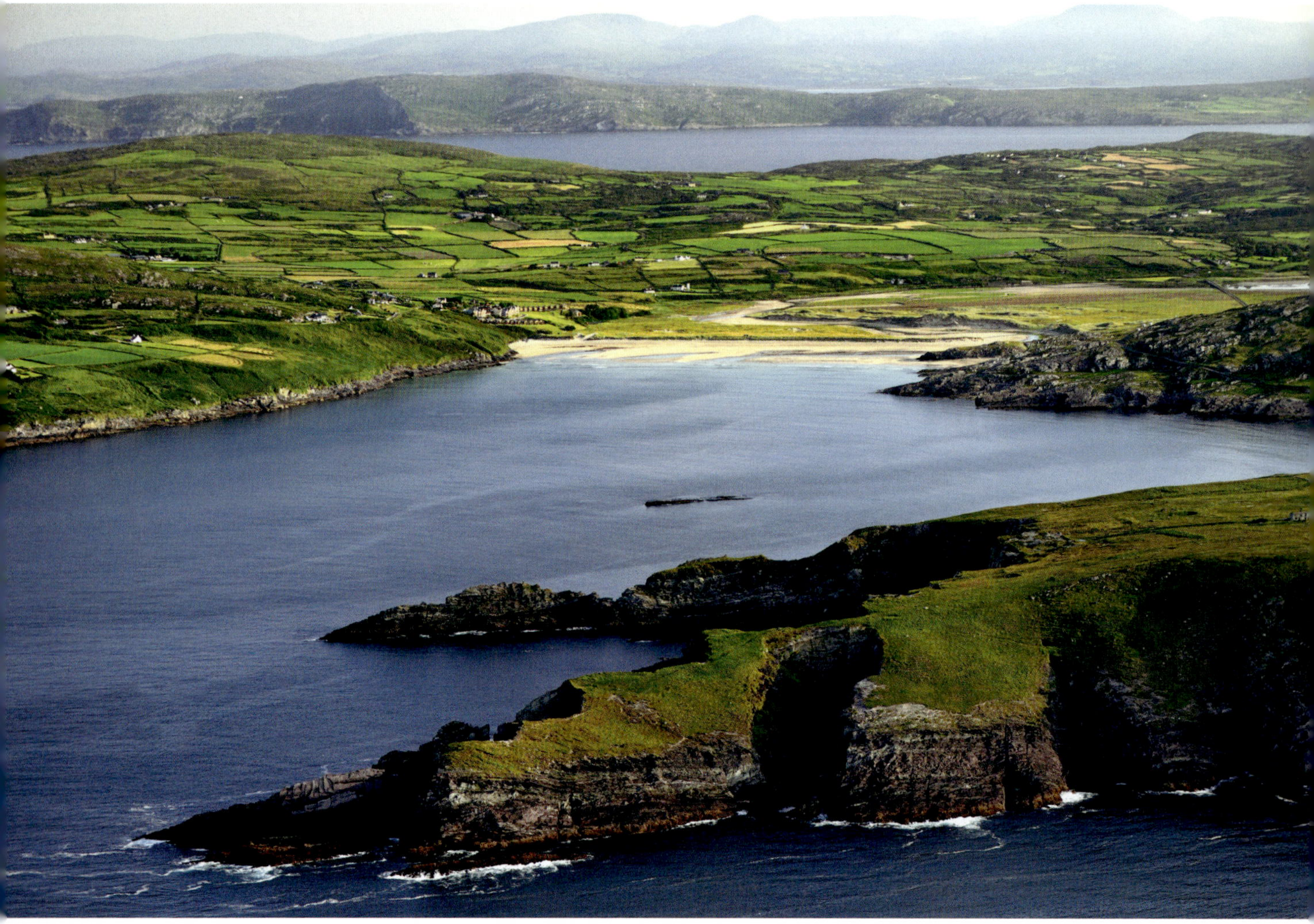

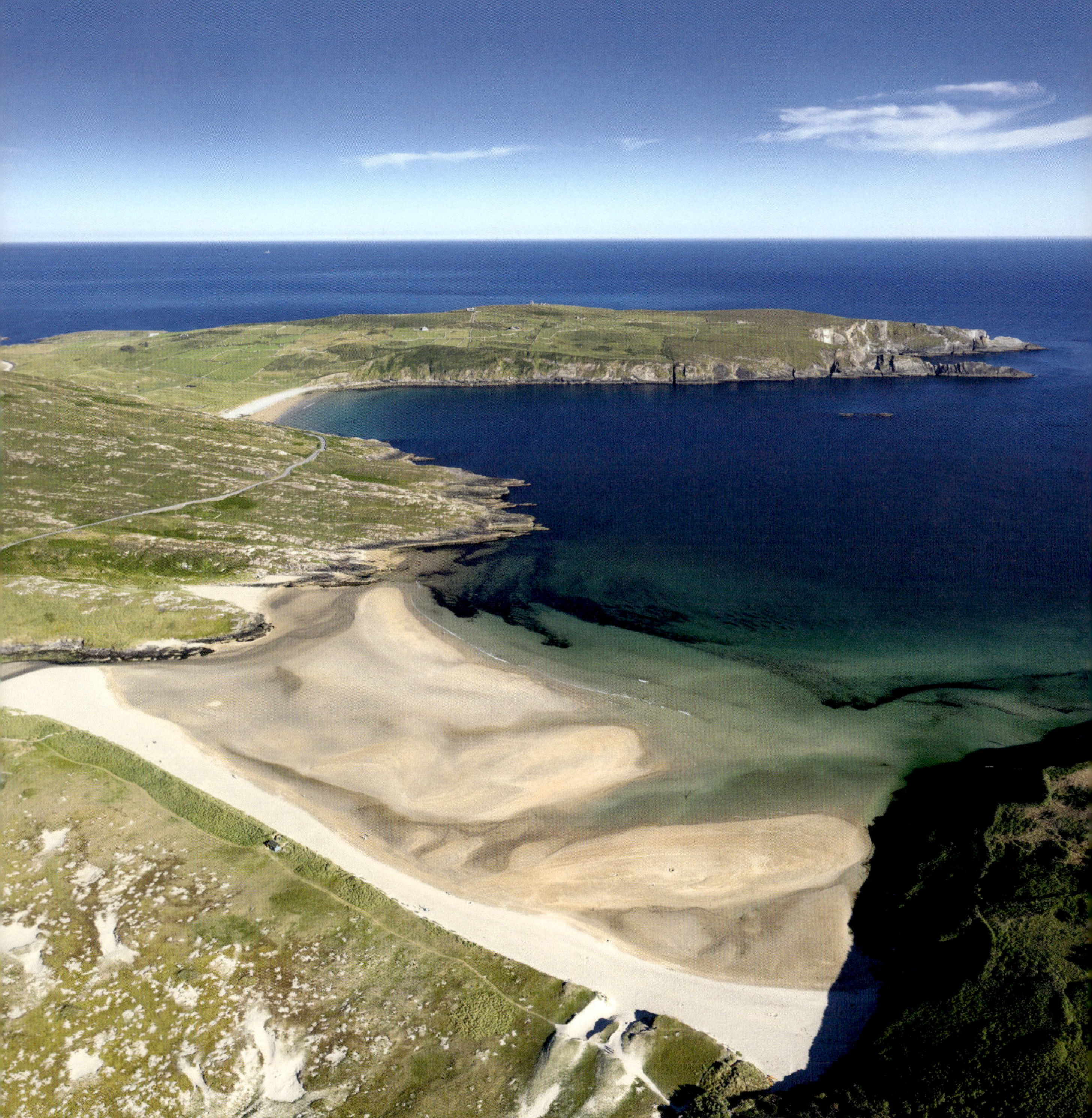

Above: The white-sand beach of Barley Cove on the Mizen Peninsula is one of the longest beaches in west Cork. Local folklore has long held that the sand dunes at Barley Cove were formed by a tsunami in 1755, following an earthquake in Portugal that measured 8.4 on the Richter scale, with science now backing up that claim.

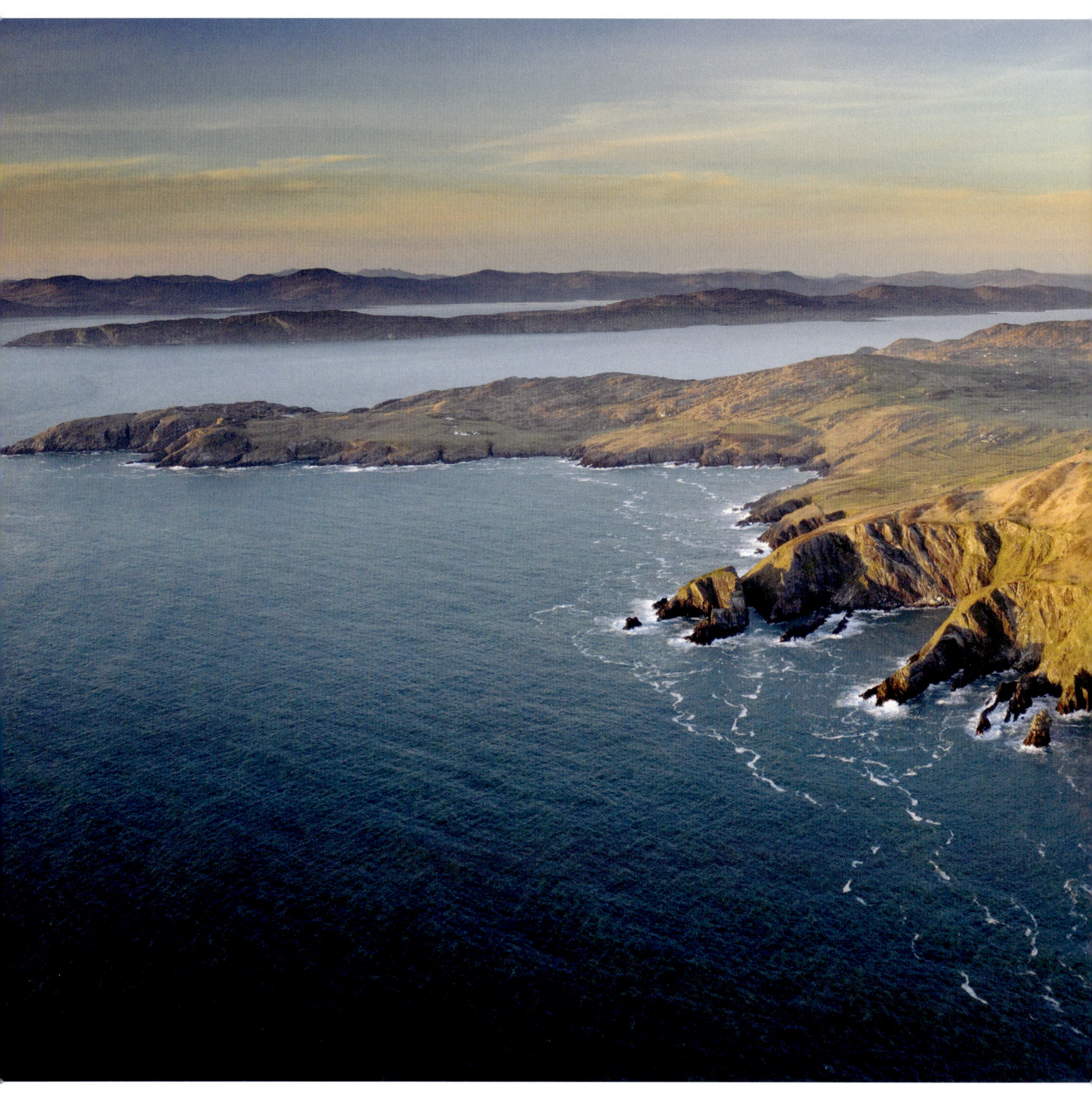

An aerial view of the Mizen Head peninsula and lighthouse.

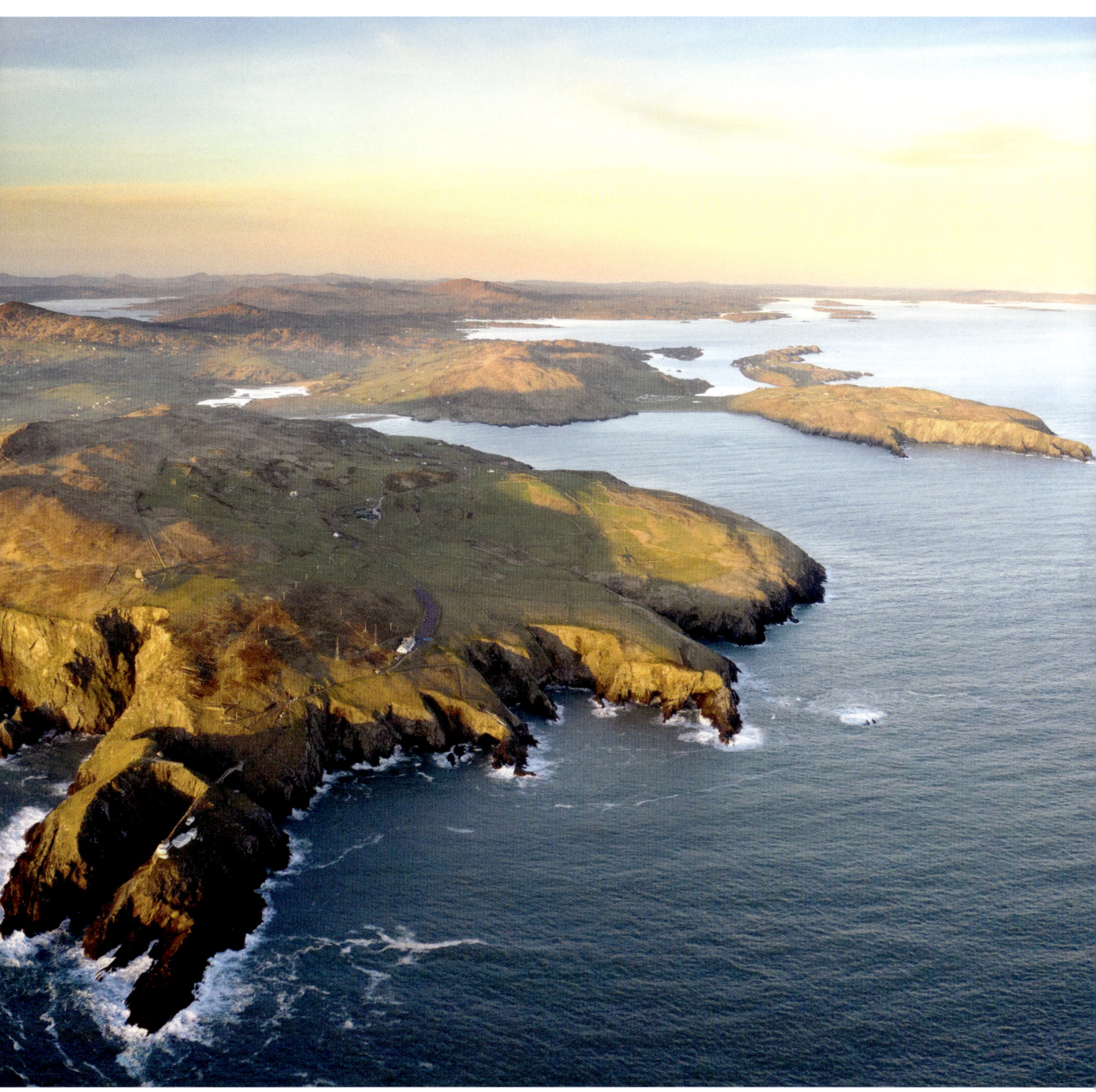

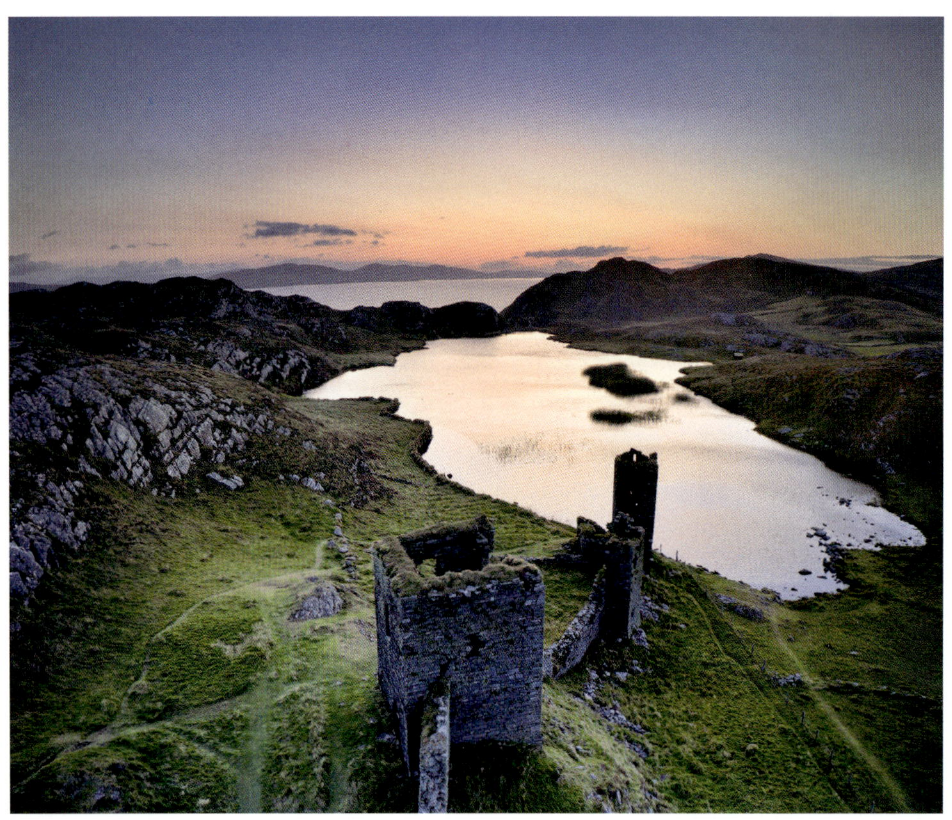

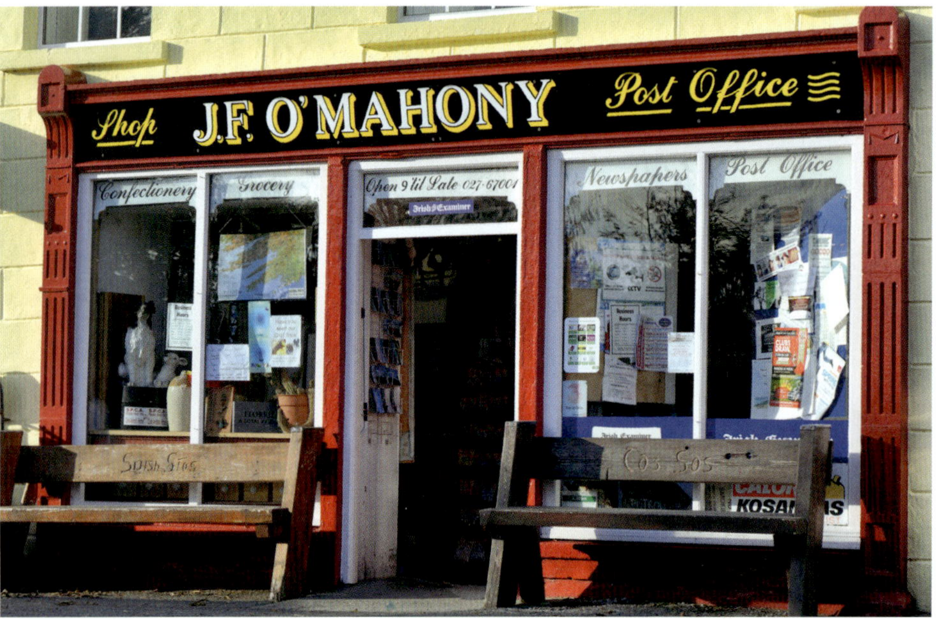

Above top: Three Castle Head, or Dunlough Castle, on the northwest tip of the Mizen Peninsula, was founded in 1207 and is one of Ireland's oldest castles.

Above bottom: Kilcrohane village shop and post office.

Opposite: Sheep's Head Lighthouse, near Kilcrohane, is one of Ireland's smallest lighthouses but the breathtaking scenery on the walk there makes it worth visiting.

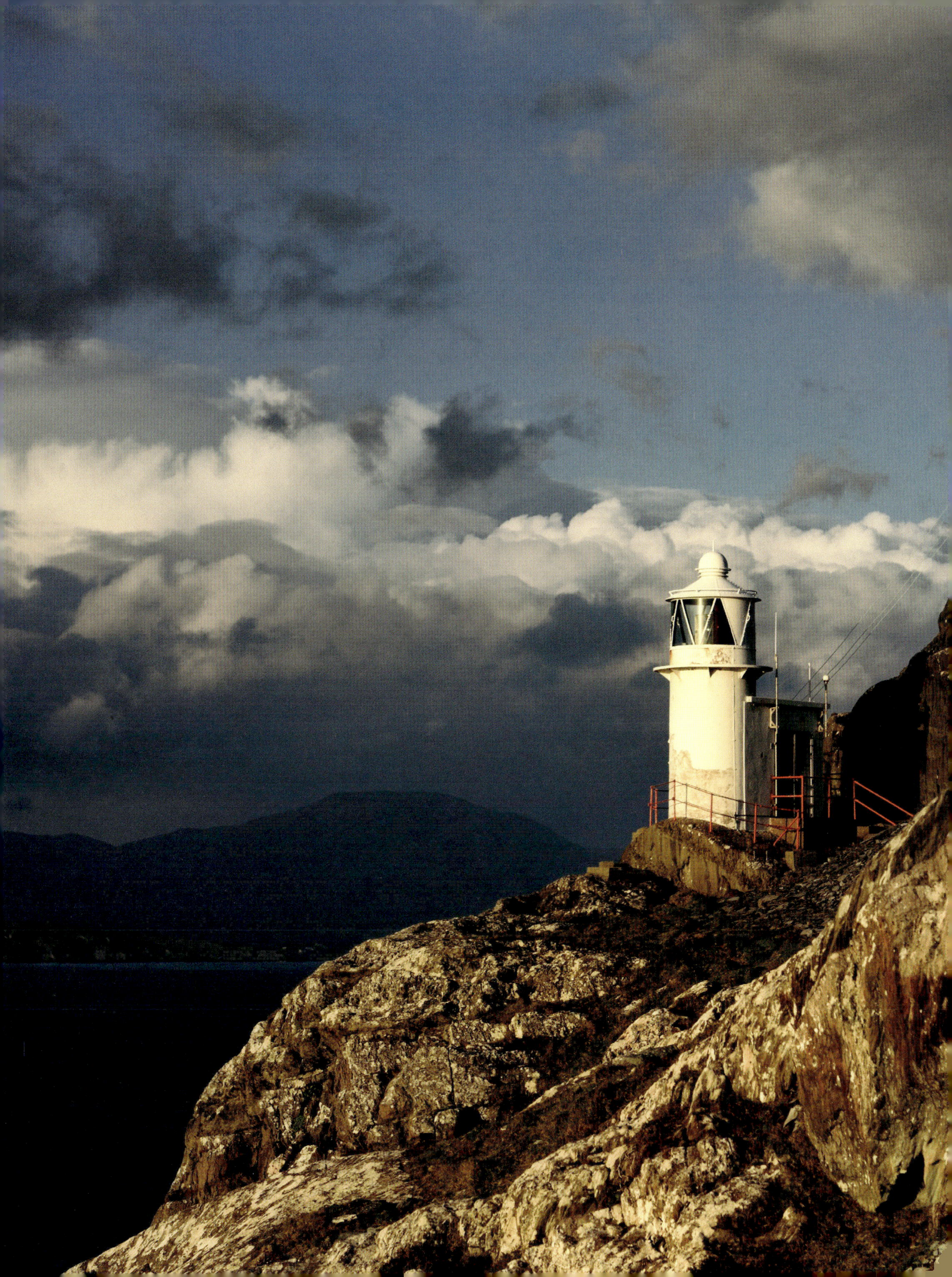

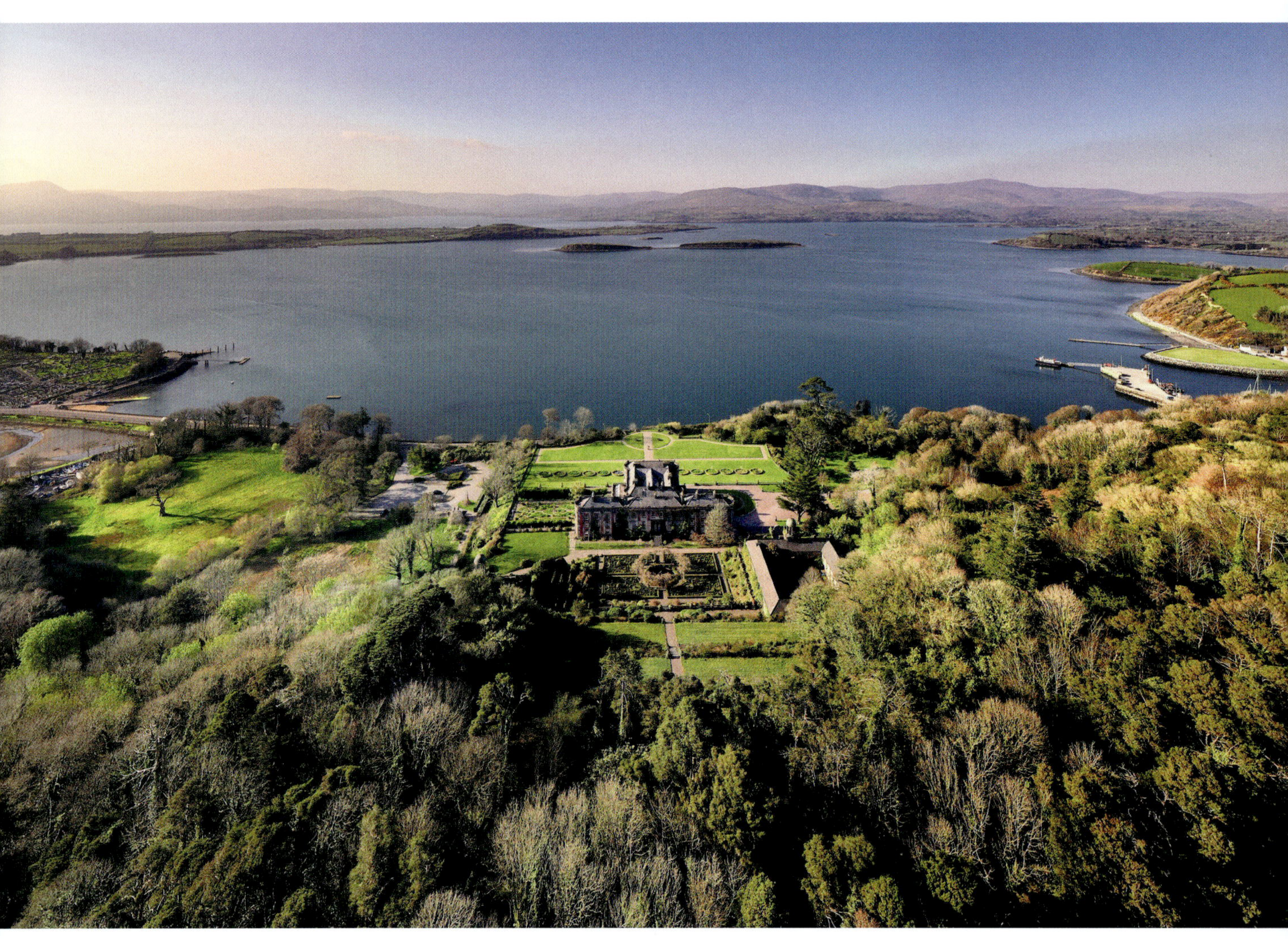

Above: Bantry House, built in 1710, overlooks Bantry Bay. Its terraced gardens are designed in the Italianate style and panoramic views can be had from the top of the hundred steps that lead up from behind the house.

Opposite: The Priest's Leap. At an elevation of 463 metres, it is the highest road in Munster and a vantage point for stunning views – on a fine day!

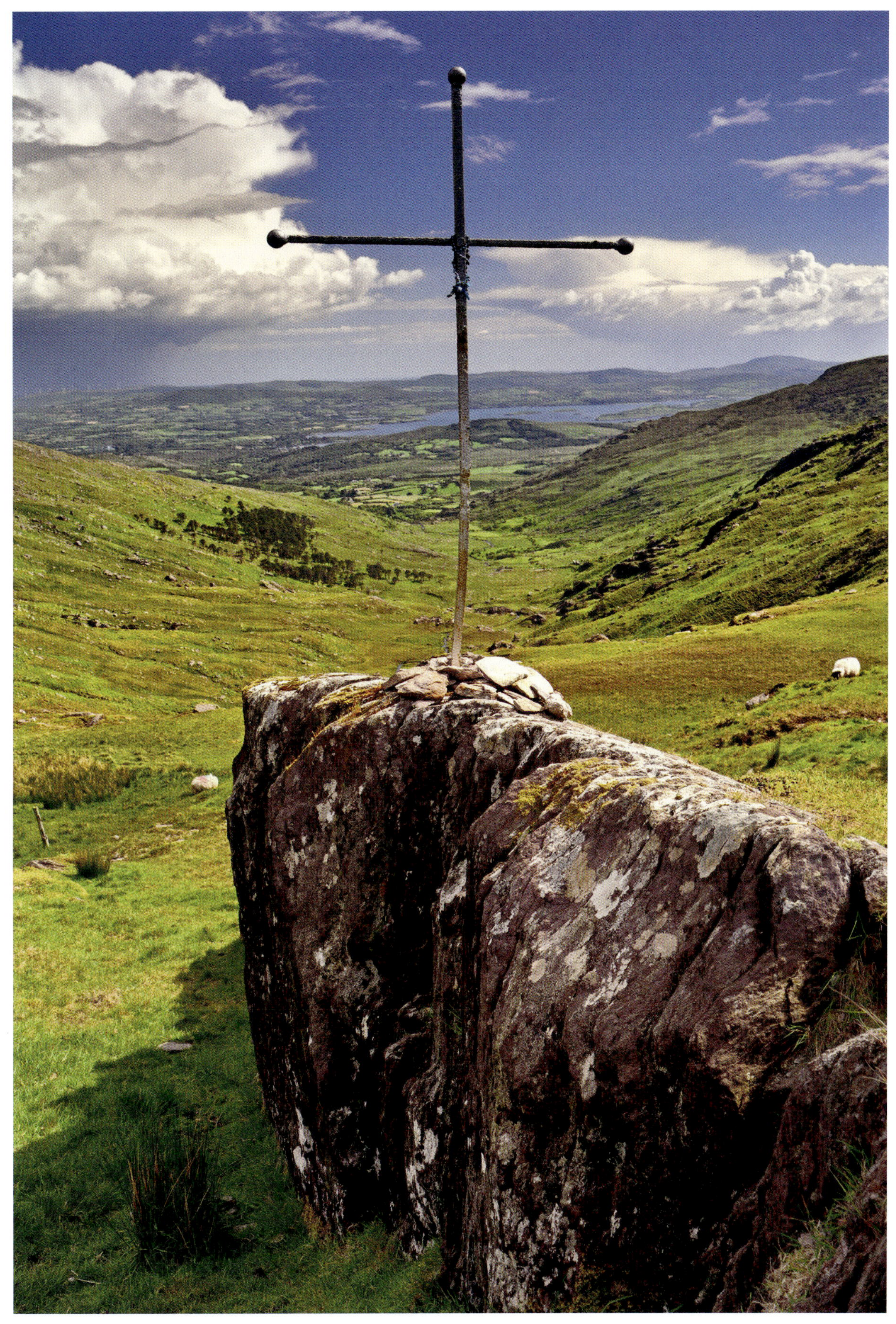

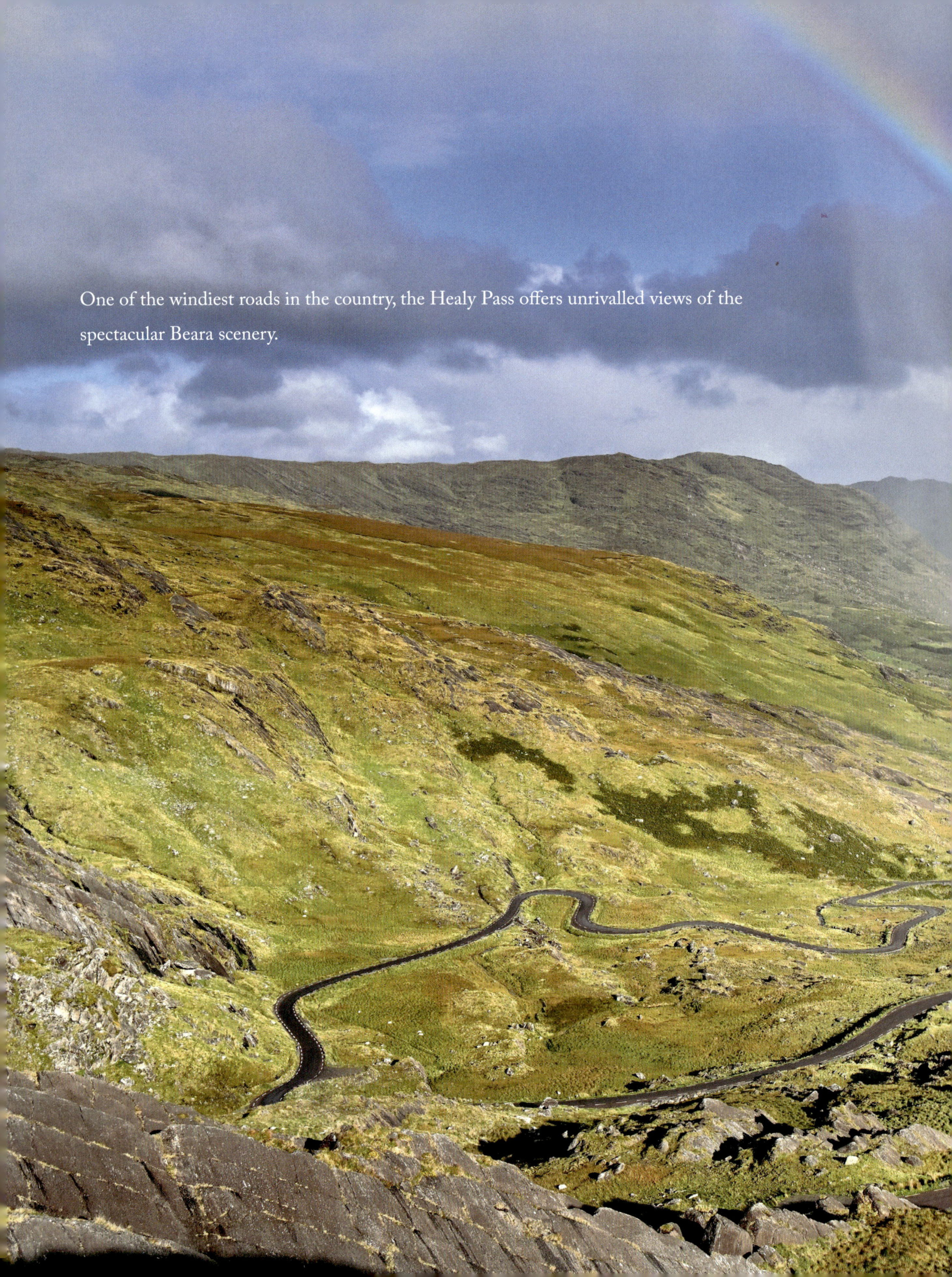

One of the windiest roads in the country, the Healy Pass offers unrivalled views of the spectacular Beara scenery.

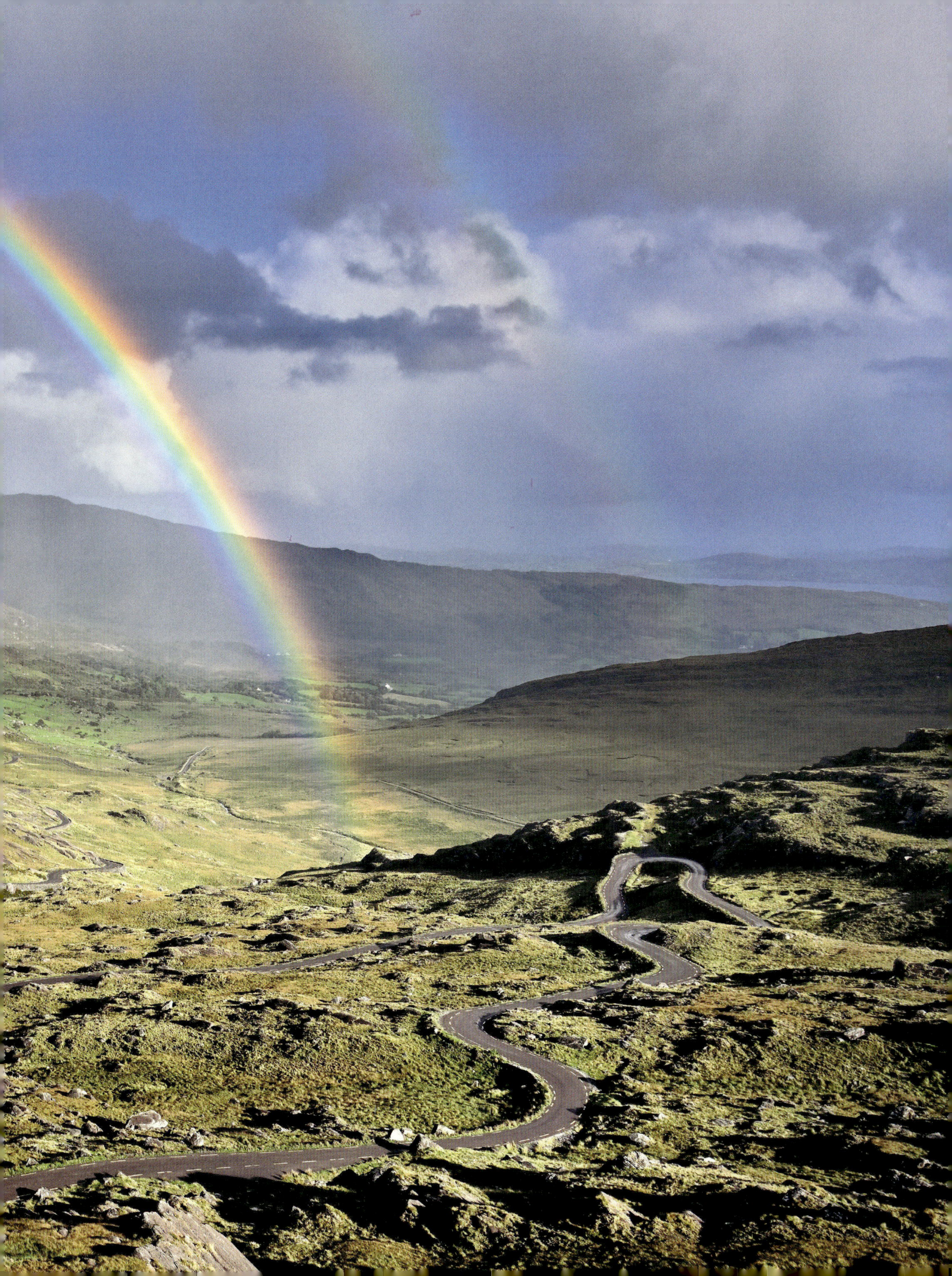

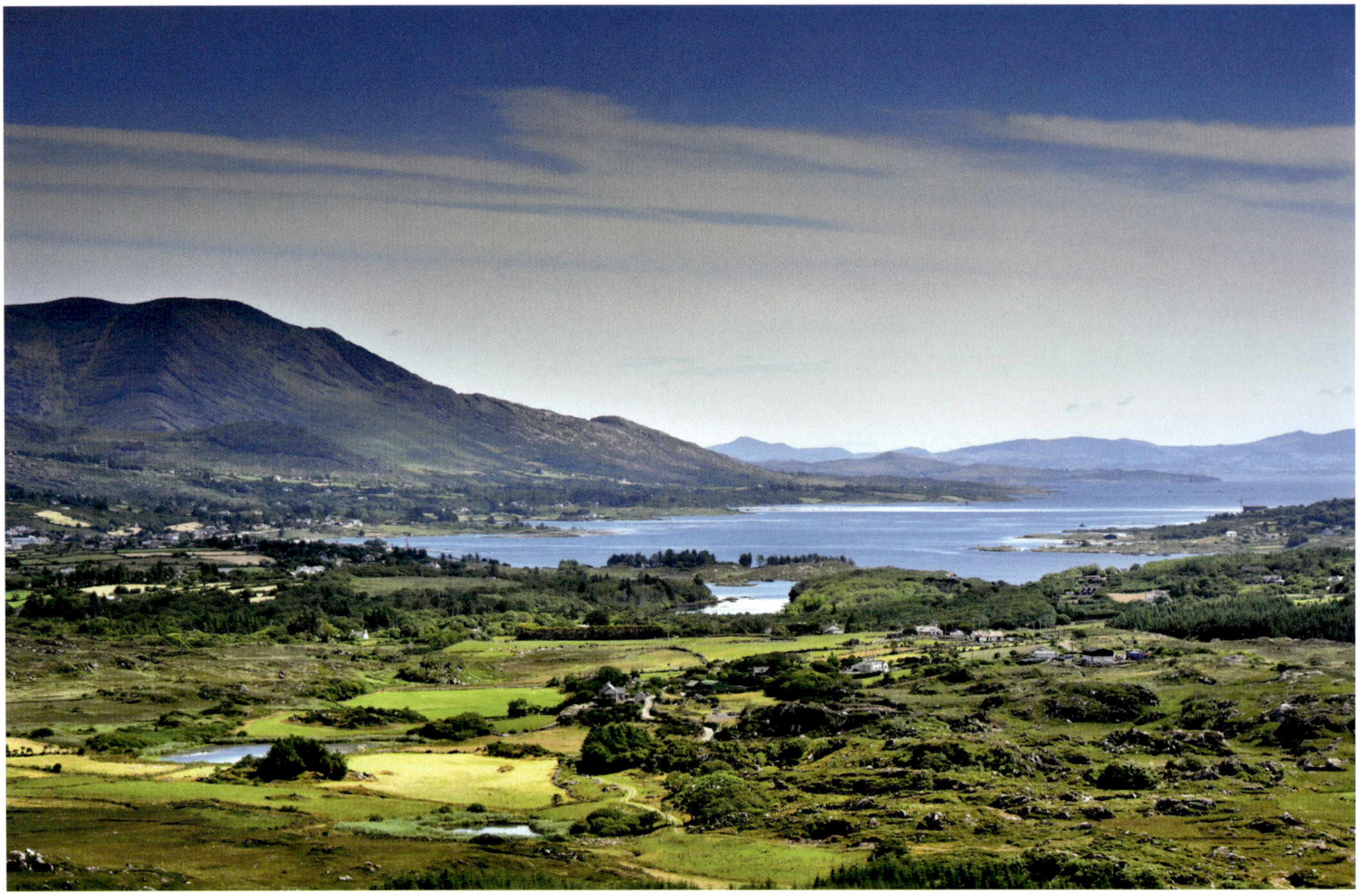

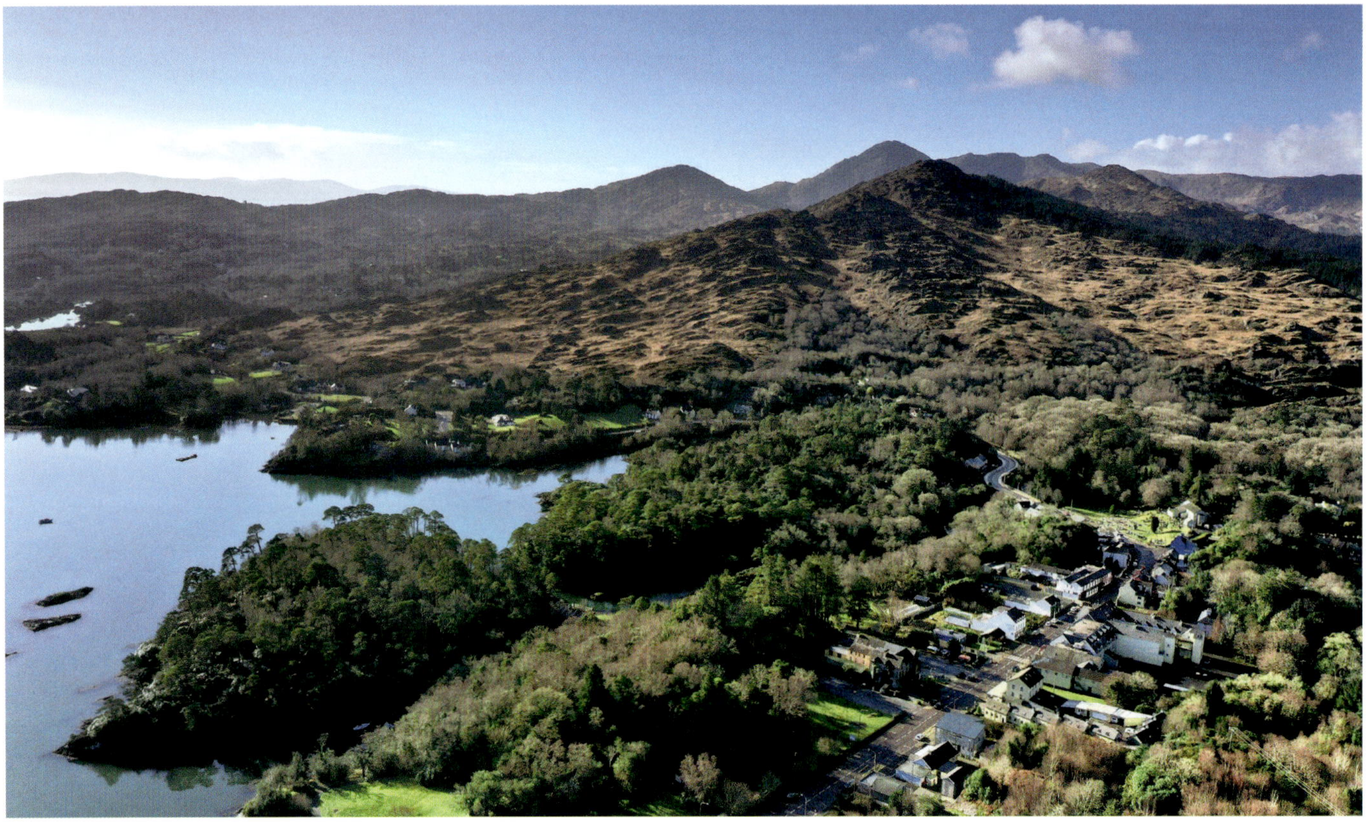

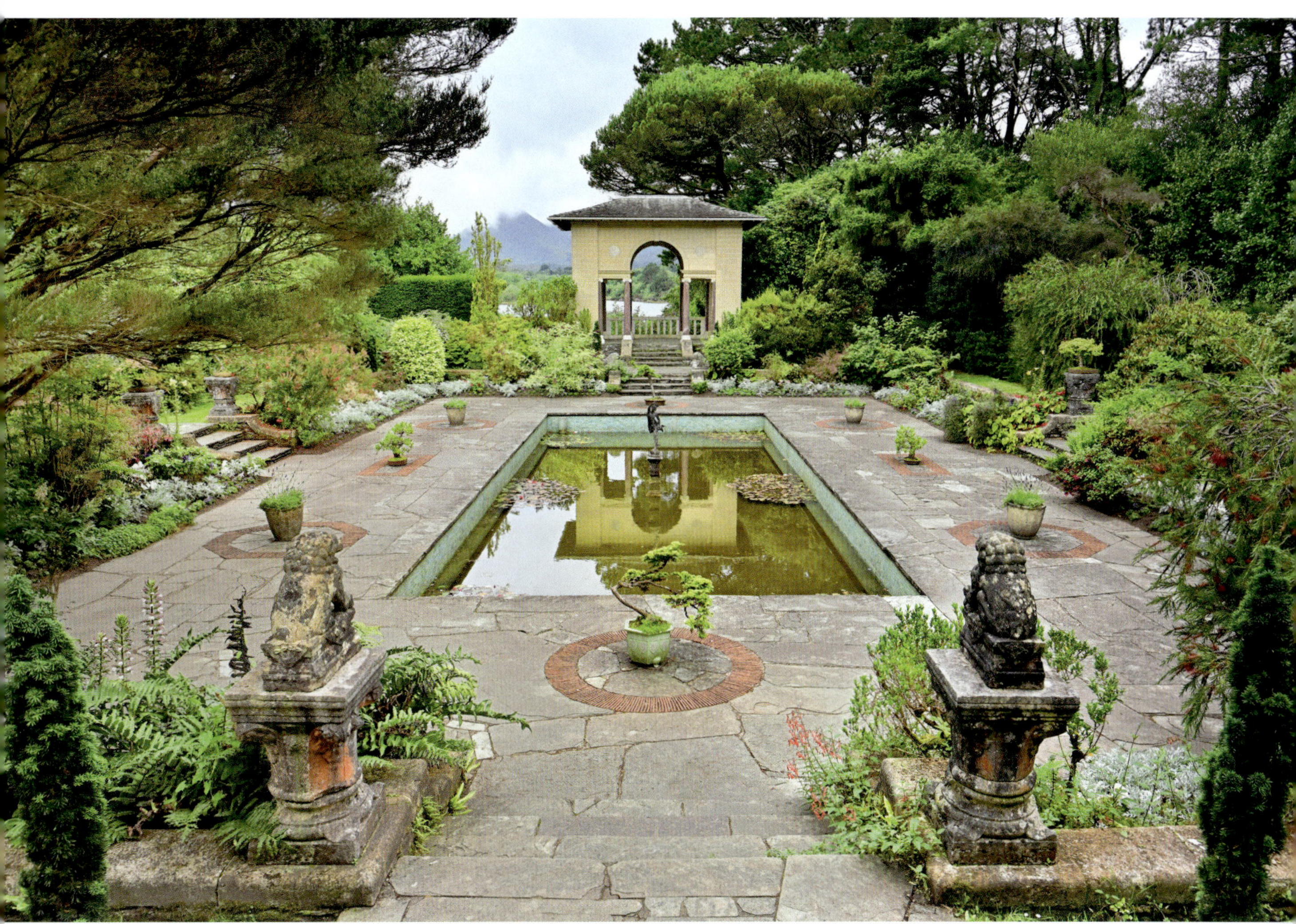

Opposite top: The rugged beauty of the Beara Peninsula.

Opposite bottom: The village of Glengarriff sits at the head of Bantry Bay in an area of outstanding natural beauty beneath the Caha Mountains.

Above: The Italian Garden on Garinish Island. This small, sheltered island in Glengarriff Bay has gardens designed by Harold Peto and a rich collection of ornamental plants from across the world. The mild, humid microclimate allows these exotic species to thrive.

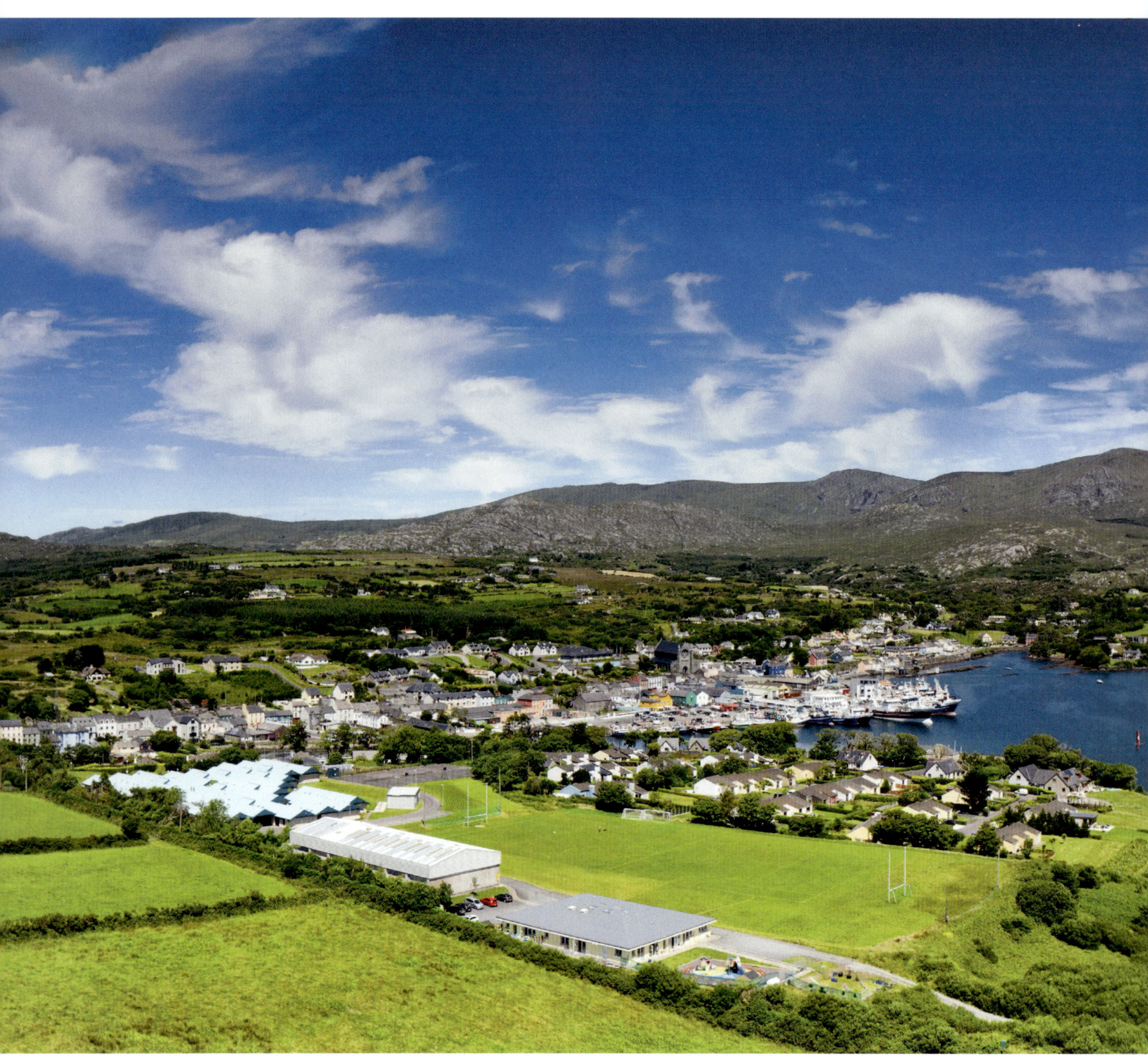

Above: The bustling town of Castletownbere, a natural deepwater port and one of Ireland's main fisheries, is popular with tourists. It is a great base for exploring the wild, pristine beauty of the Beara Peninsula. Tiny Dinish Island (right) is linked to the mainland by a bridge. It is a base for the seafood-processing industry and Castletownbere coast guard.

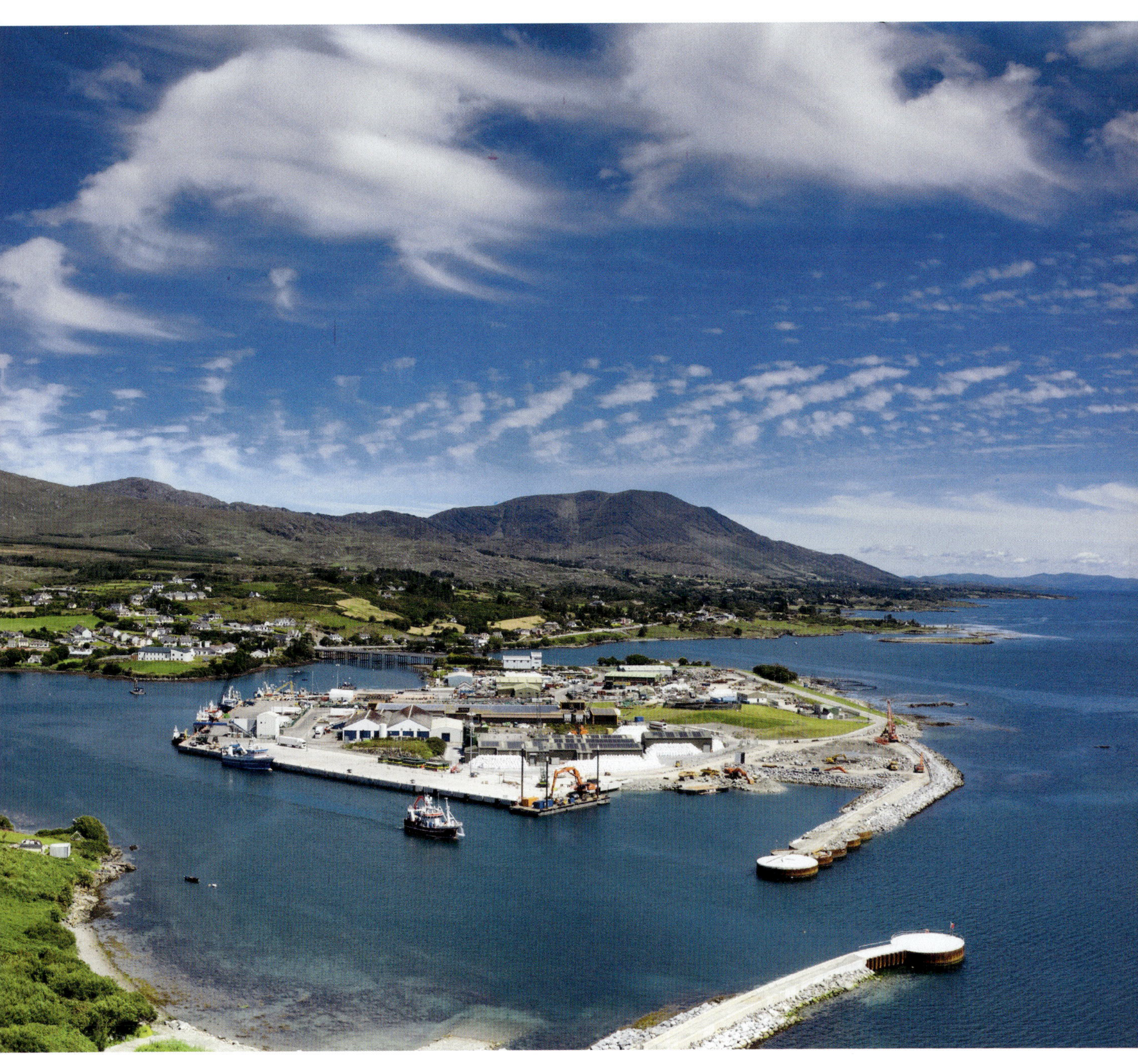

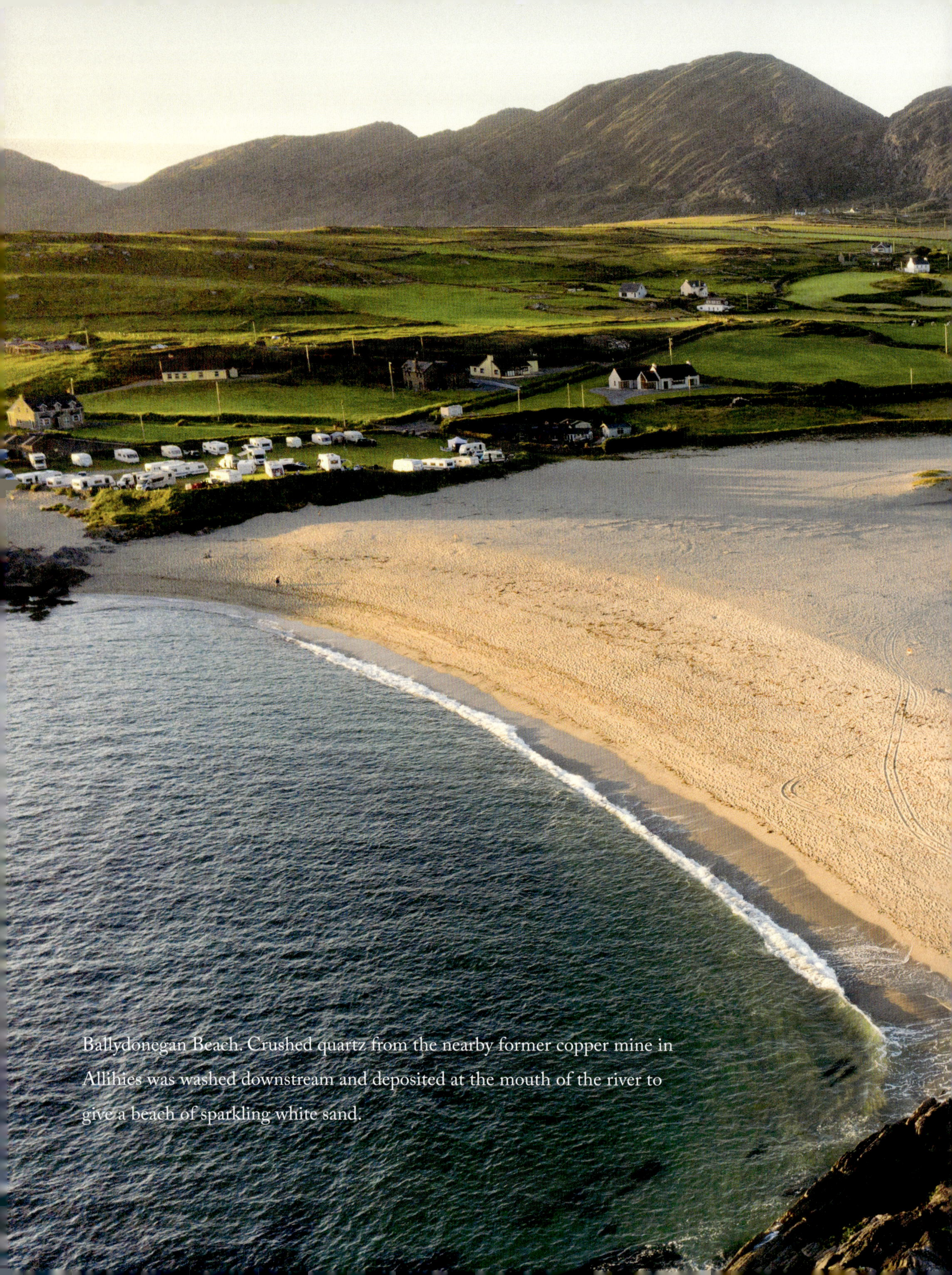

Ballydonegan Beach. Crushed quartz from the nearby former copper mine in Allihies was washed downstream and deposited at the mouth of the river to give a beach of sparkling white sand.

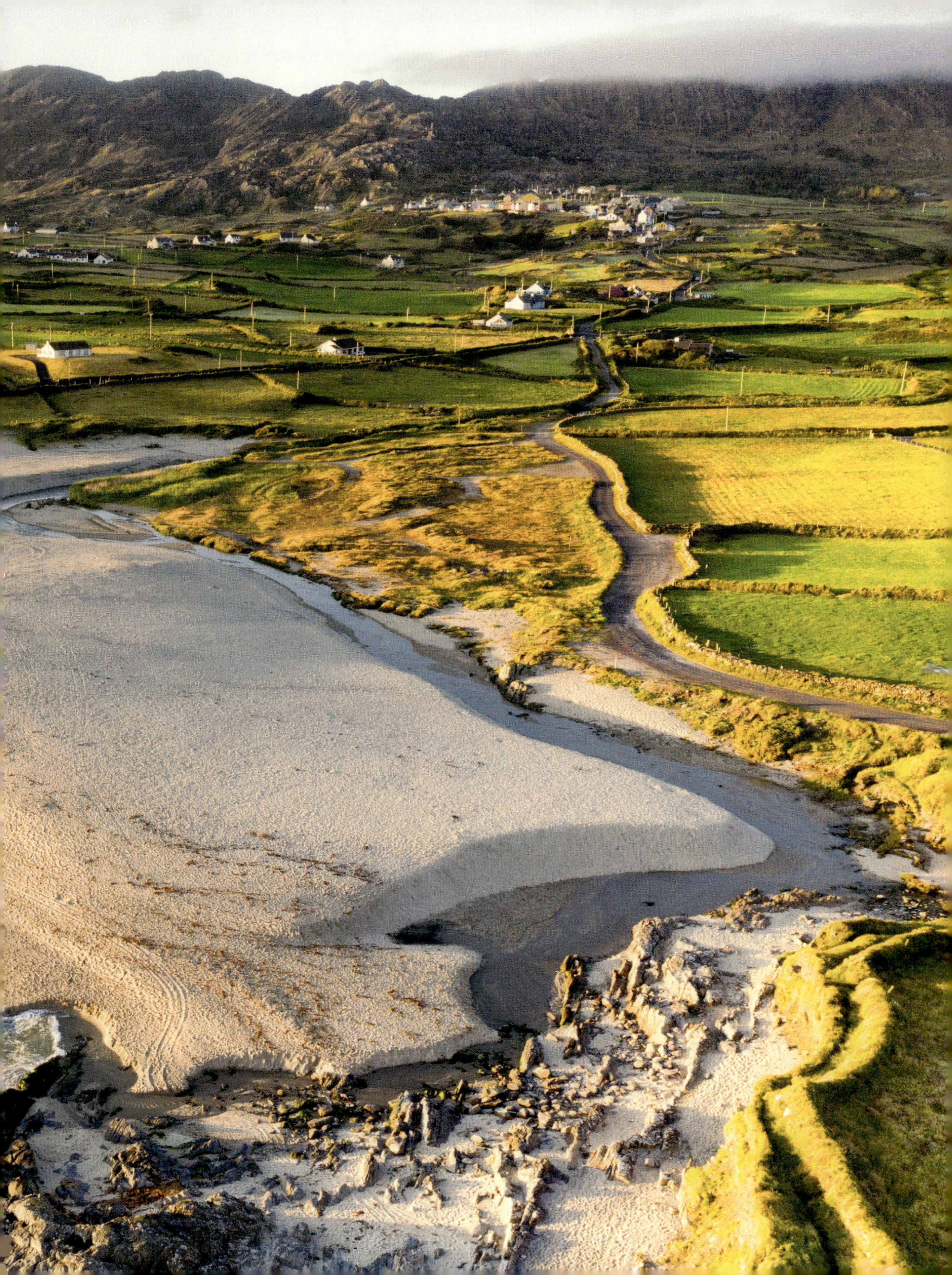

Below: Looking across to Allihies village and the mountains at the end of the Beara Peninsula, with Dursey Island in the far distance.

Opposite: One of the abandoned tunnels on the west Cork railway. The shaft turns into a waterfall in the rain.

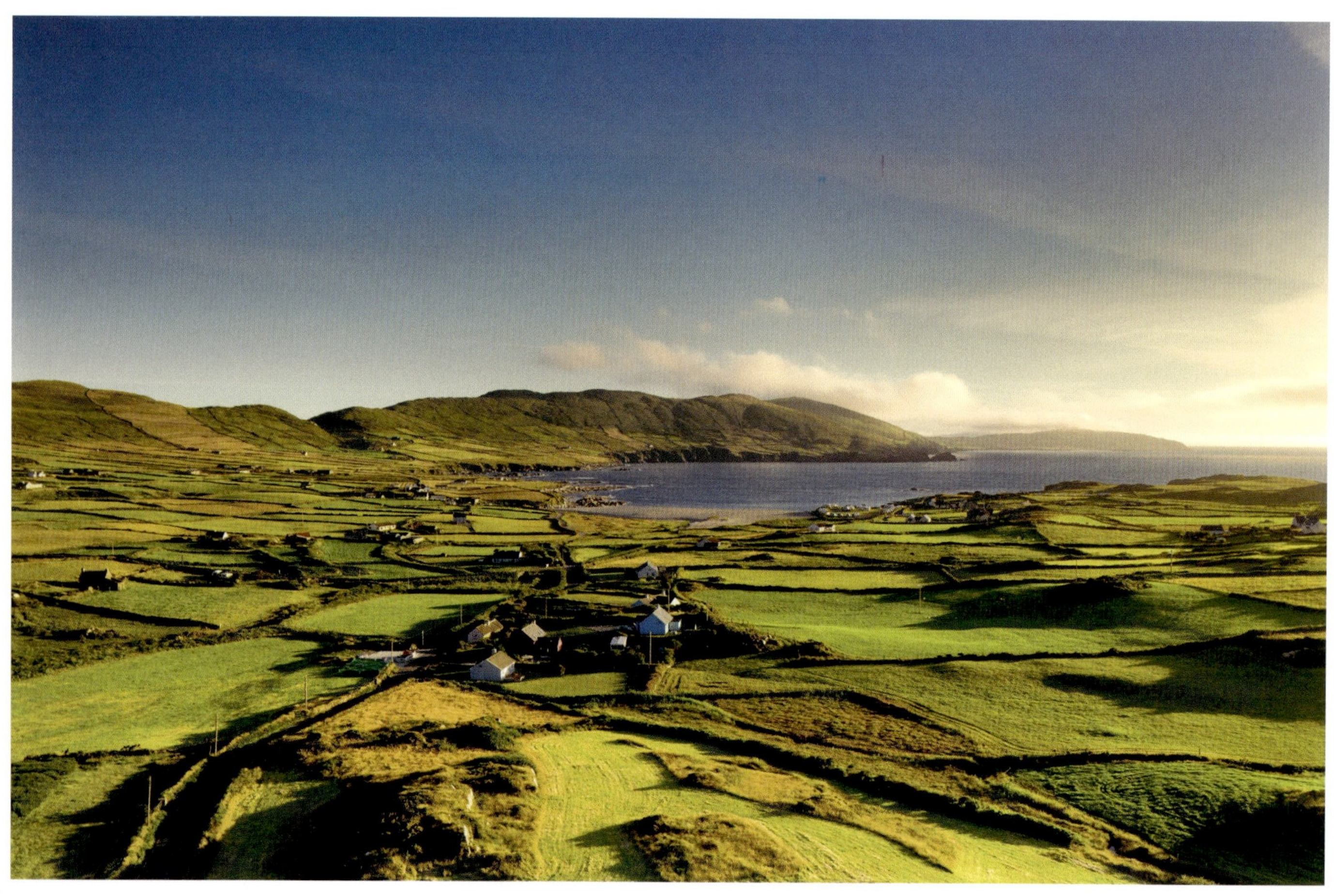

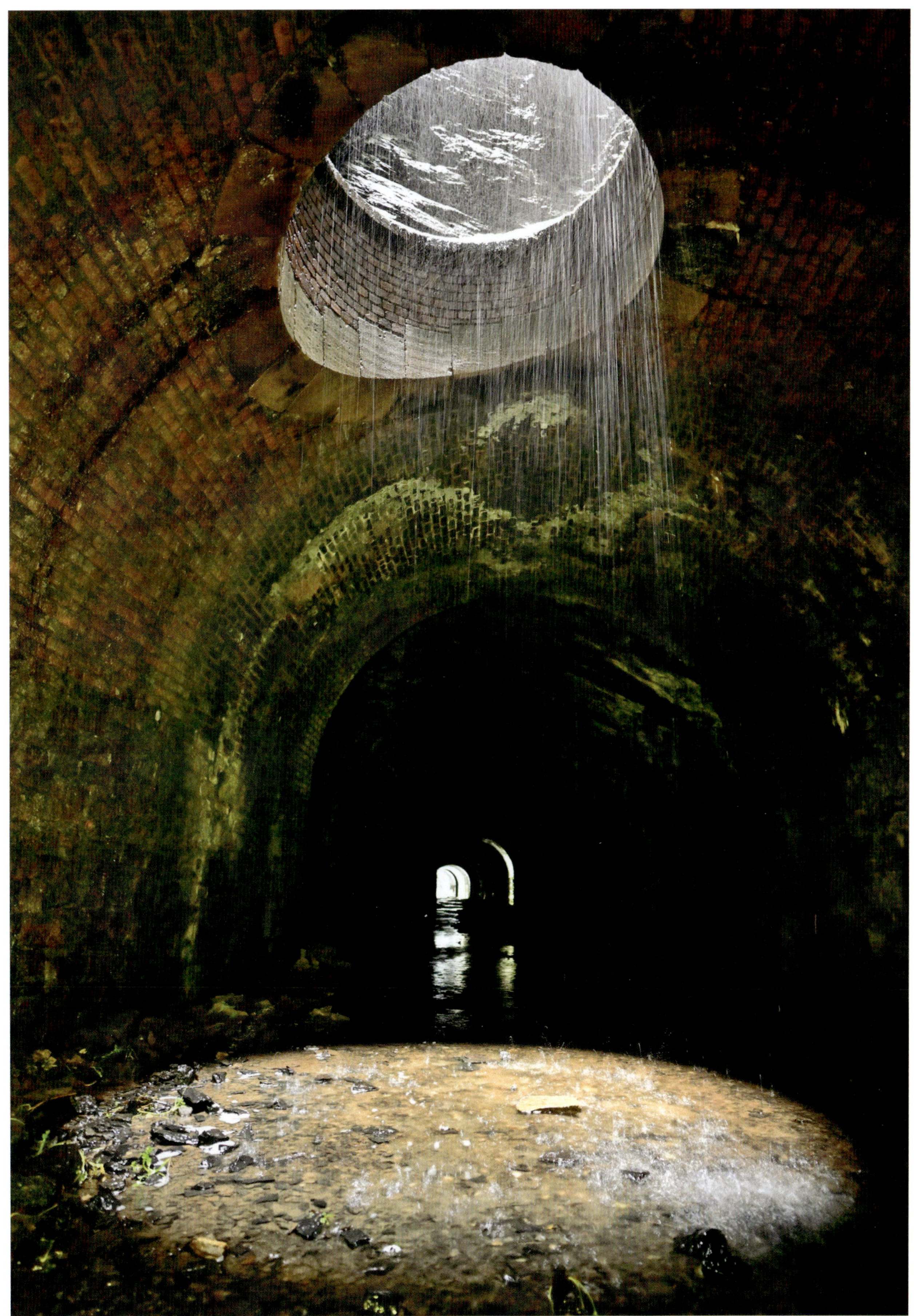

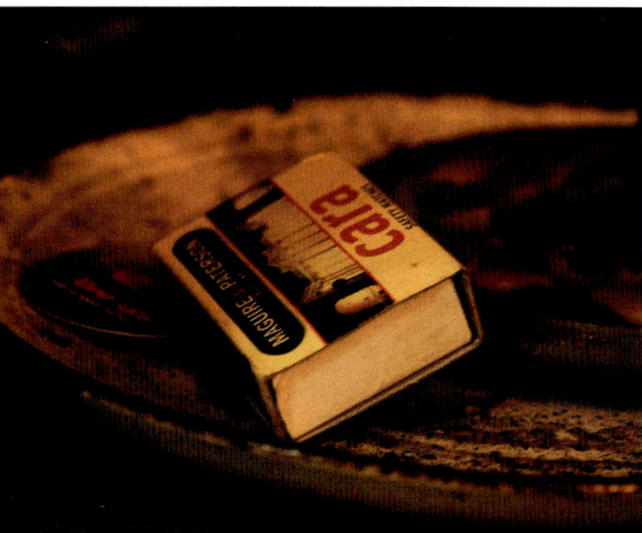

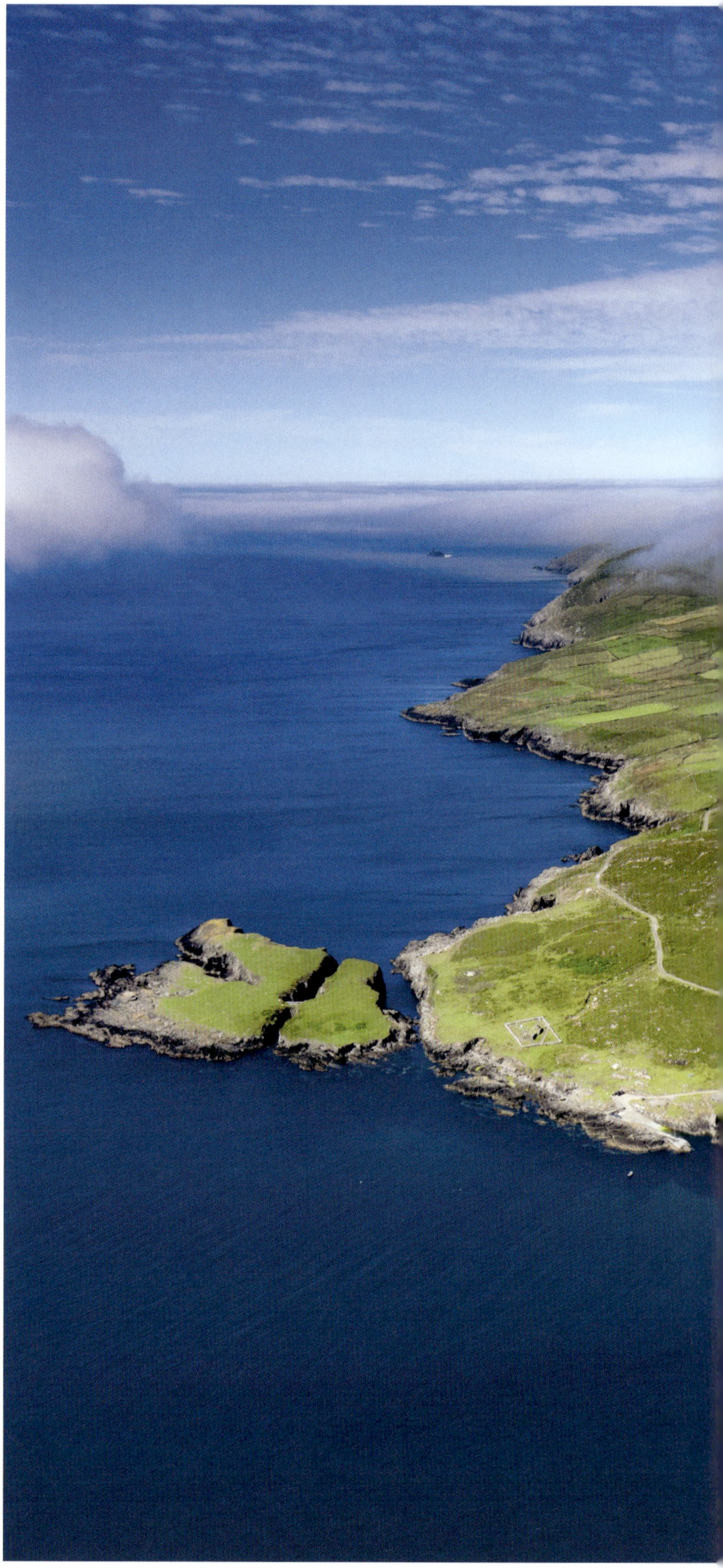

Above: A fireside scene in west Cork. Maguire and Paterson Cara matches have been used in Ireland since 1882.

Right: Dursey Island. At the end of the Beara Peninsula, this island is home to Ireland's only cable car. Just about visible are the tower on the headland (right foreground) from which the cable car runs and the terminus on the island (left of the inlet).

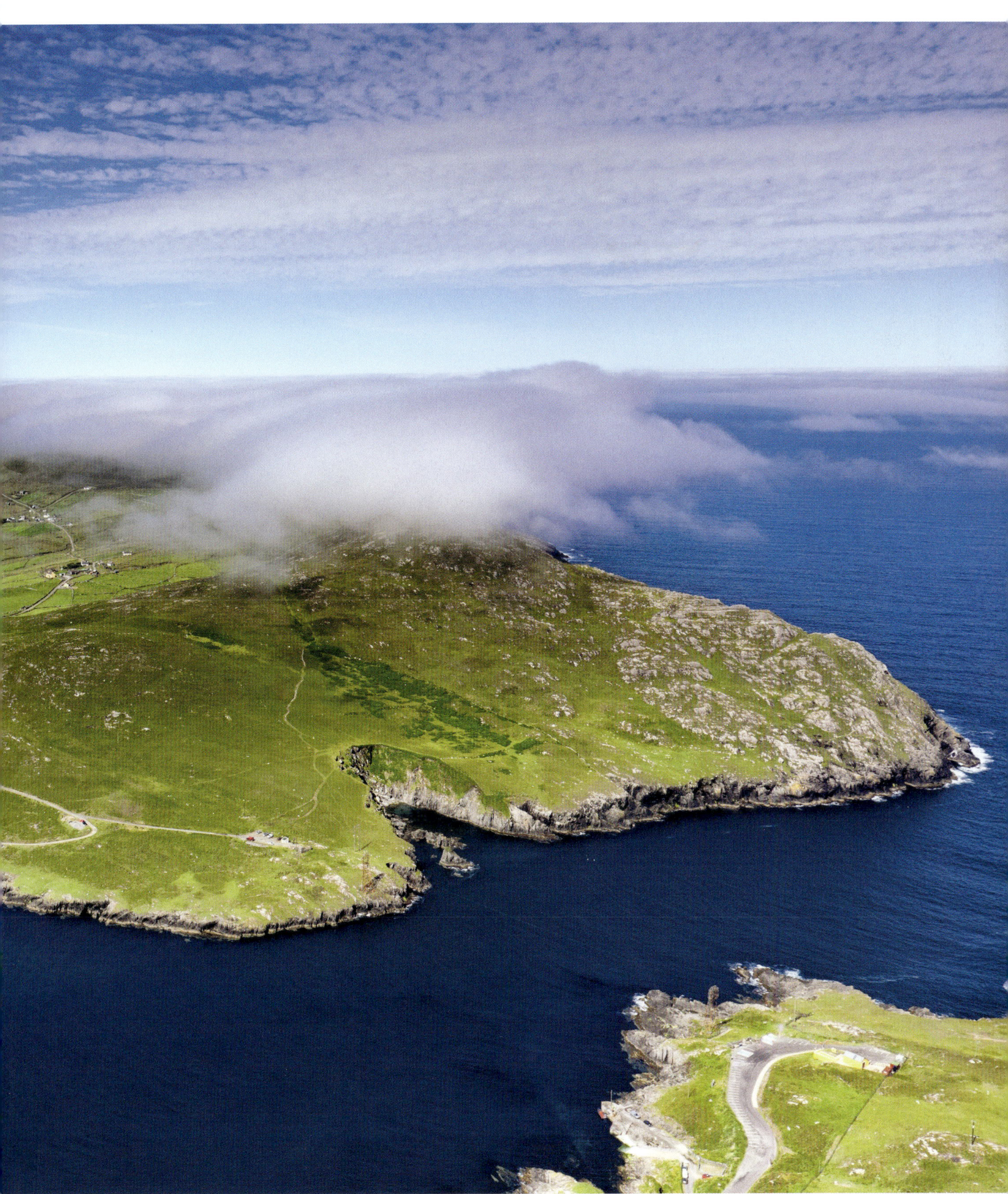

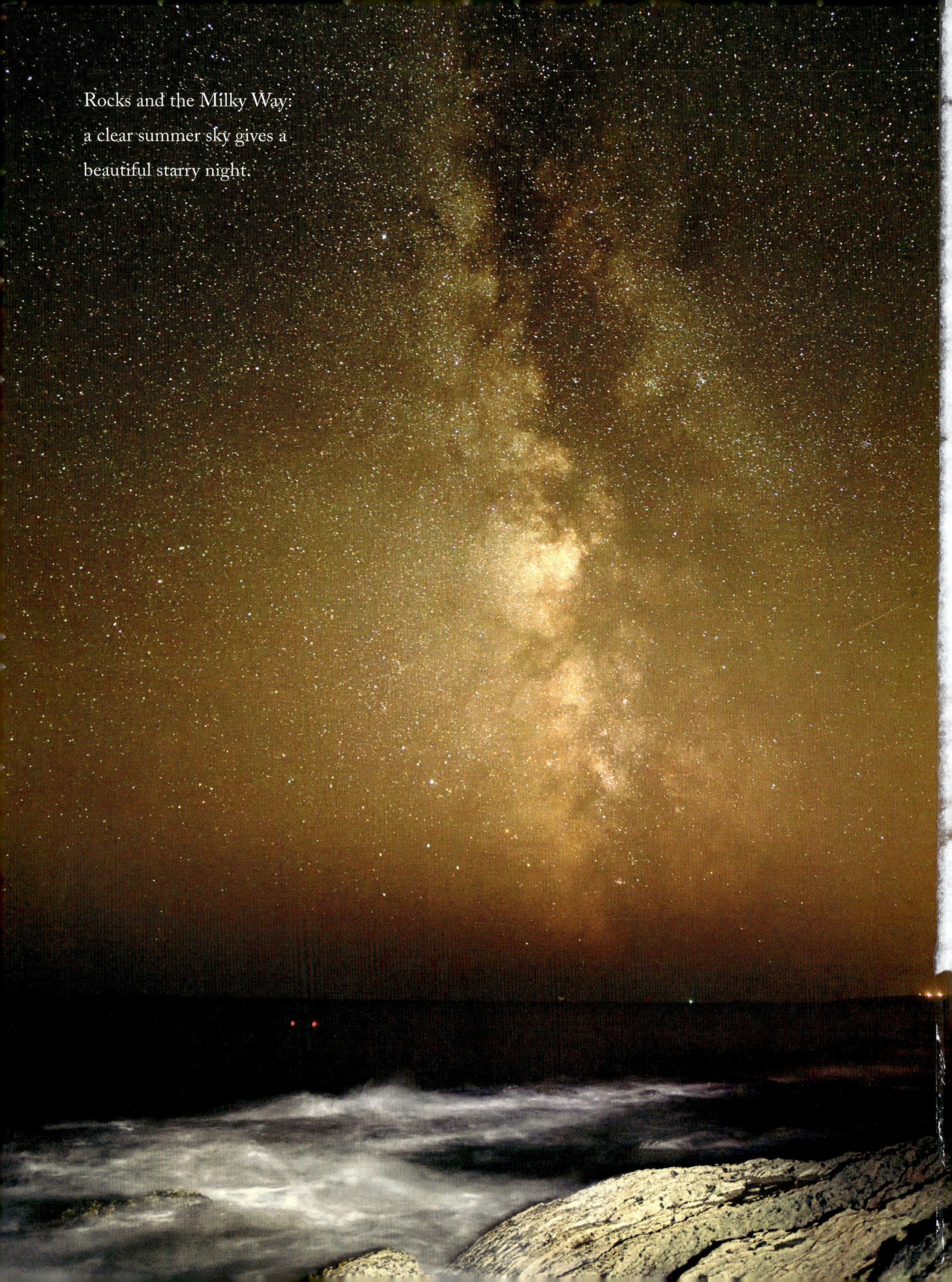

Rocks and the Milky Way:
a clear summer sky gives a
beautiful starry night.